D1559152

Balancing the Secrets of Private Disclosures

LEA'S COMMUNICATION SERIES
Jennings Bryant/Dolf Zillmann, General Editors

Selected titles in Interpersonal & Intercultural Communication (Rebecca B. Rubin, Advisory Editor) include:

Carbaugh • Cultural Communication and Intercultural Contact

Cupach/Spitzberg • The Dark Side of Interpersonal Communication

Daly/Wiemann • Strategic Interpersonal Interaction

Hewes • Cognitive Bases for Interpersonal Communication

Kalbfleisch/Cody • Gender, Power, and Communication in Human Relationships

Kalbfleisch • Interpersonal Communication: Evolving Interpersonal Relationships

Leeds-Hurwitz • Semiotics and Communication: Signs, Codes, Cultures

For a complete list of other titles in LEA's Communication Series, please contact Lawrence Erlbaum Associates, Publishers.

Balancing the Secrets of Private Disclosures

Edited by

Sandra Petronio
Arizona State University

LEA LAWRENCE ERLBAUM ASSOCIATES, PUBLISHERS
2000   Mahwah, New Jersey   London

Lawrence Erlbaum Associates, Inc., Publishers
10 Industrial Avenue
Mahwah, NJ 07430

Cover design by Kathryn Houghtaling Lacey

Library of Congress Cataloging-in-Publication Data

     Balancing the secrets of private disclosures / edited by Sandra
Petronio.
          p.   cm.
     Includes bibliographical references and index.
     ISBN 0-8058-3114-2 (hardcover : alk. paper)
     1. Self-disclosure. 2. Secrecy. 3. Privacy. 4. Interpersonal rela-
tions. I. Petronio, Sandra Sporbert
     BF697.5.S427B35 2000   302.5—dc21
     99-11093   CIP

Books published by Lawrence Erlbaum Associates are printed on
acid-free paper, and their bindings are chosen for strength and
durability.

Printed in the United States of America
10 9 8 7 6 5 4 3 2 1

Contents

List of Contributors

Walid A. Afifi
Department of Speech Communication
234 Sparks Building
Pennsylvania State University
University Park, PA 16802–5201
e-mail: w-afifi@psu.edu

Kimo Ah Yun
Communication Studies Department
California State University, Sacramento
Sacramento, CA 95819–6070

Leslie A. Baxter
Communication Studies Department
University of Iowa
Iowa City, IA 52242
e-mail: leslie-baxter@uiowa.edu

Daniel C. Brouwer
Department of Communication
Loyola University
6525 N. Sheridan
Chicago, IL 60626
e-mail: dbrouwe@luc.edu

Judee K. Burgoon
Communication Department, Bldg. 25
University of Arizona
Tucson, AZ 85721
e-mail: jburgoon@u.arizona.edu

Aileen L. S. Buslig
Hugh Downs School of Communication
Arizona State University
P. O. Box 871205
Tempe, AZ 85287–1205
e-mail: buslig@imap4.asu.edu

Rebecca J. Welch Cline
Department of Health
Science Education
University of Florida
362 Dauer Hall
Gainesville, FL 32611
e-mail: becky@nervm.nerdc.ufl.edu

Leda Cooks
Department of Communication
University of Massachusetts, Amherst
Amherst, MA 01003
e-mail: leda@comm.umass.edu

Valerian J. Derlega
Department of Psychology
Old Dominion University
Norfolk, VA 23529
e-mail: vderlega@odu.edu

Lara E. Dieckmann
Department of Theatre Arts and Dance
California State University, Los Angeles
Los Angeles, CA 90032–8103
e-mail: ldieckman@calstatela.edu

Kathryn Dindia
Department of Communication
Box 413
University of Wisconsin, Milwaukee
Milwaukee, WI 53201
e-mail: dindia@uwm.edu

Ashley Duggan
Communication Department
University of California, Santa Barbara
Santa Barbara, CA 93106–4020
e-mail: 6500apd@ucsbuxa.edu

Veronica Duncan
Department of Speech Communication
University of Georgia
Athens, GA 30602–1725
e-mail: vduncan@arches.uga.edu

Lori Folk-Barron
Virginia Consortium for Professional
Psychology
Old Dominion University
Norfolk, VA 23529

Bradley Greenberg
Department of Telecommunication and
Communication
Michigan State University
East Lansing, MI 48824
e-mail: brag@msu.edu

Kathryn Greene
Department of Communication
East Carolina University
Greenville, NC 27858
e-mail: greenek@mail.ecu.edu

Laura K. Guerrero
Department of Communication
Arizona State University
P. O. Box 871205
Tempe, AZ 85287–1205
e-mail: laura.guerrero@asu.edu

Sally O. Hastings
Department of Communication
& Broadcasting
Western Kentucky University
1 Big Red Way St.
Bowling Green, KY 42101–5730
e-mail: sally.hastings@wku.edu

Danette E. Ifert
Communication & Dramatic
Arts College
West Virginia Wesleyan College
Buckhannon, WV 26201
e-mail: ifert@wvwc.edu

Amy Janan Johnson
Department of Communication
University of Oklahoma
Norman, OK 73019
e-mail: amyjj@ou.edu

Susanne M. Jones
Hugh Downs School of Communication
Arizona State University
P. O. Box 871205
Tempe, AZ 85287–1205
e-mail: sujones@imap1.asu.edu

Nelya J. McKenzie
Department of Communication,
Auburn University
P.O. 244023
Montgomery, AL 361244023
e-mail: farish@strudel.aum.edu

Monique M. Mitchell
Department of Communication
University of Oklahoma
Norman, OK 73019
e-mail: monique@ou.edu

Victoria O. Orrego
Department of Communication
Michigan State University
East Lansing, MI 48824
e-mail: orregovi@pilot.msu.edu

Roxanne Parrott
Department of Speech Communication
University of Georgia
Athens, GA 30602–1725
e-mail: rparrott@uga.cc.uga.edu

Sandra Petronio
Hugh Downs School of Communication
Arizona State University
P. O. Box 871205
Tempe, AZ 85287–1205
e-mail: petronio@asu.edu

Michael Porte
Communication Department
University of Cincinnati
Cincinnati, OH 45221–0184
e-mail: michael.porte@uc.edu

Michael E. Roloff
Department of Communication Studies
Northwestern University
1881 Sheridan Rd.
Evanston, IL 60208–0818
e-mail: m-roloff@nwu.edu

Lawrence B. Rosenfeld
Communication Studies Department
Campus Box 3285
University of North Carolina
Chapel Hill, NC 27599–3285
e-mail: lbrosenfeld@unc.edu

Donald L. Rubin
Department of Speech Communication
University of Georgia
Athens, GA 30602–1725
e-mail: drubin@uga.cc.uga.edu

Erin M. Sahlstein
Communication Studies Department
University of Iowa
Iowa City, IA 52242
e-mail: erin-sahlstein@uiowa.edu

Pamela D. Schultz
Communication Studies Department
Alfred University
Saxon Drive
Alfred, NY 14802
e-mail: fschultz@bigfax.alfred.edu

Sandi W. Smith
Department of Communication
Michigan State University
East Lansing, MI 48824
e-mail: smiths@pilot.msu.edu

Charles H. Tardy
Speech Communication Department
University of Southern Mississippi
Hattiesburg, MS 39406–5131
e-mail: ctardy@whale.st.usm.edu

Barbara A. Winstead
Department of Psychology
Old Dominion University
Norfolk, VA 23529

Hanbi Yang
Baker & MacKenzie, Chicago
Contact: University of Georgia
Athens, GA 30602–1725

Gust A. Yep
Department of Speech
and Communication Studies
San Francisco State University
1600 Holloway Ave.
San Francisco, CA 94132
e-mail: gyep@sfsu.edu

Preface:
The Meaning of Balance

This book brings together disclosure, privacy, and secrecy to pursue a greater understanding of how people are both public and private. To be social yet autonomous, known yet unknown, independent yet dependent is essential to our communicative world. How do people manage these seemingly incongruous goals? Through its many chapters, this book argues that we actively balance revealing our public and private selves. The challenge in describing the balancing act is to recognize that a singular definition is not sufficient. Instead, balance, in this context, is more complex and variable. We want the right to keep our names private from those trying to sell us money, our telephone numbers from unwelcome callers, our social security numbers from thieves, and certain information secret from employers. At the same time, we choose to tell our family secrets, determine who knows our past, and decide who knows how we feel about others. The main issue for the public–private dialectic is to understand how to achieve goals that allow both disclosure and the ability to keep private or secret those things that make us feel vulnerable. To be able to choose who knows, when they know, if they know, and what they know about us is fundamental to our feeling in control. We do not like being compromised; therefore, we actively direct our efforts to minimize possible risks in our interactions. The way people balance their public–private tensions is essential to everyday life.

The concept of balance illustrates the interdependence of disclosure, privacy, and secrecy. We may find it difficult to let others know who we are if there is no time for solitude. We may feel conflict if we reveal to our partners without any autonomy from them. We may find it troublesome to engage in friendship relationships without time to reflect independently on the meaning of those relationships. Balancing the tensions of granting access through disclosure and managing the simultaneous needs for privacy and secrecy is an indisputable part of our interactions.

These authors illustrate many ways people balance their need to be known with their need to remain inconspicuous. Exploring issues such as HIV/AIDS, battered women, sex offenders, suppressing complaints, taboo topics, a patient's full disclosure, health, aggression, family secrets, intercultural experiences, and television talk shows, each author proposes an alternative vision of how individuals adjust the costs and benefits of revelation and concealment.

Privacy, secrecy, and disclosure are not new concepts. Yet, the authors pose new ways to consider them. For example, they suggest reframing disclosure where gender, reciprocity, and liking are concerned. We also discover that avoiding disclosures emerges as a theme. The authors demonstrate that balancing may result in de-emphasizing openness. Instead of a wish to reveal, we find that disclosure is dodged actively to conceal information in close relationships, guarding HIV status, or traumatic events.

Although we have learned a great deal by focusing on "self" disclosure, we are challenged to broaden the definition of this concept. We learn that there are many kinds of disclosure, especially in relationship to private and secret information. We see numerous examples of how disclosure goes beyond the "self." For instance, health information may initially belong to an individual, however, once it is revealed, it potentially influences partners, relatives, and friends. Individuals may need to share the information with others although it is about their husband, wife, child, or co-workers. In other words, they co-own the information. Medical staff participates in co-owning private medical information, thereby increasing the circle of people who must cooperate in managing the "disclosure." As we see, the information may include the self, yet at the same time also becomes the property of relational partners, spouses, parents, co-workers, or siblings.

This volume emphasizes the notion that balance is not a unitary concept. These authors present a more multifaceted view that goes farther than simple symmetry between the paradoxical needs of being public and private. These authors suggest several balance frameworks. First, we may define balance as a *polarization*. Polarization refers to disclosure, privacy, and secrecy as dominant forces that guide decisions about public access. In this sense, disclosure, conditions of privacy, or complete secrecy prevails over the other choices. The posture of balance revolves around one of these options and all others fall into the background. For example, in a story sent to "Dear Abby," a sister, because of a long ago conflict, withheld the death of a beloved aunt (*Sister Silences*, 1997). Secrecy reigned supreme in this story until the other sister called the nursing home. While secrecy prevailed, it was the dominant force over privacy and disclosure. People may keep secrets when they want to protect offenses or worries. When secrets take over, there is a polar shift restricting access to this information.

There may also be a polar shift to full disclosure. There are many examples of people making complete and full disclosures of information. One that is particularly noteworthy concerns a newspaper story about Jenni. We learn that Jenni, a 21 year-old woman, has a Web site. She set up a camera that lets people watch her every move, conversation, and behavior as she goes about her life in the "privacy" of her apartment (Weeks, 1997). Jenni makes a full disclosure within the range of the camera. For her, the polar force has centered on total openness without compromise. Privacy and secrecy are not interfering with her Web site disclosures.

A second type of balance is *equilibrium.* This kind of balance evolves when there is an attempt to develop stasis among disclosure, privacy, and secrecy. This represents a more traditional view of balance. The amount of disclosure is equivalent to the amount of privacy and secrecy. We give as much as we keep from others. This scenario is difficult to maintain in the long term because the type of disclosure may not be commensurate with that of privacy and secrecy. For example, if a friend tells about her divorce, she may be keeping as much or more information about her life to herself than she is willing to tell.

Aiming to equalize the amount of information a person keeps or tells may require a conscious effort to balance. Keeping secrets, for example, may require more effort than disclosing private information (Wegner & Lane, 1995). According to the preoccupation model of secrecy, when individuals strive to restrict access to secret information, they become preoccupied with mentally suppressing the information. "Secret-keepers are often placed in the unnerving position of having simultaneously to think about their cover-up and not to think about it" (Wegner & Lane, 1995, p. 31). Consequently, it is difficult for secret-keepers to balance this process in a way that reaches equilibrium between disclosure and maintaining a secret.

Third, *weighted proportions* refers to balance that gives more weight to some options and less to other options. This is different from polarization in that there are times when disclosure of some information is weighed more heavily than keeping it private or secret. Likewise, privacy might be more heavily weighted than disclosure or secrecy. A complete polar shift does not take place in any specific direction. Some measure of secrecy may be considered proportionately more important than privacy and disclosure in a particular situation. For example, in France last year, police in a farm hamlet wished to find the person responsible for murdering a young girl (Noveck, 1997). They rounded up all consenting males for a DNA test. The question posed in a newspaper article asked why the killer would ever volunteer. "The answer, some say, is the fear of suspicion and ostracism. It appears that the guilty often prefer to risk the test results … than risk drawing suspicion on themselves by not participating" (p. A12). This story illustrates a situation where there appears to be a weighted proportion of disclosure to secrecy by the murderer. The calculated risk of not disclosing and keeping the information private is considered in relationship to the risk of revealing.

Worrying may also provide an example of how weighted proportions function among disclosure, secrecy, and privacy. People who worry may talk to themselves or disclose to others about the possibility of future events that are perceived as threats. However, they may weigh the gain of revealing the future threats to others against the loss of face or risk of embarrassment. The recipients may not perceive the possibility of a threat in the same way as the discloser. In addition, talking about worries also has the potential to be harmful emotionally. Thus, the balance in favor of disclosure is considered in relationship to the potential risks and weighed against the options of privacy and secrecy.

Balancing Secrets of Private Disclosures offers many new directions using the theme of balance to shape our understanding of significant communicative problems and issues we face in today's world.

EDITOR'S RECOGNITION

There are many people to thank for their contributions to this book. Without the dedication of the authors and their insightfulness about the topic, this book would not exist.

The editor would also like to recognize Linda Bathgate for her commitment to this project and the opportunity to publish the book. Her assistant Lori Hawver also deserves credit for answering questions with promptness and good humor and Eileen Engel, Production Editor, has been a valuable resource. Jennings Bryant's enthusiasm for the project is most appreciated, as is his assistance in preparing the proposal.

Susanne Jones deserves special recognition for her continued help in finding references, following up on information, and commitment to the project. She made finalizing the book a much more pleasant task. Thanks to Mary Claire Morr for her thoroughness and professionalism. The College of Public Programs' Publication Assistance Center at Arizona State University, in particular, Mary Fran Draisker, contributed greatly to the project. My friend and companion Charles Bantz and daughter Kristen Petronio also deserve many thanks for their never-ending devotion, friendship, and support. They keep me centered.

I

▼▼▼▼▼▼▼▼▼▼▼▼▼

INTRODUCTION TO SECRETS
OF PRIVATE DISCLOSURES

1

▼▼▼▼▼▼▼▼▼

Overview of the Ways Privacy, Secrecy, and Disclosure Are Balanced in Today's Society

Lawrence B. Rosenfeld
University of North Carolina, Chapel Hill

A brief glance at the philosophical roots of self-disclosure provides insight into why most of us elect to have an approach–avoidance relationship with this form of communication. For example, Heidegger (1927/1962) considered self-disclosure essential to our understanding of our own existence and as an inevitable part of being human; indeed, talk is the way we disclose our primordial, primitive conditions of being-in-the-world. Laing (1962), on the other hand, viewed self-disclosure as a person's "making patent" his or her "true self" (p. 126). He argued that the possibility of "going forward" (as opposed to "going back," "going around in circles," or "going nowhere") exists only when self-disclosing, when a person "puts himself into his actions" (p. 126). More important than serving as a way to "go forward," self-disclosure also serves as a way to create and understand our personal selves as well as our interpersonal selves: "The act I do is felt to be me, and I become 'me' in and through such action" (p. 126).

Jourard (1971b), more than anyone else, has influenced the way we currently think about research on self-disclosure. Considering self-disclosure from an interpersonal perspective, he saw it as the way for people to express and to create intimacy, closeness, and love—as the way to be less mysterious to one another:

> When a man [woman] discloses his [her] experience to another, fully, sponta-
> neously, and honestly, then the mystery that he [she] was decreases enormously.
> When a man [person] discloses . . . to me, my perceptions of him [her] are
> altered by the facts as they come forth. . . .

3

[A] person will permit himself [herself] to be known when he [she] believes his [her] audience is . . . of goodwill. Self-disclosure follows an attitude of love and trust. If I love someone, not only do I strive to know him [her]; I *also display my love by letting him [her] know me.* At the same time, by so doing, I permit him [her] to love me.

Loving is scary, because when you permit yourself to be known, you expose yourself not only to your lover's balm, but also to a hater's bombs! (p. 5, italics in original)

Self-disclosure is a scary notion! It can explain our existence, reveal who we are to ourselves and others as we disclose and engage in an act of "becoming," and, more fundamentally, *allow* us to exist in the world. It can help us to "heal" ourselves and, simultaneously, serve as an indication of the intimacy of our relationships. Paraphrasing Jourard (1971b), self-disclosure requires courage, not only the courage to *be*, but the courage to be known and to be perceived by others as one actually is.

So, if you think about it for a moment, with all the seemingly good reasons we have for not self-disclosing, for not letting others know the private and often secret parts of who we are, it is amazing that we are open about ourselves at all. Deciding between disclosing and remaining private is an extremely complex process. This depends, for example, on how I balance the risks of disclosing with the rewards, my feelings about the information I might share, the expectations of the culture in which I live, the situation in which I need to decide whether to be more or less open, my relationship with the target of my disclosure, and the extent to which my disclosure fits the conversation. And there are still more considerations: How deeply do I need to disclose? Do I need to disclose everything, or can I disclose part of what there is to say? To what extent do I need to talk about related topics so as to provide a context for what I choose to disclose? And what are my alternatives if I choose not to disclose?

I want to be open because I want to share myself with others and get the benefits of such communication, such as receiving social support, the opportunity to think out loud, and the chance to get something off my chest. I do not want to be open because I might be ridiculed, rejected, or abandoned. Open or closed; let others in or keep others out? Every interaction has the potential for raising the tension of holding both desires simultaneously. It is not that one desire "wins" and the other "loses." Rather, they exist simultaneously. Interpersonal life consists of the tension between these opposites, otherwise there would be no problem balancing privacy, secrecy, and disclosure, and there would be no need for this collection of essays.

Whether to be open or closed is only one of the tensions that bind our interpersonal lives. Although it is what most of the authors in this book write about, there are other tensions that help define, or perhaps "round out," our understanding. The complexity of these issues becomes especially apparent when we consider the interdependence of these tensions within the context of relational communication in private and public settings. The reality of relational life is communicators seeking a variety of important, yet apparently incompatible goals. The struggle to achieve these goals creates "dialectical tensions," conflicts that arise when two opposing or incompatible forces exist *simultaneously*. Communication scholars such as Baxter and Montgomery (1996), Rawlins (1992), and Spitzberg (1994) have identified the dialectical forces that make successful communication challenging. These researchers have investigated how we interact with our relational partners and how we and our relational partners face other people whose desires clash with our own.

One dialectical tension, *integration versus separation,* addresses the tension between wanting to get involved with others while at the same time wanting to hide our entire identity in even the most satisfying relationship. The conflicting desires for connection and independence create communication challenges that can show up both within a relationship and when relational partners face the world. In this struggle we are trying to reconcile a desire for involvement with others with the desire to live our own lives, free of interference from "outsiders." Tannen (1986) captures this aspect of the integration–separation dialectic when she writes that, although we need others to survive, we want to survive as individuals as well.

Another dialectical tension, *stability versus change,* addresses our desire for predictability and our contrasting need for variety. Within a relationship, stability provides the routines that are well worn and comfortable, requiring little emotional energy and a sense of permanence. Change provides the novelty and the deviations that can stimulate growth and new ways of seeing the relational partner and the relationship. Just as boredom is the possible payoff for stability, dissatisfaction may be the payoff for change.

Also captured by the stability–change dialectical tension is the challenge that people in a relationship confront when trying to meet others' expectations as well as their own. On one hand, stable patterns of behavior emerge that enable others to make useful judgments like "good friend," or "compassionate doctor." However, those blanket characterizations can stifle people in relationships, especially those who may sometimes want to break away from the expectations others hold of them. Consider the example of the doctor who is seen as compassionate, but who feels the need to break confidentiality with a patient to reveal the patient's HIV status to a third person.

A third dialectical tension, *expression versus privacy,* brings us back to the central concern of this book and focuses attention on our need to maintain some space between self and other, which is a struggle between openness and closedness and between intimacy and distance. Historically, the notions of public and private behavior have changed dramatically (Adamopoulos, 1991; Gadlin, 1977; Trenholm & Jensen, 1990). What would be considered intimate behavior today was quite public at times in the past.

For example, in 16th century Germany, the new husband and wife were expected to consummate their marriage on a bed carried by witnesses who would validate the marriage (Adamopoulos & Bontempo, 1986). Conversely, in England as well as in colonial America, the customary level of communication between spouses was once rather formal, not much different from the way acquaintances or neighbors spoke to one another (Adamopoulos & Bontempo, 1986). Today, the notion of intimacy varies from one culture to another, although disclosure is especially high in mainstream North American society, compared to other cultures (Gudykunst, 1986).

The concept of *disclosure* is clearly related to notions of *privacy* and *secrecy.* If privacy concerns keeping things hidden, and secrets are the specific messages chosen not to be shared, then disclosure is the process that grants access to private things and to secrets. Neverthless, one might argue that it is impossible not to make yourself known once you choose to say anything; even what you choose to say about others says something about you. If every verbal and nonverbal behavior is self-revealing, however, how can self-disclosure be distinguished from any other act of communication?

Cozby (1973) suggests that in order for a communication act to be considered self-disclosing, it must contain personal information about the sender, the sender must communicate this information verbally, and another person must be the target. Put differently, the content of self-disclosing communication is the self, and information about the self is purposefully communicated to another person. This definition ignores the fact that disclosive messages may vary with respect to how revealing they are, how intentionally they are communicated, how honest and deep they are, and how positive or negative they are. The extent to which the information disclosed is available from sources other than the communicator might be another important consideration (Adler, Rosenfeld, Towne, & Proctor, 1998; D. A. Taylor & Altman, 1987; Wheeless, 1976; Wheeless & Grotz, 1976). The context is another significant aspect. Sometimes the self-disclosing nature of a statement and its intimacy value comes from the setting in which it is uttered (Officer & Rosenfeld, 1985). For instance, relatively innocuous information about family life seems more personal when a teacher shares it with a class, and highly personal information shared with a medical doctor often seems "usual" and "expected."

Although many acts of communication may be self-revealing, this definition makes it clear that few of our statements may be classified as self-disclosure. Pearce and Sharp (1973) estimate that as little as 2% of our communication qualifies as self-disclosure. Other research confirms this. For example, most conversations focus on mundane topics and disclose little or no personal information (Dindia, Fitzpatrick, & Kenny, 1988; Duck & Miell, 1986).

Derlega and Grzelak (1979) present a variety of reasons a person might have for disclosing in any particular situation. People might disclose for *catharsis,* because disclosure is a way to "get something off your chest." People disclose for *self-clarification*, because sometimes they can clarify their beliefs, opinions, thoughts, attitudes, and feelings by talking about them with others (this occurs in many psychotherapies). People also disclose for *self-validation*, because sharing personal information may elicit listeners' agreement or confirmation of a belief people hold about themselves—their self-concept. People disclose for *reciprocity*, because one act of self-disclosure often begets another. People disclose for *impression formation* because selectively disclosing personal information can serve as a way of "marketing" oneself (Wintrob, 1987). People disclose for *relationship maintenance and enhancement* because, in order to stay healthy, relationships need to be nourished by self-disclosure, by the revelations that allow partners to keep up with each other's lives (Aronson, 1984; Fincham & Bradbury, 1989; Rosenfeld & Bowen, 1991). People disclose for *social influence* because disclosure can facilitate increasing control over others, as well as serve as a means of helping others. For example, during meetings of Alcoholic Anonymous, one person's disclosure provides insight and understanding for another person in the group, or, on a larger scale, on the *Donahue* television show disclosure can be used to address injustices and remedy stereotypes (Priest & Dominick, 1994). Finally, people disclose for *manipulation* because disclosure can be used as a premeditated strategy to achieve a desired result. Rosenfeld and Kendrick (1984) found that reasons for self-disclosure differed as a function of relationship type. When the target was a friend, the top three reasons for disclosing were relationship maintenance and enhancement, self-clarification, and reciprocity. When the target was a stranger, the top reason for disclosing was reciprocity, and the second reason for disclosing was impression formation. What happens when the information concerns the HIV status of the discloser?

Although the benefits of disclosing are certainly important, there are also serious risks that make the decision to disclose a difficult and, sometimes, painful one (Henwood, Giles, Coupland, & Coupland, 1993). As the chapters in this book illustrate, avoiding disclosure seems more common than opening boundaries and revealing personal information. The scales often tip toward privacy and many of the chapters in this book are more concerned with self-disclosure avoidance than openness. For example, chapters 4–7 in this book consider the specific risks associated with disclosing and not disclosing HIV-seropositive test results with intimates and health care providers. Given the importance of this information for potential intimates, the "dance" of discovery and disclosure performed by gay men also is illustrated.

Revealing private information can be risky, both for the person who does the disclosing and for those who hear it (Petronio, 1991). These risks fall into several categories (Derlega, 1984; Derlega, Metts, Petronio, & Margulis, 1993; Hatfield, 1984; Rosenfeld, 1979). Perhaps most important in personal contexts is the fact that self-disclosure might lead to rejection by the other person. Sometimes the fear of rejection is exaggerated and illogical, but there are real dangers in revealing personal information. As Hatfield (1984) points out, "those we care about most are bound to discover all that is wrong with us—to discover that we possess taboo feelings . . . have done things of which we are deeply ashamed. Such fears are *not* neurotic" (p. 210).

Even if disclosure does not lead to total rejection, it can create a negative impression that diminishes the other person's respect and a basically satisfactory relational status quo. For example, Guerrero and Afifi (1995b) found that family members withhold a great deal of personal information from one another. Adolescents and young adults reported avoiding discussions of their dating and of negative life experiences with their parents, especially those of the opposite sex, and although men were more reluctant than women were to disclose, neither sex revealed all personal information.

With disclosure also comes a potential loss of influence in a relationship. For example, once we confess a secret weakness, control over how the other person views us can be diminished (Petronio, 1991). To reveal personal information is to risk losing control over that information and, perhaps, having it used against you—there is always "the lurking fear of what the other person would do with this [disclosed] information" (Phillips & Metzger, 1976, p. 351). The fear of loss of control may be particularly pertinent to men, stereotypically characterized as logical, objective, and unemotional (Hatfield, 1984).

There also are cultural dangers associated with disclosing (Petronio, in press). Many people view revealing personal information as weakness, exhibitionism, or mental illness. For example, people in North American culture who disclose too much too soon are judged harshly and, at the least, thought to be "peculiar" (Hatfield, 1984). Hastings, in chapter 16 of this book, considers the influence of culture on Asian Indians' decisions to self-disclose.

Paradoxically, self-disclosure often leads to increased awareness. As you reveal yourself to others, you often learn more about yourself. This awareness can expose a need for you to change, and this might be difficult or painful. If ignorance is bliss, self-awareness can sometimes be quite the opposite. This leads to the final risk of disclosure: even if revealing hidden information leaves you feeling better because you "got it off your chest" or learned something personally important, it might hurt others. Derlega, Winstead, and Folk-Barron, in chapter 4 of this book, discuss not wanting to upset others as a reason to avoid disclosing one's HIV-positive status. Cooks, in chapter 14, decides not to disclose her knowledge of who her biological father is to her brother and the father who raised her for fear of upsetting family patterns and of distancing family members.

Given the risks associated with disclosure, people might choose alternatives that include a focus on privacy, secrecy, and even deception. Deception is a problem in Western society because our moral education and common sense lead us to abhor anything less than the truth. As Jaksa and Pritchard (1994) pointed out, the very existence of a society seems based on a foundation of truthfulness. Although isolated cultures do exist where deceit is a norm (e.g., Turnbull, 1972), they are considered dysfunctional by Western standards.

Although honesty is desirable, it often has risky and potentially unpleasant consequences. Research and personal experience show that even communicators with the best intentions are not always completely truthful in situations where honesty could be uncomfortable (O'Hair & Cody, 1994). To keep information private or secret, people might use lies, equivocations, and hints.

A lie is a deliberate attempt to hide or misrepresent the truth. In a study in which respondents were asked to keep track of the truthfulness of their everyday conversational statements, only 38.5% of their statements proved to be totally honest (Turner, Edgely, & Olmstead, 1975). In another study, both students and community members reported lying daily for a variety of reasons, of which five were prominent: (a) to save face; (b) to avoid tension or conflict; (c) to guide social interaction and to make everyday relationships run smoothly; (d) to facilitate interaction with others and, conversely, to reduce interaction with others; and (e) to gain power, such as lying to get confidential information (DePaulo, Kashy, Kirkendol, & Wyer, 1996).

Although deception threatens relationships, not all lies are equally devastating (McCornack & Levine, 1990). Feelings like dismay and betrayal are greatest when the relationship is most intense, the importance of the subject is high, and there is previous suspicion that the other person is not being completely honest. Of these three factors, the importance of the information lied about is the key factor in provoking a relational crisis.

Lying is only one way to preserve a secret. When faced with the choice between lying and telling an unpleasant truth, communicators can equivocate, that is, communicate messages that are vague and that have two or more meanings. A study by Metts, Cupach, and Imahori (1992) found that equivocation can help one save face in a difficult situation. Several hundred college students were asked how they would turn down unwanted sexual overtures from a person whose feelings were important to them (a close friend, a prospective date, or a dating partner). The majority of students chose a diplomatic reaction ("I just don't think I'm ready for this right now") as being more face-saving and comfortable than a direct statement like, "I just don't feel sexually attracted to you." The diplomatic reaction seemed sufficiently clear to get the message across, but was not so blunt as to embarrass or humiliate the other person. In another series of experiments, respondents had to choose between telling a face-saving lie, the truth, or an equivocal response (Bavelas, Black, Chovil, & Mullett, 1990). Only 6% chose the lie, and between 3% and 4% chose the hurtful truth, whereas more than 90% chose the equivocal response. Similarly, Buslig and Burgoon, in chapter 13 of this book, found that requests for privacy are unlikely to be made aggressively because of the social impact of such directness.

Hints are more direct than equivocal statements. Whereas an equivocal message is not necessarily aimed at changing another's behavior, a hint is intended to get a desired response from the other person. As Motley (1992) suggests, some hints are designed to save the receiver from embarrassment, whereas others are meant to save the sender from embarrassment. In any case, the success of a hint depends on the other person's ability to pick up the unexpressed message (e.g., Petronio, Reeder, Hecht, & Mon't Ros-Mendoza, 1996).

Lies, equivocations, and hints provide a way to manage difficult situations. There are also several considerations relevant to the decision to be revealing. The first consideration has to do with the nature of our relationships with others. The more important the other person is, the more important it is to disclose.

A second consideration concerns the risk-to-benefit ratio: Even if the probable benefits are great, opening yourself up to almost certain risk may be foolish. Revealing personal thoughts and feelings can be especially risky on the job, where the politics of the workplace sometimes require communicators to keep feelings to themselves in order to accomplish both personal and organizational goals (Eisenberg, 1990; Eisenberg & Witten, 1987). Risks, however, decrease to the extent that you consider the other person trustworthy, sincere, likable, a good listener, warm, and open (Petronio, Martin, & Littlefield, 1984).

A third consideration focuses on the appropriateness of the disclosure, as well as its relevance to the situation. For instance, a study of classroom communication revealed that sharing all negative and positive feelings and being completely honest results in less group cohesiveness. In contrast, a relatively honest group climate with pleasant and superficial relational interactions has been found to foster group cohesiveness (Rosenfeld & Gilbert, 1989).

A fourth consideration centers on disclosure reciprocity. For relationships in which reciprocity is unexpected, self-disclosure creates an unbalanced relationship, one with potential problems. For example, we do not expect reciprocal disclosure from our physicians, social workers, and therapists. Of course, as Dindia points out in chapter 2, reciprocity in most relationships translates into "reciprocity over time," and not reciprocity in a tit-for-tat fashion. Although there is some evidence that the need for reciprocation is low among married couples (Rosenfeld & Bowen, 1991), other researchers argue that the greater the discrepancy between the partners' disclosure of feelings, the lower their marital adjustment (Davidson, Balswich, & Halverson, 1983). Even neurotics recognize that nonreciprocal disclosure is not as appropriate as two-way revelations (Strassberg, Adelstein, & Chemers, 1988).

Disclosure and privacy are part of a larger context, one that includes the dialectical tensions that define our relationships; the benefits and risks of being open; the alternatives to openness; the myriad considerations that go into making the decision to be open or private, to share or to hide the nature of your relationship with the other person; the risk-to-benefit ratio; the appropriateness of the disclosure; and the chance for disclosure reciprocity. Within this larger context, privacy, secrecy, and disclosure are balanced, even if the balance is a dynamic one maintained only for a moment.

DISCLOSURE, PRIVACY, AND SECRECY

The chapters of this book address disclosure and disclosure avoidance and their relationship to privacy and secrecy. Part II, on standpoints, provides not only a theoretical foundation for disclosure, privacy, and secrecy, but also draws an empirical connection to areas of social life where these concepts are highly relevant. Specifically, chapter 2 summarizes research on self-disclosure in three areas, whereas chapter 3 presents a theoretical model for understanding how people control access to private areas and secret information through choice about disclosure.

In chapter 2, Dindia looks closely at the empirical research on sex differences in self-disclosure, self-disclosure and reciprocity, and self-disclosure and liking. The relationships are not simple ones. There are a variety of contingencies and mediating variables that force us to broaden our perspective and that alert us to the need to look more closely than we might otherwise at the relations among privacy, secrecy, and disclosure. For instance, we need to look at and be sensitive to the content and form of a disclosure, the influence of the sex of the target, the discloser–target relationship, how disclosure is measured, the intimacy of the disclosure and how this intimacy "fits" the context in which the communication takes place, whether the disclosure is voluntary, and how the disclosure reflects on the person disclosing and the discloser–target relationship.

In chapter 3, Petronio uses her Communication Boundary Management (CBM) theory to explain how we negotiate the balance between privacy and openness. People give varying degrees of boundary access to others as a way to control entree to private information. In other words, we develop rules to regulate the tension between privacy and disclosure. We adjust our boundaries according to the contingencies Dindia highlights in her chapter, such as who the target of our disclosure is and the content of what we disclose, and then we adjust our boundaries further as we coordinate with the boundaries of others.

An example of physician–patient confidentiality clarifies how CBM theory operates as people communicate with one another. Physician–patient confidentiality, a topic picked up in several of the chapters of this book, is problematized by the reality that there is no such thing as absolute confidentiality. Questions of what to reveal and of how information revealed is the responsibility of both the physician and the patient force the physician and patient into an elaborate communication dance.

The chapters in Part III, on managing HIV/AIDS disclosures, are concerned with the "toughest case" scenario: the disclosure of a positive HIV/AIDS diagnosis. These chapters investigate the stigma associated with the disease and analyze the benefits and risks of disclosing HIV status to others. In chapter 4, Derlega, Winstead, and Folk-Barron focus on the reasons HIV-seropositive women and men give for choosing to disclose or not disclose their diagnosis with their sexually intimate partners. The important reasons for disclosing included seeing disclosure as a "duty" and as a way to educate the partner, as well as to experience catharsis. In an emotionally close relationship, disclosure also reflects both love and trust. The researchers found that concerns about privacy (e.g., "I don't want information being passed along to others who I didn't tell myself") and self-blame (e.g., "I felt bad about myself"—a very different reason from those found in studies of self-disclosure avoidance that focus on less-than-life-threatening issues) were the most important reasons not to disclose. Expectations affected how the information was disclosed: Those who disclosed indirectly were afraid of the partner's reaction and of being rejected, a primary fear regardless of whether the information to be shared is of the life-and-death variety or concerns more mundane matters.

In chapter 5, Cline and McKenzie switch focus from intimate relationships to the health care setting. Unlike relational partners, health care providers bring a host of obligations to their relationships with patients, obligations that may be in conflict with one another. For example, how do health care providers' obligations to society and third parties with whom the infected persons may come into contact balance with their promise to protect patient confidentiality? How does providers' right to know patients' HIV status balance with the patients' right to privacy?

Chapters 6 and 7 focus on HIV status in close relationships. Chapter 6, by Yep, applies CBM theory to the process of disclosing HIV status and begins by describing the fears of disclosing (e.g., social stigmatization, rejection, abandonment) and the fears of not disclosing (e.g., loneliness, loss of social support). Focusing on how the discloser and recipient coordinate their boundaries by using CBM theory, Yep examines the discloser's expectations for outcomes, message strategy selections, message content, the recipient's expectations, the discloser's motivation, and the message response strategies.

Without explicit HIV disclosure, how can someone find out if a potential partner is HIV-positive? In chapter 7, Brouwer looks at three texts, one concerned with explicit nonverbal disclosure, and the other two concerned with discovering the HIV status of others without their cooperation. The first text is Gregg Cadieux's "POZ" tattoo, an explicit nonverbal reference to his HIV status. The second is the practice of "trick exams," an attempt to read a potential partner's serostatus by surreptitiously feeling for swollen and hardened lymph nodes. The third text is Tom Ace's "Dire Diaries," a fictional diary that describes strategies for discovering another's HIV status in private settings, such as deducing the implications of a partner's not wanting to wear a condom (he must be infected if he is willing to have sex without a condom).

An implication of the chapters in Part III is that the disclosure of HIV status is so important that fears associated with being open are exacerbated. In fact, the information may be so risky that it borders on being a secret. If so, this may explain why it is so difficult to get people to reveal their status. However, knowing another's HIV status is so important—literally a matter of life and death—that disclosure may be something worth tricking out of another person. But is it disclosure if the information is gained without the other person's willingness or cooperation?

Part IV, on health care and illness, continues to investigate the relationship among disclosure, privacy, and secrecy. In chapter 8, Tardy reviews research supporting Jourard's contention that self-disclosure promotes physiological health and well-being: Self-disclosure relates in a positive way to self-reports of health, records of use of health services, immune system efficiency, mortality rates, cardiovascular illness, and, from Tardy's own investigation, symptoms of emotional stress. In all likelihood, self-disclosure has these positive effects because it reduces the stress associated with inhibition and helps the discloser organize her or his thoughts productively.

In chapter 9, Greene looks at two contingencies affecting disclosure: the target of disclosure—whether mother, father, sister, brother, partner, or friend—and the illness—AIDS or cancer. Respondents in Greene's study, who had neither AIDS nor cancer, supported the researcher's hypotheses of greater willingness to disclose about the less stigmatizing disease, cancer, and greater willingness to disclose to a more intimate than less intimate target. Underlying the choices of what to disclose and to whom to disclose was a careful assessment of the potential benefits and risks: What disclosure topic is least likely to lead to rejection and discrimination? Which target is most likely to offer social support?

In chapter 10, Parrott, Duncan, and Duggan expand on Greene's concern with how target and topic variations affect disclosure by including consideration of the setting. It seems logical that patients' responses to the question, "How are you?" posed by a physician would be highly disclosive. After all, saying "Fine, thanks, and you?" is likely to lead to the doctor's inquiry, "Then why are you here?" But the very nature of the questions health caregivers ask may be threatening to a patient's face—her or his self-image—and thus heighten fears of a loss of privacy. The risks associated with revealing may keep the patient from disclosing to the caregiver. These include the fear that confidentiality may be breached; fear that information provided may be used against the patient; fear of being the object of ridicule if beliefs about health care differ markedly from the caregiver's, or if ignorance or incompetence is revealed; fear that a change in behavior may be necessary, such as giving up a comfortable habit; and fear of being told something traumatic, such as having to be hospitalized. The fears associated with disclosing may outweigh the benefits, including health and well-being. Parrott and her colleagues offer suggestions designed to increase the rewards of patient disclosures. Suggestions include letting the patient speak without interruption and softening inquiries (e.g., minimizing the size of a request and speaking indirectly).

The chapters in Part V, on relational disclosure, privacy, and secrecy, are particularly concerned with disclosure avoidance. In chapter 11, Roloff and Ifert argue that the fears associated with being open are not unfounded. There are times when avoidance is a good idea, as long as it reduces arguing and does not harm the relationship. Avoidance is successful if it occurs regarding a relatively unimportant conflict; if it involves a tolerance for differences (each person needs to feel comfortable with the other person getting her or his way); if it avoids provocation, because there are other topics to talk about; and if the avoider has good communication skills—ways of communicating that emphasize commonalities rather than differences, and that stress understanding each other's perspective. Avoidance is problematic when it results in obsessing over a "minor" conflict or rationalizing that a conflict is "minor" rather than assessing it accurately.

In chapter 12, Afifi and Guerrero complement Roloff and Ifert's perspective by investigating motivations behind topic avoidance. Motivations for disclosure avoidance fall into three categories: relationship based, individual based, and information based. Relationship-based motivations include the desire to protect or enhance a relationship by avoiding a disagreeable topic (a more common motivation for males than females) and, paradoxically, the desire to de-escalate or destroy a relationship by avoiding a topic that might increase intimacy and commitment. Individual-based motivations include the desire to avoid identity-threatening disclosure and to maintain a sense of autonomy (important for teenagers, e.g., as part of the process of separation and individuation). Information-based motivations include avoiding asking for information when those to whom one would disclose are expected to be unhelpful or unresponsive, or when the topic is uninteresting to the discloser. By focusing exclusively on motivations for topic avoidance, Afifi and Guerrero add to the long list of reasons people have to avoid disclosure.

Unlike other chapters that look at the risks of disclosing, Buslig and Burgoon, in chapter 13, look at the risks involved with *not* disclosing. A denial of access to private areas may result in being seen as rude or unsociable, as rejecting, as lacking trust or positive feelings, or as betraying the relationship itself ("Aren't we friends? Why won't you tell me?"). The researchers found that respondents who were moderately aggressive in their avoidant disclosures were more satisfied with their outcomes than those who were nonaggressive or aggressive. The researchers also found that the more one feared that an attempt to gain privacy would result in negative consequences, the more one chose a less aggressive strategy.

In the last chapter in this section, chapter 14, Cooks looks at disclosure from an interpretive-critical perspective and calls into question the very nature and validity of the concept of self-disclosure (at least as envisioned in the other chapters in this book). Cooks moves us back to the philosophical roots of disclosure, where disclosure is discussed not as a dimension of interpersonal relationships but as a necessity for existence, as how we enact and simultaneously create "self." For Cooks, others play a crucial role in the disclosure–self equation: "The search," Cooks writes, "is not necessarily for a self that is/can be uncovered, bared, or disclosed but rather the ways in which the self is created, disavowed, and constructed in moments which are, ultimately, social." The self, Cooks argues, is not something already composed, a "completed entity" that we choose to disclose or not disclose, but something enacted in different contexts. The self is an entity formed in the interaction, in the telling, in the disclosure. Thus, "action" and "context" are at the center of analysis, and not, as some researchers (particularly those who devise measures for assessing self-disclosure) would have it, characteristics of the information disclosed, such as depth, amount, and honesty.

Section VI, on media and cultural issues, moves us into the cross-cultural and the popular realms of disclosure, privacy, and secrecy. In chapter 15, Rubin, Yang, and Porte compare the disclosures of Chinese and North American students. Interestingly, and contrary to the expectations of Rubin and his colleagues, there were no differences due to nationality; however, there were differences due to target and topic, confirming the importance of these contingencies when looking at disclosure. As expected, disclosure was greatest with intimates and friends and least with strangers and personal topics, such as money and personality, were disclosed less than were impersonal topics, such as attitudes and taste.

In chapter 16, Hastings shifts attention to Asian Indians. Focusing specifically on egocasting, Hastings looks at the internal messages Indian communicators offer themselves to support their decision to disclose or not to disclose. Reflecting their culture, which, for example, emphasizes social harmony (in comparison to North American culture, which emphasizes assertiveness), Indian respondents characterized their communication pat-

terns as "suppressed." They described their internal talk in ways that indicated several concerns, for example, concern about what others will think
regarding their disclosure, about whether what they say will reflect poorly
on their family name, and about the probability of the disclosure being used
for gossip. Using in-depth, ethnographic interviews, Hastings is able to
provide insight into an area ignored by researchers looking at reasons for
disclosure avoidance: the internal messages we use to justify our balance of
the expressiveness–privacy tension.

In chapter 17, Orrego, Smith, Mitchell, Johnson, Ah Yun, and Greenberg,
look at self-disclosures and "ambush" disclosures (i.e., disclosures by others
about the self-disclosing person) on television talk shows, where the talk
typically centers on private, negative information about the guests. The
researchers show how traditional North American norms are broken. They
point out that what in most relational contexts would be inappropriate
becomes fodder for discussion on national television. Analyses of self-disclosures indicate that more than 50% of the disclosures have to do with
personal attributes, such as addictions and personality traits, and with sexual
activity. Other common topics include abuse, embarrassing situations, criminal activity, and sexual orientation. Unlike nontelevised situations, responses
to disclosures were mostly negative and nonreciprocal. That is, the disclosure
process on television talk shows bears little resemblance to what happens in
other contexts. The risks of disclosure, too, are compounded by disclosing
on television: rejection, ridicule, betrayal, and exploitation take on new
meaning when the context is public and the potential for loss of face is
extremely high. The perceived benefits of self-disclosing on television must
outweigh the risks in order for people to take the gamble.

Part VII, on speaking the unspeakable, continues an examination of
disclosure, privacy, and secrecy in public contexts by exploring community
notification policies regarding sex offenders and battered women's narratives
in a courtroom setting. In chapter 18, Schultz explores the tension that results
when an individual's right to privacy and a community's right to know come
into conflict. The prevailing assumption is that a sex offender's right to
privacy is less important than the safety of the offender's community; in
other words, society's general interests, at least insofar as this particular type
of crime and illness are concerned, supersede an individual's right to privacy.
The decision to disclose, however, raises concerns because of the public
setting in which the disclosure takes place, such as the interference public
notification has on the offender's ability to readjust to life outside prison
and in the community. Schultz's analysis provides the opportunity to consider
how the benefits and risks, the advantages and disadvantages, balance when
the issue is public disclosure of sex offenders.

The interplay of the "desire for privacy, the habits of secrecy and the act
of disclosure . . . are heightened for women in abusive relationships," writes

Dieckmann in chapter 19. The relief felt from disclosing, the release granted from self-inflicted psychological abuse for keeping the secret, the possibility disclosure holds for changing the situation, that is, for ending the violent relationship—all are balanced against the likelihood of retribution, increased violence, and, perhaps, death. Disclosure, particularly as part of counseling, provides a means for self-discovery and rebuilding self-esteem, with the goal of personal and relational transformation. "Private" and "public" take on new meaning as women talk about their bodies as "simultaneously the site of knowledge, the map of violence, and the interstice between 'public' and 'private' experience." The shelter provides a safe place where battered women can experience anonymity and privacy—a place where disclosure can help the women connect and build a discursive community, which, for many, represents a gesture toward resistance.

Part VIII, and the final chapter (chap. 20), focus our attention on the future of disclosure, privacy, and secrecy. Baxter and Sahlstein point to the importance of further investigating notions of balance, the sovereign self, and the social ramifications of disclosure. The researchers close their chapter by discussing methodological and theoretical advances in the area of privacy, secrecy, and disclosure.

ON BALANCING

Together, the chapters in this book raise more questions than they answer. A simple "how to" book on methods for balancing privacy, secrecy, and disclosure would be a lie. If the research in the area has demonstrated anything (and the chapters in this book attest to this), it is that "it depends" should precede statements about how disclosure operates to regulate access to private areas and secret information. Each of us weighs the risks and benefits related to what we have to say and to whom we want to say it, the context in which we interact, and so on, and makes a personal decision—one that reflects our shared and individual cultures. In the end, what we self-disclose reflects and creates our uniqueness, at once distinguishes us from and places us within the context of our community, and serves to unite public and private in the moment of revelation.

II

STANDPOINTS ON SECRETS
OF PRIVATE DISCLOSURES

2

▼▼▼▼▼▼▼▼▼

Sex Differences in Self-Disclosure, Reciprocity of Self-Disclosure, and Self-Disclosure and Liking: Three Meta-Analyses Reviewed

Kathryn Dindia
University of Wisconsin, Milwaukee

Three issues have dominated the literature on self-disclosure. They are: sex differences in self-disclosure, reciprocity of self-disclosure, and self-disclosure and liking. The purpose of this chapter is to review three meta-analyses of self-disclosure: Dindia and Allen's (1992) meta-analysis of sex differences in self-disclosure, Dindia and Allen's (1995) meta-analysis of reciprocity of self-disclosure, and Collins and Miller's (1994) meta-analysis of self-disclosure and liking. I review the results of these meta-analyses and consider their implications for the issue of balancing disclosure, privacy, and secrecy.

A QUICK REVIEW OF META-ANALYSIS

Meta-analysis is a quantitative method of summarizing the results from multiple studies on a given issue. A meta-analysis proceeds in several steps. First, you locate all the studies on a particular topic, for example, all the studies on sex-differences in self-disclosure. Second, you calculate the effect size for each study. The effect size d is a statistic that indicates how large an effect is, for example, the degree to which women disclose more than men. Third, you calculate the average effect size across studies. Cohen (1969) offered the following guidelines for interpreting d: $d = .20$ is small, $d = .50$ is moderate, and $d = .80$ is large. The effect size d can be translated into a correlation

21

coefficient r by the approximate formula $d = 2r$ (for large values of r, the exact formula should be used, $d = 2r/[\text{sq rt } (1 - r^2)]$ (Hyde, 1993).

The fourth step in meta-analysis is to test for homogeneity of effect sizes; that is, whether an effect size varies more than would be expected by chance across the group of studies. If an effect size is heterogeneous, one can test for moderator variables, variables that systematically influence the effect size. For example, self-disclosure between strangers may be reciprocal, whereas self-disclosure between intimates may not.

SEX DIFFERENCES IN SELF-DISCLOSURE

There are probably more studies that test sex differences in self-disclosure than any other issue in the self-disclosure literature. What is the theoretical reasoning behind such studies? One perspective on self-disclosure is that self-disclosure is a personality trait. As a personality trait, self-disclosure is viewed as an enduring characteristic or attribute of an individual. An individual's "ability" and "willingness" to self-disclose is studied. Studies cast within this perspective attempt to identify high and low disclosers and to correlate individual differences in self-disclosure with demographic and biological characteristics (sex, age, race, religion, birth order), sociocultural differences, and other personality traits (Archer, 1979). Sex is the individual difference variable that has been studied most.

Dindia and Allen (1992) conducted a meta-analysis of sex differences in self-disclosure. Dindia and Allen (1992) located 205 studies involving 23,702 participants that tested sex differences in self-disclosure. The results of the meta-analysis were that women disclosed more than men, but the difference was small ($d = .18$). However, the effect size was not homogeneous across studies. In a narrative review of the literature, Hill and Stull (1987) found inconsistent findings in research on sex differences in self-disclosure. They argued that various situational factors may account for inconsistencies in sex differences in self-disclosure. Specifically, they argued that a number of situational factors have been found to affect self-disclosure (e.g., sex of target and relationship to target) and that these factors may interact with sex of discloser to mediate sex differences in self-disclosure. Thus, Dindia and Allen (1992) tested sex of target, relationship to target, measure of self-disclosure (as well as publication date and status) as potential moderators of sex differences in self-disclosure.

Sex of target (male, female, same sex, opposite sex) moderated the effect of sex of discloser on self-disclosure. Women disclosed more to women than men disclosed to women ($d = .24$); women disclosed more to women than men disclosed to men ($d = .31$); women disclosed more to men than men disclosed to women ($d = .08$); but women did not disclose more to men than men disclosed to men ($d = .03$, not significantly different from 0). In addition, sex differences in self-disclosure were significantly greater to female and same-sex partners than to opposite-sex and male partners.

What explains this pattern of results? Hill and Stull (1987) concluded that female–female self-disclosure is highest, male–male self-disclosure is lowest, and opposite-sex self-disclosure is in between. They argued that this is a result of the interaction effect of sex of discloser (women disclose more than men) and reciprocity of self-disclosure (self-disclosure is reciprocal). Thus, female–female self-disclosure is the highest because women disclose more than men and their higher levels of self-disclosure elicit more self-disclosure from their partner. Male–male self-disclosure is lowest because men disclose less than women and their low levels of self-disclosure elicit less self-disclosure from their partner. Individuals paired with opposite-sex partners will disclose in the middle, with women disclosing more than men because women are higher disclosers.

The results of the meta-analysis only partially support Hill and Stull's (1987) hypothesis. As predicted, sex differences were greater in same-sex than opposite-sex interactions. However, according to Hill and Stull, the level of female-to-male self-disclosure should have been intermediate, and the level of male-to-male self-disclosure lowest. But this was not the case. Female-to-male self-disclosure was similar to male-to-male self-disclosure.

Relationship to partner (stranger vs. friend, parent, or spouse) did not, by itself, moderate the effect of sex on self-disclosure. Sex differences in self-disclosure to strangers were not significantly different from sex differences in self-disclosure in a relationship (self-disclosure to a friend, parent, or spouse).

Measure of self-disclosure (self-report measure, report of partner's self-disclosure, observational measure of self-disclosure) moderated sex-differences in self-disclosure. When the measure of self-disclosure was an individual reporting his or her partner's self-disclosure, d was .44. Individuals reported that female partners disclosed more than male partners. This effect size was homogeneous and was significantly greater than the effect size for self-report and observational measures ($d = .17$ and .22, respectively).

Why do perceptions of other people's self-disclosure result in larger sex differences than self-perceptions or trained observer perceptions of self-disclosure? It may be the result of gender stereotypes. Perhaps we perceive that we receive more self-disclosure from women than men because there is a stereotype that women self-disclose more than men. Judgments of our own self-disclosure (and trained observer judgments of self-disclosure) may be less prone to this stereotype.

Whether studies were published in the 1960s, 1970s, or 1980s did not moderate the effect of sex on self-disclosure. Sex differences in self-disclosure have not decreased in the past 30 years. Similarly, whether a study was published did not influence the effect size. There was no evidence that studies finding sex differences were more likely to be published than studies finding no difference.

Hill and Stull (1987) suggested that interactions between situational factors may moderate sex differences in self-disclosure. Thus, Dindia and Allen (1992) tested whether interaction effects between sex of target, relationship to target, and measure of self-disclosure moderated the effect of sex on self-disclosure. The findings were as follows. Measure of self-disclosure (self-report vs. observation) did not moderate sex differences in self-disclosure to targets that have a relationship with the discloser (friend, spouse, parent). In established relationships, both self-report and observational data indicated that women disclose more than men ($d = .21$ and $.23$, respectively). However, measure of self-disclosure moderated sex differences when the target was a stranger. Men reported that they self-disclose similarly to women ($d = -.02$, not significantly different from 0). However, observational studies of self-disclosure to a stranger found that women disclose more than men ($d = .17$), and the effect size was not significantly different from the effect size for self-report and observational measures of self-disclosure to friends, parents, and spouses. Dindia and Allen (1992) interpreted the zero effect size for self-report measures of self-disclosure to strangers as a spurious result based on invalid self-report measures of self-disclosure when the target person is a stranger (individuals cannot validly report their level of self-disclosure to a generalized stranger).

Summary

Overwhelmingly, Dindia and Allen's (1992) meta-analysis provides evidence that women disclose more than men. However, sex differences in self-disclosure are small and are moderated by the sex of the person being disclosed to. Sex is not a stable individual difference variable that consistently predicts level of self-disclosure across sex of partner.

RECIPROCITY OF SELF-DISCLOSURE

Jourard (1971b) originated the idea that self-disclosure is reciprocal: "In ordinary social relationships, disclosure is a reciprocal phenomenon. Participants in dialogue disclose their thoughts, feelings, actions, etc., to the other and are disclosed to in return. I called this reciprocity the 'dyadic effect': disclosure begets disclosure" (p. 66).

There are several explanations for reciprocity of self-disclosure, including trust–attraction, social exchange, the norm of reciprocity and conversational constraints (see Chelune, 1979; Derlega & Berg, 1987; and Derlega et al., 1993 for reviews and discussions of these theories).

Although most scholars and lay persons believe that self-disclosure is reciprocal, the evidence to support the hypothesis depends on how reciprocity is tested. Reciprocity of self-disclosure has been tested a number of ways, one of the more common being the correlation between partners' self-disclosure (Hill & Stull, 1982). A criticism leveled against using relationship analysis as a statistical test of reciprocity is that it confounds base rates of self-disclosure with reciprocity of self-disclosure. For example, two persons' self-disclosure may be related due to similar personality traits (e.g., Kate and John's self-disclosure are similar because they are both high or low disclosers). Correlation confounds individual differences in self-disclosure with reciprocity of self-disclosure.

A second test of reciprocity of self-disclosure is whether an experimenter's or confederate's self-disclosure has a positive effect on a subject's self-disclosure. Typically, a subject is exposed to one of two experimental conditions of self-disclosure, high or low disclosure. The results of these studies provide evidence of a one-way effect; they do not provide evidence of reciprocity: (mutual positive influence). In addition, the generalizability of the results from these studies has been seriously questioned. As stated by Chelune (1979): "Investigators have used superficial, perfunctory remarks in the low disclosure condition and explicit, personal comments on highly private topics . . . for the high disclosure conditions" (p. 14). The results of these studies may not generalize to real-life conversations.

Sequential analysis has been used to test reciprocity of self-disclosure. Whether an individual's self-disclosure elicits a partner's self-disclosure in the subsequent turn (or near-subsequent turn), and vice versa, is tested. Only a few studies have been conducted testing reciprocity of self-disclosure using sequential analysis (Dindia, 1982, 1988; Spencer, 1993; Strassberg, Gabel, & Anchor, 1976).

A problem arises when using sequential analysis to test reciprocity of self-disclosure. An individual may reciprocate self-disclosure at a later point in the conversation, or even in a later conversation. As stated by Altman (1973):

> The dyadic effect is assumed to be a time-bound process in which people mutually regulate their disclosure to one another, at some agreed upon pace. But, little more is said about temporal aspects of reciprocity. The rate at which it occurs, how it ebbs and flows, factors which accelerate or retard reciprocity of exchange are not discussed in detail. (p. 250)

Thus, reciprocity of self-disclosure may occur in a manner other than an individual's self-disclosure, increasing the probability of the partner's self-disclosure in the subsequent turn ("My most embarrassing moment was . . ."; "My most embarrassing moment was . . ."). It may be that an individual's self-disclosure has a positive effect on his or her partner's self-disclosure, and vice versa, in some general sense that is not manifested on a turn-by-turn basis.

Kenny and La Voie (1984) provided an alternate solution to the problem of testing reciprocity of self-disclosure with what they labeled *dyadic reciprocity*. Dyadic reciprocity measures reciprocity of self-disclosure that is unique to the particular relationship, controlling for individual differences in self-disclosure. Dyadic reciprocity measures whether a partner's unique adjustment in self-disclosure (how much an individual discloses to his or her partner above or below how much he or she discloses in general) is reciprocal. Of all the tests of reciprocity of self-disclosure, Kenny and La Voie's dyadic reciprocity most closely matches Jourard's conceptual definition of reciprocity of self-disclosure.

A second issue involved in testing reciprocity of self-disclosure is how self-disclosure is measured. Research on reciprocity of self-disclosure primarily employs self-report measures of self-disclosure. Two types of reciprocity are studied with perceptual data. First, there is what has been referred to in the literature as *perceived reciprocity*, or intrasubjective perceptions of self-disclosure. Intrasubjective perceptions are perceptions of one person, that is, whether one person perceives his/her self-disclosure with the partner as reciprocal. Specifically, it refers to the correlation between an individual's perception of his or her self-disclosure to a partner (disclosure given) and the individual's perception of the partner's self-disclosure to the individual (disclosure received).

Second, there is what has been referred to in the literature as "actual reciprocity," or intersubjective perceptions of self-disclosure. Intersubjective perceptions are perceptions between persons. Specifically, it refers to the correlation between an individual's perception of his or her self-disclosure to a partner (A's disclosure to B) and the partner's perception of his or her self-disclosure to the individual (B's disclosure to A). Although this is labeled "actual reciprocity," the term is a misnomer because it is based on perceptions of self-disclosure. A few studies measure "actual" self-disclosure by employing observational measures of partners' self-disclosure.

Dindia and Allen (1995) conducted a meta-analysis to determine whether self-disclosure is reciprocal. Across 67 studies involving 5,173 participants, the effect size for reciprocity of self-disclosure was $d = .69$, a moderately large effect size; however, the results were not homogeneous. Method of testing reciprocity and measure of self-disclosure were examined as potential moderator variables. Correlational studies found the largest average effect size ($d = 1.36$), but the effect sizes were not homogeneous across studies. Studies employing social relations analysis found a similar effect size ($d = 1.18$); the effect sizes were homogeneous but were based on only four studies.

The average effect size for experimental studies was significantly smaller but still indicated a moderately large effect size ($d = .62$); again, the effect sizes were not homogeneous. Finally, studies employing sequential analysis found a small effect size ($d = .12$); the effect sizes were homogeneous but were only based on five studies.

Thus, how reciprocity of self-disclosure is tested affects the degree of reciprocity found. Relationship analysis and social relations analysis both indicate high levels of reciprocity of self-disclosure. That the studies employing social relations analysis (which controls for individual differences in self-disclosure) found large effect sizes indicates that this is not just because partners are similar in their overall levels of self-disclosure (i.e., high disclosers are paired with high disclosers). Experimental studies of reciprocity of self-disclosure found a moderately large effect of one person's self-disclosure on another person's self-disclosure. Although the results may not be generalizable beyond the artificial laboratory situation employed in these studies, they indicate a causal relationship: one person's self-disclosure causes the other person's self-disclosure. The results for the studies employing sequential analysis indicate that reciprocity does not occur on a turn-by-turn basis. However, it should be noted that two of the studies employing social relations analysis (Dindia, Fitzpatrick, & Kenny, 1997; Wright & Ingraham, 1985) tested whether self-disclosure is reciprocal within conversations and found that it was.

Method of measuring self-disclosure also moderated reciprocity of self-disclosure. Studies using self-report data had much larger effect sizes than those employing observational data. For intrasubjective perceptions of reciprocity (the correlation between one person's perceptions of his or her self-disclosure to the partner and the partner's self-disclosure to him or her), the effect size was largest ($d = 2.25$, five studies, homogeneous effect size). For intersubjective perceptions of reciprocity (the correlation between one individual's perceptions of his or her self-disclosure to a partner and the partner's perceptions of his or her disclosure to the individual), the effect size was significantly smaller but was still a very large effect size ($d = 1.37$, 10 studies, heterogeneous effect size). There was a moderately large effect size for observational measures of self-disclosure ($d = .59$, 51 studies, heterogeneous effect size).

Thus, there is overwhelming evidence that self-disclosure is reciprocal. The effect sizes range from moderately large to very large except for the studies employing sequential analysis. The degree to which self-disclosure is reciprocal depends on how reciprocity is tested, and self-disclosure is more reciprocal in correlational studies than in experimental studies. The degree to which self-disclosure is reciprocal also depends on how self-disclosure is measured; perceptions of reciprocity exceed actual reciprocity. It also appears that while self-disclosure is not reciprocal on a turn-by-turn basis, there is some evidence that it is reciprocal within conversations. Beyond these tests, most of the results were heterogeneous, indicating that there are probably other variables that moderate reciprocity of self-disclosure.

One possible moderator is the level of the relationship. Altman (1973) hypothesized that reciprocity of self-disclosure decreases as a relationship develops. Hill and Stull (1982) argued that reciprocity does not decrease as a relationship develops, but that the time frame over which reciprocity occurs increases. Regardless, strangers should reciprocate self-disclosure within conversations more than intimates.

Dindia and Allen (1995) studied the moderating effect of relationship between discloser and target on reciprocity of self-disclosure. The majority of studies (52) involved strangers and had a moderately large effect size, d = .67 (heterogeneous effect size). Unexpectedly, reciprocity of self-disclosure was significantly higher for partners who had a close relationship with each other (spouses or friends) (d = .97, five studies, homogeneous effect size). However, this could be due to the fact that studies involving spouses or friends were more likely to be self-report or correlational studies than studies involving strangers, and all of the studies employing sequential analysis involved strangers.

One study employing social relations analysis (Dindia et al., 1997) systematically analyzed the effect of level of relationship on reciprocity of self-disclosure. The results were that there were no differences in reciprocity of self-disclosure for spouses versus opposite-sex strangers. In particular, Dindia et al. (1997) found that spouses, as well as strangers, reciprocate high-intimacy evaluative self-disclosure within conversations.

Summary

The results of the meta-analysis on reciprocity of self-disclosure suggest that "reciprocity is 'normative,' meaning it is a common and expected occurrence but is not invariant or automatic" (Derlega et al., 1993). In general, the results of the meta-analysis indicate a moderately large to very large effect size for reciprocity of self-disclosure. This indicates that self-disclosure is generally reciprocal for strangers and intimates, and that it is generally perceived as being reciprocal (and it is perceived as being more reciprocal than it actually is). However, self-disclosure does not appear to be reciprocal on a tit-for-tat basis. The results of the studies employing sequential analysis indicate that one person's self-disclosure does not increase the probability of the partner's self-disclosure in the subsequent utterance.

Thus, the interpersonally competent response to self-disclosure may not be to immediately reciprocate self-disclosure. As Berg and Archer (1980) noted, "Informal observations suggest that self-disclosures are met with a variety of responses. Indeed, a common reaction to hearing about an intimate problem in another's life is to express concern or empathy" (pp. 246–247). Berg and Archer conducted an experiment in which they examined subjects' perceptions of an individual based on the individual's response to a self-disclosure. Berg and Archer (1980) found that the most favorable impressions of the respondent were formed when the respondent expressed concern for a discloser rather than when the respondent returned any level of self-disclosure. Similarly, Dindia (1984) found that self-disclosure, rather than being reciprocal, was followed sequentially by acknowledgements (such as "mm-hmm," "oh," and "yeah").

Although self-disclosure does not appear to be reciprocal on a turn-by-turn basis, studies employing social relations analysis indicate that reciprocity of self-disclosure occurs within conversations, even in developed relationships. Thus, although it may not be appropriate to immediately reciprocate self-disclosure, it appears that it is appropriate to reciprocate self-disclosure within the same conversation and that this is true for intimates as well as strangers.

SELF-DISCLOSURE AND LIKING

Self-disclosure and liking are thought to be related in at least three ways: An individual's self-disclosure to a partner leads to the partner's liking of the individual (the "disclosure–liking hypothesis"), an individual's liking for a partner leads to the individual's disclosure to the partner, and an individual likes a partner as a result of having disclosed to him or her. Collins and Miller (1994) conducted meta-analyses of all three of these relationships between self-disclosure and liking.

The first effect, that of an individual's self-disclosure on a partner's liking, has been of greatest theoretic interest, and studies examining this effect make up the bulk of the studies on self-disclosure and liking. Collins and Miller (1994) examined 94 studies testing this effect. The results were that higher levels of disclosure were associated with greater liking for the discloser ($d = .28$, a small effect size). However, the results were not homogeneous, and several moderator variables were examined.

First, like the meta-analysis of reciprocity of self-disclosure, the effect of type of study was tested. In particular, Collins and Miller (1994) examined correlational versus experimental studies (which was further divided into whether the study was a "strong," or well-controlled, experiment or a "weak," or less-controlled, experiment). The results indicated that the effect size depended on type of study. A large effect was found for correlational studies ($d = .85$), whereas small effects were found for experimental studies ($d = .27$ and .19 for strong and weak experiments, respectively). Although the effect sizes were small in experimental studies, they indicate a causal relationship: disclosure causes liking.

Why is there a larger effect size for correlational studies than for experimental studies? In addition to the lack of control in correlational studies, correlational studies employed self-report measures of self-disclosure and liking (this included both studies in which an individual reported the amount of disclosure he or she received from a discloser and his or her liking for the discloser and studies in which an individual reported his or her disclosure to a recipient and the recipient reported his or her liking for the discloser. Experimental studies manipulated high and low disclosure and then measured the subject's liking for the discloser. The larger effect size for correlational studies leads to a potential qualification of the disclosure–liking relationship. That is, like reciprocity of self-disclosure, individuals may perceive that self-disclosure causes liking more than self-disclosure actually causes liking.

Bochner (1982) noted that people tend to believe it is appropriate to engage in high amounts of self-disclosure with others they like, so when asked, they report that they engage in higher levels of disclosure to persons they like than to persons they dislike. Similarly, Bochner pointed out that people overestimate the extent to which they self-disclose to others they like, and that this too would artificially increase the correlation between self-report measures of self-disclosure and liking. Thus, self-disclosure may have a small effect on liking, but we may perceive it as a large effect.

Several additional moderator variables were studied in Collins and Miller's (1994) meta-analysis of the disclosure–liking hypothesis. The effect of study paradigm was tested. In particular, survey studies (same as correlational studies) were compared with three subgroups of experimental studies, acquaintance studies, impression formation studies, and field studies. Survey studies had the largest effect size ($d = .85$), followed by acquaintance studies ($d = .38$), impression formation studies ($d = .19$), and field studies ($d = -.31$). Collins and Miller interpreted the negative effect size for field studies as a result of an individual disclosing to a stranger in public, which may be viewed as inappropriate and a violation of social norms.

Collins and Miller (1994) also tested whether sex of discloser, sex of recipient, and the interaction of sex of discloser and sex of recipient moderated the disclosure liking relationship. The results indicated that the disclosure- liking relationship is stronger for female than male disclosers ($d = .30$ versus .11, respectively). However, the results were heterogeneous indicating that sex of discloser, by itself, does not moderate the disclosure–liking relationship. There was little evidence of differences in the disclosure–liking relationship for male versus female recipients of disclosure. The results for the interaction effect of sex of discloser and sex of recipient were significant. However, two cells contained only two observations, the difference between the two cells with larger observations did not reach significance, and the results for three of the four cells were heterogeneous.

Collins and Miller (1994) tested the effect of level of disclosure on the disclosure–liking relationship. It has been hypothesized that disclosure that violates normative expectations, specifically, self-disclosure that is too intimate or too negative, will not lead to liking (Bochner, 1982; Derlega et al., 1993; Parks, 1982). In initial interaction it is normative to engage in low-intimacy self-disclosure that reflects positively on one's self. Any self-disclosure that deviates from this norm may produce negative attributions (Bochner, 1982).

Collins and Miller (1994) did not find evidence that high disclosure, relative to low disclosure, leads to less liking. However, they indicate that their finding is limited, given the small number of studies on which the finding was based ($N = 7$) and the difficulty in comparing disclosure levels from one study to the next.

A third potential moderator of the disclosure–liking relationship, whether self-disclosure was perceived as personalistic or not, was tested. Berg and Derlega (1987) noted that people make attributions regarding another person's disclosure and that "the attributions we use to explain why someone is telling us something intimate or revealing are an important part of what the self-disclosure will mean to the relationship" (Derlega et al., 1993, p. 27). People can attribute another person's self-disclosure to the person's disposition or personality (he disclosed to me because he is generally an open person) or to their relationship (he disclosed to me because we have a special relationship).

In a narrative review of the literature, Berg and Derlega (1987) concluded that research indicates that when we perceive another person's self-disclosure as personalistic (revealed only to the target) rather than nonpersonalistic (revealed to many people), it leads to increased liking. In support of this, Collins and Miller's (1994) meta-analysis found that the mean effect size for self-disclosure where a personalistic attribution was made was $d = .453$, whereas the mean effect size for nonpersonalistic attributions was $d = .228$. Although the difference was not statistically significant, it was in the predicted direction. Collins and Miller concluded that "these studies provide some evidence that the relation between disclosure and liking may be stronger if the recipient believes that the disclosure was given because of something unique or special about him- or herself" (p. 20).

The results of research on the disclosure–liking relationship have important theoretical implications for self-disclosure. They indicate that self-disclosure causes liking, but that we may perceive that self-disclosure causes liking more than it actually does. The results also indicate that self-disclosure that is perceived as being particular to the partner or the relationship ("he or she is disclosing to me because he or she likes me") may be more likely to lead to liking than self-disclosure that is viewed as a result of a personality trait ("he or she is disclosing to me because he or she is a high discloser"). The meta-analysis did not find that inappropriate or high disclosure does not lead to liking. However, further research needs to be conducted on the latter issue.

Collins and Miller (1994) also conducted a meta-analysis of whether we disclose more to people we like (here the question is "Does liking cause disclosure?" instead of "Does disclosure cause liking?"). The results of a meta-analysis involving 31 effect sizes indicate that we disclose to people we like ($d = .72$), but the results were heterogeneous. The studies were again divided into correlational studies and experimental (strong and weak) studies. The results were that the effect sizes for strong and weak experiments did not differ from each other ($d = .45$ and .28, respectively) but both were significantly smaller than the effect size for correlational studies ($d = 1.11$). The significant, yet smaller, effect sizes for experimental studies indicate a causal relationship: liking causes disclosure. It can also be interpreted from the larger effect size for correlational studies (which also are self-report studies of self-disclosure) that perceptions of the liking–disclosure relationship may be greater than the actual effect of liking on self-disclosure. It may be that individuals believe that people disclose more to people they like, so when asked, they report that they disclose more to people they like than to people they dislike. The only other moderator that was tested was sex of discloser. The results provided little evidence that men and women differ in their tendency to disclose to people they like.

Finally, Collins and Miller (1994) conducted a meta-analysis of whether we like people as a result of disclosing to them. This meta-analysis was based on five studies, all of them categorized as strong experiments. The mean effect size was $d = .32$, indicating a positive relationship between disclosure and subsequent liking for the target. That is, people who were induced to disclose at a higher level tended to like their partner more than people who did not disclose or who disclosed at lower levels. However, the results were heterogeneous. Three of the studies found zero effect sizes and two studies had fairly large effect sizes. Collins and Miller speculated that whether the subject believed he or she acted freely in self-disclosing may have moderated the effect size. They reasoned that voluntary disclosure (rather than involuntary self-disclosure) causes us to like the person we disclosed to. However, the authors examined the studies and found no reason to believe that the studies that showed no effect differed in this dimension compared with studies that showed an effect.

Summary

A recent meta-analysis of the relationship between self-disclosure and liking (Collins & Miller, 1994) confirms that we like people who self-disclose to us, we disclose more to people we like, and we like others as a result of having disclosed to them. There are qualifications to the disclosure–liking relationship in all of its various forms (especially the latter finding). In general, in experimental studies the effect of "actual" self-disclosure (not self-reported self-disclosure) on liking is small, whereas the relationship between perceived self-disclosure and liking in nonexperimental studies is moderate to large. Nonetheless, the results for the experimental studies on self-disclosure and liking and liking and self-disclosure support a bidirectional causal relationship between self-disclosure and liking.

OVERALL SUMMARY

The meta-analysis on sex differences and self-disclosure indicates that there are sex differences in self-disclosure. However, these differences are small and are moderated by sex of partner.

The meta-analysis on reciprocity of self-disclosure indicates that self-disclosure is reciprocal. However, the effect size ranges from small to large depending on the type of study (correlational or experimental) and the measure of self-disclosure (self-report or observational). Thus, it is difficult to determine exactly how large the effect is. The results also indicate that people do not reciprocate self-disclosure on a tit-for-tat basis. In addition, the results indicate that strangers as well as intimates reciprocate self-disclosure. One study, which employed social relations analysis, indicates that spouses, like strangers, reciprocate self-disclosure within a given conversation. Thus, theories that speculate that reciprocity of self-disclosure is more important in initial stages of a relationship (to build trust or to reduce uncertainty) may be incorrect. Reciprocal self-disclosure may be necessary at all stages of a relationship. Alternatively, reciprocity may be so normative and ingrained in our behavior that we continue to reciprocate self-disclosure at later stages of a relationship.

The meta-analysis on self-disclosure and liking indicates that self-disclosure causes liking. Again, the size of the effect was much larger for correlational studies employing self-report data than for experimental studies employing observational data. The results of the meta-analysis also indicate that whether self-disclosure is perceived as personalistic versus nonpersonalistic may also moderate the effect of self-disclosure on liking. Although the meta-analysis indicates that high and low levels of self-disclosure do not differ in their effect on liking, this should be interpreted with caution. The conclusion is based on a small number of studies and the level of self-disclosure across studies is not comparable. The results of the meta-analysis on self-disclosure and liking also indicate that liking causes disclosure. Again, the results varied dramatically depending on the type of study, experimental or correlational. Thus, while it can be concluded that self-disclosure causes liking and liking causes self-disclosure, it is hard to say exactly how large these effects are.

So what does this have to do with balancing disclosure, secrecy, and privacy? The disclosure of private or secret information is not addressed in the quantitative research on sex differences in self-disclosure, reciprocity of self-disclosure, or self-disclosure and liking. Level of self-disclosure (high vs. low), self-disclosure valence (positive or negative), and self-disclosure topic were not studied as moderator variables in the meta-analysis of sex differences in self-disclosure. Few studies indicate the level of self-disclosure, and when they do, the level is not comparable across studies. Self-disclosure topic, when indicated, is also not comparable across studies. The issue of self-disclosure valence is not even addressed in the studies. Thus, we do not know whether sex differences in self-disclosure are the same for high-intimacy information as for low-intimacy information, or for negatively valenced information as for positively valenced information. We do not know if some self-disclosure topics have greater sex differences than other topics. The results of the meta-analysis cannot be generalized to the disclosure of private or secret information, such as the disclosure of positive HIV status.

The same is true for the research on reciprocity of self-disclosure. We do not know if intimate information is as likely to be reciprocated as nonintimate information, or if negatively valenced information is as likely to be reciprocated as positively valenced information. One can only assume that self-disclosure, in general, is reciprocal. The disclosure of private or secret information, such as positive HIV status, may not be reciprocal.

Although the meta-analysis on self-disclosure and liking tested whether high and low levels of self-disclosure differed in their effect on liking, and found there to be no difference, the result should be interpreted with caution. It was based on a small number of studies, and the level of self-disclosure across studies was not comparable. Thus, while it might be safe to assume that self-disclosure generally causes liking, it would be unsafe to assume that the disclosure of private and secret information, such as positive HIV status, causes liking. The results of this meta-analysis also indicate that liking causes disclosure. However, again, level of self-disclosure was not examined as a moderator variable. Specifically, individuals may not reveal private or secret information, such as positive HIV status, just because they like their partners.

The review of these three meta-analyses indicates the need for theoretical essays and empirical research that specifically deal with the issue of disclosure of private or secret information. There is an inherent bias in the self-disclosure literature that self-disclosure is good—the "ideology of intimacy" (Parks, 1982). Most of the theory and research on self-disclosure is based on the premise that intimacy is good for individuals and relationships. In general, self-disclosure theorists and researchers do not discuss the negative ramifications of intimate self-disclosure, the personal and relational risks of intimate self-disclosure, and the difficulties, challenges, and complications involved in disclosure of intimate information. In general, theory and research on self-disclosure presumes and addresses the positive outcomes of intimate interactions. Traditional research on self-disclosure ignores the issue of non-disclosure and the issue of balancing self-disclosure to meet the needs for privacy and intimacy.

Thus, traditional theory and research on self-disclosure cannot adequately explain the disclosure issues discussed in this volume. That is why this volume was written: to address the issues of nondisclosure and balance between disclosure and nondisclosure that have been for the most part ignored in the quantitative research on self-disclosure.

3

▼▼▼▼▼▼▼▼

The Boundaries of Privacy: Praxis of Everyday Life

Sandra Petronio
Arizona State University

The media constantly challenge individuals to consider ways to control their private information. For example, headlines ask, "how private is your life?" (Maas, 1998). Other reports raise privacy concerns with provocative statements such as, "in new climate, more politicians surmount imperfect private lives" (Berke, 1998), "country doctor faced tough issue of HIV privacy" (Thompson, 1997), and "don't expect your secrets to get kept on the Internet" (Quick, 1998). In a number of domains, privacy surfaces as a factor predominant in today's U.S. society.

These headlines underscore, however, the dialectical nature of privacy as it plays against an individual's need to be social and, therefore, public. The reason these headlines catch our attention is that individuals must balance the usefulness of privacy with the utility of openness. The question of how best to accomplish this goal is a matter that interests a number of scholars (e.g., Baxter & Montgomery, 1996; Derlega et al., 1993; Dindia, 1994; Rosenfeld & Kendrick, 1984). The many chapters in this book speak to ways that individuals reconcile maintaining privacy or secrecy with needing to make public disclosures. This chapter adds to the dialogue by offering a brief overview of one possible theoretical option to explain the balance between privacy and openness (Petronio, 1991). The Communication Boundary Management (CBM) theory of private disclosures proposes a scheme that provides structure to this balancing act.[1] In addition, this chapter illustrates the way this theory applies to the praxis of everyday life.

COMMUNICATION BOUNDARY MANAGEMENT

The metaphor of boundary is used in this theory to identify the border around private information. As Schoeman (1984) pointed out, "what makes things private is in large part their importance to our conceptions of ourselves and to our relationships with others" (p. 406). People define personal information as private because it reflects issues that matter deeply to them. CBM theory (Petronio, 1991) argues that understanding the way people handle private information depends on the intersection of *Boundary Structures* and a *Rule-Based Management System* that drives boundary regulation.[2]

Boundary Structures

Four related dimensions define boundary structures. These are ownership, control, permeability, and levels. Boundary structures are typically erected because revealing private information has the potential for making us vulnerable and, consequently, we need a way to control the risks. In addition, it is not simply the risk that justifies the boundary structure. We also believe that we own our private information and have the right to govern revealing and concealing. In other words, we exercise ownership rights over the information. For example, if a person thinks that a relational history is private, he or she may claim that no one else has the right to know. Salary information is often considered private and, therefore, owned by the individual. Both the ownership rights and the threat of vulnerability emphasize the need for control over the boundaries protecting private information.

We have many privacy boundaries because we co-own private information with other people. Although we have information that is uniquely our own, we also share in the responsibility of information that may start as personally private. This information can move to become a mutual obligation we hold with others. In this way, we expand our privacy boundaries based on the kind of private information and with whom we share the information. Consequently, we may enter obligations for dyadic private information, group private information, family private information, or even organization-

---

[1]To alleviate any confusion, the author is returning to the original name given this theory in the article, Petronio, S. (1991). Communication boundary management: A theoretical model of managing disclosure of private information between marital couples. *Communication Theory, 1,* 311–335.

[2]This version of the theory represents the most current articulation of CBM. The discussion of the theory focuses on a macro view of boundary management unlike the 1991 proposal that presents micro examination of boundary regulation.

ally private information. When we share the responsibility, we also institute sanctions so that each person cares for the messages in the same way. For example, organizations may punish their workers if they reveal plans for a major project to individuals outside the corporation. The strength of the sanction often is related to the degree of permeability of the boundaries. The less permeable, the stronger the sanctions for not accepting an expected level of responsibility. The more permeable, the weaker the sanctions.

Thus, boundary structures have a degree of permeability. Through the concept of permeability, we witness the way this theory addresses the dialectical issue of revealing and concealing. Boundaries may range from being completely permeable, wherein messages about private information flow openly from the individual to others, to impermeable, where secrets are tightly held. When the boundaries are permeable, people grant access, and when they are impermeable, they protect the boundaries from intrusion. Most often, people slide along this continuum, only occasionally tipping toward full disclosure or unrelentingly holding secrets.

Rule-Based Management System

The boundary structures are driven by a rule-based management system. Thus, the way the structures function to protect or grant access to private information depends on rules that are formulated to drive the management engine. This management system is defined by four essential concepts. They include: *boundary rule formation, boundary rule usage, boundary rule coordination,* and *boundary rule turbulence.*

Boundary rules are formulated to regulate the flow of information to and from others. The development of these rules is based on four criteria. First, culture plays a significant part in shaping the way that people formulate privacy rules (Benn & Gaus, 1983). Because cultures have different privacy values, they influence the decisions people make about opening up their boundaries. Some cultures are more open than others. Individual characteristics also affect the rules people develop (Collins & Miller, 1994). For example, levels of liking may alter the degree to which a person is willing to open his or her privacy boundary to others (Collins & Miller, 1994). Self-esteem is also a factor in the kinds of rules people formulate (J. Greenberg, Pyszczynski, & Solomon, 1986). People also use strategies to protect their self-esteem, especially when they feel under attack (Apsler, 1975). Individuals try to protect self-esteem by attributing failures to external causes (Berglas & Jones, 1978). As this need varies from person to person depending on the level of self-esteem, the kinds of privacy rules developed reflect the individual's needs.

Although the significance of gender differences has come under attack lately (Canary, Emmers-Sommer, & Faulkner, 1997), gender may also serve as a basis for rule formulation. Clearly, Dindia's chapter in this book illustrates that the relationship of gender and private disclosures is very much alive. The results may be better framed in terms of criteria for rule development. Men and women have a different set of criteria they use to judge whether to open their privacy boundaries. Based on these differing perspectives, they formulate rules that are not consistent with each other (Petronio & Martin, 1986; Petronio et al., 1984). However, because men and women belong to different co-cultural groups, they may not see that they are using different criteria that lead to inconsistent rules for revealing and concealing. For example, women tend to use target characteristics as criteria for developing rules, whereas men may use situational criteria (Petronio et al., 1984). Thus, if a husband and wife go shopping together and the wife wants to talk to her husband about their sexual relationship, her criteria are met by being with someone she trusts, feels comfortable revealing to, and knows will listen to her. She selects the department store as a place to disclose because of convenience, but the situation is not important to the wife. As she makes this disclosure, the husband is mortified and looks around in every direction to see if other people are listening. He cannot believe his wife would say such private things in the middle of Macy's. He becomes very quiet and does not speak. The wife is frustrated because she wants to get these issues aired and have a conversation about them with her husband. The situation is the criterion for the husband and it is not being met in this example, thus, he is not participating in the disclosure interaction. They have different criteria that lead to different rules for revealing and concealing.

Motivations also form the basis for rule development. People are motivated to grant access or protect their privacy boundaries for many different reasons. For example, a person may be lonely and motivated toward openness in hopes of becoming more social (Berg & Peplau, 1982; Franzoi & Davis, 1985). The rules that emerge are based on the desire to connect with others. In addition to loneliness, people may also be motivated to open privacy boundaries because they wish to exercise control, seek catharsis, or receive feedback about themselves. These motivation criteria for revealing and concealing serve as the basis for rules that fulfill these desires.

These criteria spell out the basis for forming boundary access rules and protection rules. Through these criteria, we determine if we want to tell and who we want to tell private information, the kinds of messages that are used to conceal or reveal, the depth and breadth of revelation or confidentiality, and, if we reveal, the timing of the message. These choices are used every day to regulate our privacy boundaries. In general, the protection and access rules reflect the decisions that we make about managing private information. Protection and access rules range from being newly developed to concrete formulas that become part of a value system.

New rules may be triggered by events such as divorce. When married people terminate their relationship, they can no longer follow the same rules for revealing and concealing. Instead, they must develop new rules for the way they will manage their privacy boundaries with each other given they are no longer intimate. Rules may also be ritualized. In other words, when we use boundary management rules, they become a manner of common practice. For instance, if someone asks a person how much money he or she makes, if the rule is ritualized, the person may reply by saying, "I really don't talk about my salary to anyone." Rules may also become concretized. Thus, when the protection or access rules have been used many times over, they form an orientation toward private disclosures. For example, families tend to have orientations toward private disclosures that exemplify values they hold in common. Most families can identify if they tend to be open or closed with each other or with outsiders as a general way of treating privacy and secrecy (Karpel, 1980; Vangelisti, 1994; Vangelisti & Caughlin, 1997).

A third part of the boundary management process is coordination. People manage many boundaries because they often co-own different types of private information with others. Consequently, they must coordinate sharing and regulating these privacy boundaries. As boundaries expand to include more than one person (i.e., dyadic, group, family, or organizationally boundaries), collective action is necessary. People who share private information co-own the rights to determine what happens to the information. Just as we do with personally private information, we develop rules to manage control over the disclosures. However, we must evolve mutually agreed-upon rules that manage co-owned private information. To ensure the use of these rules, we often build in sanctions to govern revealing and concealing. For example, if a father does not want his children talking about financial matters to people outside of the family, and the child overlooks that rule, the whole family could behave in an angry manner toward the child who violated the way the family agreed to manage privacy about this matter.

Often, the strength of the network ties influences the level of control those sharing the private information have over each other. Strangers who hear disclosures feel less commitment to using any rules the discloser might stipulate. On the other hand, those who have strong relational ties may be very influenced by the expectations for boundary management that evolves into protection and access rules. As others are involved in a disclosure of private information, they become linked by the knowledge of the information disclosed (Petronio & Kovach, 1997). Sometimes the linkage is strong where there is a density of connectedness, and other times it is weak with only loose boundary connections. Strong linkages reflect a higher level of responsibility for managing disclosed information. Weaker linkages often mean that there is less accountability for following any negotiated rules to manage the disclosed information. Consequently, with linkages that are stronger rather than weaker, there is an assumption of significant co-responsibility or co-ownership of the disclosed private information.

In addition, the extent to which the rules are explicit also affects the level of boundary control where there is co-owned information (Petronio, 1991). When a boundary management rule is implied, individuals co-owning private information may not have the benefit of understanding the expectations that others in the group have for the information. The explicit rule is easier because everyone is more able to comprehend how each person is held accountable for treating private information.

Boundary coordination brings the recipient into focus in a way that has not been considered previously. The recipient, often considered the confidant, also manages a privacy boundary. The recipient of private information may be burdened by hearing a disclosure, especially if he or she is reluctant to listen to it in the first place (Petronio, in press). For those individuals who do not want to participate in boundary coordination, being drawn into the interaction through the disclosure means they must cope with the information in some way to increase their comfort level and reduce feeling encumbered.

Predicaments found in boundary coordination, such as being a reluctant confidant, represent times when the boundary management system is in turbulence. There are many different kinds of boundary turbulence. For example, the inability to manage multiple boundaries is likely if people find it difficult to move from one boundary level to the next. A person may refuse to disclose a relational history, defining the information as personally private. However, his or her partner may have defined the information as dyadic, considering relational histories the property of both parties. If one partner defines the information as personal and refuses to reveal, the other partner might consider the unwillingness to disclose as deception. However, the individual defining relational histories as personal does not define it as deceptive. Instead, the person sees it as his or her right to have control over the information. Thus, people may remain within the personal privacy level when it is expected they move on to a dyadic or family privacy level. They may also have difficulty within a particular level coping with co-ownership of the information, as we see with the reluctant confidant.

Boundary turbulence may also occur when boundaries are invaded. Invasion compromises ownership and control over private information. For example, when parents invade their children's privacy by telling them what to do, the parents' behavior shifts the center of ownership away from the children and to them as a way to exercise control (Petronio, 1994). Alterations in control and ownership that arise from invasion may be ignored if strangers impose them. However, when family members and close friends question a person's perceived rights of ownership, turbulence in the boundary management system occurs. Turbulence also takes place when situational stresses call for boundary rule change.

A life event, such as an earthquake or catastrophic disease, often requires a change in privacy rules (Pennebaker, 1990). For example, after the San Francisco earthquake several years ago, people felt a need to disclose about their experiences using different access rules than they might when their lives were more mundane. People had a need to talk about their personal situation to give meaning to the events. However, by so doing, people often heighten the level of disclosure and open their privacy boundaries to others in ways that are not "typical" patterns of revealing and concealing. This turbulence in the boundary calls for making decisions about how the rules should change and coping with the ramifications of new practices for disclosure.

As this discussion illustrates, the boundary management system is the engine that drives the boundary structure and its component parts. This theoretical proposal frames a way to understand the dialectical nature of revealing and concealing. Not only are the dialectical forces identified, but also the theory gives a way to see how people regulate the tensions in their private disclosure interactions. The choice-making for managing these tensions is at the heart of the CBM theory. Dindia (1998) pointed out that understanding the communicative actions and reactions to dialectical contradictions is important and a matter of praxis. CBM provides an explanatory tool by which we can comprehend the nature of praxis.

THE PRAXIS OF BOUNDARY MANAGEMENT

Boundary management reflects praxis through focusing "attention on the concrete practices by which social actors produce the future out of the past in their everyday lives" (Baxter & Montgomery, 1996, p. 14). Dindia (1998) argued that "one way to view self-disclosure as praxis is to view it as a privacy regulation mechanism" (p. 92). Because privacy regulation serves a sense-making function, we are able to understand the choices that people make to cope with dialectical tensions or contradictions in everyday life. Rule formation and usage exemplify the way that people "practice" controlling the dialectic of revealing and concealing. Interestingly, the most obvious way to witness how people manage their privacy boundary is through boundary coordination. Boundary coordination requires negotiation of ownership, rule formation, and rule usage. Boundary coordination is the place where it is easiest to understand how the structure and management system blend together to form the praxis of boundary management. However, because boundary coordination does not always reach equilibrium, we also see the difficulties of management when boundaries become turbulent. There are many situations where people coordinate privacy boundaries, for example, in nursing homes between elders and care staff (Petronio & Kovach, 1997), in families (Petronio, 1991), and between partners. Coordination of privacy boundaries is also seen between physicians and patients as they manage medical confidentiality. Although people generally understand the notion of confidentiality, the specific requirements of boundary coordination can be challenging for both the physician and patient. Status differences and the relationship between doctor and patient make it difficult to determine rules, define ownership, and balance revealing and concealing. The following exemplar highlights some of the more perplexing boundary coordination issues.

Exemplar: Praxis of Physician-Patient Confidentiality

Doctor–patient confidentiality often presents a dilemma that makes coordinating boundaries and regulating rules a challenge. Generally, when individuals co-own private information, they share the responsibility and development of rules that govern accessibility and protection of the information. A mutual interdependence evolves out of jointly controlling private information. In this way, people coordinate a boundary around shared information and enter an agreement about how to regulate disclosure and confidentiality. Thus, coordination sets the parameters for how each co-owner of private information is expected to share control over revealing and concealing. The expectations of coordination, however, may be constrained by contradictory needs or differing perceptions that co-owners have about ways to govern private information. This is particularly true for confidentiality between physicians and patients. Boundary coordination for doctor and patient may be turbulent because they do not always agree on the way that medical information should be revealed or concealed.

For the most part, physicians argue that keeping medical information confidential is essential to developing a trusting relationship with their patients. Yet, physicians also agree that there are circumstances where information must be disclosed (Lako & Lindenthal, 1991). Physicians believe that they must balance ethical expectations for performing a medical role with practical needs of administering medical care (Robinson, 1991). However, they also take into account their needs in conjunction with the needs of the patient.

The equation for coordination is not simple. Consequently, the ability to synchronize mutually agreed-upon rules may be troublesome and lead to disturbances in the management system. For instance, some physicians may feel highly accountable to their patients and are more likely to negotiate with their patients and keep the medical information confidential in ways that satisfy both physician and patient. On the other hand, the type of medical information may influence the willingness of the physician to coordinate with the patient (Lako & Lindenthal, 1991). For example, as HIV/AIDS cases have illustrated, there are both ethically and legally mandated exceptions to the rules for keeping confidences (e.g., Cline & McKenzie, chap. 5). Thus, medical conditions may change the way physicians develop boundary rules. The physician may also change rules when the medical condition is fully revealed or if it is clear that the information poses some threat to the physician, other patients, the patient's friends, or family members (Friedland, 1994). In addition, some physicians hold tightly to the Hippocratic Oath, which states, according to Friedland (1994):

> What I may see or hear in the course of the treatment or even outside of the treatment in regard to the life of men, which on no account one must spread abroad, I will keep to myself holding such things shameful to be spoken about. (p. 256)

They may see little flexibility in how they "should" control the co-owned information. Thus, they aim for unconditional protection of the medical information, at times even from the patient.

In a number of cases, physicians shift the balance of control to themselves. They argue that they are in a better position to judge the potential effect of the information on their patients (Beisecker & Beisecker, 1990). In addition, physicians point out that keeping confidences about medical information is important because it protects the patient and affords the person freedom to disclose otherwise risky information (Lako & Lindenthal, 1991). Physicians believe that regulating confidentiality according to their rules leads to building a trusting doctor–patient relationship and enables the physician to give better care. Yet, sometimes physician may forget that the information belongs to both the patient and physician. The ideology of physician as protector is so prevalent that patients often accept this vision and transfer their rights of ownership. Thus, the physician may be given the role of informational gatekeeper (Backlar, 1996).

"Confidentiality is ultimately about the restriction of the flow of information. The management of information presents a powerful gatekeeping role more generally available to the doctor rather than to the patient" (Robinson, 1991, p. 282). This is particularly true within the health care community (Robinson, 1991). The physician's status in the community may contribute to granting him or her the role of gatekeeper. Often lines of communication are marked so only physicians are credible sources regarding medical information (Lindenthal & Thomas, 1982). Physicians may independently develop rules for routing the medical information without explicitly negotiating them with their patients. They might also delay, modify, or partial out the patient's medical information. When functioning as gatekeepers, physicians may disseminate test results (Greene & Serovich, 1996) or lists of donors for artificial insemination (Baran & Pannor, 1993), which may be considered highly private information to the patient. Boundary rules for disclosure to the medical community tend to be defined completely within the purview of the physician. The patient is not necessarily consulted. In

some circumstances, the gatekeeping function is even defined by legal parameters (Hoge, 1995). Yet, with patients taking a more proactive role in
medical care and increasing access to medical information, boundary management concerning confidentiality between physician and patient is not
always clear. Thus, the "interpretation of the idea of confidentiality is prac-
tically problematic . . . difficulties involved in the meaning of confidentiality,
are compounded by the ways in which the concept is used in practice"
(Robinson, 1991, p. 281).

For some physicians, there is ambiguity in the boundary management
system concerning the balance between negotiating with patients over ownership rights and the physicians' desire to make independent judgments about
controlling medical information. For others, the gatekeeping role is defined
in an uncompromising way. Thus, they find it difficult to take into account
the patient's role in controlling medical information. In either case, there is
the potential for abuse on the part of both the physician and the patient.

The story of Dr. Joseph DeMasi is a case in point (Bruni, 1998). Dr.
DeMasi disclosed that he was a pedophile in a therapy session. He told Dr.
Ingram, his psychiatrist and a faculty member with whom he was undergoing
psychoanalytical training while he was in medical school, about his problem.
Dr. DeMasi was completing his residency in child psychiatry at the time of
the disclosure. Reportedly, "Dr. Ingram, by his own admission, did nothing
to remove Dr. DeMasi from his rotations as a resident" (Bruni, 1998, p. 24).
Apparently, Dr. Ingram did not act because he did not want to breach
physician–patient confidentiality. After Dr. DeMasi molested a 10-year-old
boy in a hospital, the lawsuit filed by his parents claimed that Dr. Ingram
should have helped prevent the attack (Bruni, 1998).

In this case, Dr. Ingram based his decision about boundary protection
on his rule to maintain a patient's privacy. For Dr. Ingram, this rule seemed
to be routinized. In other words, initially Dr. Ingram did not seem to question
the parameters of his definition for confidentiality. Instead, he acted on a
taken-for-granted view that restricted all second-party disclosure. However,
after events unfolded, Dr. Ingram had second thoughts about his understanding of confidentiality. Yet, Dr. Ingram's initial desire to provide un-
limited protection of the patient's disclosure made possible certain outcomes
for himself and for the child Dr. DeMasi molested. Because Dr. Ingram did
not stop the abuse, the child lived with the incident into adulthood. The
child said that he could never forget this terrible experience (Bruni, 1998).
Dr. Ingram stated in the newspaper report that he was tormented by inde-
cision and by the seeming inability to resolve this case (Bruni, 1998). In
addition, there is a possibility that Dr. DeMasi acted on his desires in other
cases not yet known.

Dr. Ingram took responsibility for the private information in his role as
boundary gatekeeper protecting this information from outsiders. However,

there appeared to be an implied agreement between these two doctors that the information would be concealed as long as there were no confirmed incidences of child sexual abuse. Having the desire to engage in sexual activity with children and acting on those desires were two different matters for Dr. Ingram. Dr. Ingram reported that Dr. DeMasi appeared to understand the constraints. As the newspaper account notes,

> Dr. Ingram's deposition suggests that it was unlikely Dr. DeMasi would admit any sexual abuse of children, because Dr. Ingram warned him that such a disclosure would supersede confidentiality. "He knew what he could say and what he couldn't say" Dr. Ingram said in his deposition. (Bruni, 1998, p. 24)

This kind of boundary coordination between the physician and patient illustrates the complexity of negotiating co-owned rules for boundary management. When two parties are involved, each has to provide enough information about the way that he or she defines the expectations for boundary management. Dr. DeMasi depended on indirect messages, thereby keeping his definition purposefully ambiguous. He appeared to capitalize on Dr. Ingram's feelings of ethical constraints and manipulate the process of boundary coordination to fulfill his own needs. Had Dr. Ingram not been in his role as psychiatrist, he might have negotiated an alternative rule that supported full disclosure of these confessions. However, for Dr. Ingram, keeping confidences was a matter of adhering to an ethical dictum and Dr. DeMasi used this to his advantage.

"Physicians generally have seen the need for ethical behavior as necessary to further the goals and strengths of the physician–patient relationship" (Friedland, 1994, p. 255). Ironically, it is exactly the debate of ethics regarding boundary management that makes Dr. DeMasi's case an issue. The rule serves an important function that "encourages patients to bare themselves fully to their physicians so that an accurate diagnosis may be made and appropriate treatment instituted" (Friedland, 1994, p. 256). However, there are times when "courts, physicians, and commentators recognize that absolute confidentiality is neither possible, nor desirable" (Friedland, 1994, p. 257).

As Robinson (1991) pointed out, "such ethical problems raise more general issues of balance between the collective benefit which may result from the breaking of confidences, against the individual or (in certain cases) the collective harms that may result from that action" (p. 283). Rigid definitions might be less productive in certain circumstances. In addition, there is some legal precedence for a physician being expected to shift the rule that would allow disclosure of the information to a third party if he or she believes a patient is likely to harm someone (*Tarasoff v. Regents of the University of California,* 1976). In coordinating boundaries with Dr. DeMasi, Dr. Ingram had to assess the extent to which Dr. DeMasi's disclosures revealed him to be a known threat. According to the newspaper account, Dr. Ingram did not see Dr. De Masi's disclosures about his pedophilia "as a cry for help" (Bruni, 1998, p. 24). This case underscores the difficulty physicians and patients have in coordinating privacy boundaries around medical information. This particular situation is interesting because the patient was also a physician, which may have reinforced the expectation of complete confidentiality for the physician. However, the alleged pedophile capitalized on the physician's role as his therapist and took advantage of the therapist's restricted vision of confidentiality. In each instance, coordination by the patient depended more on maintaining the physician's definition than exercising his views on confidentiality. The incidences in this case also stress the management difficulties that exist when people feel caught in a boundary dilemma and illustrate the way coordination may be problematic.

CONCLUSION

The CBM theory is helpful in determining the rules to regulate revelation or concealment of private information. As illustrated in this exemplar, the theory facilitates an understanding of how individuals coordinate boundary management with each other.

At the core of boundary coordination for physician–patient interactions is the question, for whom is confidentiality an issue and from whom do we keep confidences? The exemplar shows how one person used the expectations of restricted boundary access to his advantage. He skirted the issues in a way that did not reveal the true nature of his alleged criminal activity. The physician confidant did not explore the nuances of the patient's messages. Thus, he did not acknowledge liability for the patient's actions. The physician did not investigate the way the patient was defining the boundary rules and the patient seemed determined not to dissuade the physician of the need for restricted confidences. Instead, the patient played on the physician's unwillingness to negotiate explicitly the boundary rules for protection.

The physician may have initially operated within a closed awareness context because he did not wish to take responsibility for his patient's revelation (Glaser & Strauss, 1970). Thus, he did not want to acknowledge the larger ramifications of his patient's behavior. Unfortunately, being unwilling to move out from behind a restricted boundary definition resulted in a dilemma for the physician because he was also a professor and advisor to the patient (student). The physician did not balance his two roles as therapist and professor in a productive way. Consequently, he was blamed for his inability to consider the weight of his roles as advisor and professor in determining his course of action. On the other hand, the patient pretended to be unaware of the larger issues in order to protect his criminal activities and his position in medical school.

The CBM theory considers motivations for developing rules that manage privacy boundaries. In the case of confidentiality between physicians and patients, these criteria may be an important factor in establishing the way boundary rules are established. Thus, physicians may be motivated to reveal or conceal the patient's medical information depending on their goals for medical care. For example, the physician may determine that it is a health benefit to disclose a hereditary disease to the children of a patient (Friedland, 1994). Most likely, the physician and patient would discuss such a revelation before it was made to the children. Part of the decision might entail deciding the extent of the information to be revealed, when the revelation should be made, and whether all children should be told at the same time. However, turbulence could erupt if the patient did not want the physician to tell his or her children.

Who has ownership rights over this information? If physicians feel that they have the right to determine who knows because they are in the position to make a medical decision, they may make the disclosure. If patients feel that they have sole rights, the physicians may not be given as much responsibility in the matter as they might like. Each side may have a good case for developing protection or access rules. However, the ramifications for not coordinating may have a number of consequences.

To avoid such unpleasant circumstances, it is useful to consider the fact that when people share privacy information they must establish loyalties to safeguard information that may make them vulnerable. The decision to make boundaries permeable is regulated by boundary rules, yet, for boundary maintenance to work, everyone must agree on those rules. When one person has a different idea about the way rules are formed and used, the management system may be disrupted and lead to turbulence. Conflict may emerge because one person involved in the coordination has incompatible definitions with the other boundary members. Because boundary coordination requires negotiation to succeed, instability may follow because there are incompatible goals. Physicians and patients unavoidably must interact to accomplish the goal of medical care. Yet, how they collectively manage the information is an issue. As the example in this chapter shows, sometimes one person in boundary coordination may have more responsibility or hold more weight with certain audiences. However, if the relationship is framed in terms of coordination, each person is granted some degree of ownership. Each person privy to the information is expected to negotiate the way information is controlled.

III

BALANCING PRIVATE DISCLOSURES
OF HIV/AIDS IN RELATIONSHIPS

4

▼▼▼▼▼▼▼▼

Reasons for and Against Disclosing HIV-Seropositive Test Results to an Intimate Partner: A Functional Perspective

Valerian J. Derlega
Old Dominion University

Barbara A. Winstead
Old Dominion University

Lori Folk-Barron
Virginia Consortium for Professional Psychology

There is a double-edged sword associated with the disclosure of personal information to others. Self-disclosure may provide psychological and concrete benefits, such as access to social support, the growth of personal relationships, and useful information and advice in coping with one's difficulties. However, there are also risks associated with revealing personal information. If others know personal information about an individual, there is the possibility of being rejected and exploited by others, or the disclosure may cause others distress (Derlega et al., 1993).

In this chapter, we present information about the personal reasons HIV-seropositive persons have given for disclosing versus not disclosing about the diagnosis to others. This information may shed light on the pros and cons of disclosing about the HIV-positive diagnosis to others. The manner in which someone balances the reasons for and against disclosure may influence actual disclosure and perhaps how the information is divulged.

Anyone can have private information about a distressing event that they may want to divulge or keep secret. However, concerns about disclosure/nondisclosure are heightened for virtually all persons infected with HIV because of the stigma associated with the disease and the fact that HIV is life-threatening and not yet curable (Chidwick & Borrill, 1996; Derlega & Barbee,

1998). Hence, we may learn about the processes involved in divulging potentially stigmatizing information by examining how persons with the HIV diagnosis make these decisions.

REASONS FOR DISCLOSURE VERSUS
NONDISCLOSURE OF THE HIV DIAGNOSIS

In our research we sought to develop scales that tap the different reasons for and against self-disclosure. Building on a functional model of self-disclosure (Archer, 1987; Derlega & Grzelak, 1979; also see Mason, Marks, Simoni, Ruiz, & Richardson, 1995), we assumed that the reasons for and against self-disclosure could be divided into three categories, based on the self-, other-, and relationship-focused benefits or risks that the HIV-positive person has to face:

1. Self-focused reasons for and against self-disclosure deal with the psychological or tangible benefits or costs to self based on divulging information about the diagnosis. For instance, a self-focused benefit would be the opportunity to vent personal feelings about HIV or to access emotional or tangible help in coping with the disease. Self-focused risks or concerns about disclosure might deal with the possible loss of privacy or being socially rejected.

2. Other-focused reasons for and against self-disclosure deal with the benefits or risks to others based on divulging about one's seropositive status to others. For instance, an other-focused reason for disclosure would be based on the other person's "right to know" about the HIV diagnosis or to educate the other person about HIV. An other-focused reason for not disclosing might be to protect the other person from having to make sacrifices or to keep her or him from becoming upset.

3. Relationship-focused reasons for and against self-disclosure deal with the benefits and costs that are associated with the relationship between the HIV-positive person and his or her partner. For instance, a relationship-focused benefit or reason for disclosure might be the perception that the partners have a close and satisfying emotional relationship or that they share a lot in common. A relationship-focused reason for not disclosing might be the perception that the partners do not know one another very well.

A study we conducted on personal accounts or narratives of disclosing and concealing HIV-positive test results provided evidence consistent with this functional approach (Derlega, Lovejoy, & Winstead, 1998). For instance, individuals with HIV cited personal benefits that might occur from disclosing about the diagnosis to various others, including obtaining emotional support, help, and catharsis. There was also an "other focus" involved in disclosure to others, based on a duty to tell (such as enabling someone to anticipate the discloser's future health-related problems). Participants also cited the closeness of the relationship as a reason for disclosing.

Concerns about risks to the self, such as fear of rejection and gossip, were bases for concealing information from someone about an HIV diagnosis. There was also an other focus for not disclosing to someone, based on a desire to protect another person, frequently a parent, from excessive worry or having to make sacrifices. The superficiality of relationships was a relationship-based reason for not disclosing.

Using a functional perspective and results from the personal accounts study, we constructed scales that measured the various reasons for and against self-disclosure of the HIV diagnosis to an intimate partner. These scales emphasize self-, other-, and relationship-based considerations in weighing the pros and cons of disclosing about the HIV diagnosis. If we were to construct reliable scales of reasons for and against disclosure of the HIV diagnosis, we could then use them to test how influential various reasons were in people's decisions about self-disclosure of the HIV diagnosis.

METHODS

Research Participants and Administration of Questionnaire Materials

All the results reported in this chapter are based on data collected from a sample of 64 individuals with the HIV infection. The participants were recruited from HIV/AIDS service agencies in southeastern Virginia and were asked to fill out an anonymous questionnaire about their decisions to self-disclose to an intimate partner about being seropositive after they had learned about their HIV diagnosis. The sample consisted of 35 males, 23 females, and 6 persons who did not list their gender. The mean age of the participants was 36.18 years (SD = 8.26 years). The participants were 39 African Americans, 19 Caucasians, 5 Hispanics, 4 Pacific Islanders, and 3 who did not identify their ethnicity. A majority of the sample had completed 12 or more years of school (79.7%). Twenty-five people (39.1%) in the sample described themselves as homosexual, 30 (or 46.9%) as heterosexual, and 9 (14.1%) as bisexual.

In filling out the self-disclosure questionnaires, participants were asked to think of the first person with whom they started a romantic, dating, or sexual relationship after learning about the diagnosis, or someone with whom they were in a romantic, dating, or sexual relationship when they learned about the HIV diagnosis. Thirty-one (48.4%) of the respondents mentioned someone with whom they were involved in a serious relationship at the time they found out about the diagnosis, 20 (31.3%) mentioned someone whom they were getting to know at the time they found out about the diagnosis, and 8 (12.5%) mentioned someone who was the first person they had a relationship with after finding out about the diagnosis. Five persons (7.8%) did not complete the information about the type of relationship they had with the other person.

Measures of Reasons for and Against Self-Disclosure

The scales for assessing the reasons for and against disclosing about the HIV diagnosis are presented in Appendices A and B. Participants (all of whom were HIV seropositive) were asked to indicate, on five-point scales ranging from (1) "not at all a factor" to (5) "very likely a factor", how much various reasons may have influenced their desire in disclosing or not disclosing about the HIV diagnosis to the relationship partner. The scales focusing on reasons for self-disclosure dealt with: (a) catharsis (expecting to feel better by releasing pent-up feelings), (b) seeking help, (c) duty to inform the other, (d) education of the other person about the disease, (e) testing the other's reactions after learning about the HIV-positive person's diagnosis, (f) being in an emotionally close relationship with the other person, and (g) similarity with the other person (such as sharing similar backgrounds).

The six scales focusing on reasons for not disclosing about the HIV diagnosis dealt with: (a) fear of rejection (e.g., fears about losing a relationship partner, others' lack of understanding, and being treated differently), (b) privacy (the respondent's fears that the other person would spread the information to others if he or she knew about the diagnosis), (c) self-blame or self-concept concerns (difficulty accepting that one has the HIV infection), (d) communication difficulties (not knowing how to tell the other person), (e) protecting the other person (the respondent does not disclose the diagnosis because she or he is afraid that the information about the HIV diagnosis would upset the other person), and (f) being in a superficial relationship (the respondent does not know the other person very well or only casually). The coefficient alphas for the scales were above .70, except for catharsis, which was .67, indicating satisfactory internal reliability for these measures.

Measuring Actual Disclosure to the Partner

Participants were asked if they actually disclosed to the relationship partner about the HIV-positive diagnosis. Forty-eight persons (75% of the sample) answered that they did disclose to the partner, 10 (15.6%) said that they did not disclose, 4 (6.3%) were not sure, and 2 (3.1%) did not respond to this question.

Direct or Indirect Disclosure

If research participants disclosed to the other person about being HIV-sero-positive, they were asked if they told the information directly (e.g., saying "I am HIV-positive"), or indirectly (e.g., talking in general about HIV). Thirty-six (56.3%) said they told the other person directly, and 15 (23.4%) said they told the other person indirectly. Thirteen (20.3%) did not answer this question.

Attachment Styles Measure

Research participants also completed a measure of attachment (Bartholomew & Horowitz, 1991). This questionnaire is made up of four short paragraphs, each describing one of four attachment styles (secure, preoccupied, fearful, and dismissing) as it might apply to one's close relationships in general. For instance, the secure paragraph reads, "It is easy for me to become emotionally close to others. I am comfortable depending on them and having them depend on me. I don't worry about being alone or having others not accept me." Participants rated on 5-point scales how accurately each paragraph described them, ranging from "not at all like me" (1) to "very much like me" (5). The association between attachment and endorsement of reasons for disclosure versus nondisclosure will be discussed in a subsequent section.

PARTICIPANTS' ENDORSEMENT OF REASONS FOR AND AGAINST DISCLOSING ABOUT THE HIV-POSITIVE DIAGNOSIS TO THE INTIMATE PARTNER

Recall that participants were asked to rate the degree to which certain reasons might have influenced their interest in disclosing as well as not disclosing about the HIV diagnosis to the relationship partner. This data allowed us to compare the relative importance of reasons for and against disclosing. A one-way within-subjects analysis of variance with reasons for self-disclosure as the independent variable was conducted. The dependent variable was the participant rating of how much each of the seven reasons for self-disclosure influenced interest in divulging information about the diagnosis. A one-way within-subjects analysis of variance with reasons for not disclosing as the independent variable was also conducted. The dependent measure for this analysis was how much each of the six reasons for not disclosing influenced their interest in concealing information about the diagnosis from the rela-tionship partner.

There was a significant effect on the reasons-for-self-disclosure inde-pendent variable, $F(6,366) = 8.22$, $p < .001$. The results of the post hoc test (using the Tukey procedure) provides information about the relative importance of reasons for one's interest in disclosing (see Table 4.1). The duty to inform and the desire to educate the partner, both other-focused reasons for disclosure, played a significantly greater role in influencing interest in disclosing compared to the desire to test the other's reactions, need for help, or perceptions of similarity with the other person.

Catharsis and being in a close or supportive relationship were also important factors, at least relative to the desire to test the other's reactions. These results suggest the importance of the desire to protect the other and to educate him or her, as well as of catharsis and having a close relationship, especially in contrast to the low importance given to the desire to test the partner's reactions.

There was a significant effect on the reasons-against-self-disclosure independent variable, $F(5, 295) = 5.15$, $p < .001$. The results of the post hoc tests indicate that concerns about privacy and self-blame/low self-concept were the most highly rated reasons for one's interest in not disclosing to the intimate partner (see Table 4.2). They also were rated as significantly more important than being in a superficial relationship as factors in not disclosing. These findings indicate the importance of self-focused issues (about one's personal right to privacy as well as negative self-image) in affecting one's interest in withholding information about the seropositive diagnosis from an intimate partner.

ATTACHMENT AND REASONS
FOR DISCLOSING OR NOT DISCLOSING
THE HIV SEROPOSITIVE DIAGNOSIS

The reasons generated for and against disclosure reflect the personal and interactional dilemmas faced by individuals with HIV about disclosing information about the diagnosis to the partner. Although individuals may "need"

TABLE 4.1
Impact of Reasons That Might Influence Disclosing

	Endorsement Ratings
Catharsis	3.415[ac]
Seek help	2.989[bc]
Duty to inform	3.857[a]
Educate	3.500[a]
Test other's reactions	2.730[b]
Emotionally close relationship	3.352[ac]
Similarity with the other person	3.073[bc]

Note. Within the column, numbers that do not share a letter are significantly different from one another based on the Tukey test ($p < .05$).

TABLE 4.2
Impact of Reasons That Might Influence Nondisclosing

	Endorsement Ratings
Fear of rejection	2.894[ab]
Privacy	3.300[a]
Self-blame/Self-concept concerns	3.037[a]
Communication difficulties	2.920[ab]
Protect other	3.018[ab]
Superficial relationship	2.417[b]

Note. Within the column, numbers that do not share a letter are significantly different from one another based on the Tukey test ($p < .05$).

to be open (for instance, from a sense of duty to inform the other or to educate the partner about HIV), there may also be a "need" to exercise restraint about telling the partner (for instance, concern for one's own privacy or self-blame or low self-esteem). Individuals may, however, differ in their assessments of the benefits and risks of divulging personal information. For instance, individual differences in attachment styles (based on how positive or negative people generally feel about intimate others as well as about themselves) may have an impact on this appraisal of benefits and costs. Let us consider predictions about the effects of attachment (Bartholomew & Horowitz, 1991) on one's reasons for and against disclosing about the HIV-positive diagnosis.

"Secure" individuals have positive images of the self and intimate others. Secure individuals have a high expectation that others are trustworthy and reliable as well as a high sense of their own lovability. Hence, secure individuals should not be too worried about the negative consequences to the self of self-disclosing. They might emphasize the positive benefits to the partner and to themselves of disclosing. For secure persons, reasons for not disclosing might be based on the desire to protect the other person.

"Preoccupied" individuals have a positive image of others but a negative image of self. Preoccupied persons, with their negative image of self, may exaggerate perceptions of the degree of threat posed by disclosing information about the HIV diagnosis to others.

Individuals who are "fearful" have a negative image of others and a negative image of themselves. Fearful persons may perceive few benefits from disclosing about the HIV diagnosis (e.g., unlikelihood of social support). They may also see risks (such as social rejection) if they disclose.

"Dismissing" individuals have a negative attitude toward others but view themselves as worthy of love. Dismissing adults deny their attachment needs and they may assert that relationships are not important. Because dismissive persons feel little emotional commitment to an intimate partner, they may not anticipate socially mediated benefits from disclosure or be concerned about negative social consequences.

The results of correlational analyses between attachment style measures (adapted from Bartholomew & Horowitz, 1991) and individuals' endorsements of reasons for and against self-disclosure to the intimate partner are presented in Table 4.3. There was no significant association between the preoccupied attachment style and reasons for or against self-disclosure. For the secure attachment style, the higher someone scored, the more he or she endorsed the desire to educate the other person as a reason for self-disclosure. Given that secure individuals tend to have a positive view of themselves and of others with whom they might want to have an intimate relationship, education may fit in with a desire to benefit the partner (and perhaps the relationship) by helping him or her understand the disease. Also, the higher someone scored on the dismissing attachment style the more they endorsed similarity with the intimate other as a reason for disclosure. There was no association between endorsement of the dismissing attachment style and any other reason for or against disclosure. If we assume that "similarity with the other" reflects "respect" as opposed to "affection" for the other, perhaps the dismissing style highlights the importance of a practical concern (the other person may be useful as a comparison person with whom to talk about similar experiences) in assessing the benefits of disclosure.

There were several significant negative correlations between the endorsement of the fearful attachment style and reasons for disclosure: catharsis

TABLE 4.3
Correlations Between Attachment Styles and Reasons for and
Against Disclosing the HIV Diagnosis to an Intimate Partner

Reasons for Disclosing	Secure	Preoccupied	Fearful	Dismissing
Catharsis	.085	.122	−.275*	.133
Seek help	.136	−.024	−.370**	.080
Duty to inform	.017	−.162	−.276*	.038
Educate	.269*	−.204	−.287*	−.039
Test other's reactions	−.072	.064	.030	.028
Emotionally close relationship	.140	.033	−.259*	.034
Similarity with the other person	.220	.012	.036	.256*
Reasons Against Disclosure				
Fear of rejection	−.123	−.193	.030	.052
Privacy	.058	−.106	−.042	.107
Self-blame/Self-concept concerns	−.133	.168	.101	−.156
Communication difficulties	−.105	.112	.200	−.055
Protect other person	.039	−.070	.044	−.021
Superficial relationship	−.152	−.035	.188	.185

*p < .05; **p < .01.

($r = -.275$), seeking help ($r = -.370$), duty to inform ($r = -.276$), desire to educate ($r = -.287$), and being in an emotionally close relationship ($r = -.259$). Thus, persons who are more fearful (with a negative image of others and of themselves) are less likely to endorse benefits to themselves (such as catharsis and access to help), obligations to an intimate partner (duty to inform), or interpersonal closeness as reasons for disclosure.

Overall, there were relatively few significant correlations between attachment style and reasons for and against self-disclosure about the HIV diagnosis. However, the results indicate that people who do not feel good about others or themselves (the fearful attachment style individuals) may be less likely to anticipate benefits to themselves or to their partner if they were to disclose. These findings are promising in suggesting how individual differences in valuing others and oneself (based on the attachment model) may influence decision making about disclosure.[1]

TESTING THE RELATIONSHIP BETWEEN DISCLOSING VERSUS NOT DISCLOSING ABOUT THE HIV DIAGNOSIS AND REASONS FOR AND AGAINST DISCLOSURE

Participants were asked whether they had disclosed their HIV-seropositive status to the intimate partner. Forty-eight individuals reported telling the partner, whereas 10 reported not telling the partner. We examined via t-tests (two-tailed) how endorsement of various reasons for and against self-disclosure were actually related to whether or not someone disclosed to the partner about the HIV-positive diagnosis.

There was no significant association between the decision to disclose versus not disclose and the endorsement of the various reasons for and against disclosure. Previous research indicates that HIV-positive persons mention different reasons for disclosure and nondisclosure to various target persons (such as parents, friends, lovers). Given that most of the sample had disclosed to their intimate partner and that we were only examining self-dis-

---

[1]The quality of the relationship with the partner may also have an impact on the reason for disclosure. We found a significant effect of the type of relationship on the degree to which respondents endorsed having an emotionally close relationship as a reason for disclosure, $F(2,56) = 4.661$, $p <$ .05. Results on the Tukey post hoc test indicated that respondents who were in a serious relationship at the time they found out about the diagnosis (mean = 3.690) compared to those who were getting to know someone at the time of finding out about the diagnosis (mean = 2.875) were significantly more likely to endorse having an emotional close relationship as a reason for disclosure. Respondents who were in a relationship with the first person after they found out about the diagnosis had scores (mean = 3.475) that were not significantly different from the other two groups on having an emotionally close relationship as a reason for disclosure.

closure issues raised by interacting with an intimate partner, we must leave to future research to answer the question about the association between actual disclosure and endorsement of reasons for and against divulging information about the diagnosis.

RELATIONSHIP BETWEEN DISCLOSING DIRECTLY VERSUS INDIRECTLY ABOUT THE HIV DIAGNOSIS AND REASONS FOR AND AGAINST DISCLOSURE

We were not able to document whether reasons for and against disclosure are related to the actual disclosure. However, there is evidence in the data that reasons for and against disclosure are related to how someone disclosed about the HIV diagnosis to an intimate partner. Thirty-four persons in our sample reported they had told the partner directly (e.g., "I am HIV-positive"), whereas 14 said they had told the partner indirectly (e.g., by talking in a general way about HIV). We sought to examine the relationship between direct–indirect disclosure and endorsement of reasons for disclosure and nondisclosure about the diagnosis.

Participants who disclosed indirectly compared to those who disclosed directly were more likely to be concerned about testing the other's reactions as a reason for disclosure ($t = -2.06$, $p < .05$). They were also more concerned about fear of rejection ($t = -2.06$, $p < .05$) and difficulty in communicating ($t = -.54$, $p < .05$) as reasons for not disclosing. Thus, an indirect manner of disclosure is associated with a need to test how the intimate partner "really" feels about the HIV-positive person, with fear of rejection, and with discomfort over one's inability to communicate to the partner about the seropositive diagnosis.

Indirect disclosure about the seropositive diagnosis seems designed to provide protection from being hurt or rejected by the intimate partner. The participants in the study were able to regulate the way they communicate, which may have served to minimize potential negative consequences (cf. Petronio, 1991). If the intimate partner reacted negatively to the indirect disclosure, the HIV-positive person could perhaps deny being seropositive or say nothing further about the diagnosis. If the reaction of the intimate partner was supportive, then the respondent could continue with a full revelation about the seropositive diagnosis.

IMPLICATIONS

HIV-infected persons live with many burdens. They live with a potentially fatal disease that requires considerable medical attention. But they also are concerned with the social consequences of the disease, such as the need to balance the benefits of self-disclosure about the diagnosis to others (including an intimate partner) against the risks to self and others. Hopefully, our research will be useful in documenting how HIV-infected persons weigh the pros and cons of self-disclosure.

The present research provides a preliminary sketch of how HIV-infected persons think about the advantages and disadvantages of disclosure. Other-focused reasons predominate when considering the disclosure of information about HIV. For instance, the duty to inform and to educate the partner was considered the most important influence on disclosure. Self-focused reasons explained nondisclosure. Concerns about privacy as well as self-blame/low self-concept were the most important influences on not disclosing. In the context of disclosing information about HIV to a romantic, dating, or sexual partner, benefits to the other weigh most heavily in deciding to disclose and must be balanced against the concerns about self that influence decisions not to disclose.

Duty to inform encompasses several highly correlated motives. With intimate partners, HIV-positive individuals feel an obligation to disclose HIV status so that protective measures can be taken and/or safer sex can be practiced. HIV-positive persons also do not want their partners to hear that news from someone else or to be surprised by this disclosure later in the relationship. There is also a strong sense that one simply must tell this kind of important, life-changing information to someone with whom one has or might have had an intimate relationship. The duty to inform probably applies to any important personal information, but the desire to educate may be unique to HIV. Because information about HIV was initially hard to come by and at times confusing, and because there may be resistance among uninfected individuals to learn about HIV, persons with HIV have been placed in the role of the educator. Our data suggest that they are generally willing to see their self-disclosures as serving the purpose of helping others learn about the condition. Other highly rated reasons for disclosure were catharsis and being in an emotionally close relationship. The relief of talking about something upsetting and the desire to share with a loved one are reasons we often associate with self-disclosure. It is interesting that in the case of an HIV-positive diagnosis, obligation and education may take precedence over these more well understood reasons for self-disclosure. These findings suggest that on learning they are HIV-positive, individuals begin to see themselves in a different role vis-à-vis their intimate partners. In some ways they seem to feel that disclosure is not a choice, but an obligation.

Whereas other-focused reasons were most often cited for self-disclosure, self-focused reasons were most highly rated for nondisclosure. Concerns about privacy as well as self-blame/low self-concept were the most important explanations given for not disclosing. For all disclosures of personal information, the possibility that the person receiving the information may pass it on to others without permission and /or knowledge is always a concern. The discloser must ask himself or herself how important it is to control the information and what will happen if unknown others hear about the information. Controlling the dissemination of HIV status may be particularly important to the discloser because it not only conveys information about illness, but also may be understood (rightly or wrongly) by others to convey information about lifestyle. The HIV-positive person may be particularly concerned about knowing who knows and therefore not wish to have others pass along the information. If this is true, then the discloser must judge the degree to which she or he can trust a confidante. The self-protective nature of not disclosing HIV-positive status is further emphasized by the relatively high rating given to "self-blame/self-concept concerns." Participants indicated that feeling ashamed and blaming themselves for their condition was an important reason for not disclosing. Almost as highly rated, however, was a desire to protect others from this painful information. Reasons for not disclosing an HIV-positive diagnosis, then, tend to be wanting to maintain one's privacy and to control who has the information, feeling bad about oneself, and wanting to protect others from hearing difficult and upsetting information.

The results of the fearful attachment style also indicated the possible impact of individual differences on thinking about reasons for disclosure. Thus, persons who were high on the fearful attachment measure, which pertains to individuals who have an image of others as untrustworthy and an image of oneself as unlovable, were relatively unlikely to endorse self-, other-, or relationship-focused reasons for disclosure. Fearful persons basically perceive less reason to disclose in terms of catharsis, seeking help, duty to inform, desire to educate, and having an emotionally close relationship. People who are more fearful about their personal relationships (due to intrapersonal or interpersonal concerns) perceive fewer advantages to themselves or their intimate partner from disclosing.

Our results also suggest how weighing the pros and cons of disclosure may affect how the HIV-infected person discloses about the diagnosis. Thus, HIV-infected persons are more likely to give only partial access to the information about the diagnosis if they fear rejection, want to test how the other will react to information about the diagnosis, and have difficulty communicating. Respondents who rely on an indirect mode of disclosure may be attempting to protect themselves from being hurt by an unscrupulous person or by their own communication deficits.

It is interesting that there were no significant associations between disclosure–nondisclosure and reasons for and against disclosure. We would like to examine, with a larger sample of HIV-positive persons who disclosed versus did not disclose information about the diagnosis to significant others (such as parents, friends, coworkers, and lovers), how the actual decision to disclose or not is related to the endorsement of reasons for and against disclosure.

Many chapters in the present book examine the topic of privacy regulation, dealing with how individuals seek to maintain control over the amount and kind of information exchange that they have with others. The emphasis on reasons (or functions) for and against disclosure may provide a useful framework for understanding how individuals seek to strike a balance between the need to disclose and the need to protect themselves and others from the consequences of disclosure.

APPENDIX A: SCALES MEASURING REASONS FOR DISCLOSURE ABOUT THE HIV-SEROPOSITIVE DIAGNOSIS TO AN INTIMATE PARTNER

Scales and Items

Catharsis

11. It would be a relief to me to vent or express my feelings.
18. I didn't want to have to carry this information around all by myself.
24. I would be able to get the information off my chest.
31. It would be "cathartic" (releasing pent-up feelings) to be able to tell the other person.

Cronbach's alpha = .67

Seek Help

17. This person could provide valuable advice to me.
27. This person could be of help.
30. This person would be able to provide support.
33. This person could provide me with assistance.

Cronbach's alpha = .79

Duty to Inform

1. I "owed it" to this person to tell them.
9. I didn't want the information to come as a surprise to this person later on.

10. I wanted the person to know about possible health consequence when having sex.
14. I felt obligated to tell this person.
20. I didn't want to risk any more health problems for me or the other person.
22. I wanted this person to know what they were getting into being in a relationship with me.
23. This person had the right to know what is happening to me.
26. I felt a sense of duty to tell this person.
28. I wanted to emphasize the importance of taking protective measure for safer sex.
32. I wanted to prepare this person for what might happen to me.
35. I didn't want this person to hear first from someone else about what happened to me.
36. I am concerned about the other person's and my own health.
37. If there is a chance that the other person might be (or would be) infected I wanted them to find out.

Cronbach's alpha = .89

Educate

6. I wanted to educate the other person about what the disease is like.
13. My goal is to teach others about the disease.
15. I want to make sure that people know how serious this disease is.

Cronbach's alpha = .73

Test Other's Reactions

3. I wanted to test this person's reactions about being in a relationship with me.
12. I wanted to see how the other person would feel about me after I told them.
29. I wanted to find out if this person still wanted to be with me after I told them.
34. I wanted to see how this person would react when I told them the information.

Cronbach's alpha = .79

Emotionally Close Relationship

4. We love one another.
8. Telling the other person about the diagnosis would bring us closer together.
19. We had a mutually supportive relationship.
21. We had a close relationship.
25. I trusted the other person.

Cronbach's alpha = .72

Similarity With the Other Person

2. We shared a similar background.
5. We had a lot in common.
7. We both had similar types of experiences.
16. We tended to think alike about things.

Cronbach's alpha = .77

APPENDIX B: SCALES MEASURING REASONS
AGAINST DISCLOSURE OF THE HIV-SEROPOSITIVE
DIAGNOSIS TO AN INTIMATE PARTNER

Scales and Items

Fear of Rejection

4. I was concerned that this person wouldn't understand what I was going through.
5. I didn't want to do something that would threaten our relationship.
10. I didn't want to be treated as if I were different from other people.
16. I didn't want to scare the other person away from me.
17. I worried that this person would no longer like me if he or she knew about my HIV diagnosis.
21. I was concerned about how this person would feel about me after hearing the information.
29. I didn't feel this person would be supportive.
32. I didn't want to be treated as if I were "sick."

Cronbach's alpha = .78

Privacy

2. People have big mouths and they might go running around telling other people.
20. Information about the diagnosis is my own private information.
22. I don't have to tell anyone if I don't want to.
23. I have a right to privacy.
32. I didn't want the information being passed along to others who I didn't tell myself.

Cronbach's alpha = .80

Self-Blame/Self-Concept Concerns

7. I felt that there was something wrong with me.
8. I blamed myself for being infected.
11. I felt ashamed about having the IIIV-positive diagnosis.
13. I had difficulty accepting that I was HIV positive.
25. I felt bad about myself.

Cronbach's alpha = .77

Communication Difficulties

1. I just didn't know how to tell this person.
12. I would get tongue-tied when I tried to say what happened.
15. I didn't know how to start in telling this person about the diagnosis.
19. I didn't know how to put into words what happened to me.
32. I just couldn't figure out how to talk about the diagnosis.

Cronbach's alpha = .85

Protect Other

6. I didn't want to upset this person.
14. I didn't want this person to have to make any sacrifices for me.
18. I didn't want this person to have to wind up needing to take care of me.
26. I didn't want to put this person's life into an uproar.
27. I didn't want this person to worry about me.
33. I didn't want this person to experience any pain over things I was going through.

Cronbach's alpha = .81

Superficial Relationship

   3. We didn't know one another very well.
   9. Our relationship wasn't very serious.
  24. We weren't very close to one another.
  29. Our relationship was pretty casual.

Cronbach's alpha = .85

5

▼▼▼▼▼▼▼▼▼

Dilemmas of Disclosure in the Age of HIV/AIDS: Balancing Privacy and Protection in the Health Care Context

Rebecca J. Welch Cline
University of Florida

Nelya J. McKenzie
Auburn University, Montgomery

Disclosure in the context of HIV/AIDS differs sharply from traditionally studied self-disclosure processes. Secrecy and stigma surround HIV/AIDS. In turn, HIV disclosure issues challenge traditional medical ethics.

Traditional self-disclosure research emphasizes personal revelations in therapeutic contexts and personal relationships. Scholars stressed developmental processes involving a multiplicity of disclosures, often manifest in reciprocal processes, and largely governed by relational rules. In contrast, the significance of HIV disclosure lies largely in: (a) stigma and attendant potential for destructive relational consequences, and (b) health care and public health. HIV disclosure issues in health care center on a single piece of information, disclosed unilaterally, and largely governed by external policies.

SECRECY, STIGMA, AND HIV DISCLOSURES

A unique combination of features associates HIV/AIDS with secrecy. Researchers estimate the average latency period from infection to developing AIDS as 10 years (Quinn, Narain, & Zacarias, 1990); thus, people *can* conceal their disease for years. HIV is associated symbolically with crime (e.g., intravenous drug use) and moral judgments (e.g., about homosexuality), themselves often secrets. Finally, recognizing one's own stigma leads to shame and encourages concealment.

AIDS is a stigmatizing disease. According to Goffman (1963), stigma is "an attribute that is deeply discrediting" (p. 3). In Goffman's terms, a person

71

with HIV is "discreditable" and becomes "discredited" through disclosure. People with HIV face repeated episodes of disclosure roulette, risking stigma by disclosing their disease or the loss of potential social support by failing to disclose (see Cline & McKenzie, in press).

The person with HIV who chooses disclosure loses control over that information and is subject to stigmatizing consequences. Despite legal protection (e.g., through the Americans with Disabilities Act [ADA]), often HIV disclosure results in loss of employment, housing, access to public education, insurance, and health care (Evans, 1994). People who disclose their HIV disease often lose friends, family, lovers, spouses, and the emotional and instrumental support those relationships might otherwise provide. Thus, it is not surprising that HIV/AIDS is a disease in which individuals prefer privacy. In health care contexts, that desire often conflicts with medical ethics.

BALANCING PRIVACY VERSUS PROTECTION: MEDICAL ETHICS AND HIV/AIDS

Modern medical practice is governed by a code of ethics traceable to ancient Greece and the Hippocratic oath (Leong, Silva, & Weinstock, 1992). Contemporary medical ethics include interpersonal obligations to patients to treat while maintaining confidentiality, to provide informed consent, and to protect or prevent harm. Today, practitioners' obligations extend to third parties and society at large, often conflicting with those to patients.

Medical Ethics in Conflict

Beauchamp and Childress (1989) suggest four principles to resolve ethical conflicts: autonomy, beneficence, nonmaleficence, and justice. They invoke a balancing model that weighs the risks of upholding/violating one ethical tenet against another.

Autonomy. Autonomy is the right to self-determination (Beauchamp & Childress, 1989). Patients have the right to make decisions regarding their bodies and health care and the right to privacy, including the right to control personal information. Autonomy undergirds both confidentiality and informed consent.

The principle of confidentiality is rooted in the need for patients to disclose personal information in order to facilitate health care (Leong et al., 1992). Informed consent requires explanation of medical procedures (tests, treatments, and research protocols), potential risks and benefits, alternative procedures, and the risks of not having the procedure (Derse, 1995).

Beneficence. The principle of beneficence involves "doing good" (Lo et al., 1989) and preventing harm. What benefits patients, third parties, and society may be in conflict. Beneficence, together with justice, provides a foundation for health care professionals' "duty to treat." Prior to the AIDS epidemic, the "duty to treat" applied only after the physician had entered into a physician–patient relationship; physicians had the right to choose their patients, except in emergencies (Krajeski, 1990). Beneficence and nonmaleficence often are synonymous in practice.

Nonmaleficence. Nonmaleficence mandates that caregivers "do no harm" by avoiding injury to patients, as well as others (Lo et al., 1989). Nonmaleficence is manifest in the "duty to warn." The duty to warn was established in *Tarasoff v. Regents of University of California* (1976). During therapy, a client disclosed his intention to kill a fellow student (Tarasoff), whose identity was known to the therapist. Two months later, the client killed Tarasoff, who had not been warned. The court ruled that when a "patient presents a serious danger of violence to another," the therapist "incurs an obligation . . . to protect the intended victim against such danger" (p. 346). Three conditions predicate the duty to warn: likelihood of real harm to self or others, a special relationship between therapist and client, and identifiable victims (Schlossberger & Hecker, 1996). However, *Tarasoff* leaves many questions unanswered; the duty to warn remains one of the most controversial in medical ethics.

Justice. The principle of justice recognizes that providers' ethical duties may result in conflicts of interests among patients, third parties, and society. Justice requires providers to make decisions that distribute benefits and risks fairly (Lo et al., 1989).

HIV/AIDS and Medical Ethics

Traditionally, when individual and societal interests competed, public health policy favored societal interests (Bayer, 1994). However, the AIDS epidemic challenged that tradition. Early in the epidemic, individual rights were so protected over those of society that Bayer coined the term "HIV exceptionalism" (p. 155) to characterize the break with tradition. However, the voluntary approach, emphasizing education as well as voluntary and confidential testing, was replaced in the second decade by a move toward greater restrictions, including contact tracing, third party warnings, and demands for professionals' HIV disclosures to patients.

Two reasons account for the change (Bayer, 1994). As epidemiology shifted focus to more disenfranchised populations, from the gay community (an organized population with political clout) to drug users and minorities, the emphasis on individual rights diminished. Furthermore, the development of promising early therapeutic interventions argues for greater coercion in testing and disclosure. This shifting balance changed the course of HIV disclosures in health care.

BALANCING PRIVACY
VERSUS PROTECTION IN PRACTICE

HIV disclosure issues emerge in health care from testing through the course of the disease.

Initial Disclosures: HIV Testing

The "cornerstone of public health policy" with regard to HIV testing, informed consent and confidentiality (Singleton, 1993), is now in jeopardy. Ostensibly, individuals may not be HIV-tested without permission. Although consent is assumed for routine blood tests, HIV testing requires specific consent (J. T. Berger, Rosner, & Farnsworth, 1996). While most HIV testing is *voluntary,* some *mandatory* testing is argued to benefit other individuals as well as society. Disclosure issues vary with type of testing.

Voluntary Versus Mandatory Testing. Lo et al. (1989) distinguish among three types of voluntary testing. *Unlinked testing,* used for epidemiological purposes, involves taking blood samples without attaching personally identifying markers. Thus, disclosure issues are moot. *Anonymous testing* employs codes ensuring that only the individual tested can discover the result. *Confidential testing* typically is ordered by a provider at the client's request; the results become part of the client's medical record and thus are vulnerable to disclosure. Evidence indicates that anonymous testing increases the number of persons being tested by as much as 50% over confidential testing (Lo et al., 1989).

Although voluntarily tested people are assumed to *want* to know their test results, the symbolic meanings associated with HIV testing may make that assumption incorrect (Lupton, McCarthy, & Chapman, 1995). People seek testing for numerous non-risk-related reasons: to negotiate a sexual relationship, due to pressures from others, or to bring symbolic closure to an ended relationship. Generally these individuals assume they will test negative and rarely seek follow-up tests despite engaging in recent risky behavior.

Whether testing is voluntary (e.g., for insurance, blood donation) or mandatory, most states require disclosure of results to the individual, especially if the result is positive (Closen, 1991). Closen argues that, as matter of personal choice, people should have the *right not to be informed* of their

HIV test results. Generally, voluntary testing is argued to better serve the public's health than mandatory testing and disclosure.

Mandatory disclosure often follows from mandatory testing. Military recruits, Job Corps and Peace Corps applicants, some Foreign Service personnel (Evans, 1994), and, in some states, convicted prisoners are subject to mandatory testing. Debate continues about mandatory testing of health care workers and newborns. Proponents argue that mandatory disclosed testing of newborns protects the infant, who can be treated early, and the mother who can be treated and counseled against breastfeeding, future pregnancies, and unprotected sex (J. T. Berger et al., 1996). However, mandatory testing of newborns is tantamount to testing the mother without her consent (Fleischman, Post, & Dubler, 1994). Disclosing the newborn's results discloses the mother's results, violating her individual rights (Bayer, 1994).

Opponents contend that mandatory testing of newborns is based on faulty assumptions. Most children born of HIV-infected mothers are not themselves infected; only 15% to 30% are infected (J. T. Berger et al., 1996). Second, an HIV test on a newborn is unreliable. An accurate HIV test of an infant can be made only between age 3 months to 18 months (Dumois, 1995; Fleischman et al., 1994). Third, test results are not readily available. In the 15 to 30 days necessary to obtain test results, a mother who intends to breastfeed her baby has begun to do so. Women who do not want their HIV status known, and women who suspect their infection and fear judgment as unfit mothers, are unlikely to return for test results (J. T. Berger et al., 1996). Fourth, medical treatment is not always available for infants or mothers. Treatment is expensive and HIV is most likely to affect those least able to pay (Bayer, 1994). Finally, the mother whose HIV status is disclosed is subject to stigmatizing consequences that may jeopardize social support for both mother and infant (J. T. Berger et al., 1996). In short, no health benefit is necessarily gained by mandatory newborn testing.

Confidentiality in Practice. Arguments for mandatory testing invariably emphasize benefits to society over individuals (Derse, 1995). However, disclosure of test results may provide false reassurance.

Many advocates of HIV testing assume it provides a "once and for all" definitive diagnosis. In turn, such information will benefit the individual, by allowing treatment, and the public, by preventing transmission (Krajeski, 1990). However, a negative HIV test does not assure that a person is not infected. The body may take three to six months to generate sufficient HIV antibodies to register a positive test (Scheerhorn, 1995). Second, no evidence supports the assumption that informed infected individuals will change behavior and cease risky activity (Krajeski). However, once a person tests positive for HIV, confidentiality becomes both an ethical and legal aspect of the disease.

Ordinarily, only professionals treating patients have access to medical records. In the case of HIV/AIDS, reporting requirements jeopardize confidentiality. Thus, in the case of HIV testing disclosures, the balance has been tipped in favor of public interests over private interests. Therefore, informed consent for HIV testing should include an honest discussion of the limits of patient confidentiality and the potential consequences of possible disclosures.

Patients' HIV Disclosures to Health Care Professionals

People with HIV/AIDS must decide whether to disclose their HIV status to health care professionals. The dilemma pits confidentiality against beneficence.

Balancing Access to Health Care Against the Risk of Discrimination. Patients fear violations of confidentiality, discriminating care, and refusal of care upon disclosing their HIV status to health care professionals (Opperer, 1995). Despite the "duty to treat," many providers prefer to avoid patients with HIV.

Prior to the AIDS epidemic, the American Medical Association's (AMA) code of ethics afforded physicians the right to choose clients (Krajeski, 1990). As a result of the fear and stigma associated with AIDS, refusal of care was common (Derse, 1995). The prevailing view today is that professionals have the *duty to treat* within their professional competence.

The duty to treat people with HIV disease is supported explicitly in the ethics codes of numerous professional organizations, including the AMA (Hirsch, 1994). Because people with HIV/AIDS are disabled, the duty to treat is protected by the ADA and the *Federal Rehabilitation Act* (Hirsch). Although the total number of providers and specialists providing AIDS care has increased, many providers prefer to avoid people with HIV/AIDS. A survey of primary care physicians showed that while 68% believed they had the responsibility to treat people with AIDS, 50% would not choose do so (Gerbert, Maguire, Bleecker, Coates, & McPhee, 1991).

Providers' Right to Know Patients' HIV Status. Providers' often-claimed "right to know," a matter of self-protection, conflicts with patients' right to privacy.

In 1987, the Centers for Disease Control and Prevention (CDC) documented the first case of patient-to-provider HIV transmission (Centers for Disease Control and Prevention [CDC], 1987). Estimates fix the risk of HIV transmission from infected patients to providers as three to nine times greater than from infected providers to patients (Oddi, 1994). To date, the CDC reports 52 documented cases of occupational transmission of HIV and 114 potential cases (CDC, 1997). Nurses and laboratory technicians account for the majority of exposures.

When health care workers are exposed to blood from patients suspected to be HIV infected, in most jurisdictions, the patient can be tested only voluntarily except under court order, which is a rarity (Evans, 1994). Patients' privacy rights generally outweigh providers' need to know.

Some legal analysts argue for nonconsensual HIV testing of patients when health care professionals have been exposed. Seeking a more equitable balance between patients' rights to privacy and providers' rights to protection, Singleton (1993) argues that patients ought to be required to be HIV-tested when the patient's HIV status is unknown and a health care provider has been exposed.

Singleton (1993) notes parallel contexts; California law allows mandatory testing when law enforcement, fire and rescue personnel, and victims of sex crimes potentially have been exposed to HIV in criminal contexts, but does not protect health care workers. In 1993, a jury in the Los Angeles Superior Court agreed with that reasoning in a case where a technician was exposed to a patient's blood during surgery (Singleton). The patient, who provided false medical information, was ruled responsible for fraudulent concealment of HIV infection.

Disclosure in Practice: Patients' Disclosures of Their HIV Status to Providers. The best-known case of a patient withholding HIV status from a doctor is Greg Louganis, the 1988 Olympic diver who cut his head while diving and was stitched up by a physician in order to continue competing (Marks, Mason, & Simoni, 1995). Although this incident called attention to the need for patients' HIV disclosures to providers, little research documents the frequency of such disclosures.

A dental-care study found that 70% of HIV-infected patients, in a sample of mostly gay white males, disclosed their HIV status, but only half of those who were not asked volunteered their status (Barnes, Gerbert, McMaster & Greenblatt, 1996). (These results, from a dedicated clinic in the San Francisco area, likely are not generalizable.) Marks et al. (1995) studied patients' HIV disclosures to physicians and dentists who were not treating the patient's disease; 21% did not disclose their infection to *any* providers.

Receiving care specifically for HIV requires disclosure. Thus, people with HIV/AIDS must balance the prospects of access to health care against risks of discrimination, as well as concerns that the health care professional will disclose his or her HIV status to others.

Health Care Professionals' Disclosure
of Patients' HIV Status to Third Parties

Health care providers confront questions regarding disclosure of their patients' HIV status. Their decisions weigh the value of patients' confidentiality against beneficence to others.

The Value of Confidentiality. Arguments in support of sustaining patients' HIV confidentiality include the potential for discrimination, damage to the provider–client relationship, and the ultimate failure of such disclosures to protect anyone.

Disclosure of a patient's HIV status to others opens the floodgate of potential discrimination. Cassidy (1994) recounted the case of a man involved in a traffic accident who, while receiving emergency care, disclosed his HIV status to a doctor. A newspaper article titled "Ambulance Men in AIDS Scare" provided sufficient detail to make the patient identifiable. As a result, his employers learned his HIV status, he experienced stigma on the job, and he felt he was forced to disclose his status to his previously uninformed family. The price of breach of confidentiality potentially is "ruinous" and protecting it "compelling" to providers who also serve as patients' advocates (Kalinowski, 1994, p. 9).

Confidentiality permits the patient to entrust providers with HIV information; that trust protects both patients and providers. Confidentiality advocates fear that patients who know that their confidentiality is vulnerable will avoid seeking care, leave care, or avoid being testing (Lo et al., 1989). The basis for HIV disclosures to third parties is their enhanced protection. However, such disclosures are disputed by two lines of reasoning: the *Tarasoff* case, used as justification, does not apply to HIV; and third-party notification fails to protect anyone.

Opponents of third-party disclosure argue that the *Tarasoff* doctrine does not apply to HIV because:

1. Sex is a voluntary activity; most third parties know what constitutes risky behavior, that is, are not unsuspecting victims (Daniolos & Holmes, 1995).

2. *Tarasoff* mandates warning for illegal, but not legal, actions (Schlossberger & Hecker, 1996).

3. The threat of HIV infection is neither certain nor imminent (Driscoll, 1992).

Compelling arguments contend that third-party disclosure fails to protect anyone and may do more harm that good (Daniolos & Holmes, 1995):

1. Third-party notification has potentially negative social, psychological, and emotional consequences for patients, partners, and providers (Leong et al., 1992).

2. Breaching confidentiality may escalate a patient's high-risk behavior (Daniolos & Holmes, 1995).

3. The third party may retaliate against the patient or the provider, increasing the potential for violence (Leong et al., 1992).

Confidentiality in Transition.   Prior to the AIDS epidemic, confidentiality was not absolute, but the principle was held "almost sacred" (Krajeski, 1990). Precedents for breaching confidentiality include: reporting cases of gunshot wounds, venereal disease, and suspected child abuse, and the duty to warn potential victims (Daniolos & Holmes, 1995). Early in the AIDS epidemic, many jurisdictions specifically protected HIV patients' confidentiality "to the exclusion of anyone else" (Hirsch, 1994, p. 222). Over time, those laws generally have been repealed or replaced. The three most frequent targets for disclosure are public health officials, other health care professionals, and personal contacts at potential risk.

Health care professionals are obligated by AIDS reporting laws in all 50 states (Hirsch, 1994). A few states require reporting AIDS cases by code only, but most require reporting the names and addresses of the person with AIDS. The duty to warn includes warning other health care professionals. Although universal precautions and infection control procedures provide most of the protection providers need, casualness about those procedures may create a need for warning (Oddi, 1994). However, the greatest dispute about patients' HIV confidentiality involves personal contacts at risk.

Tipping the Balance: Disclosure of HIV Information to Personal Contacts at Risk.   The principle to "do no harm" extends to personal contacts. Proponents of disclosure often cite *Tarasoff* to defend their position and argue that disclosure protects people who can avoid infection, avoid transmission, and seek treatment if infected (Daniolos & Holmes, 1995). Health professionals' organizations and the courts take conflicting positions on this issue.

No consensus exists among professional organizations regarding the duty to warn personal contacts regarding HIV infection. Some organizations direct professionals to protect third parties against harm, but fail to define harm (Driscoll, 1992). Others endorse the *permissibility* of violating confidentiality in order to protect third parties (Green, 1995). However, the AMA maintains that physicians are *obligated* to notify HIV-threatened third parties. The AMA Code states that physicians "should" notify the third party when the physician has attempted but failed to persuade the patient to make the disclosure, and has notified public health authorities who have not contacted the third party (Opperer, 1995).

Health professionals *may* be held liable for failure to disclose a patient's HIV status to third parties at risk. Precedence exists for failures to warn of psychiatric danger, medication side effects, and disease transmission (Closen, 1991). However, no health professional has yet been held liable for failure to disclose a client's HIV status (Daniolos & Holmes, 1995). Such cases are expected, but the third party's voluntary behavior and failure to take precautions likely will be considered by the courts (Closen, 1991).

Although legal opinion increasingly protects third parties, analysts agree that, within that leaning, patients still should be afforded as much privacy as possible. The issue of whether a health care professional is permitted or even obligated to disclose a patient's HIV status to third parties at risk remains disputed. Where breaches of confidentiality are allowed, numerous unanswered questions put the decision in the professional's hands. Health care professionals are left to balance patients' privacy against protecting third parties.

Disclosure to Patients: The Health Care Worker with HIV

Patients' and professionals' autonomy rights collide in the issue of whether HIV-infected health care professionals should be required to disclose their status to patients. Professionals' rights to privacy conflict with patients' rights to informed consent.

The David Acer Legacy: Irrational Fear.   In 1990, the CDC reported the first known case of a patient infected by a health care worker with AIDS (Singleton, 1993). That patient, Kimberly Bergalis, became a nationally known advocate for mandatory testing of health care workers. Further study found that her dentist, Dr. David Acer, had infected six patients (Evans, 1994). As a result of the Acer case, the public harbors irrational fear of contracting HIV from health care workers, despite the fact that Acer's practice is the only known instance of provider-to-patient transmission, and the exact route of that transmission still is unknown (Mariner, 1995).

In July 1991, following the public's near hysteria over the Acer case, the CDC recommended that, in addition to practicing universal precautions, health care providers who perform exposure-prone procedures should know their HIV status. In turn, infected providers should consult with an expert review panel to determine procedures they may perform, and, when performing them, should disclose their HIV status to patients (Singleton, 1993). Shortly thereafter, Congress passed a law requiring states to adopt the CDC or equivalent guidelines.

Despite widespread public education about HIV transmission and the small risk in health care, the public's fear continues (Oddi, 1994). About 95% of the public believes providers should disclose their HIV status, and 65% would completely discontinue treatment from an HIV-infected provider, regardless of procedure (Hard, 1993).

The Risk of Provider–Patient Transmissions: Clinical Evidence.   Arguments against disclosure by health care workers point to the small risk involved and disclosure's invasion of privacy (Scheerhorn, 1995).

The probability of HIV transmission from physicians to patients is so small as to be characterized as "minuscule" (Derse, 1995, p. 220). Surgeons, perhaps more than any other health profession, work under conditions conducive to

HIV transmission. Yet, the chance of surgeon-to-patient transmission is estimated to range from 1 in 42,000 to 1 in 420,000 (Derse). According to Mariner (1995), the risk of death from general anesthesia during surgery is greater than the risk of contracting HIV from a health provider. In contrast, the chance of patient-to-provider transmission is far greater (Opperer, 1995).

Researchers have conducted retrospective, or "look-back," studies to identify possible cases of provider-to-patient HIV transmission. Tests on over 20,000 patients, treated by HIV-infected physicians, failed to document a single case of doctor-to-patient transmission (Derse, 1995). Thus, clinical evidence fails to support the medical benefits of routine disclosure by HIV-infected health care workers.

Defining "Acceptable Risk." Although various health professions disagree on the issue of providers' HIV disclosure to patients, the courts have taken a clear stand.

The CDC and AMA recommend mandatory HIV disclosure by health care workers (Oddi, 1994). However, numerous professional organizations (e.g., the American Hospital Association, the American College of Physicians) oppose mandatory disclosure (Oddi).

Although no federal legislation directly mandates HIV disclosure by health care workers, some states require disclosure as part of informed consent (Scheerhorn, 1995). Generally, courts have upheld both hospitals' right to require HIV testing and disclosure by providers and patients' right to know, when weighed against providers' privacy and freedom from discrimination.

In *Behringer v. The Medical Center at Princeton* (1991), the court upheld the medical center's right to restrict an HIV-infected physician's practice and require disclosure to his patients. The court agreed that Behringer's confidentiality was violated, but refuted discrimination by weighing the potential harm to others as greater than the harm to Behringer (Hard, 1993). In *In re Hershey Medical Center* (1991), the court rejected a physician's privacy argument, contending that by becoming part of a surgical team, his HIV status became a public concern. Thus, disclosure fulfilled a compelling state interest.

The courts consistently have upheld patients' rights to informed consent, allowing patients the choice of avoiding risk, no matter how small. In *Canterbury v. Spence* (1973), "the court held that a doctor must disclose all risks which a prudent patient would consider material in deciding whether to consent to the medical treatment" (pp. 786–787). Cases following from *Canterbury* defined "material risk" in terms of whether a patient's decision is likely to be influenced by knowing the risk, however small (Mousel, 1992). In the case of HIV, "material risk" creates a "logically impossible" standard of "zero risk" found nowhere else in health care (Price, 1991). That standard allows patients to make decisions based on "public hysteria" (Hard, 1993, p. 305) rather than on a rational evaluation of risks.

Disclosure in Practice: The Effects of Demands for "Informed Consent."
Ironically, mandates to disclose have made health care workers reluctant to
be tested (Hard, 1993). Theoretically, HIV-infected health care workers find
their work restricted to procedures that are not "exposure prone." However,
in practice, because health organizations, including the CDC, have given up
on identifying such procedures (Mariner, 1995), providers' disclosure of HIV
infection is tantamount to unemployment (Derse, 1995).

Arguments favoring mandatory testing of health care workers privilege
the patient, or more accurately, public opinion. Clearly, the public's perceived
risk of contracting HIV from a provider is beyond justification by clinical
evidence and far exceeds actual risk (Mariner, 1995). The chance of being
struck by lightening is greater than the chance of HIV transmission from
provider to patient (Mousel, 1992). Nevertheless, the courts have tipped the
balance in favor of public over private interests.

CONCLUSION

One often-unnamed "victim" of the HIV/AIDS epidemic is the medical ethic
of autonomy, particularly confidentiality, when weighed against beneficence
to third parties and society. Prior to the AIDS epidemic, rapidly emerging
threats jeopardized confidentiality, including team approaches to health care,
computerized records, and changes in legal mandates. As the epidemic was
beginning, one analyst already characterized confidentiality as "a decrepit
concept" (Siegler, 1982).

Challenges to confidentiality are likely to occur in HIV/AIDS cases due
to the deadly nature of the disease and the stigma inflicted on the infected.
The AIDS epidemic wrought further erosion of confidentiality via professional codes of ethics reinforced by legal opinion. Today confidentiality is
so deeply eroded as to call it a "myth" (Kalinowski, 1994). The arenas in
which medical ethics are played out in the AIDS epidemic have shifted from
the interpersonal health care relationship to the health care and legal systems.
In practice, the balance of privacy versus protection has shifted even further
toward protecting third parties and society over the privacy of patients,
whose forced HIV disclosures ironically function to further jeopardize their
health and well-being.

6

▼▼▼▼▼▼▼▼

Disclosure of HIV Infection
in Interpersonal Relationships:
A Communication Boundary
Management Approach

Gust A. Yep
San Francisco State University

> *Betty has been diagnosed HIV-positive and she is terrified that if her husband, Tim, tests HIV-negative, he will take their child and leave her. During a difficult period in their marriage they separated, and she had a brief affair with a man whom she later learned has AIDS. . . . Betty did not tell her husband about this affair when they reconciled, and she can't bring herself to reveal the secret to Tim in this time of crisis. In her desperation, she prays that Tim will also test positive for HIV so that he will not discover the affair and desert her. . . .*
>
> —Black, 1993, p. 355

The HIV/AIDS epidemic has dramatically changed our world and, as Coates states, "HIV is here to stay" (Kalichman, 1995, p. xi). HIV infection can exhaust an individual's intrapersonal, interpersonal, economic, and material resources (Kalichman). At the intrapersonal level, individuals living with HIV experience denial (Adam & Sears, 1996; Black, 1993; Earl, Martindale, & Cohn, 1991; Yep, Reece, & Negron, 1997), isolation and emotional turmoil (Black, 1993; Cherry & Smith, 1993; Morin, Charles, & Malyon, 1984; Yep & Pietri, 1999), extreme uncertainty (Adam & Sears, 1996; Siegel & Krauss, 1991; Weitz, 1989, 1991; Yep et al., 1997), fear and anxiety (Catania, Turner, Choi, & Coates, 1992; Fullilove, 1989; Gochros, 1992), and depression (Hays, Turner, & Coates, 1992; Perry, Jacobsberg, et al., 1990; Rabkin & Rabkin, 1995). At the interpersonal level, people living with HIV encounter social stigmatization (Clemo, 1992; Douard, 1990; Herek & Glunt, 1988; Petronio & Magni, 1996; Pryor & Reeder, 1993; Siegel & Krauss, 1991; Weitz, 1991), difficulties in interpersonal and intimate relationships (Black, 1993; Cameron, 1993; Crandall & Coleman, 1992; Yep et al., 1997), abandonment and physical rejection (Black, 1993; Mooney, Cohn, & Swift, 1992; Siegel & Krauss, 1991; Stulberg & Buckingham, 1988), and discrimination (E. A. Anderson, 1989; Cameron, 1993; Rowe, Plum, & Crossman, 1988, Yep et al., 1997), among others. Finally, individuals living with HIV also face financial drains, as the estimated lifetime cost of HIV infection is $119,000 per person (Hellinger, 1993). In short, there are few, if any, domains of life that are not affected by an HIV diagnosis.

As the number of cases of HIV infection continues to grow (Kalichman, 1995; Yep & Pietri, 1999), recent medical developments like protease inhibitors and combination therapies have instilled the hope of increasing the life expectancy and maintenance of relatively good health for individuals living with HIV infection (R. Baker, 1996). This promising and hopeful scenario also has important implications in the interpersonal domain for this growing group of survivors: More and more people will have to face disclosure of their HIV status in their interpersonal relationships.

Research on disclosure of HIV infection has increased in recent years (e.g., Gard, 1990; Greene, Parrott, & Serovich, 1993; Marks et al., 1992; Marks, Richardson, & Maldonado, 1991; Ostrow et al., 1989; Perry et al., 1994; Schnell et al., 1992; Serovich & Greene, 1993; Serovich, Greene & Parrott, 1992). With a few notable exceptions (Greene & Serovich, 1996; Petronio & Magni, 1996), however, much of this research lacks a coherent theoretical framework. Greene and Serovich (1996) note that "there is an available model to assist in understanding how HIV-positive individuals might want to regulate information about their serostatus" (p. 51) and such a model is Petronio's (1991; Petronio & Kovach, 1997; Petronio et al. 1996) communication boundary management (CBM) theory. The purpose of this chapter is to propose a coherent theoretical framework to understanding the process of disclosure of HIV infection in the interpersonal context. To accomplish this, the chapter is divided into three sections. First, it examines the complexity of this communication process in terms of balancing secrecy, privacy, and self-disclosure in interpersonal relationships. Second, it applies Petronio's (1991; Petronio & Kovach, 1997; Petronio et al., 1996) CBM theory to disclosure of HIV infection in interpersonal relationships. Finally, it discusses the implications of CBM theory for further theoretical development, research, and praxis in the domains of disclosure, privacy, and secrecy associated with HIV infection.

DISCLOSURE OF HIV INFECTION:
BALANCING SECRECY, PRIVACY, AND OPENNESS

The decision to disclose about one's HIV infection is likely to trigger psychological conflicts (Cline & Boyd, 1993; Gard, 1990; Marks et al., 1992;

Yep et al., 1997). To describe the nature of this internal struggle, Cline and Boyd (1993) write:

> The dilemma faced by persons with HIV/AIDS is this: either risk becoming stigmatized by disclosing their condition, in order to take a chance on gaining the potential health benefits of social support or avoid being stigmatized by engaging in information control and nondisclosure, thereby losing the potential health benefits of social support. (p. 132)

The struggle between fear of stigmatization and the need for social support is omnipresent in individuals living with HIV.

The social and interpersonal impact of HIV/AIDS-related stigma has created, in Goffman's (1963) terms, a "spoiled identity" characterized by "shameful differentness" (p. 10). According to Goffman (1963), there are three different types of stigma: (a) abominations of the body (e.g., physical deformities), (b) perceived blemishes of personal character (e.g., drug abuse, homosexuality), and (c) tribal odium (e.g., division by HIV status, race, religion). Individuals with HIV infection can potentially be considered "fatally flawed" (Douard, 1990, p. 37) in all of the three areas just mentioned (e.g., an injecting drug user [IDU] from a minority community with overt symptoms of opportunistic infections associated with AIDS). For these stigmatized individuals to engage in daily social interaction with minimal discomfort, they must learn to "pass" (Goffman, 1963, p. 42), which is a complex process of management of secrecy and disclosure.

The intricate interplay between secrecy and privacy, and openness and self-disclosure is further complicated for individuals living with HIV in at least two ways. First, past research (Cline, 1989; Gerbert et al., 1991; O'Donnell, O'Donnell, Pleck, Snarey, & Rose, 1987; Triplet & Sugarman, 1987) indicates that a typical HIV-diagnosed individual who discloses his or her health condition is more likely to experience stigmatization than to receive social support. Although gender (Cline & Johnson, 1992; Dowell, Lo Presto, & Sherman, 1991; L. S. Lewis & Range, 1992) and ethnic differences (Herek & Capitanio, 1993; Herek & Glunt, 1991, 1993) have been identified in this research, findings generally are consistent with those found for HIV-diagnosed individuals. Second, concealment of one's HIV infection can result in loneliness and inadequate social support (Cline & Boyd, 1993). Past research by Pennebaker and associates (Pennebaker, 1989; Pennebaker & Beall, 1986; Pennebaker et al., 1990; Pennebaker, Kiecolt-Glaser, & Glaser, 1988) indicates that concealment of any information that is threatening to the self (e.g., an HIV/AIDS diagnosis) is associated with physical and emotional difficulties. Pennebaker (1989) argues that disclosure of traumatic events is associated with lower overall stress levels as well as increased understanding and assimilation of such events and better psychological health. More recent research supports this position. For example, M. A. Greenberg and Stone (1992) found that disclosure of severe traumas has health benefits for the discloser as manifested by fewer self-reported physical symptoms in the months following the study. On the other hand, inhibition or nondisclosure of thoughts and feelings exerts persistent stress on the body and increases the individual's susceptibility to physical ailments. Such negative effects associated with nondisclosure are particularly devastating to individuals with already compromised immune systems (Kiecolt-Glaser & Glaser, 1988).

The process of HIV disclosure in interpersonal relationships is extraordinarily complex. To understand this enormous complexity, Petronio's (1991; Petronio & Kovach, 1997; Petronio et al., 1996) CBM theory is proposed as a theoretically appropriate, conceptually relevant, and pragmatically useful framework for describing, understanding, and explaining the process of HIV disclosure in the interpersonal context.

COMMUNICATION BOUNDARY MANAGEMENT

According to Petronio (1991), individuals regulate disclosure of private information in their relational systems. Disclosure regulation in relationships has been viewed as an essential ingredient in the development and maintenance of satisfying personal relationships. More specifically, Petronio (1991) argues that regulation of disclosure increases a sense of spontaneity and unpredictability in the relationship and protects the individual in the relational system from personal vulnerabilities associated with risky information. During this course of regulation, individuals manage their communication boundaries: "Management is critical because it is the process through which the partners balance giving up autonomy by disclosing and increasing intimacy by sharing private information" (Petronio, 1991, p. 312). Thus, this approach views self-disclosure in relationships as a strategic balance between self-revelation and self-restraint.

CBM theory appears to be particularly relevant to the examination of disclosure of HIV infection in interpersonal relationships for several reasons. First, the model focuses on disclosure of unsolicited private information. Although a number of individuals engage in partner questioning as a means to reduce their risk of HIV exposure, this procedure is neither consistent nor effective (Mays & Cochran, 1993). For example, Cochran and Mays (1990) found that many individuals were reluctant to disclose honest personal information that was perceived to be threatening to the relationship. For those individuals who choose to reveal their HIV diagnosis, the communication context generally becomes a confession characterized by disclosure of unsolicited personal data (Cline & Boyd, 1993). Second, this approach, as indicated earlier, focuses on disclosure of private information potentially involving high levels of risk. In the case of HIV infection, the potential risks of disclosure are great, ranging from sadness and discomfort to complete rejection, withdrawal, and abandonment (Black, 1993; Cameron, 1993; Cline & Boyd, 1993; Yep et al., 1997). Third, this model introduces the notion of communication boundaries as a protective means for both discloser and disclosee. In other words, this approach emphasizes the transactional nature of disclosive communication in which both partners actively exchange, negotiate, manage, and process information. More simply stated, Petronio's (1991) model directs our attention to both partners, as opposed to only one member of the dyad, in a disclosure situation. For example, some HIV-diagnosed individuals are not only anxious about admitting their own serostatus but are apprehensive that telling others, like parents, will make them "fall apart" (Gard, 1990). Fourth, CBM theory is applicable to all types of dyadic interactions. This is especially relevant for understanding disclosure of HIV infection as individuals manage their communication boundaries within various personal relationships to seek social support and minimize potential costs. For example, a person living with HIV may choose to disclose the condition to carefully selected individuals in the family system, friends, potential partners, or intimate others while tactfully avoiding disclosure in other relational systems. Finally, recent research findings (Greene & Serovich, 1996; Serovich & Greene, 1993; Serovich et al., 1992) support this boundary management approach to the revelation of information regarding HIV.

CBM theory is based on three fundamental assumptions (Petronio, 1991). First, partners in a relational system erect boundaries to maintain a balance between autonomy and vulnerability when disclosing and receiving private information from the other. Second, individuals in a relational system strategically regulate their communication boundaries to minimize risks and potential vulnerability. Third, partners coordinate the intersection of their own individual boundaries by following specific relational rules that determine the sending and receiving of disclosure information in terms of timing, amount, and context to establish an equilibrium between personal autonomy and relational intimacy.

Disclosive messages inherently contain a demand or expectation for appropriate response. Petronio (1991) outlined a number of factors that must be taken into consideration before disclosure of private information takes place. For the disclosing partner, there are three potential issues: (a) expectations communicated through the disclosive message regarding desired response of partner, (b) selection and production of appropriate message strategy to disclose, and (c) content of the message in terms of both breadth and depth. Similarly, the receiving partner needs to consider several factors before responding to the disclosure, including (a) evaluation of expectations associated with the response, (b) search for attributions and motives behind the disclosure, and (c) determination of message response strategy. Boundary coordination is the extent to which partners match the demands expressed in the disclosive message and the demands in the response message.

Expectations of the Discloser

As noted earlier, disclosure of one's HIV infection entails an implied expectation of a response from the partner. The expected response, in turn, is influenced by the discloser's purpose for revealing unsolicited information about himself or herself. Derlega and Grzelak (1979) and Petronio (1991) identified five possible reasons for sending a disclosive message to one's partner: (a) personal expression, (b) self-clarification, (c) social validation, (d) relational development, and (e) social control and influence.

Personal expression is a reason for disclosing private information about the self to others. In this instance, the discloser has the need to talk about his or her feelings, thoughts, and actions (Petronio, 1991). This mode of disclosure typically conveys the expectation that the partner should actively listen, support, and empathize with the discloser. Personal expression is important in disclosure of HIV infection. Past research (Cline & Boyd, 1993; A. Lewis, 1988) indicates that, after an initial adjustment period, some individuals report that their primary goal associated with revealing their HIV condition—seropositivity or AIDS diagnosis—is to educate others. Some individuals do this educating more privately, for example, speaking with friends and family members, while others become AIDS educators and activists (Cline & Boyd, 1993). However, before individuals "go public" with their HIV condition, they carefully assess the potential consequences of the disclosure, for example, balancing between worrying others and the need to receive social support (Gard, 1990; Marks et al., 1992) or examining the relevancy of the information to the target (Serovich & Greene, 1993).

Self-clarification is another reason for disclosure of personal data. In self-clarification, the disclosers discuss their feelings and thoughts about a specific issue and the expectation communicated to the recipients of the disclosure is one of acknowledgment and reflection (Petronio, 1991). In terms of informing others about their HIV infection, some individuals rely on the disclosure to increase their own self-understanding. Cline and Boyd (1993) describe what an individual said about his own disclosure: "It wasn't so much because I didn't know what AIDS meant to others but I wasn't sure what AIDS meant to me at the time" (p. 136). Telling others about one's condition can enhance the meaning of the condition itself.

Social validation is a third reason for disclosing private information. For the discloser, social validation is the process of receiving social support and confirmation about the self. When a partner is disclosing for social validation purposes, the expectation communicated to the listener is one of affirmation of the discloser's self-esteem and ratification of self-worth (Petronio, 1991). As indicated earlier, past research (Cline & Boyd, 1993; Gard, 1990; Siegel & Krauss, 1991) reports that disclosure of HIV infection in interpersonal relationships has been met with lack of social validation or outright rejection. However, with the onset of HIV-related symptoms, a number of individuals are motivated to self-disclose to others out of personal respect and responsibility while hoping for validation and social support (Marks et al., 1992). Others disclose because of their wish for the recipient to be extraordinarily understanding and supportive of their health condition (Gard, 1990).

Relational development is another reason for revealing unsolicited private information about the self. In this instance, disclosure is done to enhance the quality of the relationship, increase intimacy, and develop a greater sense of closeness with the receiver. The expectation for the disclosure may be one of reciprocation, understanding, and greater intimacy (Petronio, 1991). In terms of disclosure about HIV-related risk factors, Cochran and Mays (1990) indicate that both women and men are hesitant to disclose their past sexual histories because of fear of halting their developing relationships or damaging their developed relationships. Contrary to these fears, Schnell et al. (1992) report that 82% of the seropositive gay men (in a sample of 200 men) who disclosed their status to their significant others indicated no relationship disruption during a 6-month follow-up visit.

Although research on HIV disclosure and relational development appears inconclusive, Cameron (1993) observes that most of the HIV-diagnosed participants in her study articulated the desire for healthy and serious relationships. One of the concerns associated with serious relationships is to avoid infecting others (Ostrow et al., 1989). Cline and Boyd (1993) described how an individual living with HIV expressed his need to inform potential romantic partners: "When I date, I tell people about being HIV positive before we go out so that they can make a decision before anyone gets involved. It is not just protecting the other person, it is protecting myself as well" (p. 143). Finally, Marks et al. (1992) found that individuals living with HIV were more likely to inform their more significant others (e.g., parents, friends, intimate others) than their less significant others (e.g., employers, landlords, religious leaders). Consistent with CBM theory, these findings suggest that individuals' expectations about disclosing private information vary according to intimacy levels and relationship types.

Social control is the fifth and final reason for disclosure of private information. Social control is the process of revealing personal data to influence the recipient of the message, and the communicated expectation may be compliance by the partner (Petronio, 1991). Adam and Sears (1996) noted how an individual may use an HIV diagnosis to persuade a relational partner to end the relationship: "Actually I was hoping that [my HIV diagnosis] would drive her off. . . . At first she was angry at me . . . and I just thought that when I found out, this would be the final straw . . ." (p. 82).

Discloser's Message Strategy Selection

Petronio (1991) maintained that once individuals have determined their expectation for disclosure, they must select specific message strategies that will enhance the accomplishment of their goals. There are several conditions that affect strategy selection: (a) emotional control, (b) anticipated outcomes, (c) need for disclosure, and (d) perception of privacy associated with the information.

The degree to which the discloser has emotional control before and during the revelation process affects message strategy selection. Petronio (1991) argued that, for example, if disclosers have relatively little control over their feelings during disclosure, they may suspend considerations of politeness and face-saving tactics in the interaction. As stated earlier, psychological responses to HIV testing, seropositivity, and AIDS diagnosis that have been reported in past research include distress and suicidality (Ostrow et al., 1989; S. E. Taylor, Kemeny, Schneider, & Aspinwall, 1993); depression, anxiety, and psychiatric symptoms (Ostrow et al., 1989; Perry, Jacobsberg, et al., 1990); fear, anger, and powerlessness (Cameron, 1993); loneliness and emotional and social isolation (Cherry & Smith, 1993), all of which might ultimately lead to difficulties coping with and adjusting to the new condition (Adam & Sears, 1996; Yep et al., 1997). Thus, the degree of emotional control over the disclosure process appears to be contingent upon the extent to which individuals have adjusted to their HIV diagnoses.

Predicted outcome associated with disclosure of private information also affects disclosive message strategy selection (Petronio, 1991). For example, if disclosers anticipate positive reactions to the disclosure, they may select a more candid and direct approach to conveying private information. If, on the other hand, a negative outcome is expected, they may use a more ambiguous disclosive message to test the situation and protect the self from possible unfavorable reactions. This appears to be true for HIV disclosure. Cline and Boyd (1993) described how one individual carefully assesses the potential outcome of disclosure before using a direct approach: "I wait for the situation to be right. It's not just something you blurt out. You have to know if they are going to be caring or not. I can tell and, like I said, I haven't had any bad responses" (p. 136).

The intensity of the need for disclosure also influences disclosive message tactic selection. In his fever model of disclosure, Stiles (1987) maintained that certain life events create a tremendous need to disclose because of the psychological distress associated with them. For example, an individual after testing positive for HIV may feel an enormous pressure to discuss the experience, to "get it off the chest." Petronio (1991) argues that if the need for disclosure is high, the discloser may be more concerned about himself or herself and less worried about politeness or face management strategies for the receiving partner. Conversely, if the need for disclosure is low, the discloser may be more other-oriented (e.g., more considerate of the partner's feelings, reactions, and freedom to control his or her communication boundary).

Because people living with HIV can feel extremely vulnerable (Douard, 1990, Yep et al., 1997), their need to inform others may be intensified. For example, Marks et al. (1992) found that the severity of disease, manifested by visible physical symptoms of HIV-related illnesses, triggered individuals to increase disclosure of their health condition regardless of relationship. More specifically, their study revealed that individuals with AIDS and symptomatic diseases had a greater tendency to inform close relatives, employees, and coworkers as compared to their asymptomatic counterparts. Because of their potential risk for becoming HIV-infected, one may also expect that individuals would have a greater need to disclose to intimate others. To examine this issue, Serovich and Greene (1993) found that the marital subsystem (spouses, former spouses, lovers) was the most appropriate recipient of disclosure of HIV testing information for the participants in their study.

Finally, perception of privacy associated with the information about to be disclosed also affects strategy selection. *Informational privacy* refers to the type of data about the self that are released or become accessible to others (Carroll, 1975). Informational privacy is positively correlated with perceived risk associated with disclosure of such information. In other words, the greater the privacy associated with the information, the greater the risk of disclosure, and the lesser the privacy, the lower the risk of revealing such information. Petronio (1991) noted that the more private the information, the more likely it is that the discloser will select an indirect message strategy; conversely, the less private the information, the more likely it is that the individual will select a direct disclosive message tactic.

In terms of disclosure of HIV testing results, informational privacy is extremely important. For example, Marks et al. (1992) found that gay and bisexual men were more likely to disclose their HIV condition to others of the same sexual orientation (less privacy, lower risk) and to those who were aware of their sexuality (less privacy) than to heterosexuals (greater privacy, higher risk). Other studies (Greene & Serovich, 1996; Serovich & Greene, 1993; Serovich et al., 1992; Yep et al., 1997) suggest that the highly private nature of HIV testing information creates clear boundaries for disclosing such data. More specifically, Serovich et al. (1992) observed that individuals, responding to the desire for privacy in HIV testing, have a tendency to tighten family system boundaries. In another study, Greene et al. (1993)

found that an individual's perception of privacy was the best predictor of the willingness to reveal HIV test results.

Discloser's Message Strategy Production

After consideration of the process of selecting a specific message strategy for disclosure of private information, individuals encode their communication. Such message strategies can be classified into two groups: explicit and implicit (Petronio, 1991).

Explicit message strategies are those communication tactics that contain high certainty demand characteristics (Petronio, 1991). Such messages contain clear intentions, low ambiguity, obvious demands, and low uncertainty. In terms of communication boundaries, these messages give little autonomy to the recipient of disclosure. In other words, less control is given to the receiver, and therefore, the listener is placed in a more threatening position where protection from vulnerabilities is more difficult to attain. Because less autonomy is given to recipients of the disclosive message, they have fewer options available as a response to the information delivered. For example, if Nora tells her boyfriend, Chris, that she is HIV-positive (a direct disclosive message), Chris must respond to such a direct statement and has fewer communication options (e.g., acknowledgment, a supportive message).

Implicit message strategies are those communication tactics that are characterized by low certainty demand features (Petronio, 1991). These messages contain a lot of ambiguity and uncertainty, thus, allowing the partner more autonomy to respond to the implicit demand in the communication. Implicit message tactics protect the communication boundaries for both the discloser and the recipient of the disclosure. The receiving partner has the freedom to probe for clarification, continue exploring the subject, or simply acknowledge the original message. If, in the example just mentioned, Nora talks about people infected with HIV (an indirect disclosive message), Chris has many available options as a response (e.g., he may choose to stay indirect by talking about HIV infection in general, people infected with HIV, or his views regarding HIV/AIDS, or he may decide to be direct by asking Nora about her HIV status).

Message Content of the Disclosure

Disclosers, after assessing their own expectations and message strategies, must make a decision about what to tell. In other words, the individual needs to formulate the actual content of the disclosive message. In terms of disclosure of HIV infection, the individual must consider telling other events associated with the condition, like mode of infection, lifestyle, sexual orientation, drug use, and current health status, among others. In a sense, revealing one's HIV seropositivity or AIDS diagnosis is, for many, a "double coming out"—the process of telling about one's health status and sexual orientation at the same time (Adam & Sears, 1996; Gard, 1990). This process appears especially difficult in a social and cultural context where strong homophobic and heterosexist attitudes and antihomosexual behaviors exist (Gross, Green, Storck, & Vanyur, 1980; Herek & Berrill, 1992; Yep, 1997).

Receiving Partner's Evaluation of Expectations

As noted earlier, disclosive messages contain specific demands regarding appropriate responses to them. To assess the expectations for responding to the disclosure of unsolicited private information, the receiver of the disclosure must consider his or her sense of obligation to act and the extent to which he or she has autonomy in responding (Petronio, 1991). Further, this sense of responsibility to act is inversely related to perceived autonomy. More specifically, the more the receiving partner experiences a sense of responsibility to act on the basis of the disclosure, the lesser the perceived autonomy or choice; conversely, the lesser the sense of obligation, the greater the freedom the partner has for deciding on available options to respond. For example, a mother, on hearing that her son has been diagnosed with AIDS, would presumably experience a tremendous sense of obligation and duty to help her son (i.e., greater responsibility, lesser autonomy). In this situation, she may perceive very few alternatives to being helpful and supportive of her child.

Receiving Partner's Attributional Searches

For recipients of disclosure to respond appropriately, they must assess the motivation behind the discloser's communication of private information. To evaluate the reasons for the disclosure, the receiver needs to consider several issues: (a) relational memory or related past experiences with the discloser; (b) message content or the information conveyed in the actual disclosure; (c) the situation or context in which the disclosive message is sent; (d) the physical (e.g., a private location) and psychological (e.g., disclosure made in the context of sharing) environment associated with the interaction; and (e) the nonverbal behavior accompanying the verbal disclosure (Petronio, 1991).

Receiving Partner's Determination of Message Response

Once receivers of private information have examined the expectations and motives behind the disclosure, they must decide how to appropriately respond. There are two possible types of response strategies. The first, direct message response, is characterized by high certainty, directness, and clarity in the fulfillment of the obligations implied in the disclosive demand message (e.g., telling the discloser that he or she will do certain things after listening to the disclosure). The second, indirect message response, features high degrees of ambiguity and uncertainty in relationship to the demand associated with the disclosure (e.g., telling the discloser that he or she is feeling emotional about the information).

Communication Boundary Coordination

The extent to which the response matches the demand of the disclosive message determines whether there is boundary coordination or "satisfactory fit" (Petronio, 1991, p. 326) within the communication episode and the relationship. Because disclosure of extremely private information, such as a diagnosis of an incurable and highly stigmatized disease, is affected by internalized prejudices, biases, preconceptions, expectations, strong emotions, and uncertainty on the part of both discloser and receiver, communication boundary coordination may be difficult to achieve (Cline & Boyd, 1993; Gard, 1990). When boundary coordination is attained, individuals report experiencing a greater sense of social support (Adam & Sears, 1996; Cherry & Smith, 1993). Cherry and Smith describe how communication boundary coordination can remove stigma, increase intimacy, and affirm the person living with HIV:

> My best friend, when I told her [about my diagnosis], she took the glass of tea that I was drinking and took a big drink out of it. That made me cry. She showed me that in her mind I was still okay. . . . She made me feel like I was still a person in the world no different than anybody else. (p. 196)

IMPLICATIONS OF CBM THEORY
AND HIV DISCLOSURE

In this chapter, the complexity of the HIV disclosure process and the potential relevance of CBM theory are examined. Potential disclosers usually go through a process of adjustment (Adam & Sears, 1996; Gard, 1990). Because HIV/AIDS is a chronic health condition, these individuals need to cope and integrate HIV into their lives. Siegel and Krauss (1991) identify three major adaptive challenges of people living with HIV infection: (a) confronting the possibility of a curtailed life span (e.g., dealing with a greater sense of urgency to achieve life goals, deciding whether or not to invest in the future); (b) dealing with social and personal reactions to a stigmatizing health condition (e.g., deciding who to tell about their HIV status, coping with feelings of social isolation, shame, guilt, and contamination); (c) developing a set of tactics to maintain optimal physical and emotional well-being (e.g., dealing with treatment decisions, maintaining a sense of emotional balance and stability). Given the complexity of this adaptive scheme, disclosure of HIV infection may be viewed as a slow, gradual, judicious, and strategic communicative process. CBM theory appears to be an especially relevant framework for understanding HIV disclosure in personal relationships. It focuses on the transactional nature of communication and disclosure of unsolicited and potentially risky personal information, balance of privacy and openness, and use of communication strategies to minimize personal risks.

Although CBM theory appears to be a promising framework for understanding HIV disclosure behaviors, its explanatory potential has not been fully tested. As indicated earlier, some data have been collected using this model as a framework (Greene & Serovich, 1996; Petronio & Magni, 1996), and future research can build on those findings. For example, future research can focus on factors leading to disclosure of HIV testing information in both gay and heterosexual relationships. Although HIV/AIDS has become an accepted reality in the gay community (Shilts, 1987; Yep, Lovaas, & Pagonis, in press), the picture is very different among heterosexuals. In spite of growing concern about heterosexual HIV transmission (Bowen & Michal-Johnson, 1989; DiClemente, 1990; Yep, 1993b), tremendous denial and unrealistic optimism still persist (Curran, 1988; van der Pligt, Otten, Richard, & van der Velde, 1993).

In addition, the HIV/AIDS epidemic has disproportionately affected minority populations (Choi, Yep, & Kumekawa, 1998; Diaz, 1998; Jemmott & Jones, 1993; Michal-Johnson & Bowen, 1992; Ostrow et al., 1989; Spigner, 1998; Yep, 1992; Yep & Pietri, 1999). Needless to say, the process of communicating private information about the self, for example, disclosing one's desire to practice safer sex or telling others about HIV infection, is influenced by cultural beliefs and value systems (Choi et al., 1998; Michal-Johnson & Bowen, 1992; Yep, 1992, 1993c, 1995, 1998). For example, Marks et al. (1992) report that Latino men had a tendency to disclose less than their European American counterparts. Such disclosure patterns may be associated with gender roles, machismo, and homophobia within Latino culture (Diaz, 1998; Yep, 1995). Similarly, African Americans have a tendency to disregard the homosexual aspects of HIV transmission (Jemmott & Jones, 1993). For Asians and Pacific Islanders, Yep (1993c, 1998) identifies communication difficulties associated with discussion of sexuality, homosexuality, drug use, and terminal illness in these populations. Finally, HIV disclosure among transgenders and transsexuals may be affected by their distinct social and cultural realities (Yep & Pietri, 1999). Therefore, further work must be done to ascertain social and cultural similarities and differences in the disclosure process.

Understanding how discloser and recipient of disclosure manage and coordinate their communication boundaries has important implications for praxis. A thorough assessment of the variables affecting the disclosure process, for instance, may provide specific guidelines and suggestions that can be easily incorporated into both pre- and posttest counseling offered in HIV antibody testing centers. Such suggestions may prove helpful for individuals undergoing testing regardless of results. For example, seronegative individuals may be able to assess potential risks and receivers' attributions associated with their disclosure of HIV testing information (e.g., others' assignment of motives for testing which may include assumptions of drug use, past sexual history, and sexual orientation). For seropositive individuals, careful assessment of the disclosure process may lessen emotional distress, stigma, and social isolation while enhancing social support, relational intimacy, and quality of life as HIV becomes a chronic manageable health condition.

7

▼▼▼▼▼▼▼▼

Nonverbal Vernacular Tactics
of HIV Discovery Among Gay Men

Daniel C. Brouwer
Loyola University, Chicago

That gay men continue to serve as major subjects of HIV/AIDS discourse—
"subjects" in terms of both "topics" and "discourse producers"—is not surprising. Over the last two decades discussions and debates about gay male
sexuality and gay male sexual practices have been invigorated among the
"queer" community, narrowly cast, and the "general public," more broadly
cast,[1] because of persistent associations between HIV and homosexuality.
    Amidst public discourse about HIV infection, gay men continue to play
out the mundanities and spectacularities of their sexual lives. Ultimately, it
is hoped, gay men make decisions about HIV disclosure and sexual behavior
that help to reduce the risks and rates of HIV transmission. Epidemiological
data fail to bear this hope out, however, for rates of HIV infection among
gay men began an upswing in the mid-1990s. Although there are several
explanations for the increase in HIV infection rates among gay men in the

---

[1]The mid-1990s have been an especially lively deliberative time for the topic of gay men's
sexuality and sexual practices. During these years, several books on those topics were published,
including Rotello's (1997) *Sexual Ecology: AIDS and the Destiny of Gay Men* and Rofes' (1995)
Reviving the Tribe: Regenerating Gay Men's Sexuality and Culture in the Ongoing Epidemic. These
books offer conflicting diagnoses and prognoses of HIV infection among gay men. The year 1997
also saw the formation of Sex Panic!, an antigovernmental regulation activist group, and a rather
public conflict between Sex Panic! and the Gay and Lesbian HIV Prevention Activists, which
advocates both greater personal responsibility and stronger state action in the cause of reducing HIV
transmission rates.

United States, an increase in risky sexual behaviors coupled with an unwillingness to verbally communicate serostatus and risk behaviors are among
the primary reasons for the rise of HIV infections (Doll et al., 1994). Throughout the brief but chaotic history of the epidemic, public health advocates,
legislators, and HIV/AIDS activists have typically agreed that encouraging
individuals to verbally communicate and negotiate themselves through potentially infective sexual situations is a key component to sound AIDS public
health policy. Advocates and activists have typically put forth another recommendation: that participants in a sexual encounter behave as if their
partner were infected with HIV. Obviously, this latter recommendation recognizes that HIV risk management can be practiced even in situations where
adequate verbal communication does not or will not take place. Some gay
men practice either or both of these risk management strategies—verbal
disclosure coupled with verbal negotiation of sexual behavior, or silence
coupled with "universal precaution." Other gay men, however, choose neither. Instead, during a sexual encounter with someone whose serostatus is
unknown, these men employ nonverbal "vernacular" tactics of HIV discovery
in order to make decisions about sexual behavior.

I am interested in examining occasions when gay men (at least one of
whom is HIV-positive) come into sexual congress and use means other than
explicit verbal communication to determine the serostatus of their partner.
In this chapter, I examine nonverbal, vernacular tactics of HIV discovery
by seropositive and seronegative men in the gay community. By "vernacular,"
I refer to those behaviors, practices, gestures, and discourses that individuals
and groups perform in the course of their everyday lives. By "tactics," I refer
to "the local methods that individuals use to make meaning of their own"
(McLaughlin, 1996, p. 16). In the absence of explicit communication about
serostatus, gay men might employ vernacular tactics such as the "sushi test,"
wherein an acquaintance, friend, or partner's refusal to eat sushi is read as
a likely indication that the person is HIV-positive.[2] Or, one might read
another's sudden change in weight or attendance at certain events as indicative of seropositive status.

This chapter examines two distinct tactics of HIV discovery. The two
vernacular tactics chosen for this analysis come from two radical AIDS
"zines": *Diseased Pariah News* (DPN) and *Infected Faggot Perspectives* (IFP).
Elsewhere, I argued that these zines function as textual subaltern counterpublics in which gay men with HIV and/or AIDS exploit the semiprivate
nature of the forum (Brouwer, 1995). This is done in order to experiment
with gay male subjectivity and sexuality and to promote modes of discourse

[2]Physicians recommend that individuals with compromised immune systems (including people
with HIV) avoid uncooked foods like sushi for fear of the exceptional havoc that parasites could
wreak on the individuals' health. I thank Gust Yep for reminding me of the sushi test.

and styles of address that are not always received as legitimate.[3] Created and sustained by seropositive gay men, the zines are exemplary vernacular fora which create, employ, and promote vernacular discourses and practices.

The first vernacular tactic that I examine is the practice of "trick exams," or the physical yet clandestine discernment of the serostatus of a sexual partner. The trick exam appears in "Examinations" in IFP. In his article, Karr (1992) narrated his experience of being subjected to forcible handling by a potential sex partner who was examining Karr for swollen and hardened lymph nodes. Ultimately, Karr was rejected as a sexual partner because his swollen lymph nodes betray his serostatus. The second vernacular tactic is the practice of "trick intuitions," or the careful appraisal of certain nonverbal behaviors as indicative of serostatus. Trick intuitions are dramatized in a semifictive piece by Tom Ace that appears in DPN. In this text, "Dire Diaries," the author presents diary entries from each of two men who participated in a trick encounter; the diary entries describe the same sexual event from the two different perspectives of the men. Notably, the diary accounts allow the reader to witness the men's internal description and justification of their ability to read their partner's infection status in the absence of explicit verbal disclosure.

While both texts describe the vernacular tactics of HIV discovery in gay male sexual situations, they also critique these nonverbal practices of HIV discovery. For instance, Karr (1992) condemns the trick exam practice not only as one that confirms the betrayal of his body, but also as a practice that reiterates the sexual "undesirability" of those who are infected. Ace (1995) critiques trick intuitions by pointing to the potential inaccuracy (and by extrapolation, the potential danger) of such a practice.

My critical approach to these texts is textual analysis, close reading that excavates the implicit and unstated assumptions about the conditions of secrecy and disclosure that underlie the vernacular practices that are described. Although the number of texts is very limited, each text is symptomatic of the concerns of a larger community of gay men and of the coping strategies that emerge from those concerns. Both tell us something about the nature of communication practices, the "erotics of making-do" (Patton, 1996, p. 142), that exist between gay men nearing the end of the second decade of the epidemic and coping with the nexus of illness, risk, and pleasure. In the next several pages, I first define the term *vernacular* in more detail

---

[3]The essay to which I refer here is *The Charisma of "Responsibility": A Comparison of U.S. Mainstream Representations of Gay Men with AIDS and Representations of Gay Men with AIDS in U.S. AIDS Zines*, my unpublished master's thesis written in 1995 at Northwestern University. The concept of subaltern counterpublics as "parallel discursive arenas where members of subordinated social groups invent and circulate counterdiscourses" (Fraser, 1990, p. 67) derives from the critical work of Nancy Fraser.

and explain the significance of a study of vernacular practices. Then, I perform a close reading of both texts, paying particular attention to the ways in which the texts describe the performances of vernacular tactics of HIV reading. Throughout, I consider the theoretical and practical implications of what I have excavated from the texts, including consideration of why vernacular practices such as these emerge, how they function, and their relative degree of efficacy.

Nonverbal Vernacular

"People who have HIV, we have a vernacular other people don't."
—Jeffrey Reed (Christie, 1996, p. 54)[4]

As I assert above, the performance of trick exams and the discernment of someone's serostatus based on nonverbal gestures and cues should be considered "vernacular" practices. At this juncture, it is imperative to provide a synopsis of vernacular theory and to explicate its significance to this study. H. A. Baker (1984) introduced vernacular theory as a term and as a unique line of inquiry. He noted that the etymological roots of "vernacular" push vernacular studies toward consideration of both "a slave born on his master's estate" and "arts native or peculiar to a particular country or locale" (p. 2). He introduces his groundbreaking book as another installment in his decade-long "quest . . . for the distinctive, the culturally specific aspects of Afro-American literature and culture" (p. 1). In 1988, Baker's fellow literary scholar, Gates (1988) offered his own contribution to the field of African American literary vernacular theory. In that book, Gates examined how African American vernacular discourse practices form the basis for Black literature.

Scholars intrigued by Baker and Gates' explorations into the Black vernacular have attempted to employ and adapt those theorists' insights into examinations of other kinds of vernacular communities and vernacular practices. If one defines the vernacular as "the practices of those who lack cultural power and who speak a critical language grounded in local concerns" (pp. 5–6), as McLaughlin (1996) does, then vernacular theory and vernacular studies open up to a broad range of concerns and populations. In line with this effort to broaden the scope of vernacular studies beyond their African American literature roots, communication scholars Ono and Sloop (1995)

---

[4]This epigraph comes from Jeffrey Reed, an HIV-positive worker at a marijuana buyers club in San Francisco, who explained to a newspaper reporter how he was able to determine which clients had legitimate, AIDS-related medical claims to marijuana and which put forth bogus claims. Using "intuition and knowledge of the AIDS culture" (Christie, 1996, p. 54), Reed confidently asserts his ability to discern the HIV- or AIDS-diagnosed.

set forth a definition of vernacular discourse as well as a justification for studying it from a critical rhetoric perspective.[5] In their definition:

Vernacular discourse is speech that resonates within local communities. This discourse is neither accessible in its entirety, nor is it discoverable, except through texts. However, vernacular discourse is also culture: the music, art, criticism, dance, and architecture of local communities. . . . [V]ernacular discourse is unique to specific communities. (Ono & Sloop, 1995, p. 20)

Ono and Sloop note that "vernacular discourse" (p. 20) is constituted not only by the everyday speech of a specific community but also by other forms of social, cultural, and aesthetic expression. Thus, although in their case study they examine World War II printed-word texts of a Japanese American newspaper, *The Pacific Citizen,* their claims about the vernacular are broad enough to warrant inclusion of nonverbal practices such as HIV-discovery practices.

Ono and Sloop (1995) treated *The Pacific Citizen* as a textual forum for discussing vernacular-discursive practices. Like Ono and Sloop, I go to a textual source for examplars of vernacular discourse: the radical AIDS zines, DPN and IFP. Zines are a unique forum wherein vernacular practices of discursive and visual representation typically thrive. "Zines establish vernacular interpretive communities" (McLaughlin, 1996, p. 66), and editors and writers in the zines "become vernacular theorists, subjects who take up the work of dismantling the ideology they encounter in pop culture" (McLaughlin, 1996, p. 57). In DPN and IFP, editors and writers speak to and for an interpretive community of seropositive gay men. They employ numerous vernacular representational tactics such as camp humor, eroticization of the male body, appropriation of personae, and hyperbole that are familiar to or characteristic of gay male culture. In each issue of the zines, one can easily find an article, poem, or short story that challenges public discourse, even liberal discourse—even gay male liberal discourse—that in any way elides, evades, ignores, or discounts the experiences, needs, desires, and concerns of seropositive gay men. In short, DPN and IFP serve as exemplary vernacular sites wherein topics or issues that are unique to or especially characteristic of seropositive gay male culture are taken up with great frequency and often receive vernacular description, translation, and/or theorization.

Trick Examinations

The next two sections of this chapter focus explicitly (and, to some readers, perhaps luridly) on vernacular practices in sexual settings. In this section, the tactic of the "trick exam" is explored. It is used by some in an effort to

___

[5]I am less interested in positioning myself within the tradition of critical rhetoric initiated by McKerrow (1989) than in broadly defining vernacular discourse for an audience of communication studies scholars.

discover—absent explicit verbal communication—if their sexual partner is HIV-positive. The nature of the "trick" sexual encounter should be described before the "trick examination" can be understood as a vernacular practice performed by some gay men. The trick is a type, or genre, of sex perhaps more recognizable as a "one-night stand." Although the communicative dimensions of trick encounters certainly are variable, I will hazard a few generalizations about the genre. Nonverbal behaviors such as sustained eye contact and bodily positioning, whether exhibited in a bar or on the street, are constitutive of trick encounters. In addition, it is not uncommon for individuals who will later trick together to engage in some sort of phatic or low-level verbal exchange. For a portion of gay men, trick encounters are predominantly nonverbal, and for some, the absence or minimal presence of verbal communication is a large (or overriding) part of the attraction of this genre of sex. Finally, tricks are characterized by little expectation of intentional future encounters. What this means, of course, is that trick encounters are sometimes not focused on the demand for or negotiation of safer sex that one would expect or hope for between two sexual partners.

Given the communicative qualities that characterize some trick encounters, gay men have developed a number of vernacular HIV reading strategies for trick situations. One of these strategies is the trick exam. Karr, cocreator and coeditor of IFP, a radical AIDS zine from Los Angeles, writes about his initial awareness of trick exams:

> I first heard of trick "examinations" in Mexico last summer [1991]. I was told how men who didn't like to ask a lot of questions or discuss [sero] status had found ways to determine it anyway by camaflouging [sic] their investigation in cloaks of massage or seemingly innocent and playful tickling of the neck or underarms. (Karr, 1992, p. 5)[6]

In a more recent article in *The Village Voice*, Schoofs (1994) recounts the following narrative in his "Love Stories in the Age of AIDS":

> Even [HIV sero] negatives have their war stories. My friend George remembers one tryst in particular. In the middle of necking, his partner pulled back and asked, "Do you have a cold?" George said he was just getting over one. "And this guy said, 'Oh, that must be why your glands are swollen,' " George recalls. "I mean, he was feeling my glands as we were making out!" (p. 21)

Having experienced physicians' probing lymph node exams themselves, or cognizant of friends' medical regimens, or competent enough to make the

---

[6]The main lymph node clusters occur on both sides of the neck, underneath the armpits, in the groin area, and deep under the sternum bone.

connection between what they read physicians doing and their own behaviors, the men about whom Karr and Schoofs write have created and practiced a vernacular tactic of HIV discovery. They belong to an interpretive community in which such vernacular exams are intelligible. A trick exam is the centerpiece of Karr's text, which begins with a lusty and explicit description of the events taking place already into the sexual portion of a recent trick. In this description, Karr expresses the extreme pleasure that he derives from the forceful and deliberately rough handling by his partner. Karr's admitted masochism is confirmed in this account of the erotic choking:

> Enormous and powerful fleshy fingers made for exceedingly large hands which cuffed my neck. . . . My hand-cuffed neck surrendered to the tightening grasp; gasping, I was very close to home [attaining orgasm] and I had no reason to believe he wouldn't take me there. (Karr, 1992, p. 5)

Yet amidst the seemingly all-consuming lust and passion from which Karr joyously suffers, a budding recognition begins to compete for his psychical attention.

> A fat forceful finger . . . then two or three more on either hand pushed deeply into the flesh of my neck. . . . [Y]et something was happening, something vaguely familiar . . . not quite known but I knew whatever it was it was not good. I let go of the vague recollection. (p. 5)

To his dismay, Karr never "went home" because his trick partner made a hasty retreat, pathetically justified by his claim that Karr was too emotionally and sexually intense. Momentarily surprised, Karr then describes how he began to assess his partner's sudden departure.

> As I was falling off [to sleep] that familiar vagueness—the fingers plunging deep into my neck—returned. This time I chose not to ignore it. Fingers . . . neck . . . fingers . . . neck. Fingers pushing . . . no not pushing . . . fingers plunging . . . no . . . not pushing or plunging . . . but . . . palpating . . . like the Doctor . . . probing for tell-tale signs of infection—lymph nodes permanently swollen and immovable . . . in my neck. Hard rocks . . . that we the infected wear in our bodies . . . our scarlet letter . . . our tattoo . . . our number. (p. 5)

In this dramatic account, Karr's assessment of his trick encounter involves most notably his increasingly precise discernment of the quality of the touching and choking to which he submitted. More specifically, there is a burgeoning recognition that the choking which he had first registered as erotic had instead masked its diagnostic intentions. Ultimately, Karr realizes that his partner's pushing/plunging/palpating fingers found the information source that gave him (that is, one of his immune system's responses to HIV infection) away.

Certainly, Karr's comparisons of his lymph nodes to a scarlet letter, a tattoo, or a number function metaphorically, but an important truth emerges when we consider Karr's comparisons on a literal level. Compared to his swollen lymph nodes, the scarlet letter, tattoo, and number are "on" the body and visible whereas his hard lymph nodes are "in" the body but palpable. Swollen lymph nodes lie like buried clues just beneath the surface of the skin. They are palpable. Because they are palpable, they can be read. Unlike a scarlet letter or a tattoo, however, which are meant to be visibly legible, Karr's swollen lymph nodes have to be felt in order to provide information. The palpable legibility of swollen lymph nodes requires a skilled reader.

How accurate or legible are swollen lymph nodes for detecting HIV status? Or, to what extent could someone who performs the exam be confident in the accuracy of his reading? Clearly, feeling/reading swollen lymph nodes as indices for HIV infection runs risks of inaccuracy. Although it is true that Karr's examiner accurately assessed Karr's seropositivity through palpation of his lymph nodes, the lay examiner in Schoof's narrative above misread the swollen lymph nodes that he encountered. It is likely that an individual might actually reduce the risk of HIV infection by choosing not to engage in potentially infective behaviors with anyone whose lymph nodes are swollen; it may also be the case that swollen lymph nodes may not be present in a seropositive partner.

Having briefly considered the efficacy of the trick exam, I wish to revisit Karr (1992) in the aftermath of his examination. Naturally, his rejection as a sexual partner was devastating, for the stigma of HIV infection was reinforced: "I am infected. One more time I am reminded that I am dirty, unclean and unwanted" (p. 5), he laments. Karr decries the fact that he forfeits the privilege of consent when his hard-as-rocks lymph nodes betray his serostatus against his permission. He is angry, but should not Karr have disclosed his serostatus in the first place? In this text, might we may misplace our sympathies with a humiliated Karr who should have preempted the use of a clandestine serostatus reading practice by explicitly disclosing his status? Indeed, in ultimately condemning "men who didn't like to ask a lot of questions or discuss status" (p. 5), Karr implicitly condemns himself, for he does not allege to have initiated discussion about serostatus in this trick encounter. There are, however, at least two mitigating factors against Karr's total culpability. First, the reader should be reminded of the communicative norm of silence or near silence that strongly influences many trick encounters. Still, "the context made me do it" hardly suffices as a justification. What must also be noted, then, is Karr's implied commitment to safer sexual practices in the absence of verbal disclosure of HIV serostatus in his lament: "that we were safe becomes unimportant" (Karr, p. 5). In the aftermath of his examination, Karr does not draw attention to his "need" for explicit verbal communication, but to his assumption that in place of verbal communication, risk-reducing behaviors are epidemiologically and morally sufficient. For Karr, the moral offense lies not in his silence about his seropositivity but in his examiner's secretive searching.

Trick Intuitions

Another example of nonverbal vernacular HIV reading tactics in trick situations is dramatized in a semifictional account that appears in DPN.[7] The zine article consists of 1-page diary entries "pulled" from each of two different men's diaries. As the reader soon discovers, the diary chroniclers are describing the same event, a trick encounter in San Francisco. The unnamed first participant, a San Francisco resident, recounts a late evening walk home during which he saw, "met," and had unprotected oral and anal sex with a handsome out-of-town visitor. The diary entry describes and justifies the nonverbal negotiations of the sexual practices in which they engage. "We were very much on the same wavelength sexually," the San Francisco resident remarks—"we didn't need any words" (Ace, 1995, p. 31). Concern about HIV transmission and infection arises in the diary entry where the chronicler briefly explains how he determined his trick's serostatus in the absence of explicit discussion and disclosure: "I figured he must've been positive when he went to fuck me without a rubber. No negative guy would have ever have [sic] been so calm about taking a risk like that" (Ace, p. 31). In the absence of explicit verbal communication, this participant observes a specific behavior of his partner and then reads the "emotional tenor" with which his partner performs that behavior; finding his partner "so calm," he assures himself of his serostatus-discovering acumen.

---

[7]I wrote to Tom Ace, the author of "Dire Diaries," in order to confirm my initial perception about the semifictional nature of the events depicted. Ace promptly wrote back:

There is no one encounter that was the basis for the narrative. . . . It's a synthesis of elements of various encounters, and a bit of pure fiction. The circumstances of the encounter (meeting on the street) and the description of Russell are fictional. . . . Parts of the first entry (p. 31) are based on experience, either mine or the experience of others. (personal communication, December 31, 1997)

Ace's narrative control over the voices and behaviors of his characters permits him to expose and interrogate what he believes to be all-too-common justifications for risky sexual activity. Ace's critique succeeds to the degree that readers of "Dire Diaries" recognize the justifications as familiar and problematic.

On the basis of the first four paragraphs, the reader of "Dire Diaries" cannot yet determine whether the first chronicler is seronegative and does not care about getting infected, or whether the man is seropositive and does not worry enough about reinfection to insist on protective latex barriers. What makes this unprotected sexual encounter all the more urgent, however, is the fact that the San Francisco resident reveals to the reader later in his entry that he is, indeed, seropositive: "I have no problem with having unprotected buttsex with guys *who are also positive"* (Ace, 1995, p. 31, italics added).

This man's decision not to disclose his seropositive status or to insist on protective latex barriers is not left unremarked, for Ace has this man devote almost half of his diary entry to the ethics of disclosure.

> But it felt wrong that we didn't talk about it first. Like I said, I can't imagine he was negative, but I would've felt better if we'd gotten it all out in the open. . . . Maybe I oughta talk about my status first. (Ace, 1995, p. 31)

The San Francisco resident expresses a twinge of ethical unease—"it felt wrong"—about his decision not to disclose, and he momentarily considers a course of action for the future—"Maybe I oughta talk about my status first" (p. 31). Despite these brief musings, however, the San Francisco resident does not indict himself or his partner for their silence, nor does he fully resolve to perform full disclosure in future encounters. "Part of the attraction," he admits, "was keeping it all nonverbal" (Ace, 1995, p. 31). Undermining an ethic of full disclosure, the chronicler's appreciation of the erotics of the nonverbal and his confidence in his serostatus-reading ability are justifications with which readers of the zines are certainly familiar. Consequences of such justifications are amplified through the inclusion of a second diary entry, this one by the other participant.

The second chronicler, whose name the first chronicler remembers to be "Russell," is discovered to be writing in his diary on his return flight home to Boston. "I have only one trick to report," Russell informs his diary, and then he briefly describes the cruise on the street, the walk back to his friend's residence, and his anal penetration of the first man. Like his counterpart, Russell briefly, yet confidently, describes his ability to read the serostatus of his trick partner: "I could tell he was HIV-negative without asking, so I didn't bother with a rubber. Guys who know they're infected have it written all over their faces" (Ace, 1995, p. 32).

Like the San Francisco resident, Russell describes his interpretive strategy as an ability to read the "emotional tenor" of another man. For the first participant, reading serostatus required detection of his partner's "calmness." For Russell, reading serostatus requires interpreting nonverbal cues in the face of the other man. Russell does not clarify for the reader, however, which facial characteristics convey seropositivity and which convey seronegativity.

Furthermore, Russell never explicitly discloses his own serostatus, although it is strongly implied that he is negative. The potential tragedy that emerges is Russell's infection with HIV. His faulty assumption about his trick's serostatus and his subsequent decision not to engage in safer, barrier-using sexual practices promote this outcome. For, unlike Karr's narrative, in which the encounter is interrupted before potentially infective behaviors occur, these trick participants consummate.

In both diary entries, gay men give expression to their ability to accurately read nonverbal signs of HIV infection. Placed side by side, however, the diary entries dramatize to the reader that these men's confident (albeit vague) assertions of their reading abilities are dreadfully inaccurate. The first writer announces his seropositivity and his assumption about Russell's seropositivity. Russell, on the other hand, implies his seronegativity and announces his assumption about the first writer's seronegativity. What the reader witnesses in these diary accounts, then, is a dual-perspective recollection of a possibly infective encounter.

Conclusion

The two texts examined in this chapter describe nonverbal vernacular tactics of HIV discovery in trick encounters that, because of the very nature of the trick encounter, demonstrate seeming devotion to secrecy. Still, the devotion to secrecy about serostatus is not total. In both texts, gay men demonstrate a concern for balancing the mystery and excitement of silence with an effort to determine serostatus (and thus risk level) by other means. In the case of the trick examination, Karr's (1992) examiner was able to accurately ascertain Karr's seropositivity through skilled palpation. In the "Dire Diaries" encounter, the trick participants' intuitive judgments ultimately fail to deliver them accurate serostatus results. The two texts that I have examined demonstrate that the effort to balance secrecy and privacy with accurate knowledge is not always a successful one. Vernacular practices, although they originate from often rich and complex repertoires of knowing, can be problematic. In Ace's (1995) semifictional piece, the reader witnesses paltry and vague justifications for inaccurate and potentially infective HIV reading practices. In Karr's confession, the humiliation that Karr suffers from the trick examination tempers valorization of the practice as "accurate."

Throughout this chapter, I refer to "Examinations" and "Dire Diaries" as "vernacular texts." At this point, a few comments about their nature as "texts" and about their significance as "vernacular" are warranted in understanding the limitations and contributions of a study such as this. As written documents, the zine articles are enduring expressions, not subject to the evanescence of face-to-face interactions. They are documents that demonstrate the reflection and control of narrative events that are characteristic of writing, and they contribute to the development and maintenance of an interpretive community of seropositive gay men. Because they are print media texts, they are certainly easier to acquire than interviews or ethnographic data. Yet, despite their ease of acquisition and despite the critical function that they play in fostering an interpretive community, their status as print media texts does not, as McLaughlin (1996) claimed, "invite more prolonged analyses than do casual, short-lived discursive forms" (p. 26). The vernacular critic should also be wary of Ono's and Sloop's (1995) claim that "[vernacular] discourse is neither accessible in its entirety, nor is it discoverable, except through texts" (p. 20). As skilled ethnographers demonstrate, meticulous observation and participation in the nonprint vernacular artifacts of a community invite prolonged, nuanced, and "deep" analyses. For some cultures and communities, in fact, print texts might be the most desiccated source of vernacular knowledge. Written texts, as these and many other critics acknowledge, hardly exhaust how and where the vernacular is discoverable. Face-to-face conversations, support group discussions, and gossip in bars, for example, all foster discussion of and critique of vernacular practices of HIV discovery. Finally, my choice of vernacular texts should not suggest that they hold privileged epistemological or political positions or that the critic is warranted in fetishizing vernacular texts as more pure or more authentic. On the contrary, while the two texts examined do offer a critical perspective, writings in DPN and IFP are not uniformly progressive. Here, the critic should heed the warning that "constructions are not necessarily, because they are vernacular, liberatory" (Ono & Sloop, p. 38).

IV

BALANCING PRIVATE DISCLOSURES FROM HEALTH CARE TO ILLNESS

8

▼▼▼▼▼▼▼▼▼

Self-Disclosure and Health: Revisiting Sidney Jourard's Hypothesis

Charles H. Tardy
University of Southern Mississippi

In a 1959 article in the journal *Mental Hygiene,* Sidney M. Jourard set forth the ideas, propositions, and beliefs that subsequently came to be recognized, and vilified, as an "ideology of intimacy" (Bochner, 1982; Parks, 1982, 1995). Jourard argued that self-disclosure both signified and provided a means of achieving a "healthy personality." The importance of self-disclosure could not be overestimated:

> Activities such as loving, psychotherapy, counseling, teaching, and nursing all are impossible of achievement without the disclosure of the client. It is through self-disclosure that an individual reveals to himself and to the other party just exactly who, what and where he is. Just as thermometers, sphygmomanometers, etc. disclose information about the real state of the body, self-disclosure reveals the real nature of the soul of the self. Such information is vital in order to conduct intelligent evaluations. All I mean by evaluation is comparing how a person is with some concept of optimum. You never really discover how truly sick your psychotherapy patient is until he discloses himself utterly to you. You cannot help your client in vocational guidance until he has disclosed to you something of the impasse in which he finds himself. You cannot love your spouse, your child or your friend unless he has permitted you to know him and to know what he needs to move toward greater health and well-being. Nurses cannot nurse patients in any meaningful way unless they have permitted patients to disclose their needs, wants, worries, anxieties, and doubts. Teachers cannot be very helpful to their students until they have permitted the students to disclose how utterly ignorant and misinformed they are. Teachers cannot

provide helpful information to the students until they have permitted the students to disclose exactly what they are interested in. (p. 505)

Over the next 20 years these ideas, although not necessarily these words, spawned hundreds of empirical studies and influenced much of the writing about interpersonal communication and relationships. From 1969 to 1974, the first five years of the *Social Sciences Citation Index* (SSCI), Jourard's articles were cited an average of 110 times a year. In 1973, 187 articles cited his research. Although much less prominent, Jourard was still cited by an average of 44 articles a year from 1991 to 1997. Clearly, Jourard's legacy endures more than 20 years following his death.

Embedded within the *Mental Hygiene* essay, however, was an idea that even future adherents to the ideology found extreme: the contention that self-disclosure facilitates physiological health and well-being. In this article, Jourard (1959) took an innovative and risky position. In a period when society, and the academy, embraced a view of illness that associated disease with pathogenic microorganisms, Jourard suggested that ill health can result from behavior, the failure to self-disclose:

I believe that in the effort to avoid becoming known a person provides for himself a cancerous kind of stress which is subtle and unrecognized but nonetheless effective in producing not only . . . assorted patterns of unhealthy personality . . . but also . . . [a] wide array of physical ills. (p. 503–504)

He even suggested that gender differences in self-disclosure might account for known gender differences in mortality rates, implying that women live longer than men do because they disclose more. Although he was not alone in suggesting connections between social processes and health, Jourard's position was unique due to its specificity.

Despite, or perhaps even because of, the provocative proposition, the *Mental Hygiene* article has to be one of the least influential of Jourard's works. During the period 1969 to 1973, when Jourard's work was cited in more than 500 articles, only four authors mentioned this essay. In the last 7 years there have been no citations in the SSCI. However, the influence of the version of this article in Jourard's (1971b) book *The Transparent Self* is more difficult to assess.

Jourard's position, which appeared so radical and unacceptable as to not warrant consideration, is perhaps the proposition from his work that remains the most viable today. This chapter reviews evidence that is consistent with the hypothesis that self-disclosure promotes physiological health and well-being. Researchers from a variety of disciplines—clinical psychology, psychophysiology, epidemiology, psychiatry, and communication—have examined health implications of self-disclosure. This chapter reviews this research and describes data supporting the hypothesis.

SELF-DISCLOSURE AND RESISTANCE TO ILLNESS

Research on epidemiology and immunology now examines not just the etiology of specific diseases but also the role of psychosocial factors that affect the general susceptibility of the human organism to illness (Berkman, 1995). Typically people develop illness when an infectious agent enters the body externally or a preexisting one proliferates within the body. Both result in ill health only when normal immune system defenses fail. Thus, understanding disease depends not only on knowledge of pathogenic microorganisms but also on knowledge of factors that affect the body's ability to protect itself. Accumulating evidence suggests that self-disclosure promotes resistance to disease.

Several studies of self-reported disclosure, both as a trait and as a behavior, demonstrate a link between openness and health. One study that conceptualized self-concealment as a personality trait observed that people with lower scores on this variable reported fewer physical and psychological symptoms of illness than people with high self-concealment scores (Larson & Chastain, 1990). In an attempt to isolate the unique contribution of this personality trait on health, the authors statistically controlled for the effects of trauma, trauma disclosure, and social support on health and still observed a significant relationship between self-concealment and health. Another study (Blotcky, Carscaddon, & Grandmaison, 1983) that directly assessed the relationship between reports of physical illness and self-disclosure suggested a curvilinear relationship between the two variables. The authors claimed that subjects with the highest and lowest trait self-disclosure scores reported more incidents of acute and chronic illnesses than other subjects did. In a study of patients with breast cancer and Hodgkins' disease, Mesters et al. (1997) observed that people who reported more openness in discussing their illness with family members reported better outcomes after 13 weeks of treatment, for example, fewer physical and psychological complaints.

Pennebaker (1989, 1997), who conducted the most important work on this subject, developed a theoretical model and conducted numerous empirical tests of the relationship between disclosure and health. He argued that the repression of personal reactions to traumatic events harms, whereas the expression of these feelings facilitates health and well-being. His theory suggests that traumatic experiences are common occurrences. People inevitably experience disappointment, disillusionment, rejection, loneliness, and loss. Explaining, not merely describing, personal feelings about such significant life events helps people assimilate those events into their memory. Repression of these feelings, literally, requires physiological effort that detracts from normal biological functions. Continued repression requires continued effort, leading to decreased physiological efficiency, and therefore susceptibility to disease and illness. Additionally, encoding these experiences as narratives may serve a cognitive function by helping to more efficiently store these events in memory (Pennebaker, Mayne, & Francis, 1997). A series of nonexperimental and experimental studies supports these conclusion.

In one of the nonexperimental studies, Pennebaker and O'Heeron (1984) observed that people who talked more about the unexpected death of a spouse had better physical health during the year following their bereavement than those who talked less. Several studies indicated that people who reported never discussing childhood traumas experienced more symptoms of illness than those who talked about those events (Pennebaker & Sussman, 1988; Pennebaker, 1989).

In the controlled studies, college students spoke (Pennebaker, Hughes, & O'Heeron, 1987) or wrote (Pennebaker & Beall, 1986; Pennebaker, Colder, & Sharp, 1990; Pennebaker et al., 1988) about either their day's activities or an event that was the most distressful they had ever experienced. Consistent with the predictions, subjects in the traumatic disclosure condition reported feeling healthier following the experiment. Physiological measurements taken during the experiment indicated that traumatic disclosure condition subjects evidenced improved immunological efficiency, reduced skin conductance, and greater consistency in brain wave activity between left and right hemispheres, but also greater heart rate and blood pressure than trivial disclosure condition subjects. Even more impressively, an audit of student health clinic records revealed that individuals in the traumatic disclosure condition visited the clinic less during the 6 months following the experiment than did those in the trivial disclosure condition.

A subsequent study of adults (Francis & Pennebaker, 1992) indicated that writing about traumatic events improved absentee rates as well as positively affected indices of blood chemistry related to liver functioning. The effect of this experimental manipulation of disclosure has been replicated in other laboratories as well (M. A. Greenberg & Stone, 1992; M. A. Greenberg, Wortman, & Stone, 1996).

Several studies dramatically demonstrate the impact of confession on health. A study of Holocaust survivors utilized documentary interviews in which the participants recounted their experiences in concentration camps (Pennebaker, Barger, & Tiebout, 1989). These stories were rated for openness. Physicians assessed the health of the participants. People who disclosed the most upsetting experiences showed better subsequent health. These data are particularly impressive given the length of time between the events and their recounting in the interview, and also considering the difficult life circumstances experienced by the participants. Cole, Kemeny, Taylor, Visscher, and Fahey's (1996) 9-year study of homosexuals with HIV indicated that men who concealed their gay identity had an immune system that deteriorated faster, a shorter time to onset of AIDS, and a shorter time to AIDS mortality than men who revealed their identity. Moreover, not only was there a dose-response relationship between concealment and health, but the relationship obtained even after controlling for sample characteristics and alternative explanations. These studies provide strong support for the idea that how we communicate life experiences, in addition to the events themselves, is important.

Thus, several types of data provide results consistent with Jourard's hypothesis. Self-reports of health, records of use of health services, blood tests assessing immune system efficiency, even mortality rates have been found to vary with measures of self-disclosure. Likewise, these indices of health have been associated with measures of self-disclosure that include self-reports of trait-like behavior, self-reports about the discussion of specific stressful events, and experimentally manipulated behaviors. Thus, the association of self-disclosure and health is not limited to single conceptualizations or operationalizations of these variables. However, I should also note that this research does not attempt to describe with any precision the nature of, or contingencies associated with, the relationship between self-disclosure and illness.

SELF-DISCLOSURE AND CARDIOVASCULAR DISEASES

Cardiovascular disease is the leading cause of death in the United States and responsible for more hospital admissions than any other disease (American Heart Association, 1998). Psychosocial factors have long been recognized as important elements in the etiology, development, and treatment of cardiovascular diseases (see Krantz, Baum, & Singer, 1983). One prominent psychophysiologist attributes great importance to communication: "The response of our hearts, blood vessels, and muscles when we communicate with spouse, children, friends, colleagues, and the larger community has as much to do with our cardiovascular health as do factors such as exercise or diet" (Lynch, 1985, p. 10). A growing number of studies identify self-disclosure as a behavior that impacts cardiovascular health.

Hypertension, commonly identified when resting systolic blood pressure exceeds 140 mm Hg or diastolic blood pressure surpasses 90 mm Hg, is one cardiovascular disease that has been related to self-disclosure. Handkins and Munz (1978) compared self-reported and observed self-disclosure of normotensive and hypertensive adult males. Hypertensive subjects revealed less information in response to intimate, but not nonintimate, questions during an interview. The two groups did not differ on the Jourard Self-Disclosure Questionnaire (Jourard, 1971a). Jorgensen and Houston's (1986) experiment examined normotensive subjects with a parental history of hypertension to normotensive subjects without a parental history of hypertension. They reported that people with a predisposition to high blood pressure who repressed their negative affect during the experiment were characterized by exaggerated blood pressure reactivity to stressful tasks. A third study compared the self-disclosure of subjects who differed in blood pressure reactivity to a mental stress test (Hahn, Brooks, & Hartsough, 1993). Subjects who showed the most blood pressure change had significantly lower self-reported disclosure scores than subjects who were less reactive. Moreover, normotensive subjects whose parents had hypertension disclosed less in response to queries for information by the experimenter than did normotensive subjects whose parents had no history of hypertension. The authors suggested that their data support theories of essential hypertension based on repression and coping with stressful events. Thus, these three studies suggest that maladaptive cardiovascular processes are associated with decreased self-disclosure.

Another group of studies examines cardiovascular changes that occur as a result of self-disclosure (Tardy, 1993). Many studies have examined heart rate and blood pressure changes that occur while people talk about themselves. Some of these noted that this form of discourse is self-disclosure (Cumes, 1983; Pfiffner, Nil, & Battig, 1987), whereas most did not (e.g., Siegman, Dembroski, & Crump, 1992). These studies asked participants to answer personal questions ranging from the mundane; for example, "What have you been doing today?"; to moderately intimate; for example, "What makes you angry?" Although people can give intimate or nonintimate replies to any question, generally the intimacy of the response will reflect the intimacy of the question. Thus, many studies have documented that heart rate and blood pressure increase when people self-disclose (e.g., Tardy, Thompson, & Allen, 1989). However, the importance of this finding is limited by the lack of control conditions. None of these studies compared the cardiovascular reactivity of self-disclosive to nondisclosive speech on the same topic. Fortunately, one study makes that comparison.

Christensen and Smith (1993) provided the most direct assessment of the effect of self-disclosure on cardiovascular reactivity. The authors confirmed the prediction that subjects with high cynical hostility scores would show greater systolic and diastolic blood pressure reactivity when discussing a personal, distressing event than when talking about a fictional stressful event that they read about. Subjects low in hostility did not evidence differential reactivity to the disclosive and nondisclosive speaking tasks. The authors suggested that people high in cynical hostility are at heightened risk of physical illness because their physiological reactions to self-disclosure may foster social isolation and a subsequent deficit in social support.

The publication of a single-subject case study supporting the disclosure–health hypothesis by the journal *Psychosomatic Medicine* suggests that Jourard's idea must be gaining widespread acceptance. Mann and Delon's (1995) report described 9 years of treatment by a patient for virtually uncontrollable hypertension. Six years of multiple drug treatments failed to produce normal control of blood pressure. However, after a spontaneous revelation of a repressed traumatic experience and associated emotions, the patient's blood pressure stabilized. Most important, this reduction was sustained for two years following the disclosure. Though case studies have many limitations, this publication dramatically illustrated the cathartic benefits of self-disclosure, or conversely, the deleterious consequences of failure to self-disclose claimed by Jourard, Pennebaker, and others.

Although there are fewer self-disclosure studies of cardiovascular illness than of resistance to disease, the available evidence also suggests that self-disclosure is associated with positive outcomes. Again, the relationship between self-disclosure and health was not contingent on single operational definitions of these variables. As with the research on illness, the literature on cardiovascular processes only provides a rudimentary depiction of the relationship between self-disclosure and this index of health.

SELF-DISCLOSURE AND HEALTH
IN THE M.C.R.S. STUDY

I collected data relevant to Jourard's hypothesis as part of a study funded by the National Institutes of Health entitled Moderators of Cardiovascular Reactivity to Speech (M.C.R.S.). This project investigated factors that affected cardiovascular activity occurring during speech. Results related to both self-reported and observed self-disclosure are described below.

Subjects were 156 college students whose ages ranged from 18 to 35, with a median of 20.90. The sample contained approximately equal numbers of men and women, and African American and Caucasian students.

An occluding cuff was placed on the participant's arm with the microphone placed over an area where the brachial artery could be palpated. The participant then sat quietly for an initial rest period of approximately 10 minutes. Blood pressure and heart rate were measured at 3-minute intervals during this period with an Industrial Biomedical Sensors 700A automated blood pressure and heart rate monitor. Following the rest period, participants engaged in a series of four speaking tasks, each of which required subjects to answer two questions and each of which was followed by a 5-minute resting period (e.g., "What are your plans for the day?"; "What are your best or worst characteristics or traits"). Half of the questions required the subjects to talk about themselves, whereas the other half required subjects to talk about another person. Subjects were asked to talk for at least a minute in answering each question. Subjects' blood pressure and pulse rate (PR) were measured while they answered questions and during each post-task rest period. Thus, 15 physiological recordings were made for each subject: three during the initial resting period, eight during the four task periods, four during post-task resting periods.

Composite resting measures of the three physiological variables were computed by averaging the last two recordings of systolic blood pressure (SBP), diastolic blood pressure (DBP), and PR from the initial resting period. The eight physiological recordings of each variable were also averaged to compute a single score as the task measure.

Subjects completed several self-report questionnaires. The health perceptions and the mental health subsections of the Medical Outcomes Survey (MOS) short form (A. L. Stewart, Hays, & Ware, 1988) were used to measure health. The self-disclosure scale (L. C. Miller, Berg, & Archer, 1983) asked subjects to rate how fully they had disclosed to a close friend on a series of topics (e.g., personal habits, deepest feelings, worst fears). Both scales have been utilized frequently and validated. The sample median was used to divide subjects into high- and low-discloser groups.

In order to examine the relationship between self-disclosure and health, two types of analyses were conducted. First, data were analyzed with a series of separate 2×2 analyses of variance (ANOVAs) with task (resting vs. speaking) and trait self-disclosure (low vs. high) as the independent variables and SBP, DBP, and PR as dependent variables. Second, the self-disclosure scores were correlated with the self-reported health subscales.

Trait self-disclosure produced a significant main effect on DBP ($F(1,153)$ = 5.13; $p < .025$) but not on SBP or PR. Figure 8.1 illustrates the finding that subjects high in trait self-disclosure exhibited lower blood pressure while resting and while talking ($M = 68.45$) than subjects low in trait self-disclosure

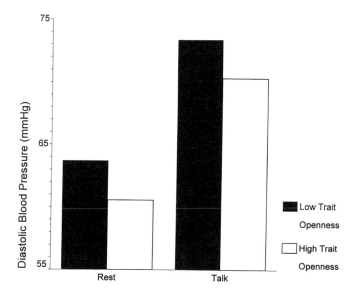

FIG. 8.1.   Diastolic blood pressure while resting and while talking for subjects high and low in trait self-disclosure.

(M = 65.45). The ANOVA also revealed significant task effects for all three variables, but these will not be discussed here. There were no self-disclosure trait by task interactions.

Simple Pearson correlation coefficients indicated a significant association of trait self-disclosure with mental health (r = –.16; p < .05) but not with general health perceptions. The direction of this relationship indicated that increased openness was associated with reports of decreased mental distress. Figure 8.2 illustrates this relationship. I formed three approximately equal-sized groups based on the self-disclosure scores and compared these groups on the mental health scale.

Another report of the M.C.R.S. study (Tardy & Allen, 1998) described the factorial analysis of these data. We compared the physiological responses of subjects as they answered the interview questions about themselves (i.e., self-disclosed) to their responses as they answered questions about someone else. These procedures elicited low-intimacy self-disclosures that were very different from the disclosures elicited in Pennebaker's research. Our results indicated that people exhibited significantly higher DBP when talking about someone else (M = 74.36) than when talking about self (M = 70.84).

The M.C.R.S. study provides additional evidence that self-disclosure relates to health and well-being. These data extend earlier reports that subjects who are more open evidenced signs of better physical health than subjects who are relatively closed. Interestingly, DBP proved to be the physiological variable most sensitive to self-disclosure. DBP was associated with both

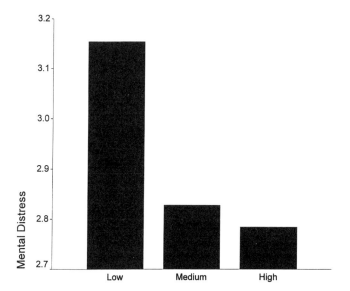

FIG. 8.2.   Self-reports of mental distress by subjects low, medium, and high in trait self-disclosure.

self-reported trait self-disclosure and with the experimentally manipulated disclosure behavior. In both cases self-disclosure produced lower DBP, whereas SBP and PR were unaffected. Because constriction and dilation of the vasculature affects DBP more than SBP and PR, perhaps self-disclosure invokes some type of adaptive response that moderates the changes that occur normally when people speak. However, at present it is not clear whether these differences are due to parasympathetic processes being invoked by self-disclosure, by increased sympathetic responses produced by nondisclosure, or by some combination of both. Regardless of which mechanisms account for these differences, over time these patterns may foster better cardiovascular health. However, I should note that the mean differences in DBP detected in this study were statistically but not clinically significant. How these differences relate to the health and life expectancy of these 156 college students is a much more complex and uncertain issue. Nonetheless, discovering these patterns in a laboratory experiment helps identify mechanisms and processes that may be studied further in clinical settings or with attention to other risk factors.

The correlation between trait self-disclosure and mental distress was also consistent with the hypothesis. People who reported more openness in discussing important issues also reported fewer symptoms of emotional distress, though the coefficient was rather small. People with below-average self-disclosure trait scores apparently report more symptoms of psychological illness than people with average, or above-average, scores do. However, no relationship between self-disclosure and reports of physical illness was detected. Because the sample consisted of college students with a median age less than 21, the range of scores for the physical illness variable no doubt would be attenuated. A more sensitive measure of physical health may be needed for studies of this population.

These results should not be interpreted to suggest that indiscriminate openness leads to improved health and well-being. Rather, I think the findings are consistent with the idea that people can and should strive to maintain a balance between openness and privacy in their relationships with others. For example, the M.C.R.S. results indicated a linear relationship that was far from perfect between trait openness and psychological health. Complete openness was not invariably associated with reports of fewer symptoms of mental or emotional distress. Nor was openness always associated with lower DBP. Moreover, the experimental manipulation in this study focused only on low- or moderate-intimacy disclosure. When people made appropriate disclosures, their DBP was lower than when they made appropriate responses that were nondisclosive. However, these data do not indicate that more intimate responses to these questions would produce incremental decreases in blood pressure. Quite probably the reverse would be true. Thus it would be inaccurate to infer that these results support indiscriminate openness.

Rather, a more realistic interpretation of the data and methods suggests that these results support the idea of balance.

CONCLUSION

What, then, is the status of Jourard's hypothesis? There is not only a great deal of evidence supporting a link between self-disclosure and health but also an emerging acceptance of this connection. This research has examined numerous indices of health, including self-reports of physical and psychological symptoms, assays of various components of the immune system, cardiovascular functioning, and morbidity and mortality rates. Various types of self-disclosure, likewise, have been examined, ranging from self-reports of typical behavior to accounts of traumatic experiences. Given the diversity of these measures, the consistency of the results is impressive. Moreover, the idea that health and disclosure are connected is becoming widely accepted. The publication in a scientific, medical journal of a single-case study illustrating a connection between disclosure of a traumatic event and hypertension (Mann & Delon, 1995), described earlier in this chapter, suggests that scholarly gatekeepers are no longer skeptical. One book even discusses this phenomenon (Derlega et al., 1993). The increasing number of studies of the self-disclosure and health linkage indicates that researchers from a wide variety of disciplines find the idea useful. Thus, Jourard's hypothesis appears to be quite healthy itself.

However, as research focuses on the scope, explanatory processes, and limitations of the relationship between self-disclosure and health, Jourard's contribution becomes diminished. He provided the framework for the research but not the details. New theories are needed to identify the facets of disclosure that are linked to health outcomes, to identify the physiological processes that account for these linkages, and to understand the limitations on self-disclosure imposed by social relationships. Currently the ideas of Pennebaker supplant Jourard's hypothesis because of their specificity and empirical support. Pennebaker now suggests that self-disclosure facilitates health by not only eliminating the deleterious consequences of inhibition but also by organizing thoughts and memories in more productive ways. Specifically, encoding experiences in ways that indicate self-reflection and causal thinking promote well-being (Pennebaker et al., 1997). Whether these linguistic processes account for the beneficial effects of disclosures about non-traumatic experiences remains to be discovered. Thus considerable work remains to be conducted to understand how self-disclosure relates to health.

Increased attention to the social dynamics of the self-disclosure and health hypothesis is also warranted. Most of the research to date has focused on the discloser and not on the relationship between disclosers and listeners.

Obviously indiscriminate revelations can produce negative consequences, regardless of how they might theoretically affect the speaker's health. Fear of reprisals perhaps keeps people from revealing important information in the first place (Rosenfeld, 1979). Moreover, negative disclosures can produce negative emotions in the recipient (Hatfield, Cacioppo, & Rapson, 1994). What may be healthy for the speaker may not be for the listener. These issues are not new but may warrant reexamination in light of their implications for health. Research should seek to identify the optimal balance in revealing and concealing personal information for maintaining health of relational partners.

The advancements in the health and self-disclosure hypothesis, however, should not detract from the importance of Jourard's contribution. He was at least partly responsible, and maybe even largely responsible, for the efforts that have led to the acceptance of the idea that self-disclosure produces demonstrable health benefits. Ironically, the idea that appeared so radical in its initial formulation has become so commonplace that its origin is frequently overlooked.

ACKNOWLEDGMENTS

This research was supported by grant 1R15HL52296–01A1 from the National Institutes of Health.

The assistance of Diane Berry, Mark Lambert, Frederick Lee, Erika Selenberg, Patti Smith, and J. T. Johnson in conducting the study was greatly appreciated.

Parts of this paper were previously reported at the Annual Convention of the Southern States Communication Association, Memphis, TN, in 1996 and at the International Conference on Language and Social Psychology, Ontario, Canada, in 1997.

9

▼▼▼▼▼▼▼▼▼

Disclosure of Chronic Illness Varies by Topic and Target: The Role of Stigma and Boundaries in Willingness to Disclose

Kathryn Greene
East Carolina University

Research continues to increase at a critical juncture between the fields of communication and health care, particularly disclosures of illnesses. As the number of patients with chronic illnesses as such as AIDS and cancer continues to increase, more people must decide how to balance decisions to reveal or conceal their illnesses. Disclosure is widely recommended by health care practitioners, in part due to the link between disclosure and physical and mental health. Decisions to disclose chronic illness, however, are threatening and problematic for many patients. Stigma surrounding illness has contributed to the unwillingness to disclose. People must balance competing needs to obtain benefits from disclosure yet avoid negative consequences from sharing.

The goal of this chapter is to explore patients' willingness to disclose a diagnosis of chronic illness to members of their family. This study will examine if the topic of the illness (e.g., AIDS or cancer), the potential target or recipient of the information (e.g., mother or brother), or some combination of the two best explains willingness to disclose. Research on stigma and self-disclosure is reviewed. The effects of stigma on balancing disclosure are examined first.

STIGMA

Decisions to disclose can be inhibited by negative images of the information or stigma. Goffman (1963) described stigma as a deeply discrediting attribute, deviating from a prototype. Stigma is not mere prejudice; it indicates a preference for avoidance and carries a mark of shame or discredit (Herek & Glunt, 1988). Stigma originates in shared reactions of groups of people that are inherently comparative (Leary & Schreindorfer, 1998). Deviance is often labeled as illness, and certain illnesses carry meanings other than biomedical, such that the illness becomes a metaphor for characteristics attributed to the person (Sontag, 1989). Originally, cancer fit this definition for stigma, but cancer is perhaps not currently stigmatized in this way. HIV/AIDS fits all of these qualifications for stigma, though that also may be lessening.

Stigma and HIV/AIDS

AIDS has been socially defined as a disease of marginalized groups (Herek & Glunt, 1988). HIV/AIDS itself is stigmatized, but there are things that intensify stigma, including assignment of blame (see Leary & Schreindorfer, 1998). Sexual activity and drug use are more stigmatized than perinatal transmission or transfusion as modes of contracting HIV. Thus, the AIDS stigma has been layered upon preexisting stigma. J. A. Kelly and associates (J. A. Kelly, St. Lawrence, Hood, Smith, & Cook, 1988; J. A. Kelly, St. Lawrence, Smith, Hood, & Cook, 1987) had physicians, medical students, and nurses read vignettes describing how a patient contracted HIV/AIDS. The results of the studies by Kelly and associates indicate a clear prejudice against AIDS and homosexuals, with most specific findings for unwillingness to interact with people with AIDS (see Crawford, 1996). More recently, a meta-analysis by Crawford reported (based on 21 published studies) more stigma towards AIDS than other illnesses, with more stigma among college students than among health professionals.

Stigma functions differently for various groups, likely based on blame or perceptions of control over infection. Being homosexual is stigmatized even without adding HIV-positive status (see Derlega, Lovejoy, & Winstead, 1998), but some people with HIV/AIDS must deal with the double stigma of AIDS and homosexuality. Group perceptions/stereotypes of HIV/AIDS as a White gay male disease has isolated HIV-infected persons who do not fit this description (e.g., women or black men). Stigma is also a problem for HIV-positive women and for children, two groups who have not been widely addressed by media images of HIV/AIDS.

The effects of stigma can be widespread. People with HIV/AIDS "must bear the burden of societal hostility when they are most in need of social support" (Herek & Glunt, 1988, p. 886). For interpersonal relationships, there is potential for physical withdrawal, avoidance, and fear of rejection (Leary & Schreindorfer, 1998). In psychological terms, stigma can lead to a sense of alienation, lost social support, anxiety and depression, and decreased self-concept (look, e.g., at the suicide rate). For health consequences, stigma could lead people to resist HIV testing (see Serovich et al., 1992) and may also lead to nondisclosure, thus further increasing the possible spread of HIV/AIDS. To manage stigma, many HIV-infected persons report "passing" or deliberately concealing their stigmatized attribute (infection). Clearly, stigma has effects on willingness to disclose HIV infection.

Crawford's meta-analysis (1996) revealed more stigma towards AIDS than other illnesses. For example, St. Lawrence, Husfeldt, Kelly, Hood, and Smith (1990) compared AIDS and leukemia. They explained that many diseases are as lethal as AIDS, yet few have created the level of fear and irrational hysteria associated with AIDS, including proposals to quarantine and tattoo people with AIDS/HIV.

Stigma and Cancer

In the past, cancer evoked the same intense negative reactions now associated with HIV/AIDS. Bolund (1990) pointed out that "There is only one disease, AIDS, that has a similar strong attribution of dread" (p. 13). The blaming or labeling associated with HIV/AIDS stigma, however, does not generally occur with cancer, although different types of cancer are viewed differently. For example, compare perceptions of breast cancer with those of leukemia, and cancer associated with sexually transmitted diseases (STDs) or smoking is viewed still differently. The continuum of "deserving" versus "being inno-cent" has not been applied to the public perception for cancer. Public stig-matization of persons diagnosed with cancer has decreased. Although disclosure of a cancer diagnosis may still be risky in terms of potential loss of health insurance and employment due to missed workdays, disclosure to intimates, such as family members, may not be as threatening now as it was in the past.

Clearly, stigma can function to inhibit self-disclosure for both AIDS and cancer victims. If stigma is intense, the potential consequences could over-whelm any possible disclosure. This could result in potential lost social support and possible health precautions through failure to disclose.

SELF-DISCLOSURE

Several theories of disclosure have been proposed, but Communication Boundary Management (CBM) theory (Petronio, 1991) has the possibility to incorporate variables such as topic and target to explain disclosure decisions. Petronio's (1991) theory of boundary management describes how people control potential risk to self when disclosing. Individuals regulate disclosure of private information in their relationships to attain a balance between disclosure and privacy, and between intimacy and autonomy (Petronio, 1991).

Individuals erect a metaphoric semipermeable boundary to protect themselves and reduce their chances of losing face. The risks associated with disclosing chronic illness are tremendous, perhaps leading to more rigid boundaries (little or no disclosure). Clearly, disclosure is a double-edged sword: it is possible to lose social support through disclosure, yet potential support can also be eliminated through failure to disclose (Hays, Turner, & Coates, 1992).

There are benefits from self-disclosure, and people struggle with decisions to disclose in order to receive support while avoiding negative consequences associated with stigma (see Greene & Serovich, 1996; Yep, 1993a). Potential benefits from disclosing include feeling loved and accepted, gaining information, and possibly making safer sex decisions (for HIV).

There are risks for people who disclose their chronic illness, and decisions to disclose are likely fraught with fear and anxiety (Marks et al., 1992; Yep, 1993a). Risks can include potential rejection and discrimination, and emotional distress for others. The potential impact is wide ranging, from ostracism in interpersonal relationships to self-identity crises, from threats to basic survival (loss of employment, housing, insurance or health care) to loss of social support. A person must see benefits (and how they outweigh risks) before being willing to expose themselves by disclosing (Hays et al., 1992).

Disclosure may be a means of obtaining social support, and social support may serve a significant role in mediating between stress and health (e.g., Albrecht & Adelman, 1987; Greenblatt, Becerra, & Serafetinides, 1982; Kulik & Mahler, 1989). Disclosure of traumatic experiences has been reported to reduce stress (e.g., M. A. Greenberg & Stone, 1992; Pennebaker, 1990) and physical and mental health problems (e.g., Pennebaker, 1990; Susman, 1988). In addition, satisfaction with social support increases both psychological (J. J. Kelly, Chu, & Buehler, 1993; Zich & Temoshok, 1987) and physical well-being (Hays et al., 1992; Zich & Temoshok, 1987).

Researchers have also established that the target of self-disclosure constrains how people reveal information about themselves (see Stokes, Fuehrer, & Childs, 1980; Tardy, Hosman, & Bradac, 1981). The factors in decisions to disclose to one target (e.g., mother) are likely different from another (e.g., partner; see Simoni et al., 1995). An important step in the coping process for people with chronic illness is the disclosure of this information to others, however, at present, there is a lack of clarity about who is considered an appropriate recipient of that information. Next, specific research on disclosure of HIV/AIDS and disclosure of cancer will be reviewed.

Self-Disclosure and HIV/AIDS

There is a small but growing body of research on how people decide who to tell about their HIV infection (see Derlega et al., 1998; Greene et al., 1993; Greene & Serovich, 1995, 1996; Hays et al., 1992; Marks et al., 1992; Serovich et al., 1992; Serovich & Greene, 1993; Serovich, Kimberly, & Greene, 1998; Yep, 1993a). Findings indicate that people disclose their HIV/AIDS status very selectively. These disclosure decisions are based, in part, on the degree to which others are expected to respond in a positive way.

The target or recipient of HIV information is significant in explaining how people balance disclosure decisions. Members of the marital subsystem (lovers, spouses, ex-spouses, friends) have been viewed as the most appropriate targets for disclosure of HIV infection, with the nuclear family (e.g., parents, siblings, children) rating next highest (Greene & Serovich, 1996; Marks et al., 1992; Serovich & Greene, 1993; Simoni et al., 1995), extended family and the general public rating lowest.

Serovich et al. (1992) looked at the potential recipient of HIV testing information. Individuals overall reported most desire to restrict access to HIV testing information to the general public, less to the community, and least to the marital subsystem. Serovich and Greene (1993) expanded this work by looking at potential family targets for release of HIV testing information. Overall, participants reported most support for access to HIV testing information for members of the marital subsystem (e.g., lovers, spouses), moderate support for access for the nuclear family (e.g., mother, son), and least support for access for the extended family (e.g., aunt, mother-in-law).

Greene and Serovich (1996) replicated these studies and reported that HIV-infected persons have clear distinctions in perceptions of appropriate recipients of information about HIV infection. In addition, HIV-infected persons reported less desire (compared with other groups) for disclosure of HIV infection to members of all subsystems. Marks et al. (1992) similarly reported that HIV-positive men were highly selective in choosing targets of disclosure and tended to inform significant others (parents, friends, and lovers) more than nonsignificant others (employers, landlords, and religious leaders). Next, we review research on disclosure to various family targets, including partners, parent(s), siblings, children, and friends.

Disclosure to Partner(s).   Disclosure to partners is not just done to obtain social support, as there is an added benefit of possible safer sex practices. The partner of an HIV-positive person is in a significantly different position from others in that he or she may be at substantial risk for exposure to HIV. Nondisclosure could also affect the health of an HIV-infected person. An infected person is at risk for reinfection with a possibly more drug-resistant strain of HIV; additionally, other STDs are dangerous to HIV-infected persons. Therefore, decisions to disclose to partners are defined by different senses of obligation, both moral and legal. There is concern that some HIV-infected individuals continue to put others at risk for infection, and Perry and Markowitz (1988) reported that significant numbers of HIV-positive gay men (30% to 63%) continued to engage in unprotected anal intercourse with multiple partners after their diagnosis. Similarly, Marks et al. (1992) reported that for HIV-positive gay men, disclosure decreased with number of sexual partners.

Rates of reported disclosure of HIV infection to sexual partners have varied and range from 31% of a sample of homosexual HIV-positive men (Stempel, Moulton, Bachetti, & Moss, 1989) to 89% of an HIV-positive sample (Mansergh, Marks, & Simoni, 1995). Perry, Ryan, Fogel, Fishman, and Jacobsberg (1990) reported that 53% of HIV-positive gay men had disclosed to all present sexual partners, but only a lower rate had disclosed to past or casual sexual partners. Clearly, some people who know themselves to be infected with HIV/AIDS fail to inform their sexual partners of this fact, but these figures indicate that reported disclosure to partners may be increasing.

Disclosure to Parent(s). People who test HIV positive report great distress over decisions to tell parent(s) (Kimberly, Serovich, & Greene, 1995). HIV-infected persons may fear parents' rejection, and perhaps withdrawal of financial or emotional support (Gard, 1990). HIV-infected persons cite health, age, and lack of education or sophistication as reasons for not disclosing to parents (Gard, 1990; Kimberly et al., 1995). One problem with disclosing HIV-positive status to parents is that it may also provide information about an HIV-infected person's associated behavior (e.g., sexual or drug using). Gard labeled this phenomenon a "double coming out" (p. 254). In fact, virtually no one in Marks et al.'s (1992) study revealed HIV infection to parents if parents did not already know about their gay/bisexual orientation. Reports of disclosure to parents vary. Marks et al. (1992) reported that 23.8% of the HIV-positive people in the sample had disclosed to their mothers, compared with 8.1% who had disclosed to fathers, but Simoni et al. (1995) reported moderate disclosure, with 59% to mothers and 31% to fathers. This is in sharp contrast to a sample where 82% of mothers and 78% of fathers had knowledge of a child's HIV infection (Greene & Serovich, 1996). (These figures were also adjusted for people without target mothers or fathers.) Regardless of the discrepancy in numbers, results of these studies indicate that disclosure of HIV infection to fathers is significantly lower than to mothers.

Disclosure to Siblings. There is less information available about disclosure of HIV infection to siblings. For example, Marks et al. (1992) reported that 34.4% of their HIV-positive sample had disclosed to their sisters compared with 30.7% to brothers, and these levels are higher than disclosure to parents. Mansergh et al. (1995) also reported moderate disclosure (49%) to brothers and (53%) to sisters. HIV-infected persons may also choose to disclose incrementally, first to siblings to get support for disclosing to parents and possibly to obtain additional information about how parents might respond.

Disclosure to siblings may be slightly higher than to parents and is higher for sisters than brothers.

Disclosure to Friends. Studies of disclosure have often added "friend" as a target person. Reports that individuals disclose most to friends are not surprising, because a friend is a voluntary relationship, likely marked by similarity. Perry, Ryan et al. (1990) reported 68% disclosure to a friend, but Marks et al. (1992) reported 58% disclosure to a male friend and 43% to a female friend. This is in contrast to Hays et al. (1992), where 95% had disclosed to a gay friend.

Disclosure and Cancer

Although several researchers are currently examining the process of disclosing HIV infection, less is known about disclosing a cancer diagnosis. Some researchers assumed that patients disclosed a cancer diagnosis (e.g., Pruyn, Van den Borne, & Stringer, 1986; Weir, Deans, & Calman, 1985). Years ago, over 90% of physicians reported that they never told patients of their illness, revealing it only to the families (Oken, 1961), but more recently, more than 95% of doctors surveyed informed patients directly of their cancer diagnosis (Novack et al., 1979). Thus, there have been clear changes in the process of how a cancer diagnosis is revealed.

A diagnosis of cancer is often accompanied by emotional responses such as fear of death, pain, vulnerability, loss of control, guilt, isolation, and hopelessness (Bolund, 1990; L. R. Martin, 1982; Revenson, Wollman, & Felton, 1983). Cancer patients speak of themselves as lepers and speak of fear of being rejected by others (Severo, 1977), much like reports from those infected with HIV. In addition, Funch and Mettlin (1982) found that women recovering from breast cancer reported feelings of being overprotected and misunderstood when seeking support. Dunkel-Schetter, Feinstein, Taylor, and Falke (1992) investigated coping in cancer patients and reported that those who attended support groups used more and a wider variety of social support. Interestingly, in this study, coping was measured by items such as "talked to someone," and "let my feelings out somehow," and these clearly tap self-disclosure as well. Thus, we still need to understand more about disclosure and cancer.

Research Question

The role of stigma in willingness to disclose chronic illness cannot be overlooked. For both AIDS and cancer, stigma has potential effects but it is not known if disclosure is different by topic. It is also possible that the target or recipient of the information is a crucial factor in the decision to disclose illness. The topic of the information and the potential target of the information might also work together to explain willingness to disclose. Based on this, the following research question is posed:

RQ: Is the topic (cancer or AIDS), the potential target (specific family member), or some combination of topic and target most important in predicting a person's willingness to disclose chronic infection?

METHOD

Participants

Participants (N = 168) in the present study were drawn from a larger study (N = 826) of disclosure and attitudes toward AIDS conducted in 1994 (the smaller final sample included only those participants who responded to all six target family members). Participants were overwhelmingly Caucasian (64%) or African American (32%). Participants ranged in age from 18 to 74 years (M = 30.6), and the sample was 45% male and 54% female.

Participants were recruited by students trained in an undergraduate research methods course. This project is part of a larger study of relationships and disclosure. Student researchers completed a mock interview with the author before collecting data, and each researcher had to sample participants meeting specific criteria. Random call-backs were conducted (25% contact) to ensure participation. Each participant was given the questionnaire and instructions, and the surveys were returned sealed.

The instructions on the questionnaire stated: "We are going to ask you to think about specific people in your family and your relationships with them. We will ask you to think about things happening to you that might cause you to volunteer information to members of your family. Next, we will ask you if you think you would, indeed, tell members of your family if these things happened to you."

Measurement Instruments

The primary goal of this study was to examine if the topic (cancer or AIDS) or the potential target (specific family member) was more important in predicting a person's willingness to disclose. Likert-type items were developed by the author, following the format for disclosure of AIDS items developed previously (Greene & Serovich, 1996; Serovich et al., 1992). The instructions asked participants to think about disclosing to family members. The first item stated: "Think about your [target such as mother]. How likely would you be to tell [him/her] if you had [AIDS/cancer]?" Responses ranged from "Absolutely" (1) to "Never" (5). The second item substituted "cancer" for "AIDS." Participants then thought about various targets and how willing they would be to disclose to each target person. Target family members included: mother, father, partner, sister, brother, and best friend. Thus, the primary variable of interest in the present study, likelihood of disclosing illness, was composed of 12 items: six targets for two diseases.

RESULTS

Data were analyzed using factor analyses, confidence intervals, and MANOVAs. Analyses were conducted to explore both target and topic effects, as well as a combination of target and topic effects. The level of significance was set at $p < .05$ for all tests.

The factor analysis indicated a three-factor solution accounting for 65% of variance using varimax rotation. Thus, it is clear that neither topic nor target alone can account for differences in disclosure in these data (the solution was neither one nor two factor). The factors did, however, tend to group according to target rather than topic. Primary factor loadings were all above .60, with no secondary loadings above .4 except for the sister disclosure items. The first factor was labeled "friend/sibling" (eigenvalue = 4.97; 41% variance) and included friend/AIDS (.76), friend/cancer (.69), brother/AIDS (.75), brother/cancer (.70), sister/AIDS (.65), and sister/cancer (.67). (However, the loadings for the sister items were also above .5 on the second factor, indicating the sister items split loaded.) The second factor was labeled "parent" (eigenvalue = 1.47; 12% variance) and included mother/AIDS (.80), mother/cancer (.59), father/AIDS (.86), and father/cancer (.68). The third factor was labeled "partner" (eigenvalue = 1.39; 11% variance) and included partner/AIDS (.73) and partner/cancer (.83). Thus, there were some differences by target in these data. Mean score comparisons using 95% confidence intervals were also calculated to explore these differences (see Table 9.1).

Participants did distinguish between disclosing cancer and disclosing AIDS. Participants were generally more willing to disclose cancer than AIDS (the confidence intervals for that disclosure of AIDS and cancer generally did not overlap for a particular target person), but participants reported that disclosing both AIDS and cancer was likely. This difference did not hold for the partner item, however, as participants reported they would tell partners equally (as often) about either AIDS or cancer diagnosis. Thus, there were some differences by topic in these data.

To better explore the nature of the target and topic disclosure differences, a MANOVA was performed. The 12 likelihood-of-disclosing items were the dependent measures, with two within-subject factors, topic (AIDS or cancer) and target (six family members). The design included tests for main effects of topic and target as well as the interaction of topic by target. The MANOVA for disclosure items indicated statistically significant main effects

TABLE 9.1
95% confidence intervals (CIs) for 12 disclosure items

Disclosure item	Mean*	SD	CI
Partner AIDS	1.18	.59	1.14–1.22
Partner cancer	1.18	.60	1.14–1.22
Mother AIDS	1.83	1.08	1.75–1.91
Mother cancer	1.46	.87	1.31–1.53
Father AIDS	2.21	1.31	2.09–2.33
Father cancer	1.63	1.03	1.54–1.72
Sister AIDS	1.83	1.08	1.74–1.92
Sister cancer	1.59	.96	1.51–1.67
Brother AIDS	2.05	1.16	1.95–2.15
Brother cancer	1.71	1.00	1.63–1.79
Friend AIDS	1.66	.94	1.59–1.73
Friend cancer	1.40	.72	1.35–1.45

*Lower score indicates more likelihood of disclosing

for both topics (Wilks's Λ (1, 167) = .554, p = .002) and target (Wilks's Λ (5, 163) = .606, $p < .001$). Follow-up analyses for the topic effect indicated that participants were more willing to disclose cancer than AIDS. Follow-up analyses for the target effect indicated that participants were more willing to disclose to partner than to friend, mother, or sister and even less to brother or father. There was also a significant interaction between topic and target (Wilks's Λ (1, 167) = .763, $p < .001$). This effect was more difficult to explain, but the most notable effect was for partners. For most family targets, there were differences in disclosure by topic, with disclosure of cancer more likely, but participants reported equal likelihood of disclosing AIDS and cancer to partners. Thus, the MANOVA revealed effects for both topic and target, but the interaction between target and topic cannot be ignored.

DISCUSSION

Results of the present study indicate that both topic and target explain willingness to disclose chronic illness. The assumptions proposed by Petronio's (1991) CBM theory and the balance of privacy have utility in explaining these findings. Petronio focuses on the permeability of informational boundaries, and these data do show differences in informational boundaries or by target. Previous researchers have reported that people create boundaries in willingness to disclose AIDS (e.g., Greene & Serovich, 1996; Marks et al., 1992; Serovich et al., 1992). The order of the means in likelihood of disclosing (see Table 9.1) is the same for both AIDS and cancer. For both diseases, partner and friend were most likely, mother or sister next most likely, and brother or father least likely disclosure recipients. The differences by target alone imply that people do balance competing needs in disclosure decisions. People clearly make distinctions in how they balance private information and to whom they choose to disclose chronic illness.

Theories of stigma indicate that people might be more likely to disclose cancer than AIDS, and this was supported by these data. The stigma surrounding AIDS is clearly more intense than for cancer today. Examination of stigma will be crucial, as it has been shown to affect social support, decisions to disclose, coping, and identity (see Derlega & Barbee, 1998). Unfortunately, not many relational theories incorporate stigma explicitly in their models. Stigma is based on assumptions about cancer and HIV/AIDS status, and, at times, about mode of transmission.

Interestingly, these topic differences between AIDS and cancer did not hold for the partner items, and this should be explored further. Participants reported equal likelihood of disclosing AIDS or cancer to a partner. The implications are significant, because people clearly underestimate the difficulty of disclosing HIV/AIDS to their partner. For AIDS but not cancer, the partner is at significant risk for infection. Others (e.g., Perry, Ryan et al., 1990; Stempel et al., 1989) confirm that an astonishingly low number of HIV-infected people do in fact tell their partners. Thus, this partner disclosure is an area researchers should continue to explore.

LIMITATIONS

There are several limitations to this study worth noting. First, the sample was not comprised of people with cancer or HIV (to the best of our knowledge). Thus, items tapped only individual perceptions of likelihood of disclosing infection. Previous research (Greene & Serovich, 1996), however, has shown remarkable similarity between HIV-positive and non-HIV-positive people's formation of groups of (or boundaries for) disclosure recipients; even further, they show how willingness to disclose infection and actual disclosure patterns were significantly correlated. The format used to measure disclosure in this study was an improvement over previous research because it was specific to a target person and by disease. It would be useful, however, to have multiple item measures, but this would be difficult to obtain without rather obvious redundancy. Only one perspective was taken into account, where obtaining responses from target family members would provide valuable additional information (though only one perspective is a major factor in a decision to disclose). The operationalization here also involved an intent to perform a hypothetical behavior, and the hypothetical situation did not include how they contracted the disease, if significant other was aware of risk behavior, and so on. An additional limitation was the design: a longitudinal design, studying the process of disclosure through the course of disease would add insight.

Implications

There are implications in these data for people working with patients and their families, for message design, and for theory.

Implications for Health Care Workers. The data presented here may be useful for people who work with persons diagnosed with cancer and HIV/AIDS and/or their families. The value of disclosing disease information to family members has been well documented (cf. Berg & Derlega, 1987; Pennebaker, 1990). However, for those who are not willing to disclose, or for those who have reservations about doing so, sensitivity to these disclosure differences must be respected.

Health care workers may develop programs (or incorporate the information into social support groups) to help individuals with difficult decisions about disclosure. Specific discussion of disclosure problems could be useful, perhaps with role-plays. Although only cancer and HIV/AIDS were examined in this study, it is reasonable to assume that other illnesses may have stigma associated with them that could decrease likelihood of disclosure. Health care workers should continue to be sensitive to differences in willingness to disclose, and the means in this study indicate that brothers and fathers may be especially problematic recipients for this type of disclosure. It may be that people are more comfortable disclosing health information to women.

Implications for Message Design. Clearly, stigma is still a problem that inhibits disclosure. Specific campaigns portraying how HIV (or cancer) affects families and the support families can provide might be useful in reducing this stigma and labeling. More messages with positive portrayals of people with cancer and AIDS might serve to reduce stigma and increase likelihood of disclosing. Campaigns also need to be specific about how and why to disclose chronic illness, in particular to partners.

Implications for Theory. Additional work to test Petronio's CBM theory and Yep's (1993a) application to HIV/AIDS would be fruitful. There is also a need for more information on decision-making criteria and disclosure strategies (Petronio et al., 1996; Yep, 1993a). Because disclosure is a relational event, variables associated with both the sender and the receiver need to be examined (Yep, 1993a). Social exchange theory has been used to describe relationships, but it has also been used to describe disclosure decisions in relationships. People balance positive and negative potential consequences of disclosure before being willing to make decisions about illness. For some, the sheer relief of not keeping a secret and anticipation of support outweigh fears of negative consequences. Derlega and Barbee (1998) indicate that HIV-infected persons have some level of awareness of the positive and negative consequences of disclosure, much like the anticipated response variable in Petronio's (1991) boundary management model.

Future Research. Research such as this study can contribute to understanding how people deal with chronic illness. Insight into how people live with diseases will become increasingly important as treatments progress. Balancing the need to disclose infection to obtain social support with avoiding stigma is a part of this process. Researchers examining disclosure must continue to do so within a theoretical framework, for example, a boundary management, social exchange, or uncertainty reduction model. Examination of other variables that predict likelihood of disclosing infection would be useful (e.g., gender, relationship with target, expected response). It would also be helpful to understand if disclosure functions in the same way for those outside the nuclear family (e.g., grandparents, in-laws, etc.) or for nonfamily members (e.g., teachers, employers). Clearly, asking people with cancer or HIV about their disclosure patterns over time would prove beneficial, and this would be a way to study actual message strategy selection for disclosure. At present, very little information is available about the content of disclosure messages, especially regarding chronic illness. The present study makes a significant contribution to explaining how people balance decisions to disclose chronic illness, and more research would be useful.

ACKNOWLEDGMENTS

Completion of this project was made possible by travel funding provided to the author from the East Carolina University College of Arts and Sciences Dean's Office.

10

Promoting Patients' Full and Honest Disclosure During Conversations With Health Caregivers

Roxanne Parrott
Veronica Duncan
University of Georgia

Ashley Duggan
University of California, Santa Barbara

Sometimes willfully, and at other times without awareness, patients fail to disclose important personal information to health caregivers. Physicians in rural south Georgia, for example, used to be puzzled by the fact that so many of their patients experienced severe anemia. The medical professionals came to understand that rural Southern culture views the habit of eating kaolin, white clay or dirt, as "relatively harmless," and so, patients seldom disclosed the practice to their caregivers (Beasley, 1993, p. B2). Some Hispanic, Arabic, South Asian, and Chinese communities use lead in folk medicine, and many Mexican American households cook with lead-glazed pottery (Trotter, 1990). Again, patients are unlikely to disclose these practices to health caregivers because these actions are simply part of the daily routine. The behaviors may contribute to lead poisoning, however, and patients' failure to talk about these practices and others associated with health risk, disease, and illness inhibits health caregivers' ability to diagnose and efficaciously treat patients. Politeness theory (P. Brown & Levinson, 1978) and an impression management (Goffman, 1959) framework suggest why patients may hesitate to be fully disclosive during medical interaction and how health caregivers might encourage patients' honest disclosure, balancing the caregivers' need to know with efforts to safeguard patients' identities.

POLITENESS THEORY: IMPRESSION MANAGEMENT
DURING DISCLOSURE ABOUT HEALTH

Politeness theory focuses on individuals' goals to satisfy both a desire to be liked by others, their positive face wants, and the desire to behave without others' intervention, negative face wants (P. Brown & Levinson, 1978). Medical interaction provides a classic case of a situation in which a listener, the patient, is likely to encounter threats to both his or her positive and negative face wants in the content of what the speaker, a health caregiver, says. Patients often expend considerable personal resources to be present and interact with medical professionals. Yet, the questions that health caregivers ask and the routines required as part of the medical interview may put a patient in the position of withholding some information to present an image that is most consistent with the patient's identity and self-concept. For example, most people's diets contain ingredients unique to their familial or cultural background. However, the usual medical interview fails to provide opportunities for these habits to be discussed without a caregiver appearing to be critical. Sometimes, this gives the appearance that the patient is irresponsible. These outcomes allow little freedom to manage one's impression, one of the most important goals of human communication (Goffman, 1959). Thus, although patients may answer physicians' questions, patients' responses are likely to be suitable for self-presentation purposes, making a good impression, and engendering feelings of liking, which satisfies positive face wants. Such responses may fall short, however, of revealing all the information health care- givers need to know in order to make the most appropriate diagnoses and apply the most efficacious treatments.

Beyond patients' efforts to manage their impressions during medical interaction, patients may sometimes avoid disclosing to health caregivers because caregivers might request a change in behavior that the patient does not want or feels unable to make. Such communication constitutes a negative face threat. If patients are able to predict that particular revelations will lead to health caregivers making such demands, patients may simply avoid telling the whole truth in some cases. Understandably, health caregivers may regard the patient's response in this regard as beyond the scope of the caregiver's responsibility and concern. Sometimes, however, the patient's desire not to change a behavior is connected to cultural beliefs and practices, as when some communities use lead in folk medicine. In other situations, the behavior may represent one that the patient believes must be performed in order to maintain a livelihood, as when farmers expose themselves to the sun during peak hours of ultraviolet intensity. Medical interaction is particularly likely to limit such revelations, as both the power or status of a listener relative to the speaker, and the degree of imposition associated with a listener's hearing and understanding influence how face-threatening an interaction is for a listener (P. Brown & Levinson, 1978). The social distance between health caregivers and patients may reduce the likelihood that patients will be comfortable communicating in ways that appear to challenge health caregivers' power and authority. A farmer whose physician recommends that he avoid the sun between the hours of 10 a.m. and 3 p.m. to reduce the harmful effects of exposure on the farmer's skin is unlikely to tell the health care provider, "That's easy for you to say. You have an office job where you can be working inside during that time. I have to be outside working between 10 a.m. and 3 p.m. if I want to make a living."

Health caregivers who act and communicate in ways that reduce the barriers of status and social distance between themselves and their patients may promote patients' self-disclosures and learn something about the patients that enables the caregivers to accommodate patients' lifestyles, work, and cultural beliefs. Socially competent speakers have been found to make attempts to mitigate threats to face by avoiding, for example, embarrassing a listener (Lim & Bowers, 1991). Situations leading to embarrassment include violations of privacy (Burgoon et al., 1989; Sharkey & Stafford, 1990), with privacy having been found to have particular salience in health care settings (Campbell, 1990; Greene, Parrott, & Serovich, 1993; Halperin, 1988; Parrott, 1995; Parrott, J. Burgoon, M. Burgoon, & LePoire, 1989; Serovich, Greene, & Parrott, 1992). Conceptualizing privacy from a communication perspective encompasses: (1) an informational component, recognizing one's desire to decide who and what information others will have about oneself; (2) a physical dimension, relating to an individual's ability to control access to the physical self; (3) a psychological element, concerning access to one's thoughts and feelings; and (4) a social dimension, addressing the freedom to determine with whom one interacts (Burgoon, 1982), each with specific relevance to medical interaction. Organizational, cultural, personal, and interactional variables may predict when patients' privacy is most likely to be threatened during medical interaction, reducing patients' comfort with self-disclosure. Caregivers' awareness affords potential opportunities to address these possible problems and promote patients' comfort with revealing personal information about thoughts, feelings, and behaviors.

HEALTH CARE ORGANIZATION CHARACTERISTICS AND THREATS TO PATIENTS' PRIVACY

Over the past several decades, the health care delivery system in the United States has adopted practices that may threaten patients' privacy, including the use of team treatment, patients as models in teaching, and computerization of health information (Coleman & Shellow, 1995; Williams, 1971). Team treatment refers to the situation in which a patient's condition is evaluated by more than a single health caregiver. This increases the number of people who have access to confidential information, examine and judge the patient's attitudes and behaviors, and make demands on the patient relating to his or her physical body, including undressing and participating in medical testing. Just as some physicians have reported that they failed to disclose fully to patients because a particular setting was viewed as inappropriate for informing patients about issues regarding their health status (Fallowfield, 1997; Gostin, 1995; Mitsuya, 1997), patients, too, may more often fail to disclose intimate information in these settings. One way to balance requests for information from patients and address organizational threats to privacy is for the caregiver to consider whether he or she would reveal sensitive information about a patient to the patient in a particular setting. For example, if a caregiver would not disclose information about the results of a patient's HIV test to the patient in a particular context, the health caregiver should not ask a patient about the number of sexual partners he or she has had during the previous 6 months in that context. Such considerations should increase caregivers' awareness of potential face threats associated with requests for information or invitations to disclose that operate in particular settings, and, as a result, caregivers may strive to provide more appropriate settings for their own and patients' sensitive disclosures.

Sometimes, promoting patients' disclosures in a setting with multiple caregivers present is important for purposes of the team's evaluation or for medical students' training. In these situations, caregivers could provide verbal explanations to a patient about the benefits associated with having so many persons present, especially when the patient is being asked to give access to his or her body, thoughts, and/or feelings to so many others. Previous research has demonstrated that when a primary caregiver explained to a patient the need for having medical students participate in the attending physician's activities, this explanation was found to increase patients' comfort with the medical education situation and to increase the rate of disclosure (Milligan, 1987).

Beyond threats to privacy posed by the presence of multiple caregivers, the perceived threats associated with computer information systems used in health care settings today may inhibit patients' disclosures. These computer systems afford a way to protect patients' rights in many ways, as they document patient care, reducing redundancies by providing a record of treatment for the patient's protection in a court of law (Coleman & Shellow, 1995; Sugarman & Powers, 1991). Computer systems, however, also increase patients' perceptions that sensitive information is being widely disseminated. Patients' privacy can be legally threatened by the very same information systems that sometimes afford protection in a court of law. For example, when the need to know arises in a court, it often overshadows patients' privacy, and private data may be released to courts of law (Kornstein, 1987; Spielman, 1992). Patients' general sense that this has happened in the past can erode confidence in their relationships with health caregivers, especially for some groups who may believe that they will be singled out as targets for violations of confidentiality through the dissemination of computerized information.

African American patients may be particularly concerned about what health caregivers do with the personal information they receive. Unfortunately, sensitive information has sometimes been used against African Americans, as exemplified by the move of some in the United States towards forced sterilization of African American and low-income women (Cline & McKenzie, 1996; Watson, Trasciatti, & King, 1996). Moreover, there is historical precedent that raises African Americans' concerns about whether health caregivers want to collect information to help African Americans or to use them for the sake of science (Wilkinson & King, 1987). A salient example is the Tuskegee syphilis experiment. In these unfortunate experiments, African American males were diagnosed as having syphilis but were not treated for the disease, and the immoral use of information allowed the disease to spread in the community, resulting in the death of those men (Jones, 1993). Hispanic migrant farm workers may also distrust the collection and computerization of information about them (Blair & Zahm, 1991). Migrant farm workers' complex health problems have been documented, yet many resist seeking care due to fear regarding their legal status in the United States and lack of understanding about the health care system's reporting function in connection with legal services (Decker & Knight, 1990).

Caregivers might directly address the specter of doubt regarding their motives for collecting information by explaining the safeguards developed within the organization to protect patients' confidentiality when information is computerized. Health caregivers can also address the organizational barriers to patients' disclosure imposed by computerized information systems by limiting requests for sensitive disclosures to those that are really necessary at a given point in time. Too often, health caregivers solicit information that might be useful at one time in the future but has no direct relevance to a current problem. Focusing on the immediate need for specific information affords balance in the setting, encouraging patients to disclose personal beliefs and practices because the information is needed for diagnosis and treatment, instead of part of a larger system of gathering details about patients' personal lives.

CULTURAL CHARACTERISTICS AND THREATS TO PATIENTS' PRIVACY

For many patients, disclosure of health information is directly associated with evaluations of trust and perceptions of attitude similarity relating to cultural beliefs (Sue et al., 1982). Patients may believe that their disclosures will convey cultural beliefs and practices for which health caregivers within the formal U.S. system of health care have little or no regard (Eng, Hatch, & Callan, 1985). For example, among many Mexican American families, as well as in the African American community, the relationship between religion and illness is central. The African and African American cultures do not separate the physical from the spiritual, as the formal health care system in the United States is often perceived to do; religious rites are viewed as an integral part of the healing process (Krajewski-Jaime, 1991). Some individuals may have people at church "lay hands" on them and pray their illness away by faith. Faith healing demands that an individual continue to believe that the illness will be healed even when the presence of objective symptoms suggests that the illness is not being resolved (Griffith, English, & Mayfield, 1980). Sometimes, in such situations, taking medicine to treat the illness may be perceived as implying that the person lacks faith in God's ability to heal. In turn, this lack of faith may cause people in the church to view the illness as an individual's own fault, because God gave a healing, but the individual failed to take it (Griffith et al., 1980).

A patient's belief in faith healing may pose a barrier to communication between a caregiver and patient, as the patient may assume that the caregiver will invalidate the patient's belief (Davis et al., 1994). This is particularly unfortunate because the likelihood is great that there exists much common ground between patients and caregivers regarding religion and health, as research has demonstrated time and again that many who choose the health care profession have deep and abiding religious faith (Nuland, 1988). Communicating in ways which afford a balance between support for patients' spiritual beliefs and health versus promotion of medical therapies and regimens may be one of the greatest challenges faced by health caregivers in efforts to establish trust with patients.

Culture shapes individual patients' reactions to the content and structure of medical interaction. Navajos, for example, believe that the language and thoughts of individuals can constitute reality. Within this worldview, the discussion of negative information, even objective results from valid medical tests, may be viewed as having harmful outcomes by Navajos (Carrese & Rhodes, 1995). Awareness of this cultural belief may guide caregivers' talk away from the negative test results and toward the positive avenues available to address the medical findings in efforts to promote patients' health and well-being. Thus, respect for individuals' cultural beliefs may achieve a great deal in efforts to involve patients with the provision of care. The challenge is to gain a patient's trust so that he or she will feel comfortable disclosing information about important cultural beliefs and practices, as few caregivers will be familiar with the range of cultural backgrounds seen within the formal system of health care in the United States.

One way to promote patients' disclosures about cultural beliefs relating to health and health care is to encourage a patient to have whomever they want to be present during the medical interaction. Although organizational barriers to privacy imposed by the presence of multiple caregivers may inhibit patients' disclosures, respect for cultural practices and the inclusion of family members and others whom a patient wants to be present may promote disclosure. For more than two decades, research regarding Mexican Americans' utilization of formal health services, including prenatal care, has demonstrated the importance of including family members in the decision-making process (Hoppe & Heller, 1975). Sometimes, the family may be included in every phase of treatment, providing a natural support system. Family members may also contribute insights about cultural beliefs and practices related to health and health care, enlarging health caregivers' understanding and improving medical outcomes. The balance between respecting patient privacy and including family members proves challenging, however, when family members convey beliefs that conflict with medicine. For example, family members may describe death as "God's will," whereas the caregiver regards such an expression as a sign of giving up or not valuing human life (Guendelman, 1983).

Beyond the cultural traditions associated with particular group membership, patients may also belong to communities with strong traditions and heritage by virtue of where they live and/or work. In rural and small town communities, the extended social interconnectedness has been found to impact patients' confidentiality (Ullom-Minnich & Kallail, 1993). In such cases, particularly vigilant efforts may be required for caregivers to safeguard patients' social and informational privacy. Balancing the patient's right to grant access to some members of a social network, while restricting access to others should be viewed as a critical goal of medical interaction to gain patients' trust and comfort with disclosing private information about thoughts, feelings, and behaviors. These efforts include limiting the dissemination of information about patients' visits, including the types of medical tests ordered and the outcomes associated with medical exams. Health caregivers should consider whether a patient's health status is likely to become available to friends, family, and neighbors simply because of the links among social network members. For example, a member of the community who works in a health care organization may know the patient whose medical results are being reported or documented. As with computerized information, caregivers may directly address such concerns with the patient, and if the patient is concerned about confidentiality, caregivers could suggest treatment options outside of the community to protect patient confidentiality (Ullom-Minnich & Kallail).

Culture influences a patient's attitudes about self-medication and self-treatment as well (Igun, 1979). Health caregivers who ask patients what they have done to treat their symptoms afford patients an opportunity to describe personal beliefs and practices relating to illness. Patients' responses may include treatments for the illness that are inconsistent with what health caregivers trained in Western medicine would suggest for the same illness but that are consistent with a patient's beliefs about illness, many of which are culturally specific. Awareness of patients' beliefs about self-medication and self-treatment may enhance caregivers' ability to balance what they regard as necessary practices with what a patient may believe to be acting in his or her own best health interest. Incorporating conversation about cultural issues into medical interaction may also enhance the likelihood that caregivers will gain insights about particular personal characteristics that could inhibit patients' revelations of significant information during medical interaction.

PERSONAL CHARACTERISTICS
AND THREATS TO PATIENTS' PRIVACY

Health caregivers may carefully address organizational characteristics potentially impinging on patients' privacy and consider cultural constraints on patients' revelations only to find that individual characteristics, including patients' knowledge levels, socioeconomic status, age, and other developmental criteria, limit the likelihood that patients will be fully forthcoming during medical interaction. Patients cannot disclose what they do not understand, and failure to understand what a health caregiver is talking about may threaten a patient's self-concept and identity, causing not only a failure to self-disclose, but hesitation to seek medical care as well. This may occur in situations where the patient is asked to disclose information about something that the patient is unable to discuss due to a lack of knowledge. Lack of knowledge about sex, physiology, and reproduction, for example, has been observed to contribute to the ways in which Hispanic women talk about these issues with health caregivers (Amaro, 1988).

When caregivers provide opportunities for patients to ask questions and express their own needs for information, the patient's requests give some sense of how much the patient knows about a topic, as well as affording a sense of reciprocity in the information seeking and giving that transpires. When a newly diagnosed diabetic patient fails to keep an accurate record of blood sugar levels to report at the next medical exam because the patient was too intimidated to ask the physician to write down instructions about the required record keeping, future diagnosis and treatment is impaired. Moreover, caregivers should recognize that the limits of their own understanding might foster patients' reluctance to self-disclose. Physicians seldom recognize children's mental health problems, for example, a finding which has been used to explain why parents are reluctant to disclose information about their children's behavioral or emotional symptoms (Wissow, Roter, & Wilson, 1994). Parents may fear that the caregivers' inability to make a diagnosis will lead to caregivers invalidating parents' claims, blaming parents for children's conditions, and/or misdiagnosing children. Physicians can limit these misgivings by limiting statements that dismiss patients' observations and claims.

Another individual characteristic likely to affect patients' willingness to disclose during medical interaction is the patient's socioeconomic status. A patient may feel that he or she cannot afford to completely disclose medical information to caregivers because they will tell patients that they are seriously ill and/or have to be hospitalized. This fear is often caused by the economic and social reality of the lives of many patients who are unlikely to disclose this reality due to pride, embarrassment, or even fear of legal repercussions (Guendelman, 1983). Many Americans lack sufficient health insurance to cover the costs incurred by illness, let alone hospitalization. Also, a large number of Americans live in single parent households, where the parent cannot afford to miss work or leave children unattended to obtain health care.

Beyond the limitations imposed by knowledge and socioeconomic status, individuals' age and some other developmental criteria may predict when patients are more or less likely to reveal personal information during conversations with health care providers. Older patients may suffer from loss of hearing, so that they are, at times, unable to understand requests for information but are too embarrassed to acknowledge such deficit or loss (Chatters, Taylor, & Jackson, 1985). Once more, this demonstrates the need for health caregivers to be socially competent in the following ways: anticipating the need to compensate for elderly patients' poor hearing, looking at the patient to provide an opportunity for them to read the caregiver's lips, repeating information to afford additional opportunities to be understood, and offering instructions in writing. Just as hearing acuity may affect patients' disclosure levels, other developmental characteristics, including visual and mental acuity, might well affect patients' abilities to understand requests for information and the likelihood that they will reveal information, including information about their disability. In the absence of such revelations, health caregivers have only their own perceptions to rely on in considering whether a patient appears to understand and to be forthcoming during conversation. The caregiver's perceptions may be enhanced by giving attention to avoiding specific communication behaviors which discourage disclosure and adopting other behaviors found to encourage the patient's full and honest interaction.

INTERACTION CHARACTERISTICS
AND THREATS TO PATIENTS' PRIVACY

To breach a patient's confidentiality assumes that a health caregiver has gathered information from and about a patient that is shared with others (Parrott et al., 1989). Too often, however, research examining medical interaction reveals that physicians fail to allow patients to complete statements about their concerns (Beckman & Frankel, 1984), conveying that patients' opinions are not worth hearing. When health caregivers behave in such ways, it should not be too surprising that patients develop an attitude of resistance with regard to medical interaction. One way to promote patients' disclosure and safeguard patients' privacy is to provide opportunities for disclosure without interruption and without directing questions at specific caregiver concerns while neglecting patient concerns (de Carpio, Carpio-Cedraro, & Anderson, 1990).

The form and function of caregivers' communication should be carefully considered as a strategy to increase patients' revelations. Caregivers' direct verbal questions, for example (even about cultural beliefs and practices in efforts to gain insights about such matters), may invade patients' psychological privacy, reducing the ability to control their thoughts and feelings. Strategies that might lessen the impact of such inquiries include the use of supportive statements (Wissow et al., 1994), the expression of hesitancy about a possible imposition on the listener's freedom, or the minimization of the size of a request (Brown & Levinson, 1978; Craig, Tracy, & Spisak, 1986). Within the African American community, adults seldom ask children to label and discuss obvious object attributes for which children know the adult already has the answer, nor are children socialized to feel compelled to answer questions in the first place (Slaughter & Epps, 1987). Caregivers might balance a more typical direct question-asking approach to information seeking with requests for narratives about "a typical day," "usual breakfast or supper," and other approaches that provide the patient with an opportunity to tell a story that affords broad insights into the patient's life.

Even when verbal communication does not directly reveal that an invasion of privacy has occurred, nonverbal communication provides insight into recognizing invasions of privacy. Laboratory studies have long suggested that emotional states are often more clearly expressed nonverbally than verbally (Argyle, 1975; Ekman & Friesen, 1976; Mehrabian, 1972). In addition, nonverbal behavior tends to encourage the verbal expression of the inner experience (Chawla & Krauss, 1994; Enelow & Swisher, 1986; Feyeriesen, 1987; Krauss, Morel-Samuels, & Colasante, 1991) and emotional expressiveness (DiMatteo, Linn, Chang, & Cope, 1985), both of which are so critical to understanding a patient's health status. Because concerns related to psychological privacy are not usually made explicit, but instead are expressed in subtle cues, the health care provider will only pick them up if he or she listens attentively (McCann & Weinman, 1995; Waitzkin, Cabrera, DeCabrera, Radlow, & Rodriguez, 1996). Additionally, the health care provider should observe the subtleties of patients' nonverbal cues, such as gaze aversion and postural shifting (M. Y. Smith & Rapkin, 1996).

To create an environment where patients feel comfortable revealing their expectations, feelings, and fears associated with ways that their illness affects roles and relationships, health care providers may seek to establish rapport with patients (Chackes & Christ, 1996). Certain features of the health care provider's communicative conduct and certain elements of the interaction have greater impact on health care evaluations than do other behaviors (Harrigan, Oxman, & Rosenthal, 1985). High-rapport health caregivers sit facing the patient with their legs and arms uncrossed, arms in symmetrical side-by-side positions, and engaged in moderate eye contact with patients. They avoid asymmetrical arm postures, backward lean in their chairs, gestural and postural inactivity, and eye contact sustained for excessively long periods of time (McCann & Weinman, 1995; Street, 1991; Wissow et al., 1994). As a result of adopting these behaviors, together with the verbal strategies suggested earlier, caregivers are likely to increase patients' rates of full and honest self-disclosure during medical interaction. These patient revelations should contribute to caregivers' increased understanding of the personal characteristics that may limit patient disclosures, and the cultural experiences that shape patients' perceptions regarding medical interaction.

CONCLUSION

If medical interaction is to attain efficacious health outcomes, there must be a balance between disclosure and privacy (Schain, 1990). The balance between the caregivers' politeness and the patients' impression management, and between the caregivers' efforts to obtain sensitive information and the patients' honest self-disclosure is a delicate one to achieve. Efforts to attain it must encompass organizational, cultural, personal, and interactional strategies. Several characteristics of the health care system in the United States at the end of the 20th century foster patients' resistance to full and honest disclosure, enhancing the status differences and social distance between caregivers and patients and inhibiting patients' free expression regarding familial, cultural, and personal practices and beliefs. Awareness of these contributes to the health caregiver's ability to engage in appropriate communication and to acknowledge the patient's individual concerns. Understanding the contribution that culture brings to medical interaction may motivate health caregivers to encourage patients to convey such beliefs, which may, in turn, reveal important information for making accurate diagnoses and recommending appropriate treatments. Individual patients' knowledge levels, socioeconomic status, and other personal characteristics may also comprise an important part of the equation in promoting full and honest disclosure. Perhaps most important is the sensitivity with which health caregivers interact with their patients. They should recognize that the messages they convey—even when they are saying nothing at all—will guide patients in their decision making about whether to tell the whole truth, or only that part which the caregiver seems most receptive to hearing.

V

▼▼▼▼▼▼▼▼▼▼▼▼

BALANCING THE SECRETS
OF PRIVATE DISCLOSURES
IN CLOSE RELATIONSHIPS

11

▼▼▼▼▼▼▼▼▼

Conflict Management Through Avoidance: Withholding Complaints, Suppressing Arguments, and Declaring Topics Taboo

Michael E. Roloff
Northwestern University

Danette E. Ifert
West Virginia Wesleyan College

As relationships become more intimate, relational partners acquire greater amounts of information about each other, and especially data of a personal nature (Taylor & Altman, 1987). Such information acquisition can result from direct observation of another's behavior and/or from self-disclosure by the person (C. R. Berger, 1987). Although the acquired information could be positive, it is also possible that insights into some part of the partner's disagreeable nature might emerge. Indeed, intimates often engage in actions that stimulate negative emotions in their partners (Scherer & Tannenbaum, 1986). When discovering a partner's negative behavior, individuals must decide whether to disclose their disapproval and run the risk of an argument, or to keep their feelings secret and, perhaps, live with an ongoing provocation. To help with such decisions, communication scholars have turned their attention to conflict management.

Research on communication and conflict has grown dramatically over the last two decades. During the mid-1970s, edited volumes began to explore issues related to conflict resolution (e.g., Jandt, 1973; Miller & Simons, 1974). As is typical of such initial works, the content covered was quite diverse, and it was difficult to identify underlying theoretical perspectives on communication and conflict from which one might recommend ways of resolving disputes. However, the heuristic value of these volumes is evident in the conflict literature of the 1990s. One can point to useful volumes that articulate theoretical perspectives used to understand conflict processes (e.g., Cahn, 1992) and recommend research-based conflict-management behaviors (e.g.,

151

Cupach & Canary, 1997; Folger, Poole, & Stutman, 1997; Hocker & Wilmot, 1995).

Despite these important strides, there remain critical gaps in our knowledge. To a large extent, communication scholars have been preoccupied with discovering how individuals might develop solutions to overcome the cause of their conflict and thereby prevent its recurrence. Because people often describe their typical conflicts negatively (McCorkle & Mills, 1992), such a research emphasis is reasonable. This focus, furthermore, has an upbeat tone that is consistent with a desire to empower individuals to be active problem solvers. However optimistic, our prevailing scholarly approach ignores the possibility that some conflicts are effectively irresolvable or that the costs arising from trying to resolve others may be too severe to justify addressing them. In such cases, individuals may elect to keep secret their complaints and thereby avoid an argument.

To leave the conflict unresolved is a risky course of action. An unresolved conflict could fester to the point of causing an explosion (Baumeister, Stillwell, & Wotman, 1990), which would aversively impact relational quality. There are negative correlations between conflict avoidance and relational satisfaction (e.g., Bowman, 1990; Canary & Spitzberg, 1989; Kurdek, 1994; Sillars, 1980) and stability (McGonagle, Kessler, & Gotlib, 1993). As a result, a confrontational, problem-solving style rather than an avoidant one is the prevailing recommendation made by therapists (Gottman, 1993; Pike & Sillars, 1985).

In spite of the aforementioned evidence, the rejection of conflict avoidance and nearly complete endorsement of confrontation by conflict-management professionals may be premature. Some studies have found that frequency of arguing about relational problems is negatively related to relational quality (Lloyd, 1987, 1990). Frequency of arguing may be related to relational instability even if the partners calmly discuss the conflict and are satisfied with the outcome of their discussion (McGonagle et al., 1993). More importantly, Pike and Sillars (1985) found that conflict avoidance was more evident in arguments between satisfied spouses than between dissatisfied ones.

The contradictory findings with regard to the effect of confrontation versus conflict avoidance may stem, in part, from the relationships studied. For example, Rands, Levinger, and Mellinger (1981) found that conflict avoidance was positively associated with relational satisfaction among couples whose arguments made them feel less intimate afterwards and whose disputes were potentially volatile. It was negatively related to satisfaction among couples whose disagreements typically resulted in feelings of greater closeness and where there was a low risk of aggressive behavior. Among marital couples who are emotionally distant and autonomous, enacting avoidant behavior is positively related to relational satisfaction (Sillars, Pike, Jones, & Redmon, 1983).

Thus, research suggests that conflict avoidance deserves more attention than it has been afforded. Perhaps achieving successful relationships requires a balance between confrontation and avoidance. When confrontation and arguing have become the dominant form of interaction, the relationship may be endangered. In such case, nondisclosure might be a viable conflict-management technique as the parties attempt to contain the extent of their disagreements. However, the prevailing paradigm that implicitly guides conflict research views a deficit in argumentative skills as the basic cause of dysfunctional conflict (e.g., Infante, Chandler, & Rudd, 1989). Because conflict avoidance is an attempt to suppress an argument, it is often viewed as a skills deficit that should be treated rather than encouraged (Birchler, 1979). Indeed, we know of few conflict-management texts which acknowledge that there might be conditions under which conflict avoidance is a preferable response (e.g., Hocker & Wilmot, 1985; M. A. Rahim, 1986). To help close this knowledge gap, we examine research on conflict avoidance by identifying the fundamental processes involved in avoidance and the conditions under which it might be successfully used.

THE NATURE OF CONFLICT AVOIDANCE

Deutsch (1973) argued that conflict exists whenever there are incompatible activities. In his view, incompatibility occurs when a behavior contradicts, interferes with, or makes another's action less likely or effective. Conflict may also result from an action that violates a rule or norm (Metts, 1994; Roloff & Cloven, 1994). Hence, at its core, conflict involves a stimulus action perceived to be undesirable and/or inappropriate. In some cases, the action is sufficiently provocative that an observer feels compelled to confront the actor and directly or indirectly disclose a complaint or grievance to the actor (Newell & Stutman, 1991). When the actor resists this challenge, a quarrel (Vuchinich, 1987) or dispute (Stafford & Gibbs, 1993) has arisen.

The perceived existence of a conflict is distinct from the communicative responses to it. An undesirable or inappropriate action may go unchallenged and, even if confronted, may not elicit a response from the actor (e.g., Vuchinich, 1987). Such cases often reflect conflict avoidance. Conflict avoidance occurs when a person tries to prevent discussion of an undesirable or inappropriate action. In a sense, avoidance is aimed at preventing undesirable by-products of confrontation and arguing. Disagreements often stimulate behaviors such as criticism and sarcasm (Resick et al., 1981), which can cause arousal (Gormly, 1974), reduce relational satisfaction (Bowman, 1990), and stimulate regret for having spoken one's mind (Knapp, Stafford, & Daly, 1986). Hence, concern for the negative consequences of engagement is not unfounded.

Conflict avoidance may take three forms. First, an observer of an objectionable action may choose not to confront the actor. Second, once a confrontation has been initiated, an actor may engage in behaviors to prevent elaborated discussion of a conflict. Finally, the actor and observer may negotiate an agreement to stop talking about the conflict or, in effect, declare it taboo. Although we recognize that these three forms of avoidance may constitute a cluster of behaviors that co-occur, it is informative to examine each separately.

Withholding Complaints

Even in the happiest relationships, individuals engage in behaviors on a daily basis that negatively impact their partners (Birchler, Wiess, & Vincent, 1975; Kirchler, 1988). However, many objectionable acts one encounters are allowed to pass without comment. On average, individuals in dating relationships do not disclose 40% of their relational complaints to their partners (Roloff & Cloven, 1990). Similarly, observers of everyday rule violations often do not confront the transgressor (Felson, 1984). Although the volume of grievances withheld from a relational partner is negatively related to relational satisfaction (e.g., Roloff & Cloven, 1990), in some cases, withholding may not affect relational quality.

One of the most frequent reasons individuals have for not disclosing grievances is that the conflict is insufficiently important to warrant disclosure (Solomon & Roloff, 1996). This reason for withholding is especially common among individuals in highly intimate relationships (Cloven & Roloff, 1994). M. A. Rahim (1986) speculated that conflict avoidance was an appropriate response to trivial conflicts. Among individuals withholding grievances because they are unimportant, a positive rather than negative association exists between the proportion of withheld complaints and relational satisfaction (Solomon & Roloff, 1996).

Individuals choosing to withhold unimportant complaints face a variety of challenges. First, and ironically, the act of withholding trivial complaints might prompt processes that cause individuals to see the problems as serious. Conflicts often stimulate mulling or obsessive thought as individuals try to make sense of their problem (Cloven & Roloff, 1995), and the extent of mulling over minor conflicts is positively associated with judgments of problem seriousness (Cloven & Roloff, 1991). Such effects result from the tendency of individuals to think about their conflicts in ways that are insufficiently self-critical and to ignore the partner's perspective. However, these mulling tendencies can be overcome when individuals anticipate communicating about the conflict (Cloven & Roloff, 1993a). Individuals who choose never to disclose their unimportant grievances may never overcome the mulling biases and, eventually, convince themselves of the importance of their problem. It is possible that discussing the conflict with someone other than the partner could break this cycle (Cloven & Roloff, 1993a).

Second, viewing a conflict as unimportant might be a rationalization resulting from a person's powerlessness within a relationship. Withholding complaints in a dating relationship is positively related to an individual's dependence upon the partner (Roloff & Cloven, 1990). Holding back complaints about a dating partner's dominating behavior increases with expectations that the partner might respond aggressively (Cloven & Roloff, 1993b). Although suggestive, the aforementioned studies did not directly link powerlessness to withholding complaints because they are unimportant. Recently, Solomon and Samp (1998) found that both relational dependency and anticipated aggressive partner responses were related to viewing a problem as less serious and intending to avoid confronting the partner about it. However, they found no evidence that perceiving the conflict as less serious mediates the association between relational power and plans to avoid confronting the partner. Individuals who withhold complaints due to their unimportance should recognize the possibility that their judgments may be distorted by their relative powerlessness.

Finally, individuals who withhold complaints must live in silence with an unresolved albeit unimportant problem. Because the partner is likely unaware of the conflict, his or her provocative behavior may continue. As a result, those who choose to withhold grievances must cope with the reoccurrence of the problematic behavior. Research clearly indicates that selectively ignoring another's problematic behavior (i.e., looking only at his or her good points, distracting oneself with work, waiting for the problem to resolve itself) increases one's distress about the relationship (Menaghan, 1982, 1983).

However, three coping devices may be useful. First, individuals who attempt to improve the overall quality of their relationship may be able to overcome the negative by-products of unresolved, ongoing problems. Bowman (1990) found that coping with marital problems in a way that improved the emotional quality of a marriage (e.g., doing things together, paying more attention to one another, finding humor in problems) was positively correlated with marital happiness. Importantly, such an approach did not include trying to directly solve the problem. Alternatively, some individuals cope with ongoing problems by making optimistic comparisons (i.e., they think their relationship is getting better and view their relationship as better than the relationships of others). Use of optimistic comparison decreases stress (Menaghan, 1982, 1983) and although not universally effective (Menaghan, 1983), sometimes reduces the incidence of future relational problems (Menaghan, 1982). Thus, although trying to ignore an ongoing problem does not seem to work, recognizing its existence but compensating for it by engaging in positive actions or making optimistic comparisons may neutralize its negative effects. Finally, a person may withhold a complaint but monitor the situation to determine whether the problem goes away or remains insignificant. If it does not, then a confrontation may be required. Individuals judge such a "wait and see" stance with regard to a problem with a romantic partner to be as appropriate as confrontation and more appropriate than actively trying to avoid confrontation over the issue (Sternberg & Dobson, 1987).

Not all grievances are sufficiently trivial to warrant keeping them secret, and as a result, a confrontation occurs. In such cases, the person who is confronted may engage in behaviors designed to prevent discussion of the issue. We turn to that next.

Suppressing Arguments

It may seem counterintuitive that once confronted, an individual would seek to avoid discussion rather than mount a spirited defense. However, the nature of an argument may motivate individuals to end the discussion. An argument can be arousing (Gormly, 1974), and Gottman (1994) speculated that conflict avoiders attempt to prevent the affect associated with arguing from becoming a totally absorbing state. Some scholars have speculated that argument suppression is a means by which an individual who benefits from the status quo can avoid having to change (e.g., Scanzoni, 1978).

Although acts designed to avoid explicit discussion of an issue are often treated as a single cluster (Sillars, Colletti, Parry, & Rogers, 1982), to more fully understand their nature, we examine three common types. First, conflict avoiders may engage in synthetic agreement. In effect, to bring the confrontation to a quick end, they simply agree with the confronter's demands (Graziano, Jensen-Campbell, & Hair, 1996; Sternberg & Dobson, 1987), and may even apologize or promise that the offensive action will not happen again. Importantly, their agreement is not genuine but is merely an attempt to placate the offended party. Although admitting wrongdoing and losing face, ending the discussion may offset these costs. Indeed, some males report that they allow their female partners to debase them as a means of terminating their partner's behavior (Buss, Gomes, Higgins, & Lauterbach, 1987).

Synthetic agreement is likely to be problematic. Because it is not genuine, it is possible that the offender may leak cues indicating such and the confronter will see it as a transparent attempt to close off further argument. Indeed, wives who perceive that their husbands are submissive (e.g., too complacent or compliant during discussions) often attribute malicious intent or a lack of love to their husbands (Epstein, Pretzer, & Fleming, 1987). In such instances, the confronter may respond by pursuing the argument with greater vigor. Moreover, to agree with the complaint brings with it acceptance of responsibility (e.g., Wood & Mitchell, 1981) and willingness to change (Schwartz, Kane, Joseph, & Tedeschi, 1978). If synthetic agreement is simply an attempt to avoid arguing and there is no real intent to follow through, then the problematic behavior will likely reoccur and the confronter is less likely to be sympathetic.

Rather than completely give in, a second way to prevent further discussion is to admit the existence of a conflict but minimize its importance. Witteman (1992) found that some individuals try to smooth over their conflicts by telling their partners that their differences are inconsequential. This strategy seems based on the assumption that a trivial problem does not require extensive discussion.

A difficulty associated with smoothing is that it may be disconfirming to the confronter. Individuals who are angry with another's behavior often view the undesirable behavior as having been repeated on several occasions and believe that the confrontation only occurred after they could no longer suffer in silence; hence, their anger is justified (Baumeister et al., 1990). Thus, attempts to minimize the problem will likely be at variance with the confronter's own experience and imply that he or she should not be taken seriously. Such disconfirmation might be made worse if the transgressor indicates that the confronter is overreacting (Baumeister et al., 1990).

There may be cases where smoothing is effective. Gottman (1994) found a group of happily married couples who routinely minimized the importance of their conflicts and, as a result, kept arguing to a minimum. Such individuals stressed the common values that tied them together which overwhelmed the importance of any conflict they might be discussing. As a result, neither party felt it necessary to persuade the other to change.

A third means of preventing discussion is to withdraw from the conversation. In its most overt form, a partner refuses to further discuss the issue or leaves the scene (Benoit & Benoit, 1987; Lloyd, 1987). However, withdrawing may also be implicit and take the form of conversational unresponsiveness. Gottman (1994) argues that some individuals stonewall during a conversation such that while listening, they tend to remain silent after their partner is done speaking, and/or sometimes engage in incoherent speech (Gottman & Krokoff, 1989).

Scholars have identified a dysfunctional confrontation pattern in which a person demands change and the partner responds by withdrawing (Christensen, 1987, 1988). In part, this pattern may reflect fundamental roles in a confrontation. When a person complains to another, acknowledgment and agreement are the most desired responses and being ignored is one of the least preferred (Alberts, 1988). To ignore the complaint not only indicates unwillingness to change but also creates a host of other negative impressions. Being unresponsive is correlated with appearing to be unattractive, disinterested, and negative toward the conversational partner (Davis & Holtgraves, 1984; Davis & Perkowitz, 1979). Despite these negative outcomes, an unresponsive person may be able to discourage arguing and maintain the status quo.

Gottman (1994) reports in his research on marital conflict that approximately 85% of the stonewallers are male. In part, this may reflect the greater desire of wives to change their marriages and the relatively greater satisfaction with the status quo enjoyed by husbands (Jacobson, 1989). When discussing a conflict issue of importance to a wife, the frequency of the wife demand–husband withdraw pattern produces destructive conflict outcomes (Kluwer, Heesink, & Van de Vliert, 1997) and lower concurrent and long-term relational satisfaction. For issues raised by the husband, a pattern in which the husband is demanding and the wife is withdrawing should be more common than is the opposite pattern. Indeed, research indicates that for husband-initiated topics, either there is no difference in the occurrence of wife demand–husband withdraw and husband demand–wife withdraw patterns (Christensen & Heavey, 1990; Heavey, Layne, & Christensen, 1993) or husband demand–wife withdraw is more frequent (Klinetob & Smith, 1996). Although the frequency of husband demand–wife withdraw is negatively correlated with concurrent husband satisfaction, it is not significantly related to his long-term satisfaction (Heavey, Christensen, & Malamuth, 1995).

There appears to be little to recommend stonewalling. Yet, withdrawal may not be universally bad. Witteman (1988, 1992) found that withdrawal is correlated with uncertainty about how to resolve the conflict. In effect, a person may be less responsive while trying to figure out how to appropriately respond. This should be especially likely if the confrontation was a surprise and he or she is unprepared to respond. Furthermore, stonewalling among males may result from their inability, in high-intensity disagreements, to edit their statements so that they respond constructively rather than destructively to their partner's negative statements (Gottman, 1994). As a result, they may say very little rather than run the risk of saying something that will escalate the disagreement. Yovetich and Rusbult (1994) found that individuals try to control their initial proclivities to react destructively to their partner's negative behaviors but are unable to do so when forced to react quickly. Hence, M. A. Rahim (1986) suggested that conflict avoidance is appropriate when a "cooling-off period" is required. When used to postpone an argument, a problem with stonewalling arises from its unclear intent. Without some explanation, the confronter is free to make any number of negative attributions which may make the conflict worse (Epstein et al., 1987). In the absence of a clear commitment to re-engage the argument, postponement may appear to be an indirect tactic intended to maintain control (Frost & Wilmot, 1977).

However, some conflicts require more than a temporary suspension of argument. Individuals may have actively engaged one another and have been unable to find a solution to the problem. Their lack of progress may adversely impact their feelings about the relationship (Johnson & Roloff, 1995). Assuming that they have good reason to stay in the relationship, the solution may be for individuals to negotiate an agreement to remove the topic from the table. If so, it is essential that we understand how issues may be effectively declared taboo.

Declaring a Topic Taboo

Although as relationships grow more intimate individuals expand the number of topics about which they can talk (Altman & Taylor, 1973), one can identify a number of topics which are off-limits for discussion (i.e., taboo) within close friendships (Goodwin, 1990), cross-sex premarital relationships (Baxter & Wilmot, 1985), and families (Vangelisti, 1994). Individuals frequently treat topics as taboo to avoid negative evaluations from others and to maintain a positive relational environment (Vangelisti, 1994).

Recent research suggests that individuals may actually negotiate an agreement to declare a topic off of the table as a means of avoiding the negative consequences of arguing (Roloff & Ifert, 1998). The effectiveness of such a conflict-management tactic depends in part on the nature of the agreement. Agreements can vary in the extent to which they are implicit and informal or explicit and formal (Roloff & Ifert, 1998). Implicit agreements may reflect an unstated but mutual understanding that the topic should not be discussed again. Explicit agreement consists of an overt agreement to quit talking about the issue. The advantage of explicit agreements stems from their clarity and enforceability. However, they force the parties to explicitly acknowledge their inability or unwillingness to resolve their problem and commit both parties to an avoidant course of action that may not be easily adapted to changing circumstances. As a result, explicit agreements may be problematic, and there is evidence that the explicitness of agreements declaring topics taboo is negatively correlated with relational satisfaction (Roloff & Ifert, 1998).

The negative impact of explicitness may also stem from the processes that lead to it rather than from some inherent feature of such agreements. One reason individuals report for explicitly declaring topics taboo is that they are unimportant (Roloff & Ifert, 1998). Deciding that a topic is unimportant is positively correlated with extensive discussions of the issue prior to explicitly agreeing to declare the topic taboo. It is possible that such frequent engagement might prove frustrating as individuals make it clear that they are resistant to change. Although a resolution might be possible, the costs associated with continued engagement are not offset by the benefits resulting from resolution and partners choose to quit talking about their conflict. Perhaps out of exasperation, they agree to never discuss the topic again. Indeed, explicitness is positively correlated with recollections that one partner declared that he or she never wanted to discuss the issue again (Roloff & Ifert, 1998). Thus, the problem with explicitness stems from the frequent disagreements that lead to it.

Explicitly declaring a topic taboo also results from fearing that continued discussion would harm the relationship. Although anticipated relational harm is not significantly related to the amount of prior discussion, it is correlated with one partner announcing that the topic is not appropriate for discussion. The topic may be potentially resolvable but it cannot be discussed because it is so inappropriate or offensive that addressing it might seriously harm the relationship. To overcome this obstacle would require convincing the partner for whom the topic is inappropriate that his or her view is incorrect, which would mean discussing the inappropriate topic. Regardless of its importance or resolvability, then, the issue cannot be discussed.

Explicitness is negatively associated with relational satisfaction. However, the negative association between explicitness and satisfaction is moderated by relational commitment (Roloff & Ifert, 1998). The negative impact of explicitness is only significant among individuals who have low or moderate levels of relational commitment. Among those individuals who are highly committed, the negative association between explicitness and relational commitment is of trivial magnitude. This could mean that some individuals who are very committed to their relationship are sufficiently confident of its viability that they are not bothered by a conflict they cannot discuss. In effect, they can live with an explicit contract to agree to disagree.

It is unclear what communication processes might lead to implicit agreements to declare a topic taboo. One might speculate that implicit agreements result from interpreting a partner's nonverbal cues when a topic is being discussed (Folger et al., 1997), but Roloff and Ifert (1998) found no evidence of such a relationship. Alternatively, it is possible that implicit agreements result from a combination of selective information disclosure and the absence of influence attempts. Gottman (1994) found that happily married conflict-avoidant couples disclose their perspectives on a relational problem, but they do not extensively explore the emotional nature of their differences nor do they attempt to persuade their partners. Once each partner has explained his or her view of the conflict and understands the other's perspective, the confrontation has ended. In effect, there is tacit agreement that they should ignore their differences or wait for time to take care of the problem.

Our analysis thus far suggests that conflict avoidance is not the absolute evil implied by current approaches to studying conflict management. If certain conditions are met, conflict avoidance might prove to be a useful skill. In the final section, we articulate those conditions.

CONDITIONS UNDER WHICH CONFLICT
AVOIDANCE CAN BE SUCCESSFUL

Although we acknowledge that more research is needed on conflict avoidance before firm conclusions can be reached, we offer the following tentative set of conditions under which conflict avoidance might be successful. Because conflict avoidance is not aimed at resolving the fundamental cause of the dispute, we do not believe it is fair to evaluate it on those grounds. Instead, its success is determined by its ability to reduce the amount of arguing and to mitigate the harmful relational by-products of not talking about a problem.

First, successful use of conflict avoidance requires substantial tolerance. Filley (1975) characterized a conflict-avoidant style as including an ideology of tolerance in which one allows individuals to follow their own path even if disagreeing with it. Similarly, Gottman (1994) observed that happily married conflict-avoidant couples emphasize their tolerance of differences and willingness to let each other go his or her own way. Thus, conflict avoidance may be more successful among open-minded than closed-minded individuals (Rokeach, 1960), and it may be problematic among those persons whose conception of intimacy strongly endorses similarity, shared activity, and open communication (Baxter, 1984).

Second, successful conflict avoidance requires the use of coping devices. We suspect that ongoing conflict would try the patience of even the most tolerant individual. Hence, something must be done to prevent continuing provocation from harming the relationship. In effect, couples must find something positive in their relationship to balance the negative provocation. Gottman (1994) noted that happily married avoidant couples focus on positive aspects of their marriage, which allows them to minimize the importance of unresolved conflicts. We noted earlier that such an outlook might be supported by engaging in frequent mutually enjoyable activities with one's partner or by making optimistic comparisons.

Third, to be successful, conflict avoidance should be selectively rather than universally used. We doubt that avoidance makes sense for all types of disputes. There seems to be consensus that avoidance is best suited for conflicts that parties perceive to be relatively unimportant. Unfortunately, there may be little consensus about what constitutes an unimportant conflict. In one sense, a conflict is unimportant to the extent that it has few practical negative consequences. Such might be the case when a conflict is over a preference or a nuance (Deutsch, 1973). Similarly, Pruitt (1981) hypothesized that agreeing to disagree might be an integrative way to end relational conflicts over differing interests in recreational activities. In the latter case, the partners employ a laissez-faire strategy in which they are allowed to independently rather than jointly pursue their desired action (Falbo & Peplau, 1980).

However, a conflict may have few practical consequences for the parties but be important to them because it stems from their fundamental values. Values are conceptions of what should be (Deutsch, 1973) and because they are so central to a person's belief system (Rokeach, 1968), they are not easily compromised. Not surprisingly, conflicts over values are among the most difficult to resolve (e.g., Greenhalgh, 1986). As such, individuals would seem to be advised to avoid arguing over these issues. However, the ability to avoid such conflicts may be affected by the nature of the values themselves. Deutsch (1973) speculated that some values both specify what is ideal and mandate that the ideal should be imposed on others. Hence, parties with conflicting values are sometimes drawn to one another, often in bitter clashes. In such cases, avoidance is not possible.

Fourth, to be successful, conflict avoidance must be freely chosen rather than coerced. We noted earlier that powerless individuals engage in conflict avoidance to dodge the negative consequences of confronting a more powerful partner. However, such behavior is unlikely to be effective. Gelles and Straus (1988) found that victims of relational abuse often try to avoid discussing topics that might set off the violent behaviors of their partners but instead find that their avoidance is unsuccessful at preventing aggression. Individuals who anticipate that their partners would respond aggressively to relational complaints often feel unable to change their partner's behavior, which causes them to withhold complaints and feel less satisfied with their relationship (Makoul & Roloff, 1998).

Fifth, to be successful, conflict avoidance requires communication skills. This assertion may seem counterintuitive; why would the successful avoidance of communication require skills to communicate? This confusion may stem from the false assumption that conflict avoiders never communicate about their problems. To the contrary, Gottman (1994) noted that although happily married conflict avoiders talk less about their problems than do conflict engagers, avoiders discuss their relational problems in a distinct way. Unlike unhappily married conflict avoiders, the happy ones moderate their use of avoidance and supplement it with positive communication behaviors. They try to understand and accept each other's perspective. They emphasize their commonalities rather than differences and note that the conflict is not that important. Furthermore, to use conflict avoidance on a selective basis implies that when necessary, one can enact confrontational behaviors. This implies that a person must believe he or she has the ability to confront the partner and that such a confrontation will have positive outcomes. If those beliefs are absent, avoidance may be used indiscriminately and will reduce relational satisfaction (Makoul & Roloff, 1998). Thus, conflict avoidance should be one among a constellation of conflict-management behaviors within a person's repertoire.

Finally, successful conflict avoidance may require substantial perspective taking and individual problem solving. To avoid a confrontation, individuals may monitor their partner to determine when and why he or she might be upset and then try to solve the problem without being asked. Indeed, Sillars (1980) found that some roommates manage their conflicts through empathic adjustment rather than explicit discussion and agreement.

Clearly, we are not arguing that conflict avoidance should be the predominant style of managing disputes. We have acknowledged drawbacks associated with using it. However, under certain conditions, it may prove to be effective. Also, we concede that the aforementioned conditions are quite demanding. We suspect, however, that the conditions associated with successful conflict engagement may be equally demanding.

In our view, it may be important that relational partners maintain a balance between confrontation and avoidance. Although we suspect that the most desirable ratio of confrontation to avoidance varies with the couple, we are doubtful that either complete disclosure or avoidance of complaints is desirable. In the former, the couple's sense of commonality may be threatened, and in the latter, there may be little vitality and ability to address problems. Hence, effective conflict management requires an ability to be confrontational and to be avoidant.

12

▼▼▼▼▼▼▼

Motivations Underlying Topic
Avoidance in Close Relationships

Walid A. Afifi
Pennsylvania State University, University Park

Laura K. Guerrero
Arizona State University

> *A wonderful fact to reflect upon, that every human creature is constituted
> to be that profound secret and mystery to every other. A solemn consid-
> eration, when I enter a great city by night, that every one of those darkly
> clustered houses encloses its own secret; that every room in every one of
> them encloses its own secret; that every beating heart in hundreds of
> thousands of breasts there, is, in some of its imaginings, a secret to the
> heart nearest it!*
>
> —Charles Dickens, *A Tale of Two Cities*

As Dickens wrote, humans can never know one another's thoughts and
feelings completely. No matter how close two people are, they cannot get
into one another's minds and hearts to achieve total understanding. Humans
can empathize, but they can never really put themselves completely into their
partners' minds. Unlike the fictional Vulcans in the popular *Star Trek* series,
humans are unable to use a "mind meld" to fully understand what another
person is experiencing.

Indeed, individuals struggle to maintain balance in their relationships. On
the one hand, humans feel a powerful need to be connected to one another
and to feel understood. Communication is used to bridge the gap between
people. In particular, self-disclosure is a means by which people can share
their innermost thoughts with one another and peek into one another's
thoughts and feelings. On the other hand, there are times when people prefer
to keep their thoughts and feelings private, to preserve the mystery about
which Dickens so eloquently marvels. This chapter emphasizes an aspect of

165

this equilibrium between revelation and concealment that has been mostly ignored in the literature: topic avoidance.

Topic avoidance occurs when an individual strategically decides *not* to disclose information on a particular topic to another person. Some topics are avoided because they are considered "taboo" within a particular relationship or context. Baxter and Wilmot (1985) discussed several common taboo topics, including the state of the relationship, information about previous relationships, relational rules, negative self-disclosures (such as fears and embarrassing moments), and relational problems. Almost everyone in Baxter and Wilmot's (1985) study could identify at least one topic that they considered to be taboo in their relationship. Similarly, Guerrero and Afifi (1995b) found that teens saw sexual experiences and dangerous behavior as common "taboo topics" in their relationships with their parents. Secrets are another form of topic avoidance. For example, Sally may strategically avoid talking when her colleagues are discussing who will get the big promotion in her department because she knows that Mary will get the promotion, but she is supposed to keep it secret. Topic avoidance can also be part of the deception process. Buller and Burgoon (1996) discuss concealment as a form of deception that involves keeping relevant information private. People might conceal information to protect themselves (e.g., teens not telling their parents how badly they did on an exam) or others (e.g., not telling a friend that her new haircut is unattractive). Taboo topics, secrets, and deception are all related to topic avoidance, but topic avoidance is a broader construct than all three.

Research on general topic avoidance, taboo topics, secrets, and deception has established that individuals are sometimes motivated to avoid disclosure, even with their most intimate partners. Indeed, the need for equilibrium between revelation and concealment necessitates such avoidance. Unfortunately, little attention has been paid to the circumstances under which individuals are most likely to avoid disclosure. This chapter addresses this issue by presenting a motivational perspective for understanding the circumstances under which topic avoidance is most likely to occur. Our perspective is grounded in research in three theoretical areas: uncertainty reduction, social penetration, and dialectics. Thus, before discussing specific motivations underlying topic avoidance, we review relevant ideas from these three theoretical areas.

THEORETICAL FOUNDATIONS

On the surface, the prevalence of topic avoidance in relationships appears to run counter to the implicit notions underlying several theories of relational behavior. For example, uncertainty reduction theory (URT; C. R. Berger &

Calabrese, 1975) advances the principle that people seek information to reduce uncertainty and advance relationships. Relatedly, social penetration theory (SPT; Altman & Taylor, 1973) is premised on the assumption that increasingly high levels of self-disclosure accompany relationship development. However, as is shown in the following sections, current research and theory illustrate that topic avoidance can be used strategically to lower uncertainty (e.g., avoiding disclosure as a "secret test") and enhance relational progress.

URT

When articulating URT, C. R. Berger and Calabrese (1975) adopted the assumption that individuals are driven by a desire to reduce uncertainty in initial interaction. Research since the theory's inception has expanded its scope to the realm of close relationships (C. R. Berger, 1993; Planalp & Honeycutt, 1985; Planalp, Rutherford, & Honeycutt, 1988). As a result, many scholars now hold as axiomatic that individuals in relationships are motivated information seekers (for review, see Vorauer & Ross, 1996). In fact, C. R. Berger and Kellermann (1994), although recognizing that individuals pursue multiple goals, recently argued that "the acquisition of information is an important goal in almost every strategic communication episode" (p. 2).

However, information seeking occurs in many forms. Research has shown that individuals typically reduce uncertainty in one of three general ways (for review, see C. R. Berger & Bradac, 1982): (a) passively (i.e., through unobtrusive observation); (b) actively (i.e., by asking third parties or observing targets after subjecting them to a "test"); or (c) interactively (e.g., through direct interaction with the target). In one example of information-seeking research, Baxter and Wilmot (1984) investigated the techniques that people use in their attempts to discover their partners' true feelings about the relationships. These information-seeking techniques include: (a) *directness tests*, such as direct questioning; (b) *third party tests*, such as asking a friend to get information for you; (c) *public-presentation tests*, such as touching someone in public to see how he or she reacts; (d) *indirect-suggestion tests*, such as hinting and attention seeking; (e) *endurance tests*, such as seeing how many "costs" your partner will endure; (f) *separation tests*, such as seeing how your partner reacts to being separated from you; and (g) *triangle tests*, such as seeing if you can make your partner jealous. Because most of these tests involve indirectly acquiring information about a partner's level of commitment, Baxter and Wilmot (1984) referred to these techniques as "secret tests" (p. 171). The indirect nature of these tests illustrates that there are times when relational partners want information, but they refrain from direct self-disclosure and questioning. In particular, the secret test of separation shows how avoidance of a person, not just a topic, can be utilized to acquire information.

SPT

The premise underlying SPT and most research on self-disclosure is that individuals seek bondedness with others by becoming increasingly disclosive as relationships develop (e.g., Altman & Taylor, 1973; D. A. Taylor & Altman, 1987). Specifically, Altman and Taylor likened the process of developing an intimate relationship to the peeling of an onion. The outer skin of the onion represents superficial information, while the inner core of the onion represents the most intimate self-disclosure. Altman and Taylor believed that relationships are closest when communication between partners has high depth (i.e., intimate disclosure), breadth (i.e., discussion of different topical areas), and frequency (i.e., frequent dislosure). However, some scholars, such as Parks (1982), have cautioned against adopting the assumption that self-disclosure and complete openness are the pantheon of close relationships. Indeed, research on relational maintenance has shown that both openness and avoidance are key contributors to relational closeness. For example, Canary and Stafford (1994) discussed antisocial strategies (such as inducing jealousy) and avoidance (such as avoiding topics that led to disagreement) as strategies used to help maintain relationships under certain circumstances. Thus, it appears that SPT only explains part of the acquaintanceship process. Self-disclosure of private information is indeed important, but this disclosure must be balanced by discretion and privacy even in the closest relationships.

Dialectics Theory

Dialectics theory recognizes that both disclosure and topic avoidance are important within close relationships. Baxter's (1988, 1990, 1991) work rests on the assumption that people have seemingly contradictory goals in their relationships. For example, Baxter (1988) contended that couples want to be open, yet they also want to keep some information private. This is the openness–closedness dialectic. Other primary dialectics include autonomy–connectedness and novelty–predictability. Baxter argued that dyadic partners must manage these dialectical tensions if they hope to maintain satisfying relationships. Rawlins' (1983a, 1983b, 1992) work on friendships also adopts a dialectical perspective. He labeled expressiveness–protectiveness as one of the primary dialectical tensions that characterize friendships. Expressiveness includes the desire to express one's feelings and innermost thoughts. Protectiveness includes the desire to avoid disclosure and protect oneself from vulnerability. Taken together, the work on dialectics suggests that both self-disclosure and topic avoidance are crucial components within different types of close relationships. Indeed, dialectical theory captures the notion of balance very elegantly.

MOTIVATIONS UNDERLYING TOPIC AVOIDANCE

As the brief theoretical review indicates, individuals are not constant disclosers. In fact, the evidence suggests that topic avoidance is a common relational event. Unfortunately, many scholars studying uncertainty and self-disclosure have failed to acknowledge the intricate structure of motivational forces shaping avoidant behavior in relationships. However, if one adopts the notion that revelation *must* be accompanied by some concealment to maintain individual and relational development, then self-disclosure and topic avoidance share equal billing as weights that balance relationships.

We offer a motivational, goal-oriented perspective to relational behavior as a way of understanding the seemingly contradictory behaviors that emerge in relational life. Underlying this perspective are certain axioms that frame its scope.

First, we assume that individuals have a relatively complex goal structure (although its complexity depends on several factors) and they seek multiple goals simultaneously (e.g., C. R. Berger & Kellermann, 1994). Behavior is typically not the result of a singular motivating force but, instead, the product of an amalgamation of goals that are working together.

Second, a variety of different strategies may be successful at attaining the same goal (e.g., Cappella & Street, 1985). Although one might find this axiom simplistic or obvious, the implications of recognizing this relationship between goals and behavior are far-reaching. For example, individuals may seek the same goal of bondedness through disclosure or, conversely, through avoidance.

Third, several different goals may be achieved by enacting the same behavior (e.g., Haslett, 1987). The behavior may affect multiple goals simultaneously or may be used to attain different goals at separate points in time. An example of the former would be avoidance of disclosure about an issue that is face threatening (thus often protecting both the self and the relationship—two separate goals); teens report that they sometimes avoid discussing dangerous behavior, such as trying drugs or alcohol, with their parents. They avoid such discussion to protect themselves from criticism and punishment, and also to protect the trusting relationship they have built with their parents. An example of using a behavior to attain two different goals at separate points in time is when avoidance is used to increase bondedness in the developing stages of relationship (by avoiding topics that could lead to relational problems) but to increase distance in its deteriorating stages.

Finally, we assume that goal structures are hierarchically organized and that the specifics of the hierarchy vary according to personal, relational, and social contexts (e.g., Austin & Vancouver, 1996). The desire for greater certainty in a relationship (a typically salient goal) may be sacrificed at particular relational stages for the more immediate concern of protecting the relationship (e.g., Afifi & Burgoon, 1998). From within this framework of assumptions, the reasons underlying both the decision to disclose and the choice to avoid disclosure in relationships becomes more evident. Next, we briefly examine some of the more salient goals underlying relationship behavior and reflect on how they contribute to our understanding of topic avoidance patterns in close relationships.

Relationship-Based Motivations

There is a long history of research establishing the importance that individuals place on connectedness (for review, see Baumeister & Leary, 1995). Although this desire has been variously labeled, individuals' needs for initiating, developing, and maintaining social ties, especially close ones, is reflected in a litany of studies and a host of theories. For example, available evidence shows that individuals are predisposed to seek social bonds (Bowlby, 1969) and that most people seem to form them rather easily and quickly (for review, see Deaux, 1996). Once formed, individuals are often reluctant to break these bonds, even when dissolution is inevitable (e.g., Lacoursiere, 1980). Moreover, cross-cultural research has revealed that the dissolution of close bonds is typically met with protest and can have severe negative impacts on an individual's mental and physiological health (Hazan & Shaver, 1994). In fact, research on physiological and emotional consequences of attachment, overall, has demonstrated that individuals with close social bonds are more emotionally and physiologically healthy (as operationalized in a variety of ways) than individuals without such ties (e.g., Albrecht & Adelman, 1987; Baumeister, 1991). For example, individuals without close bonds report more loneliness and depression (Segrin, 1998). This desire for belongingness also comes across in small group interaction, where individuals treat in-group members much more positively than out-group members, even when groups are created randomly (e.g., Tajfel & Billig, 1974).

    Not surprisingly, this internal drive for connectedness is foundational to many theories of behavior. Attachment theory (for review, see Bartholomew, 1993) is based on the premise that a child's need for bondedness with a caregiver, and that caregiver's reaction to that need, helps shape relational behavior throughout our lives. In a similar vein, motivational theorists argue that inclusion is a basic human need (e.g., McAdams & Powers, 1981), and SPT (Altman & Taylor, 1973) assumes that individuals disclose in order to fulfill their basic need for belongingness. In this sense, it seems contradictory to suggest that this need to develop and protect social bonds serves as motivation to *avoid* disclosure. Yet, available research on topic avoidance implies exactly that.

Relationship Protection and Topic Avoidance.   Although relatively few stud- ies have examined the motivations underlying topic avoidance, those that have consistently find the desire for relationship protection (variously op- erationalized) to be a strong motivating factor encouraging topic avoidance. Baxter and Wilmot (1985), for example, found that fear regarding potential negative relational impact was the primary factor motivating topic avoidance in cross-sex relationships. Relatedly, Hatfield (1984) found that fear of abandonment (conceptualized as concern over relationship deescalation or termination) was a common concern underlying individuals' decisions to avoid certain topics in intimate relationships. Finally, our research program has shown relationship protection to be an important factor leading to topic avoidance in close relationships. Interestingly, however, the goal of relational protection motivated avoidance in certain relationships more than in others. Specifically, we have found children to be motivated by relationship protec- tion in their decision to avoid disclosure with parents more than with siblings (Guerrero & Afifi, 1995a). Relatedly, in a study of friendships (Afifi & Guerrero, 1998), our results showed that the goal of relational protection encouraged avoidance for males more than females, and with male targets more than females targets. The diversity of these patterns across relationship types reflects the influence of personal, social, and relational factors in the salience of particular goals and emphasizes the complexity of goals as pre- dictors of behavior.

Although the goal of bondedness clearly motivates disclosure and infor- mation searches, the aforementioned findings also unequivocally demon- strate that this goal sometimes underlies decisions to avoid these processes. A member of an opposite-sex friendship dyad interviewed in a recent study by Afifi and Burgoon (1998) articulated the logic behind avoidance as a relationship-protecting strategy. When asked what he avoids discussing in his relationship and why, he noted discussing the state of their relationship and explained that "If you bring that stuff back up [relationship state], you don't know what it's going to cause, you know . . . so it's safer to just avoid it . . . safer on the relationship" (p. 269). His answer reflects the perception that avoiding disclosure can sometimes protect relationships from the harm that might be brought by disclosure. In sum, individuals sometimes embrace blissful ignorance. When people are uncertain regarding the relational impact of self-disclosure, they are often willing to sacrifice the possible increased intimacy that disclosure may produce in favor of protecting their relation- ships from possible destruction.

Relationship Destruction and Topic Avoidance.   Paradoxically, in addition to using topic avoidance to help protect or enhance relationships, individuals sometimes use topic avoidance to help destroy or deescalate relationships. Knapp's interactional stage model shows how avoidance is used to accomplish relational disengagement (Knapp & Vangelisti, 1992). In the *circum-scribing* stage, individuals constrict communication, reducing the depth, breadth, and quantity of self-disclosure. In the next stage, *stagnating*, communication is at a standstill, with couples avoiding many conversational topics. Self-disclosure about the relationship itself is especially avoided during this stage. The *avoiding* stage is characterized by attempts to completely avoid interaction. When communication does occur, it is typically brief. Relatedly, Baxter's (1982) work on relationship disengagement strategies features avoidance or withdrawal as a common tactic.

In a similar vein, people may use topic avoidance as a way of preventing an existing relationship from escalating. For example, if you do not want someone to get too close to you, you might limit the conversation to superficial topics. In our qualitative data on topic avoidance between parents and children, one teen wrote the following:

> My mom remarried about a year ago. I don't like my stepdad at all. He is always trying to act like my real dad and boss me around. I resent this. He will *never* be my dad. I already have a dad. I really hate it when he tries to get all close to me by asking about my life. He'll try to cozy up to me and ask all about my friends and stuff like he's my buddy or something. I make sure I don't tell him *anything* but he never gets the hint.

This example illustrates how people can use topic avoidance to keep intimacy from developing. Some people may use this strategy routinely. The attachment theory literature, for example, describes two attachment styles that are based on intimacy avoidance. *Fearful avoidant* individuals avoid intimacy because they are afraid that if they allow themselves to get too close to others they may be rejected and/or get hurt. *Dismissive avoidant* individuals are fiercely independent and unmotivated to build close relationships (Bartholomew, 1990). Both fearful and dismissive avoidants are likely to avoid discussing relationally oriented issues that would enhance intimacy and closeness.

In sum, topic avoidance is used both when people want to protect their relationships (by avoiding disagreeable topics) and when people want to destroy their relationships (by avoiding topics that increase bondedness). Next, we explore how topic avoidance is used when people want to protect themselves as individuals.

Individual-Based Motivations

Very few motivations have received greater scholarly attention than the desire to protect one's individual identity. Decades of research have been devoted to understanding the ways in which needs related to our identities shape our cognitions and behavior. The result is an impressive corpus of knowledge that has served as the foundation for several theories of identity management (for a review, see Schlenker, 1980). Although scholars have argued about whether individuals prefer identity-enhancing or identity-verifying feedback (for discussion of this debate, see Swann, 1990), they almost unanimously agree that behavior is motivated by identity needs (for review, see Schlenker, 1985).

This interest in shaping our self-image, variously labeled impression management (Tracy, 1990), self-identification (Schlenker, Britt, & Pennington, 1996), or facework (Cupach & Metts, 1994), has been shown to directly impact behavioral choices in both routine and extraordinary circumstances. For example, Guerrero and Afifi (1998) found that jealous individuals who were motivated to maintain self-esteem tended to deny feeling jealousy and to avoid discussing their feelings with their partners. Albas and Albas (1988) succinctly explained college students' post-exam behaviors from an impression-management perspective. Evidence of the motivating nature of self-enhancement needs in more unexpected contexts is found in Afifi's (1999) examination of safe-sex behavior and Holtgraves' (1988) analysis of gambling activities. In these studies, and *many* others, the data show that behavior is directly influenced by concerns regarding impressions.

However, individuals do not only seek to present positive images of themselves; they also hope to disassociate themselves from undesirable identities (e.g., Schlenker, 1985). In fact, some have argued that this desire to distance ourselves from identity-threatening information is more motivational than is the desire to be linked with positive impressions (e.g., Leary & Kowalski, 1990). Consistent with this logic, Ogilvie (1987) found that behavior is influenced more by a desire to protect against a negative or undesirable identity than by a motivation to push toward a desirable one. For example, a child attempting to convince her parents that she is responsible may take pains to hide facts about her irresponsible behavior from her parents. These efforts may be as important to the success of her identity goals as her ability to perform responsible behavior. Further evidence for the importance of avoiding identity threats comes from research on the common use of disclaimers in everyday interaction (e.g., Hewitt & Stokes, 1975) and on the use of repair strategies following identity-threatening behaviors (Cupach & Metts, 1994). In sum, individuals avoid identity-threatening behavior and its associated negative arousal state, while also seeking to associate themselves with identity-bolstering information and its associated positive arousal state.

It is important to note that the *target* of this "identity work" has, thus far, been left unaddressed in our brief review of identity-management literature. Most of the reviewed literature adopts a conceptualization of impression management that involves an interest in studying individuals' desire to manage their impressions in the eyes of others (e.g., Baumeister, 1982). However, another conceptualization focuses on individuals' psychological needs to protect their identity within themselves (e.g., to convince *themselves* that they are competent or to protect their beliefs about their own identity; e.g., Greenwald & Breckler, 1985). In the former conceptualization, individuals' private self-impressions are less important than the success of the impression that they are able to create for others. The opposite is true for the latter definition.

Besides attending to concerns with impression formation, another individually based motivation guiding avoidance behavior is the motivation to maintain private boundaries from within which we can develop our sense of autonomy. Research on privacy, dialectical processes, and the "separation–individuation" process has found that people need to maintain their own "space" in order to feel independent and competent. In fact, dyadic needs for connection and bondedness are often balanced with individual needs for autonomy and privacy. Petronio (1991), in her work on communication boundary management (CBM) theory, recognizes this need to balance connection and privacy. She argues that even married couples must maintain a sense of separateness if they are to be fully satisfied in their relationships. As she stated,

> Marital couples are expected to tell each other private thoughts and feelings to increase openness. At the same time, they are expected to maintain a sense of their own identity by protecting themselves through controlling the flow of private information to each other. (Petronio, 1991, p. 336)

This need for privacy is also prominent in many theories about relationships and social development. For example, Baxter's (1988, 1990, 1991) work on dialectics theory shows that people have needs for both autonomy and connection and for openness and closedness. If individuals sacrifice autonomy for connection, they will be engulfed by the relationship and could lose their own individual identities. In the social development literature, Blos (1962) discusses the separation-individuation process whereby children develop an individual identity apart from their parents (see also Steinberg & Silverberg, 1986). During this process, privacy becomes of paramount importance to the child.

It is clear from the extant literature that these diverse individual-based motivations, while separate processes, work together to shape behavioral decisions (e.g., Leary & Kowalski, 1990). People are likely to use topic avoidance to protect their public identities, their private identities, *and* their needs for autonomy and privacy. These motivations are discussed in more detail next.

Identity Management and Topic Avoidance. Just as research has shown that disclosure is often enacted strategically to bolster one's identity, so it is that disclosure is *avoided* to protect identity against harm. Consistent with the past motivations research, we have conceptualized self-protection as a desire to manage both private and public identities, and operationalized it as "wanting to avoid judgment, embarrassment, and criticism, as well as wanting to avoid feeling vulnerable" (Guerrero & Afifi, 1995a, p. 280). Our research on topic avoidance has consistently found self-protection to be among the most salient motivations underlying decisions to avoid disclosure. For example, in our study of avoidance in families (Guerrero & Afifi, 1995a), we found the desire to protect the self to be the most consistent predictor of overall levels of topic avoidance across all family relationships except sisters. In fact, this motivation alone accounted for between 25% and 40% of the variance in topic avoidance across different family relationships, which provides strong evidence for its role as a motivator of behavior. In a similar vein, our analysis of topic avoidance in friendships (Afifi & Guerrero, 1998) showed self-protection to be the only motivation that predicted topic avoidance in all three relationship types: male same-sex friendships, female same-sex friendships, and cross-sex friendships. Children and teens (ranging from 10 to 18 years old) report engaging in topic avoidance with their parents to protect themselves from punishment, criticism, and embarrassment (Guerrero & Afifi, 1995b). Others studying topic avoidance have also confirmed the important role of self-protection. Hatfield (1984), for example, found fears regarding exposure and the loss of identity to be two primary reasons that individuals avoid disclosure.

Other reasons cited by participants of topic avoidance studies also fall under this motivation to manage impressions. We have found social inappropriateness (conceptualized as a perception that the disclosure would be socially unacceptable) to be a reason that is a particularly good predictor of avoiding certain topics (e.g., Afifi & Guerrero, 1998; Guerrero & Afifi, 1995a). Considerable evidence suggests that such fears about the social acceptability of a behavior are motivated by the need to protect the public identity from harm (for review, see Schlenker, 1985).

Privacy and Topic Avoidance.   Research suggests that different people have different needs for privacy, and that privacy needs change over time. Petronio and Martin's (1986) research suggests that because men have stronger needs to control privacy than women do, they practice more topic avoidance and less self-disclosure. Burke, Weir, and Harrison (1976) found that husbands tend to "compartmentalize" home- and work-related environments more often than wives do. As a result, it seems that men see home and work as separate topics, with home being more appropriate to discuss with their wives than work. Women, on the other hands, tend not to distinguish between home- and work-related topics as much. This may be because women have less rigid privacy boundaries than men do (see Petronio & Martin, 1986).

Our research on topic avoidance in parent–child relationships also suggests that individual needs for privacy play a role in regulating topic avoidance and self-disclosure. Specifically, we found a small but significant association between teenagers' needs for privacy (operationalized as how important privacy is to them) and their tendency to avoid discussing topics with their parents. In our qualitative data on children's topic avoidance in families, one of the respondents expressed her need for psychological privacy this way:

> It really pisses me off when my mom comes into my room without knocking or when she picks up the phone when I'm talking to someone. She acts like she owns me. My mom wants me to tell her everything. She thinks she has to know everything about me all the time. I get sick of it. Sometimes I want to tell her it's just not her business. I am almost an adult. I have my own life. I need my privacy.

Notice that the teen who wrote the above passage is concerned with being able to control the environment in a way that protects privacy. One way of protecting her privacy is to rebel against the mother when she wants to know "everything." Such rebellion surely involves topic avoidance.

Our research also suggests that teenagers, who have heightened needs for privacy and autonomy, practice more topic avoidance than preteens or young adults do. Specifically, we found that teens aged 15 to 18 reported more avoidance on a variety of topics (e.g., activities with friends, dangerous behaviors, failures) than did 10- to 12-year-olds or 22- to 25-year-olds. We interpreted this finding as reflecting the separation-individuation process that marks the teenage years.

In sum, the research just discussed suggests that people avoid discussing certain topics because they want to protect or enhance their self-images, or because they want to maintain autonomy and psychological privacy. A final motivation for topic avoidance revolves around the information-seeking function of communication.

Information-Based Motivations

Although it has received less scholarly attention than the two previously discussed motivations, the desire to receive information that is interesting and of high quality likely regulates when and to whom we avoid discussing certain topics. For example, C. R. Berger's research on URT (for review, see C. R. Berger, 1988) has unequivocally established the need for individuals to have a sense of control over their environment. Although the theory began as an explanation of behavior in initial interaction, scholars quickly discovered that individuals' desire to reduce uncertainty (thereby increasing control over their environment) shapes behavior across contexts. One context in which this need for uncertainty reduction surfaces is supportive interactions. Studies of comfort and social support suggest that individuals typically seek support in hopes of reducing uncertainty about an internal state, event, or person (e.g., Mishel, 1984). Ideally, in these circumstances, the support-giver will be able to offer information that will help reduce this uncertainty. Indeed, social support scholars have argued that the search for personal control—the companion goal to the desire to seek information and reduce uncertainty—is the primary factor motivating requests for support (for review, see Albrecht & Adelman, 1987). Recipients of poor support (i.e., individuals whose sense of personal control was not increased) often suffer severe circumstances, ranging from illness to depression and suicide (e.g., Rook, 1985; Seeman & Seeman, 1983). In contrast, supportive interactions that give information and reduce uncertainty have been shown to provide a host of psychological and physiological benefits (e.g., Hammer, 1983). Not surprisingly, individuals skilled at social support are highly prized, while those lacking such skills are less socially desirable (e.g., Samter, 1994).

Quality of Expected Information and Topic Avoidance. Because self-disclosure is often a risky venture that can leave a person vulnerable, people are likely to be "choosy" when deciding to whom they will self-disclose their innermost thoughts and feelings. Moreover, when people self-disclose for purposes of seeking information, they are only likely to disclose to those who they believe will be helpful and responsive to their needs. If a potential target is perceived as unhelpful and/or unresponsive, topic avoidance is likely to occur. In other words, this information-based motivation is apparent when individuals avoid disclosure due to a belief in *partner unresponsiveness* (Afifi & Guerrero, 1998; Guerrero & Afifi, 1995a, 1995b). We have operationalized this motivation as "avoiding topics because one feels the partner will be: (a) unresponsive, (b) think the issue is trivial, or (c) lack the knowledge to handle the problem" (Guerrero & Afifi, 1995a, p. 280). In our research, partner unresponsiveness has been a particularly good predictor of avoidance with male targets. Research shows males are poorer at providing the sense of control that ideally accompanies attempts at support (for review, see Cutrona, 1996). Consistent with this research, our studies of families and friends show avoidance with male targets to be, at least partially, motivated by a perception that they will be unable or unwilling to provide a quality response (Afifi & Guerrero, 1998; Guerrero & Afifi, 1995a, 1995b).

Research on topic avoidance in marriages has produced similar results for unresponsiveness. For example, Burke et al. (1976) noted that perceptions of target unresponsiveness are a common reason for topic avoidance in marriages for both husbands and wives, but particularly for wives. Specifically, 22.6% of wives and 9.8% of husbands reported avoiding disclosure because they expected their spouse to be unresponsive to their problems. Interestingly, however, 19.7% of the husbands reported that they avoided disclosure with their wives because they felt that their spouse lacked knowledge relevant to the problem at hand. None of the wives reported this motivation. Therefore, women may be more likely to avoid disclosure because they expect their partners to be unresponsive, whereas men may be more likely to avoid disclosure because they expect their partners to be unhelpful. In both cases, the perception that the information gained will be of low quality (either in terms of responsiveness or helpfulness) appears to lead to topic avoidance.

Futility of Discussion and Topic Avoidance. Individuals may also avoid certain topics because they think that talking about a particular issue is futile or because they find the topic uninteresting. For example, you might be tired of hearing a friend complain about work. Therefore, you avoid asking questions about your friend's job and you try to change the subject if your friend starts to complain. At other times, people avoid communicating because they feel that they can't change anything or consider it useless to talk about a particular issue. Here is an example from our qualitative data on teens avoiding disclosure with their parents:

> It is a total waste of time to talk to my dad about my SAT scores. We have been over it a million times and no matter how much we talk about it, it doesn't change anything. My college applications are in and I'm going to have to live with my score.

Notice that the teen in this example sees no reason to seek information about this topic and is content to simply ignore it. Of all of the motivations we have discussed in this chapter, the "futility" motivation is the least studied. Yet we expect that people routinely avoid communication or change the subject because they find a particular topic unstimulating, uninteresting, or a "waste of their time."

HIERARCHY OF GOALS AND FUTURE RESEARCH

What makes individuals willing to disclose risky information in certain circumstances and unwilling to do so in others? The answer lies in the relative importance given various goals in any particular context. Although relationship-, individual- and information-based motivations, among others, may be simultaneously operational, their relative salience shifts with the personal, relational, and social context. For example, Schlenker and colleagues (Schlenker et al., 1996; Schlenker, Britt, Pennington, Murphy, & Doherty, 1994) have outlined three antecedent conditions that influence the relative salience of impression management as a goal. The first factor is the extent to which the disclosure reflects onto highly valued and central components of the identity. For example, individuals whose identity is *centrally* tied (with a particular audience) to being "in control" will be very hesitant to disclose information about behaviors that reflected a loss of control. Second, the goal of impression management varies in salience to the extent that failure to achieve success in the goal may result in potentially vital negative consequences. For example, Leary and Kowalski (1990) note that impression management increases in importance when the target is relied upon for valued outcomes. Third, the more that the self-disclosure relates to the violation of a highly valued rule of social appropriateness (e.g., being respectful), the more salient self-protection becomes. For example, if one believes that respecting elders is an important part of noble conduct, then he or she is unlikely to disclose information to elders that may imply disrespect.

Future research may uncover similar criteria for determining the goal salience of relationship- and information-based motivations for topic avoidance. Given that individuals shy away from behavior or disclosure that may threaten a *cherished* relationship (for review, see Baumeister & Leary, 1995), we might expect the goal of relationship protection to be particularly salient in satisfying relationships. Indeed, that is what we have found (e.g., Afifi & Guerrero, 1998; Guerrero & Afifi, 1995a). Future research on topic avoidance should examine the role that relational alternatives play in predicting the salience of the relationship-protection goal. This goal may also strongly motivate individuals whose relational alternatives are low to avoid potentially relationship-threatening disclosures, as evidenced in Cloven and Roloff's (1993b, 1994) research on conflict avoidance. The salience of information-based motivations may be closely tied to the nature of the topic being avoided. Individuals may be most likely to cite target unresponsiveness as a reason for topic avoidance in situations in which advice is the desired outcome of disclosure (e.g., disclosing about a recent failure). Again, our research on topic avoidance generally supports such a prediction (e.g., Guerrero & Afifi, 1995a). On the other hand, the salience of information-based motivations may also be partly a function of the extent to which an individual displays high or low need for closure, as some research by Webster and Kruglanski (1994) has shown.

In sum, further research needs to be conducted to help explain shifts in the salience of motivations or goals underlying topic avoidance in relationships. What is clear, however, is that (a) individuals often choose to avoid disclosure rather than risk the perceived personal or relational consequences of disclosure; (b) individuals report relatively consistent motivations for why they avoid disclosure; and (c) the salience of these motivations changes based on personal, social, and relational contexts. Future research on these and other issues related to topic avoidance will help scholars understand how people balance needs for revelation and concealment within their relationships. If communication is the bridge to understanding between two people, topic avoidance may be one barrier that helps people maintain mystery and protect their personal and relational identities, thereby keeping needs for expression and privacy in balance.

13
▼▼▼▼▼▼▼▼

Aggressiveness in Privacy-Seeking Behavior

Aileen L. S. Buslig
Arizona State University

Judee K. Burgoon
Arizona State University

Although privacy is sought at one time or another in virtually every human culture, society's acceptance of one's claims to privacy is not always forthcoming (Nyberg, 1993). The reasons for this conflict are plentiful. Sometimes society's need for openness and disclosure runs counter to one's own need for closedness and privacy. Much of the work rests upon the individual to strike the balance between revealing and concealing just enough to satisfy both the individual and society.

Kottler (1990) points out that in the past, physical isolation was contrary to survival, because it was necessary for humans to live and work together simply to stay alive. Privacy has many historical and current sociocultural stigmas. The needs of the larger group outweigh the needs of the individual, and people who spend too much time alone are considered potentially dangerous (Hareven, 1991; Sillars & Weisberg, 1987). Additionally, people may be labeled "rude" or "unfriendly" when they are not forthcoming with personal information, and may be branded with the assumption of a host of undesirable personality traits because they desire privacy (Pedersen, 1988). The equation of privacy with secrecy, and secrecy with deceitfulness or shame (Bok, 1982; Warren & Laslett, 1980), has given privacy a bad reputation. Even individuals may stigmatize privacy, when they confuse privacy and aloneness with being lonely (Kottler, 1990).

LEVELS OF AGGRESSION

How persons seek privacy may be considered in terms of the aggressiveness of their actions. Previous research on privacy mechanisms by Buslig (1994) suggested that strategies used by people to procure privacy can be thought of as aggressive or nonaggressive, or a blending of the two (deemed moderately aggressive). A discussion of the biological basis of privacy by Klopfer and Rubenstein (1977) also suggests a tripartite division of privacy strategies, as they note that animals may withdraw, conceal, or threaten physical aggression to protect their privacy.

Assertiveness training reached the height of popularity in the 1970s, and it has become a truism that assertiveness is a superior strategy to either aggressiveness or nonassertiveness in obtaining goals with the most positive outcomes. However, some research does not bear out this belief. In a study of aggressive, assertive, and apologetic requests, McCampbell and Ruback (1985) found that one third of their subjects incorrectly identified which style they had been exposed to, with all claiming that the style was more aggressive than it was actually conceived to be. Related to this finding, Stern (1990) found that even the most nonassertive communication style was judged assertive by her subjects. As Hull and Schroeder (1979) suggested, it is unlikely that the typical person distinguishes assertion from aggression the way that scholars do. Therefore, it is not whether a behavior can be defined objectively as aggressive, but rather how the act is labeled that is important, and if the target of the act defines it as aggressive, he or she is likely to retaliate (Felson, 1981).

Furthermore, nonaggressive strategies are often found to be the least damaging to relationships. Although some studies comparing aggressive versus assertive styles determined that assertiveness was perceived more positively (Hollandsworth, 1977; Hollandsworth & Cooley, 1978; Woolfolk & Dever, 1979), nonassertiveness usually resulted in better perceptions than assertiveness. Epstein (1980) found that a submissive requesting style elicited the least amount of anger, and the most compliance and sympathy, of four styles and was always rated significantly more positively than assertiveness. When considering the social or relational impact of different requesting strategies, research suggests that nonaggressive strategies work best (Hollandsworth & Cooley, 1978; Hull & Schroeder, 1979; Kelly, Kern, Kirkley, Patterson, & Keane, 1980; McCampbell & Ruback, 1985).

However, while previous research has shown that the use of less aggressive requests usually results in more positive relational outcomes, the reasons for this finding are largely unexplained. People's perceptions of relational messages (Burgoon & Hale, 1984) may provide clues as to why aggressiveness may be detrimental to relationships. To the extent that levels of aggressiveness are perceived as differing in pleasantness, dominance, and composure, one may conclude that some privacy-seeking behaviors will result in more compliance or better relational communication and impression management.

PERCEPTIONS OF AGGRESSIVENESS

Privacy seekers are likely to feel the need to display pleasantness and cooperation, even while trying to disengage themselves, especially if relational concerns are present. Messages of intimacy, liking/love, friendliness, trust, affiliativeness, and general positive regard all rely on the conveyance of pleasantness (Burgoon & Hale, 1984; Wilmot, 1980). However, a desire for privacy also conveys a desire to avoid others, which is strongly correlated with feelings of displeasure (Mehrabian, 1981). The indirect conveyance of a desire for privacy lessens accountability and culpability for one's actions that is not possible with more direct methods. Although the use of indirect strategies may not be perceived as pleasant, they are undoubtedly more pleasant than directly aggressive strategies.

One's ability to influence or control others and the situation at hand is related to relational messages of dominance (Burgoon & Hale, 1984). To achieve or restore privacy, it may be necessary to display some level of dominance (Burgoon, Buller, & Woodall, 1996), but at the risk of relational harmony. People are often less well liked if they appear dominating (Bochner, Kaminski, & Fitzpatrick, 1977). Wilmot (1980) points out that greater relational control or management will result from the avoidance of obviously dominating behaviors. Therefore, indirect strategies may be chosen by privacy seekers to lessen the appearance of being dominating or domineering.

However, nonaggressive and moderately aggressive strategies are unlikely to be equally low in dominance, either in action or perception. As mentioned previously, moderately aggressive strategies are described as such because they exhibit some characteristics of both aggressive and nonaggressive strategies. Specifically, moderately aggressive strategies are expected to help people "stand their ground," neither fighting nor taking flight. Because this defense of one's privacy is neither the totally submissive or frightened posture of nonaggressiveness, nor the totally insolent or frightening posture of aggressiveness, moderately aggressive privacy strategies are expected to be perceived as moderately dominant as well.

Composure is positively valued in typical communication exchanges. People who appear composed are usually judged to be more competent or credible communicators (Burgoon & Koper, 1984; Dillard & Spitzberg, 1984) and are likely to maintain better impressions than do those who display more negative arousal. Furthermore, people may try to appear composed as a protective feature of their self-presentation style, in order to decrease the possibility of challenges from others (Arkin, 1981).

However, neither highly aggressive nor unaggressive strategies may appear particularly composed. People who seek privacy aggressively may be perceived as "out of control," while those seeking privacy nonaggressively may seem startled. Strategies that are neither highly aggressive nor unaggressive may therefore actually reflect increased control of arousal, as well as be perceived as more controlled and composed than either extreme.

Based on these arguments, three hypotheses are forwarded about the relational messages conveyed via privacy-seeking behaviors:

H1: Aggressive strategies are perceived as less pleasant than less (moderate or nonaggressive strategies.

H2: There is a direct monotonic relationship between perceived dominance and aggressiveness of strategies.

H3: Moderately (non)aggressive strategies are perceived as more composed than either more or less aggressive strategies.

RELATIONAL IMPACT OF AGGRESSIVENESS

Seeking privacy may have various undesirable effects on our relationships with others. Strangers may view privacy-seeking strategies as rude or unsociable, while friends may feel that the privacy seeker is betraying the meaning of friendship itself, interpreting the privacy behaviors as rejection, a reduction in closeness, a lack of trust, or not enough liking to share private information or time. Given that privacy seeking is fraught with potentially negative relational repercussions, a general expectation for unaggressive strategy use seems reasonable, yet the consequences of our privacy behaviors may not be the same for all types of relationships.

The contrast between friends and strangers can demonstrate the differences in relational impact that might result from privacy-seeking behavior. On one hand, it may be that one would avoid using aggressive strategies with friends (or other well-acquainted individuals) more so than with strangers, because of greater desire for relational harmony in such long-term relationships. For example, Baxter (1984) found that the use of polite strategies increased in close relationships. The relatively small possibility of establishing a relationship in the future with any particular stranger threatens fewer lasting effects of using more aggressive privacy mechanisms.

On the other hand, the increased acceptance and trust that accompanies friendship also suggests that people may be more "honest" in their expressions and disclosures than they are with strangers (e.g., Millar & Rogers, 1987). People are allowed more freedom of behavior with those with whom they feel secure, suggesting that the use of aggressive strategies with intimate others should be less risky in the long term. However, Stern's (1994) research on confrontation between friends found no significant relationship between the use of confrontation strategies and behavioral or affective interdependence. This suggests that regardless of level of closeness and interactivity, many friends are hesitant to directly express negative feelings when they have a grievance, such as when a friend invades their privacy.

Because of the transience of interaction, privacy seekers may feel freer to choose strategies with regard to instrumental effectiveness rather than relational sensitivity when dealing with strangers. As strangers, privacy seekers still face the possibility of being drawn into open conflict in response to their own aggressiveness, but the potential for extended repercussions is less, since there is little "relationship" to damage in the first place. Therefore, an argument for either more *or* less aggressive strategy use by friends, in contrast to strangers, can be made, but it is believed that increased concern for the established relationship will "win out" in this instance:

H4: People use less aggressive strategies with friends than with strangers.

The problem with using indirect or inoffensive tactics, however, is in the chance that they will also be less effective in reducing or eliminating others' intrusiveness (Hull & Schroeder, 1979). In these cases, privacy seekers may experience less privacy than they desire, and feel the need to resort to using more clear, direct, and/or aggressive strategies if indirect mechanisms have proven inadequate. Although Epstein's research (1980) found that a submissive style achieved the most compliance to a request, most other research supports the conclusion that more aggressive styles are at least more objectively effective, if not relationally effective, in gaining privacy (e.g., Hollandsworth & Cooley, 1978; Hull & Schroeder, 1979; Woolfolk & Dever, 1979).

However, there are several other mitigating factors why persons may not use aggressive strategies to defend their privacy. When one anticipates that an intruder may react negatively to a request for privacy, one is more likely to make the request as inoffensively as possible, in an effort to minimize negative consequences (Felson, 1981; Stern, 1994). Privacy seekers also may be concerned about the impact of the request on their immediate or future interactions with the intruder.

The use of aggressiveness itself is risky regardless of one's relationship to the intruder, because the confrontational nature of the most aggressive strategies opens one up to the possibility of overt conflict. Furthermore, the unpredictability of strangers may make tactful, yet assertive, comments or behaviors risky. People may interpret "negatively assertive" behavior, such as a request for privacy, as less aggressive and more acceptable when enacted by friends than by strangers (Lewis & Gallois, 1984), but nevertheless, may still be hurt by such behavior. Furthermore, expectations of negative consequences may influence privacy seekers' levels of aggressiveness, which may in turn influence their satisfaction with the outcome of the situation.

A privacy seeker's satisfaction can be considered in two parts: (a) satisfaction with the outcome of the situation, and (b) satisfaction with one's response to the situation. For example, one could be dissatisfied with the outcome (e.g., the privacy seeker revealed a piece of information deemed private), but satisfied with one's response (e.g., the privacy seeker did not appear rude or unsociable), or vice versa. It is also possible that a person could be satisfied with both the response and the outcome to the privacy situation, or dissatisfied with both, and that feelings of satisfaction may be unrelated to levels of aggressiveness. Although some research may support the belief that more aggressive behaviors will be more effective in achieving privacy, these same aggressive behaviors may be detrimental to one's relationships and one's own view of self, resulting in dissatisfaction with one's response even though increased privacy was the outcome.

Based on the above, the following hypotheses and research question are proposed:

H5:   Privacy seekers who anticipate greater negative consequences use less aggressive strategies.

H6:   There is a direct monotonic relationship between strategy aggressiveness and negative relational impact.

RQ1:   Is privacy seekers' level of strategy aggressiveness related to satisfaction with (a) their response, and (b) the outcome of the situation?

THREAT AND JUSTIFICATION

The level of threat perceived by privacy seekers may cause them to use more aggressive means of protecting their privacy. Derlega and Chaikin (1977) suggested that when self-disclosure is threatening, people will take steps to prevent the revelation of that information. If the desire for privacy is great enough, then it is likely that more aggressive strategies will be used to protect one's privacy. Furthermore, people who feel highly threatened by privacy invasions may react more impulsively and emotionally (i.e., aggressively) than those who feel less threatened, as a result of falling into an automatic mode of defensiveness or hostility.

Similarly, if the reason for seeking privacy is considered legitimate or justified, one may feel the use of more aggressive strategies is also justified (Felson, 1981; Haggard & Werner, 1990). The need to perform a task without interruption (Werner & Haggard, 1992), the protection of information for security reasons (Westin, 1970), and the desire or need to engage in socially condoned private behavior (Laufer, Proshansky, & Wolfe, 1973) may all be construed as justifiable reasons for seeking privacy. Therefore, two more hypotheses are forwarded relating to the legitimate use of aggressive privacy mechanisms:

H7: There is a direct monotonic relationship between privacy seekers' feelings of threat and the aggressiveness of their privacy strategies.

H8: There is a direct monotonic relationship between privacy seekers' feelings of justification and the aggressiveness of their privacy strategies.

PRIVACY PROTECTION AND RESTORATION

Not all privacy-seeking instances start with the same motivation to act. A brief comment should be made at this point to clarify the difference between the two privacy-seeking types, privacy protection and privacy restoration, that contribute to people's choice to be more or less aggressive. The main difference between privacy protection and privacy restoration is that protection is a proactive response to a potential loss of privacy or threat of invasion, whereas restoration is a reactive response to an invasion that has already occurred, or is in the midst of occurring.

These two privacy-seeking types may prompt the use of different behaviors. For example, a person seeking privacy protection may have a more thoughtful, less aroused or extreme, solution to his or her "problem" than someone who must deal with an unexpected invasion. Furthermore, people seeking privacy restoration often do not have the same range of options at their disposal, such as manipulating environmental features for more privacy, and may feel more behaviorally constrained by various elements of the situation. Therefore, it is important to consider whether a privacy seeker's behavior is motivated by a need to proactively deter, or to reactively respond to, an invasion of privacy.

METHOD

Participants

Participants were drawn from both student and adult nonstudent populations. A total of 152 participants (75 males, 77 females) completed the study, including 80 students and 72 nonstudents. Students, recruited from a large southwestern university for extra credit, were mostly single (86%) and White, non-Hispanics (64%), with an average age of 23 years. Nonstudents were drawn from the Southwest, Southeast, and Midwest regions of the United States via snowball sampling, and participated voluntarily (71%), or for passes to a movie theater (29%). Nonstudents were more often married (47%) than single (36%) and, like the student sample, tended to be White, non-Hispanics (72%), with an average age of 36 years. Forty-six percent of nonstudents indicated that they had earned a 4-year college degree or better.

Procedure and Measures

A self-report questionnaire was utilized rather than a laboratory experiment to allow for descriptive analyses of people's naturally occurring privacy experiences. All participants received envelopes that could be sealed to increase their sense of security and response privacy. All participants were given the opportunity to complete the questionnaire at a time and place of their own choosing (e.g., at home) and were asked to return the questionnaire within two weeks.

Open-Ended Questions. Participants were asked to provide a written description of a time when they felt they had less privacy than they desired, specifically when they were trying to work or to complete some task. Half of the participants ($n = 76$; 36 male, 40 female) were randomly assigned to describe a situation in which a stranger was involved, whereas the other half described a situation involving a friend (39 males, 37 females). Participants were also randomly assigned to describe a situation in which they attempted to protect their privacy prior to intrusion ($n = 79$) or a situation in which their privacy was invaded and had to be restored ($n = 73$).

Participants were asked to describe the situation and their response to it, including where and when the situation occurred, what they did to protect or regain their privacy and why, how they felt after the situation had passed, if there were any relational consequences to their actions, and if they would have done anything differently if they could have.

Two coders were trained to analyze participants' written responses for participants' overall level of aggressiveness in the situation. For each written account, coders were instructed to categorize participants as either aggressive, moderately aggressive, or nonaggressive, in order to allow for treatment of the participants' aggressiveness as a predictor variable in statistical analyses. Inter-rater reliability for aggressiveness was .79.

Closed-Ended Items. Participants also responded to a series of statements using 7-point Likert-type statements assessing their feelings about, and responses to, the invasion.

To verify that participants perceived different levels of intimacy with strangers and friends, the *relational intimacy scale* (Burgoon & Koper, 1984) assessed participants' amount of intimate connection to the intruder and status differences between the participant and the intruder. Participants' ratings of their own aggressiveness was measured as a double-check against coders' classifications of participants into aggressiveness categories. Cronbach alpha coefficient reliabilities for these manipulation check variables were .77 for intimacy and .60 for aggressiveness.

Relational impact measured whether the privacy response resulted in a negative relational outcome, and was expected to be related to participants' *anticipation of negative consequences* (Stern, 1994), a measure of the amount of forethought and concern about possible intruder perceptions and responses to the request for privacy. Cronbach alpha coefficient reliabilities for the above measures were .69 for impact and .60 for anticipation. Two measures, *satisfaction with response* and *satisfaction with outcome,* were combined into a general *satisfaction* rating of participants' contentment with results of the situation once it had passed due to their relatively high inter-correlation, $r(152) = .67$, and higher combined inter-item reliability, $r = .77$.

Participants' perceptions of *threat* due to the intruder's privacy invasions, and participants' own feelings of *justification* (i.e., participants felt that they were justified in their desire for privacy), were expected to anticipate more aggressive strategy use. Finally, to determine participants' perceptions of their behavior, measurements of *pleasantness, dominance,* and *arousal/composure* were also collected. Reliabilities for these measures were: threat, $r = .67$; justification, $r = .50$; pleasantness, $r = .80$; dominance, $r = .70$; and arousal/composure, $r = .79$.

RESULTS

Data were analyzed using chi-squares, correlations, and MANOVAs. MANOVAs utilized a 2 (relationship type) × 2 (privacy-seeking type) × 3 (level of aggressiveness) × 2 (participant gender) × 2 (subsample) factorial design. All blocking variables and two-way interactions, which resulted in F-ratios less than 1, were dropped from final analyses. Gender and subsample were included in analyses in order to determine whether data should be interpreted separately for male and female responses and for student and nonstudent responses. Few differences due to these factors were revealed, allowing collapse across categories for most analyses. However, a few gender and subsample differences did occur, and are reported where appropriate. The privacy-seeking condition produced no significant differences for protection versus restoration, and therefore both conditions are combined for all analyses in this report.

When specific hypotheses are addressed by the findings, significant univariate tests are reported regardless of whether multivariate tests were also significant, so that meaningful differences due to individual variables might still be recognized, even if composite multivariate effects masked those differences (Huberty & Morris, 1989). As an initial step, intercorrelations were computed among measures in order to determine whether further data reduction was necessary and MANOVA was appropriate for specific sets of variables.

As a result of this preliminary investigation, MANOVAs were performed for two sets of dependent variables: (a) situation variables (relational impact, justification, threat, anticipation, satisfaction), average $r = .21$, Bartlett's test of sphericity = 82.48, $p < .001$ (10 df); and (b) Senders' relational messages (participants' ratings of own pleasantness, dominance, composure), average $r = .30$, Bartlett's test of sphericity = 48.80, $p < .001$ (3 df). To reduce the risk of Type I error, all univariate analyses were adjusted using the Bonferroni procedure (Rosenthal & Rosnow, 1984).

Manipulation Checks

Relational Intimacy. Differences in relational intimacy are often an integral part of how we define types of relationships. As expected, participants described closer relational intimacy with intruders in the friendship condition ($M = 4.90$) than in the stranger condition ($M = 3.14$), $F(1, 150) = 58.45$, $p < .001$, $\eta^2 = .28$.

Aggressiveness. ANOVA and planned polynomial contrasts confirmed that coders' classifications of participants' responses on levels of aggressiveness coincided with participants' own perceptions of their behavior, $F(2, 149) = 24.29$, $p < .001$, $\eta^2 = .25$. A linear contrast, $t(83) = 6.94$, $p < .001$, revealed that participants classified as aggressive by coders also perceived their behavior as more aggressive ($M = 5.09$) than participants in the moderately aggressive category ($M = 3.68$), who perceived themselves as more aggressive than participants coded as nonaggressive ($M = 2.93$).

Hypotheses and Research Question

Hypotheses H1, H2, and H3. Participants' ratings of their own pleasantness, dominance, and composure were also tested and found to support hypotheses H1 and H2, but not H3, multivariate $\Lambda = .82$, $F(6, 278) = 4.78$, $p < .001$, univariate $F(2, 141) = 7.43$, $p = .001$, $\eta^2 = .10$ for pleasantness, univariate $F(2, 141) = 9.87$, $p < .001$, $\eta^2 = .12$ for dominance, and univariate $F(2, 141) = 2.91$, $p = .058$, $\eta^2 = .02$ for composure.

Repeated contrasts revealed that participants perceived their own behavior as significantly less pleasant when using aggressive strategies ($M = 2.93$) than when using moderately aggressive strategies ($M = 4.54$), $t(89) = 3.67$, $p < .001$, whereas moderately aggressive and nonaggressive strategies ($M = 4.43$) were considered equally pleasant, $t(126) = .07$, $p > .10$. A significant univariate interaction effect for subsample by aggressiveness was also found for pleasantness, multivariate $\Lambda = .92$, $F(6, 278) = 1.91$, $p = .079$, univariate $F(2, 141)$ $= 3.57$, $p < .04$, $\eta^2 = .05$. Students felt they were more pleasant when they were moderately aggressive rather than nonaggressive (Agg $M = 3.02$, Mod $M = 4.61$, Non $M = 3.87$), whereas nonstudents perceived themselves as more pleasant when least aggressive (Agg $M = 2.78$, Mod $M = 4.49$, Non $M = 5.18$), $t(126) = 2.47$, $p < .02$.

Repeated contrasts also revealed significant differences for dominance. As predicted, aggressive strategies ($M = 5.45$) were rated higher on dominance than moderately aggressive strategies ($M = 4.24$), $t(89) = 2.98$, $p = .003$, which were rated higher than nonaggressive strategies ($M = 3.76$), $t(126)$ $= 2.16$, $p < .03$.

Participants' ratings of their own composure or feelings of arousal showed the expected pattern, in which moderately aggressive strategies ($M = 3.86$) were perceived as more composed and less aroused than either aggressive ($M = 4.50$) or nonaggressive ($M = 4.28$) strategies (higher Ms reflect greater arousal). However, participants' composure ratings of moderately aggressive strategies differed significantly from aggressive strategies, $t(89) = 2.30$, $p < .03$, but not from nonaggressive strategies, $t(126) = 1.44$, $p > .10$. Additionally, a main effect for gender, multivariate $\Lambda = .94$, $F(3, 139) = 3.06$, $p = .03$, univariate $F(1, 141) = 4.01$, $p < .04$, $\eta^2 = .03$ for composure, suggests that, overall, females ($M = 4.39$) were more aroused by privacy invasions than were males ($M = 3.86$).

Hypothesis H4. Only 24 participants were categorized as having used aggressive strategies to defend their privacy, in comparison to participants who used moderately aggressive ($n = 67$) and nonaggressive ($n = 61$) strategies. Hypothesis H4, which proposed that people will seek to defend their privacy from friends less aggressively than from strangers, was somewhat supported. Participants who were categorized by coders as using aggressive strategies were more likely to be in the stranger ($n = 18$) than in the friend ($n = 6$) condition, $\chi^2 = 6.00$, $df = 1$, $p < .01$, whereas no differences for relationship type were found for moderate aggressiveness, $\chi^2 = .13$, $df = 1$, $p > .10$, or nonaggressiveness, $\chi^2 = 1.33$, $df = 1$, $p > .10$. However, participants' own ratings of their aggressiveness did not differ when the intruder was a friend ($M = 3.45$) versus a stranger ($M = 3.75$), $F(1, 142) = .01$, $p > .10$.

Hypotheses H5, H6, H7, and H8. Hypotheses H5 and H6, which predicted that use of aggressiveness would be inversely related to the anticipation of negative consequences, and directly related to negative impact on one's relationship with the intruder, were supported by MANOVA. However, hypotheses H7 and H8, which investigated the impact of threat and justification on strategy aggressiveness, were not, multivariate $\Lambda = .78$, $F(10, 284)$ $= 3.77$, $p < .001$, univariate $F(2, 146) = 5.62$, $p = .004$, $\eta^2 = .07$ for anticipation, univariate $F(2, 146) = 5.28$, $p = .006$, $\eta^2 = .07$ for impact, univariate $F(2, 146)$ = $.61$, $p > .10$ for threat, univariate $F(2, 146) = .52$, $p > .10$ for justification. Polynomial contrasts revealed an inverse linear trend for level of aggressiveness and participants' anticipation of negative consequences, $t(83)$ = -3.14, $p = .002$. Participants who chose to defend their privacy aggressively ($M = 2.39$) anticipated the fewest negative consequences, followed by those who chose moderately aggressive strategies ($M = 3.04$) and nonaggressive strategies ($M = 3.66$). Correlation between participants' own ratings of their aggressiveness and their anticipation of negative consequences also supported this relationship, $r(152) = -.28$, $p < .001$.

Planned orthogonal contrasts also revealed a linear trend for aggressiveness level and participants' ratings of actual negative relational impact, $t(83)$ = 3.09, $p = .002$. Privacy seekers using aggressive strategies ($M = 3.94$) felt the greatest amount of negative impact on their relationship with the intruder, compared to moderately aggressive strategy users ($M = 2.76$) and nonaggressive strategy users ($M = 2.33$). Participants' own aggressiveness ratings also correlated with negative relational impact, $r(152) = .25$, $p = .001$.

Research Question RQ1. The relationship between satisfaction and the use of aggressiveness was the focus of research question RQ1. An effect for strategy aggressiveness was found, multivariate $\Lambda = .81$, $F(10, 284) = 3.77$, $p < .001$, univariate $F(2, 146) = 5.35$, $p = .006$, $\eta^2 = .07$. Participants were least satisfied with the privacy situation (i.e., its outcome and their response) when they responded least aggressively ($M = 4.96$) and more satisfied when they responded moderately aggressively ($M = 5.79$) or aggressively ($M = 5.59$). However, participants' ratings of their own aggressiveness were not found to be correlated with satisfaction, $r(152) = .08$, $p > .10$ (two-tailed).

DISCUSSION

Although few people deny its necessity, seeking privacy is a risky interpersonal venture. When people cannot maintain adequate amounts of privacy, they may experience stress, but, in requesting privacy, they may experience a different kind of stress if relational ties are strained or conflict ensues. Therefore, privacy seekers find themselves in a precarious situation that requires great skill to manage successfully.

Relationship Effects

The finding that only a relatively small percentage (16%) of participants used assertive or aggressive strategies when seeking privacy lends support to the belief that few will risk arousing negative responses that might accompany such behavior, despite a general belief that we have a right to privacy. Previous research (McCampbell & Ruback, 1985) has found that others already tend to perceive all levels of compliance-gaining behavior as higher in aggression than they really are; therefore, people requesting privacy in any form may run the risk of being perceived as behaving more extremely than is objectively so.

Other research has shown that assertiveness and aggressiveness, compared to less assertive or nonassertive behavior, results in lower ratings of likability (Kelly et al., 1980), less compliance and sympathy, and more anger (Epstein, 1980), and is perceived as less polite, more hostile, and less satisfying to the recipient (Woolfolk & Dever, 1979). The disinclination to seek privacy aggressively appears to be so strong that even one's relationship to the intruder may not play a significant part. Although chi-square analysis did find that people categorized as aggressive were more likely to use such strategies with strangers than with friends, participants' own assessment of their aggressiveness did not differ for relationship type.

People's reluctance to be aggressive when seeking privacy seems relationally sound, because participants who used aggressive strategies felt that their behavior impacted their relationship with the intruder more negatively than those who used moderately aggressive or nonaggressive strategies. Participants who used aggressive strategies reported that their actions were more likely to lead to conflict and explosive responses and to put a strain on their relationship with the intruder. Such reactions are not unexpected, because aggression often begets aggression, and lend support for the belief that requesting privacy is not an easy feat and can have relational repercussions.

Perceptions of Aggressiveness

Competent communication is likely to include an emphasis on appearing pleasant, composed, and moderately dominant, and behaviors that contribute to such perceptions can lead to better relational exchanges. For this study, moderately aggressive behavior was expected to embody the best combination of these three dimensions, in comparison to aggressiveness and nonaggressiveness. Predictions about dominance and pleasantness were clearly supported, while the prediction about composure/arousal was only somewhat less conclusive.

Participants perceived moderately aggressive strategies to be more dominant than nonaggressive strategies, but less dominant than aggressive strategies. Previous research (e.g., Epstein, 1980) shows that dominant behavior may be effective in goal acquisition but potentially detrimental to relationships in high amounts. On the other hand, submissive behavior is often ineffective for reaching instrumental goals, but perceived more positively in terms of interpersonal impressions. However, people who display low dominance may also be seen as less socially competent, which can lead to negative impressions (Burgoon & Koper, 1984). Therefore, moderately aggressive strategies can be advantageous, in that such behaviors may be more effective in gaining privacy and positive relational consequences simultaneously than either aggressive or nonaggressive strategies.

Participants' perceptions of strategy pleasantness were also consistent with predictions. Privacy seekers considered their behavior much less pleasant when they used aggressive strategies than when they used moderately aggressive or nonaggressive strategies. The advantages of appearing pleasant should be obvious. Pleasant behavior is more likely to signal friendliness and cooperation, and one's desire not to be rude or threatening, which may in turn reduce the chance of conflict. Participants' perception of moderately aggressive behaviors as equal in pleasantness to nonaggressive strategies suggests that either strategy would be more relationally effective than aggressive behaviors. However, the other advantages of moderately aggressive strategies may make this strategy a better choice than nonaggressiveness.

Results for perceptions of arousal/composure were less clear cut. Participants' ratings of their own arousal did show the expected pattern for levels of aggressiveness, in that moderately aggressive strategies were perceived as less aroused/more composed than aggressive or nonaggressive strategies, but differences were only significant for comparisons of aggressiveness and moderate aggressiveness. One possibility why moderately aggressive behaviors did not differ from nonaggressive behaviors on arousal ratings is that some moderately aggressive behaviors are themselves arousing. The cognitive anxiety associated with deceptive or assertive behaviors may cause the moderately aggressive participant to feel more aroused than might be apparent to observers, which in turn would affect their composure ratings.

Preinteraction Mediators and Postinteraction Effects of Aggression

Although results of this study confirm that defending one's privacy aggressively increases the risk of negative consequences, the anticipation of such consequences apparently lessens the likelihood that one will use such force. Privacy seekers who indicated the greatest amount of fear that their attempt to gain privacy would result in negative consequences also were rated least aggressive, regardless of perceptions of threat or justification. However, attempts to avoid negative consequences via nonaggression did not translate into more satisfaction with the situation.

In fact, nonaggressiveness resulted in the least amount of satisfaction with the outcome of, and one's own response to, the invasion, suggesting that nonaggressive strategies are ineffective in achieving one's desired amount of privacy. These findings seem to confirm and coincide with a statement by

Burgoon et al. (1989), who concluded that people are reluctant to use direct and aggressive methods to restore privacy, even if these methods might be more effective. Burgoon et al. (1989) stated: "In a culture as obsessed with interpersonal relations as it is individual rights, it is likely that people in actual privacy-invading situations rely far more on passive and subtle strategies than on direct (and potentially more efficacious) ones" (p. 155).

Considering the large disparity between the frequency of nonaggressive and aggressive responses found in the present study, it seems safe to assume that people often bow to outside relational and social pressures, neglecting their own needs for privacy. Nonaggressive strategies may stave off open conflict for privacy seekers trying to avoid contact with others, but they will not necessarily avoid internal conflicts resulting from inadequate privacy. In privacy situations, the problem lies in the balancing of individual and relational needs.

CONCLUSION

The results of this study suggest that, in terms of achieving one's (multiple) goals, using moderately aggressive strategies may be better than using either aggressive or nonaggressive strategies. In their research on conversational retreat, Kellermann, Reynolds, and Chen (1991) propose that moderately aggressive strategies or tactics are likely to be seen as more socially appropriate than aggressive behaviors, and more efficacious than nonaggressive behaviors, a conclusion that might be reached for the present study as well. For example, in this study, moderately aggressive behaviors were seen as more pleasant and composed, making them more appropriate than aggressive strategies, but also more dominant, and subsequently more efficient than nonaggressive strategies. As such, moderately aggressive strategies may embody the best combination of relational message perceptions, balancing efficiency with sensitivity.

Yet one can note other good reasons for "striking a happy medium" via the use of moderately aggressive strategies when seeking privacy. In this study, privacy seekers who chose aggressive strategies perceived that they encountered greater negative consequences and that their relationship with the intruder was more negatively impacted than did those using other strategies. Yet when participants anticipated negative reactions and chose less aggressive methods to defend their privacy, those who employed nonaggressive strategies were least satisfied with their actions and the results of the situation.

The effects of people's own privacy seeking on their relationships with others seems an important, yet relatively little studied area of privacy and communication. People and societies alternate between needs for openness and for closedness, and the fulfillment of these needs must be negotiated with care. By using moderately aggressive privacy-seeking strategies, one may reap both individual and relational benefits, appearing relatively open while being sufficiently closed. The ability to maintain boundaries while maintaining relationships is an indispensable skill for the privacy seeker, yet a skill not easily mastered. The balancing act is precarious indeed.

Family Secrets and the Lie of Identity

Leda Cooks
University of Massachusetts, Amherst

It is the holidays, and as I see Christmas decorations everywhere, hear the carols blaring from loudspeakers perched on telephone poles—the commercial blitzkrieg that comes this time of year—inevitably my thoughts turn to my family. After all, who doesn't associate family with the holidays? And whether thoughts are pleasant or not so pleasant, often it seems that these are the ties that bind.

During this particular holiday season, knowing that I would be writing this chapter (illuminating the concept of self-disclosure), my thoughts are inextricably bound up with ideas of who I am today and the ways in which the stories I had heard and told about my family had always shaped ideas of who I was, and who I thought I should be. Throughout my life it had been taken as given that who you are is, at least in large part, the product of from whence you came.

Of course, years of studying about and researching identity and difference had theoretically altered my views of the stability of the signifier. Identities were multiple, fragmented, informed as much by context and interaction as by the more stable characterizations of race, class, gender, sexuality, ability, and age. I had always believed that who I was was less important than how I created myself in specific moments of interaction, and how, in responding to this "talk," others created me.

Still, I am quite conscious of the importance of family in our society as a primary identity determinant. Our kin and where we are from, how we are positioned based on race, religion, and ethnic identity are, after all, the

197

most important markers of affiliations and of difference in U.S. society. These markers are simultaneously taken to be the most public and the most private symbols of ourselves, containing the most superficial and the most intimate knowledge of our potential as citizens and as private beings. These markers often form the core of disputes over private boundaries under public policy and legislation, where, as in the theme of the women's movement, the personal is political. We learn about ourselves and our histories through family stories, what our ancestors did, the struggles they went through, and the meaning this holds for our own being. These stories are powerful in that they position us as both private and public people. Perhaps it is this talk that most orients us in a society that often bases identity on heritage and birthright.

These stories inform the "self" I share in this chapter, even as a new self is created in the reflection of my past. This chapter is an emotional (in that it is designed to evoke and elicit emotions in ourselves, the subjects of our research, the topics we choose, and the readers of our work), an interpretive (descriptive account of a socially created self), and a critical (commenting on the self, society, and institutions in positioning and informing the stories people tell and which stories are given credence) account of self-disclosure. As such, it makes use of the author's personal experience as a means to understanding the place and position of emotion in everyday life (Ellis, 1991a), even as it positions that experience within the context of communication research on the topic/construct of self-disclosure. Although perceptibly an autoethnography or self-narrative, this piece is not merely a confessional— an unloading of family laundry that needed to be aired. Rather, it is intended as a useful study of our use of stories lived and told in creating the self and what happens when that source or stories about self is revealed to be falsehood. However, the chapter is concerned more with the ways in which our identities are constantly *negotiated*, and with what happens when the family stories are uncovered as secrets, and thus identity is, according to the new account, read as a lack of history.

Accordingly, two issues inform this chapter: (a) the concept of self-disclosure and alternative ways of researching this concept; and (b) identity as it is both theorized and enacted in late modern U.S. society. As these issues are discussed, they inform connections among self-disclosure, identity, and relationships. First, the chapter examines the theoretical and methodological perspectives framing the construct of self-disclosure, the narrative, and subsequent episodes. Then, I discuss the story, my reflections, and subsequent episodes that made the enactment of my "self" (if not the self itself) a secret. In the analysis, concepts from narrative and coordinated management of meaning theories are used to show grammars of identity in the stories lived (those created in live action) and told (those recounted from past experience).

SELF-DISCLOSURE

Self-disclosure has been defined as a way of demonstrating to others who we are and what our needs are (Derlega, 1984) or, more specifically, as the revealing of intimate information about the self in conversation (Nakanishi & Johnson, 1993). In U.S. culture, reciprocal self-disclosure has been seen as a primary prerequisite to the development of healthy and meaningful relationships. This phenomenon has been widely researched in communication over the last 35 years, moving from a focus on personality traits, using scales like Jourard's Self-Disclosure Questionnaire, to an understanding of disclosure as situational and contingent on context and relationships (Duck & Pittman, 1994).

As well, this research has moved from an initial focus on self-disclosure as invariably healthy for relationships to investigating mediating variables that influence the consequences of disclosure. Here, reasons for revealing intimate information about the self are determined by complex interrelationships between an individual's expectations and predictions for relationships and norms, valence, topic, setting, and language variables (Bradac, Hosman, & Tardy, 1978; Gilbert, 1976; Tardy, Hosman, & Bradac, 1981). Self-disclosure has been studied in interpersonal (Derlega et al., 1993), family (C. M. Anderson & Martin, 1995; Buhrmester, 1992; Martin & Anderson, 1995), and intercultural (Ting-Toomey, 1987; Wolfson & Pearce, 1983) settings, among others. Across cultures, researchers have looked at the correlations between self-disclosure and other outcome variables, such as competence (self/other; Ting-Toomey, 1986), communication satisfaction (Nakanishi & Johnson, 1993), and commitment. Research linking gender and self-disclosure (e.g., Hacker, 1981; Stephan & Harrison, 1985; Tannen, 1995) has examined the differences in frequency and type of self-disclosure among men and women and have looked at the impact of these differences on both public (workplace) and private (friendship, marriage, family) lives. Stewart, Cooper, Stewart, and Friedley (1996), summarizing this research, noted that women tend to disclose personal and relational information to serve expressive and affiliative needs, whereas "men tend to disclose about task or goal oriented topics for the purpose of serving instrumental needs" (p. 114).

THEORETICAL AND METHODOLOGICAL
CONSIDERATIONS OF SOCIAL CONSTRUCTIONIST
WORK ON IDENTITY AND SELF-DISCLOSURE

Although scales measuring disclosure have proven valid and reliable, few studies have investigated the external validity of the construct in depth (Duck & Pittman, 1994). Duck and Pittman noted that:

Self-disclosure, like other forms of communication . . . acts to situate the person within particular relationships, but also the act of self-disclosure itself is crafted within the person's own view of the world. . . . Self-disclosure thus serves to regulate the individual, relational, and world view issues that the person stresses. (p. 691)

Following Duck and Pittman's call for alternative methodologies in the study of self-disclosure, interpretive researchers have provided an alternative route for research, noting that self-disclosure is a way of both creating the self and being situated/constructed by others (Leeds-Hurwitz, 1995; Shotter & Gergen, 1989). As Baker and Benton (1994) observed:

Because all knowledge is situated and local rather than based on universal truths, self-disclosure may be viewed as situated, localized, personal and self-defined. . . . Self-disclosure is a highly politicized activity of self-construction, bound up in expectations for appropriateness that are totally dependent on the dominant power structures and the individual's relation to such structures. (p. 221)

Thus, interpretivists and critical theorists have examined the phenomenon somewhat differently, sometimes to examine the construct in more depth (through reflective accounts or interviews) and at other times to question the nature and validity of the construct itself.

This essay falls somewhere in between interpretive and critical approaches, neither accepting self-disclosure as a fully formed phenomenon, observable and testable, nor rejecting its utility as a social form. The quest of this search is not necessarily for a self that is or can be uncovered, bared, or disclosed, but rather for the ways in which the self is created, avowed, disavowed, and constructed in moments which are, ultimately, social. In this view, people create the reality they know in their interactions with others. These interactions structure their reflections and, in turn, alter their actions in various situations. From a social communication perspective, the individual, society, social practices, and institutions are defined as emergent from the communication practices themselves rather than as fixed, separate entities that provide objective responses to particular needs (Pearce & Cronen, 1980; Pearce, 1989). Of the social approaches to studying communication, emotional narrative and coordinated management of meaning (CMM) theory provide the most compelling analysis of narrative as the antecedent or frame for subsequent episodes in which the self and family stories are created, and a way of looking at the consequences of those stories for the disclosure(s) of selves.

Emotional Narrative and Introspective Accounts

Ellis and Bochner (1992) noted that:

> The act of telling a personal story is a way of giving voice to experiences that are shrouded in secrecy. . . . By making intricate details of one's life accessible to others in public discourse, personal narratives bridge the dominions of public and private life. Telling a personal story becomes a social process for making lived experience understandable and meaningful. (pp. 80–81)

Rather than denying subjectivity in accounting for self or presuming that this phenomenon can or should be rendered objectifiable to be valid, emotional narrative complicates matters by sharing the complexities of self-construction with the reader, thus deliberately complicating what it means to disclose the self.

Introspective accounts, then, may be considered the building blocks of emotional narrative. Through reflective examination of one's own and others' emotional experiences, introspection is "conscious awareness of itself, a social process of self-examination involving conversation with oneself" (Ronai, 1992, p. 103). In this chapter, I use introspective narrative in combination with notes taken from actual conversation. Together, the two should provide readers with the necessary components for sharing the cognitive/emotional experience of the researcher, incorporating these descriptions into their own emotional memories, and generating new understandings of how selves are constructed and researched relationally.

Social Constructionism and CMM

Social constructionist theories, according to Pearce (1995), "describe the process of social action from the 'inside,' " seeing "research as both about socially constructed events and objects and as a specific instance of the social construction of events and objects" (p. 89). CMM theory, as social constructionist praxis, places communication at the center of social processes and conversation as the basic unit through which meaning, structure, and action emerge. Persons in conversation are material beings who embody social practices; they "create patterns of practices that constitute their forms of life" (Cronen, 1995, p. 231). Pearce (1994) emphasized that "when we communicate we are not just talking *about* the world, we are literally participating in the creation of the social universe" (p. 75).

A major strength of this approach, as it is applied to the study of self-disclosure, is that CMM analysis gives insight into the relational nature of meaning. CMM helps us understand the multiple layers and positions from which stories are lived and told. Instead of defining selves as entities that mitigate or mediate variables, CMM looks at selves as cocreated among participants in interaction, instructed by patterns of action and the contexts in which they occur. CMM looks at rules for conversation as structuring episodes or grammars of practice. Rules are built on previous interactions but are not limited to the meanings previously given to conversational events. They provide a way of "going on," of coordinating social interaction and providing coherence to social life. Grammars of practice refer to the rule-using abilities that human beings have in acting on and in the world. Furthermore, Cronen (1995) notes that CMM should (among other things) promote "socially useful description, explanation and critique . . ." (p. 231) and "coevolves with both the abilities of its practitioners and the consequences of its use" (p. 232).

In this chapter, I focus my use of this theory and method of analysis on four main concepts of CMM as these concepts illuminate the ways in which enacting identity in relation to others insures secrecy and maintains moral order and the family system: (a) contexts for action, (b) looped patterns, (c) logical forces, and (d) conversational triplets. To begin, CMM has five interrelated *contexts for action*: the self and the way in which people identify themselves under particular conditions; culture, described as a set of actions enacted by a group of people that are similarly patterned in their use of individual and societal resources; episodes, defined as specifically structured and bounded sequences of conversational actions; relationships, denoting sets of patterned links and their reflexive effects on each other; and speech acts, defined as the language used in particular situations that leads to particular meanings within that situation. Each level of meaning is interconnected to the other, yet each also has its logic of action. Thus, I might respond to a perceived attack to my self by threatening the relationship, and that response informs the way I see myself, the relationship, and the possibilities inherent in the pattern of action.

Although levels of meaning are usually hierarchical and can potentially enhance or limit responses of participants, sometimes the relationship between levels becomes looped rather than hierarchical, causing ambiguity in the message. This is known as a *looped pattern*, and is the second concept used in this analysis. Looped patterns can cause action to become locked or static, because they ignore or circumvent the potential abilities of interactants to change the grammar of the interaction. Although looped patterns are normal in most systems, in some cases, called *strange loops*, a paradox results from the actions at one level contradicting or implicating the actions at another, locking participants into negative and sometimes dangerous stories (Pearce, 1994). A woman who wants to be recognized as assertive in the workplace might respond to a challenge of her ideas by standing up for herself because such action demonstrates responsibility and maturity. Yet, if she does so she will be labeled "aggressive" or "domineering" in the context of American cultural patterns. Whichever way she responds to the challenge, her actions will reflect negatively on her perceptions of her ability to perform competently in this context.

The third concept, *logical forces,* is based on the central notion of the socially constructed nature of meaning. To be part of a society means that you must learn to function according to the rules of that society. Rule systems, or "logical forces," govern the affordances and constraints of various actions. People make choices based on what they perceive to be the forces operating in the interaction; they may be aware or unaware of the agency and consequence of their actions (Cronen, 1995).

The fourth concept, that of *conversational triplets,* brings the analysis together. To determine the forces, levels of meaning, and perceived or intended consequences of actions, CMM analysts look at what comes before the statement (the antecedent) as it frames the interaction; the utterance or act itself as it is constituted in the levels of meaning of each participant; and the consequences, the responsive action desired (regardless of whether it was known or produced; Xi, 1991). In the analysis that follows, the story and introspective narrative provide the antecedent, or frame, for the episodes (actions) that follow. The consequences are then analyzed in terms of the affordances and constraints the actions produced and the looped pattern that developed.

With this framework in mind I now turn to the title of this chapter, "Family Secrets and the Lie of Identity," and to recounting the narrative that became the antecedent to secrecy. Referring to identity as a lie points to several possible meanings: (a) that an identity has been revealed to be false, or not one's own; (b) that there are no truths that, taken together, form the sum of one's identity; (c) that, in accepting an alternative truth about identity as a secret, a now false self must be enacted to preserve the secret—and thus the family system. Thus, in discovering that the accepted stories told about one's "self" (in whatever manner that might be conceived) are not true, one must accept that identities are created and negotiated as a means toward the survival and preservation of the system. In this light it is perhaps most clear that it is the *enactment* of the story of identity and not the story as an entity apart from its social construction (lived experience of it) that makes it valid (as experience).

THE STORY OF A SECRET SELF

Using introspective narrative technique, I begin with the story told; that is, the story told to me about my identity. My mother related this story to me when I was 30 years old. The storytelling took place in an Irish pub, where my mother and I had gone for a beer one evening the day after the new year. Once we were seated and the band began to play, my mother started telling me the truth about the self I thought I knew; the secrets she had kept for 30 years unfolded as she told me the story of my birth.

"There is something I need to tell you," she said. "How do I say this?" (Her shoulders raised and frame lifted as she took a deep breath.) "Steve, the man you know as your father, is not your father. Your real father is a man I was in love with at the time you were born. He was—and is—married and has a family. He said that he was willing to divorce his wife at the time but I thought it was too big a risk for both of us to take. He always wanted to know about you, and I have kept in touch with him over the years. I have sent him pictures, although, for a time, you spoke to him on a daily basis. His name is Bill, Bill Kline. You might remember him; he was a friend of ours for a while and you were friends with his son and daughter."

I nodded my head, dumbfounded. My head was reeling and all I could think of was that this man whom I saw on an almost daily basis in high school and whom I had maintained a casual acquaintance with was my father. The second thought was that when his son, Joe, and I were heading towards a relationship in high school, my mother had uncharacteristically squelched it immediately.

My mother continued. "Steve believes that you are his child, as does everyone else. Only Bill and I know the truth. We could have taken this to our grave and indeed we were prepared to, but I felt that, at this point in time, you needed to know this. I thought maybe it would help you understand more about who you are and, perhaps, explain some of the alienation you have felt in this family. Most of all, I want you to know that you are a Jew, on both sides of your bloodline, and I want you to be proud of that, not to hide it as I have and my mother did."

My mother went on to tell me the circumstances surrounding her pregnancy and her decision to stay with my father and not to ask for help from my birth father, who had a wife and three children of his own. She told me that her choice of this man as my birth father was made carefully. He was a man with whom she was in love, who had brains and good looks and was a Jew. Although my mother was a Jew as well, the father I had grown up with was an atheist and actively anti-Semitic. There was no space to be a Jew in our household; indeed that was not an aspect of our identity that ever got mentioned. When my grandmother came to live with us and tried to teach a little bit about my heritage, this too was strongly discouraged. Religion was forbidden by my father and hidden by my mother. She had never loved my father, I heard her saying. This came as no surprise to me. Still, I couldn't help but wonder about my brother. Who was his father? As if she had read my thoughts, my mother said that she had decided (and with many misgivings) to stay with the man she had married and to have his child. My brother, at least, was who he thought he was.

She explained to me that she had been tempted to tell me once before, about 10 years ago when I was going through a tough time. I had said many times that I felt like an outsider, like I didn't have a place in the family. I didn't know who I was. She said that she had wanted to tell me then but felt that it would only make things worse for me. Now, she said, she wasn't sure if telling me this would help or hurt, but she wanted me to know my heritage, know that I came from good people.

My mother said, "You always wondered why you loved sports so much and were so athletic; Steve and I never played sports but your father, Bill, was a football player and a marathon runner."

"The irony in all this perhaps is that my own story is very similar," my mother continued. "The man who I knew as my father; the man who I called 'father' all my life was not my real father. I found this out when I was going through my mother's things in New York, when she was moving to Florida. I was 33 at the time. I found my birth certificate and my father's name was not on there." "So who was your father?" I asked. My mother replied, "That was not so easy to find out, and is part of the reason why I am telling you this now. I tried finding out from my mother, but she kept telling me she was raped. Somehow I didn't believe her. To this day I am almost sure my father was a man who she was close to for many years. I knew him quite well as a child. He was a Jew too, although Harold (the man she had married) was a Gentile. I had a picture she took of him and tried to track him down. The contacts I had told me that he was dead at that point. So I never actually got to see him again. So I want you to have that choice; the choice that I never had—to have a relationship with your father."

"So he knows you are telling me this," I said. "Yes, I told him that I would be telling you this now," my mother confessed. "He supports my reasons. He wants you to know about who you are and the people you come from. Bill thinks that Steve was a terrible father to you; he never thought I should have stayed with him. But I never thought I had a choice, not until I was much older."

Although I was confused about the rationality of any of these decisions, either 30 years ago or now, I was even more confused over how I should feel, what this information meant to me and to who I was. After this moment, this story, I was no longer the same person. Or was I? If this were only a story among many stories about myself and my life, then how and why should it make a difference?

I felt as though there had been an earthquake, some kind of natural disaster in which the earth under my feet had shifted, turned upside down. Nothing was as it should be. There were so many questions, starting with how Steve could have been so ignorant of the circumstances of my birth. Almost immediately, I began to think of the ways this information would change my relationship with my brother, with my father, and with my mother.

My brother and I had shared quite a lot over the years and were pretty close; this would be a secret I could never tell. Family meant more to him than anything, and my mother was as close to perfect in his eyes as any woman could be. No, this would have to stay with me, a burden perhaps greater for me than for my mother. In her eyes, this had changed only her relationship to me; other relationships would go on as they always had. For me, there were many decisions that needed to be made about relationships to pursue or leave behind and the impact these decisions would have on my system of family and friends.

When I was younger, I did not have a good relationship with my father, but over the years he had mellowed. I felt that he tried to reach out to me now but didn't quite know how and didn't care enough to ask. Still, I was concerned enough about him and his relationship with my mother that I would not want to reveal this. Over the years, his extended family was the only family I knew; my mother had been the only child of an opera singer, widowed when my mother was young. My grandmother was never close to her own siblings, so I did not know of aunts or uncles or cousins. So I was not related to the only family I had ever known. This may not be a strange phenomenon for many people, but strange, certainly, when all have believed and told this story for 30 years. On top of these relational negotiations, I also had to consider the link to my real father. He wanted to talk to me and, more than that, he wanted to have some kind of relationship with me. How would this affect my relations with the family I had known as my own? How would this affect my feelings for the father with whom I had been raised?

How, then, can you go about living a life when you are no longer quite sure about your position in it? And, crucial to this analysis, how did the self who was created in this story coincide with, negate, or integrate (or all of these) with the stories lived and told about my self in other interactions, in other family narratives? This issue is important to a social constructionist understanding of self-disclosure: the creation of self in interaction occurs on multiple levels and in multiple contexts. For this analysis, I briefly discuss several subsequent episodes that occurred with my family, to give greater insight into the ways in which my self (among selves) was not disclosed, revealed, concealed, or discovered, but rather enacted in light of the story described.

Enacting a Secret Identity: Episodes in the Aftermath

Several months after my mother told me her story, I visited my brother. He commented on a recent fight between my father and myself, saying "Why do you still let him get to you? After all these years I thought you had moved on. You still let him bother you." Although I wanted to tell my brother the truth about my reaction, I simply said, "I don't know . . . guess I have a short memory." I acted to preserve the secret, and thus the relationship I had with my brother.

On New Year's Eve a year after my mother told me "my story," I was again visiting my parents. As the new year approached and my father (Steve) got increasingly inebriated, he began to get sentimental. He said to me, "I know I don't tell you this often, or at all really, but I am very proud of you. You have my genes. You have my brains. You have your mother's looks, thank God, but you have my brains." I just nodded my head as my eyes welled up with tears. I had spent my life trying to please him, only to find out that he really wasn't my father. Now, as I looked at him, I knew that pleasing him would still be important to me, important enough to keep the secret.

In the months following the revelation of this information, my real father (Bill) called me several times; he asked me if I had any questions and told me that he wanted us to have a relationship. I asked him questions about his family, his relationship with my parents over the years, about his health and history. But when he pressed me about meeting me face-to-face, I backed away. Finally, after a year of phone calls, and at my mother's insistence, I met him at a secret location. He showed me pictures of himself and his family. It was obvious to me that his family, his children, and maintaining his image as a well-known and respected politician were important to him. Yet, equally obvious, was that he felt some sort of obligation to "make things right" for me.

"I never liked your father," he said, after my mother had left us to talk alone. "In fact, I thought he was a terrible father to you." He went on to talk about the things he had witnessed in my parents' home when I was a child. "I wish I could make it up to you somehow. I want you to be happy. What do you need? Do you need money?" I was insulted that he thought money would make me happy, but even more that he could attack my father. At least he had been there. "No I don't need money," I responded. "And my father has mellowed quite a bit. We get along okay." I felt trapped by my own words and the relationships they would forge, maintain, or destroy. If I created a bond with this man, what would it mean to my other relationships? Yet, despite what I did, or didn't, say to my cousins, aunts, uncles, brother, or (other) father, Steve, I felt distanced from them.

ANALYSIS

Using the CMM concepts described above, the primary *antecedent* for my actions in these episodes is the narrative account of my birth and my heritage. The antecedent story framed or provided some context for the patterns of action in the episodes that followed. In the narrative account, primary emphasis is placed on the autobiographical level of meaning. Positioning the account in this manner, we see that the consequence my mother desired was that I would change my definition of self (autobiographical level of meaning) based on the news of my real father. However, my primary level/context of meaning throughout the interactions discussed above was relational. My actions and the desired consequences were to preserve my family relationships and my patterns of action within them. Rather than moving from the relational level to the autobiographical level, in the subsequent episodes with my family I remained locked into a grammar of practice that emphasized the relational level of meaning. Thus a *looped pattern* occurred. Because the relational level was most important for me, to change this level by responding at the level of autobiography would result in a change in the family system. Any choice I made in these situations would change the patterns of action in a way that would completely disrupt the enactment of my identity within the family. If I had pursued a relationship with my real father, it would further alienate me from Steve. If I told Steve the truth about "having his brains and my mother's good looks," that too would result in alienation from my family and upheaval of the entire system. Likewise, had I told my brother why I let my father push my buttons, why I hadn't "moved past" his treatment of us as children, I would reveal the reasons for my confusion and anger. It was safer (albeit damaging either way) to keep the patterns intact.

How, then, is a self constructed? My mother told me that she had decided to tell me the story of my birth and the secret of my identity because, as she put it, I lacked a sense of self. However, as I have looked at my interactions with my mother and other members of my family it seems clear that I did have the "sense of self" to know that I depended on my position within the family system, a system that could be threatened by this information. So maintaining my role in the family meant maintaining this looped pattern, the consequences of which neither my mother nor I desired.

CONCLUSIONS, CONTRIBUTIONS, AND IMPLICATIONS

Should the target of research on self-disclosure, identity, and relationships be on what is disclosed, to whom, in which context, and at what point in the conversation? In addition, should we be concerned with the antecedents, actions, or consequences of this disclosure? What about the politics of who discloses, how that information is used, and with what consequences to individuals and groups with less power in this society?

As mentioned earlier, should the focus of our research be on the closure of a self, as a completed entity, or on the ways selves are created, maintained, enacted in different contexts and as part of social systems? Should the issue for communication researchers be not which one method of researching self-disclosure is most appropriate, but rather what the construct accomplishes in its study? If and when the research focus is on communication competence—interpersonally or inter- or cross-culturally—disclosure of a cultural or relational self seems to take the form of how much the information *reveals* about who we *really* are and the consequences this revelation has on the relationship. Such a view, while useful to those hoping to teach a sense of cultural timing in relationships, is mechanistic and totalizing. The self is always already composed. We may choose to reveal that self to others, and parts of that self may be unknown even to us, but always the self is an entity that is formed apart from interaction.

The use of social constructionist theory and methodology informs studies of the means (Wittgenstein's *language games*) through which self is created or interpreted in interaction. The focus on language as creative places action and context at the center of analysis, thus adding variety and complexity to the study of *interpersonal* communication. In this study, the use of emotional narrative adds depth to the study by including the emotional *as* cognitive and situated action, counting as data collected in the story told. Coordinated management of meaning adds complexity to the study of the "self-in-relation" through analyzing levels at and through which meaning occurs and including timing and sequence as part of that meaning.

Richardson (1992) wrote that poetry, and other alternative forms of interpretive work, "commends itself to multiple and open readings in ways that conventional sociological prose does not" (p. 126). Such work may raise questions that reflect the subtext of the interpreter, if not a universal text or textual interpretation. For instance, if readers question the validity of the story, what, specifically, are they questioning? The "truth" of identity? The validity of the story as described? The "normality" of my response to these events and to the characters depicted within? The implications of such stories on Jewish identities? On the identities of Jewish women? Each of these questions reflects not only the notions of validity as both inside of (that is, the story's structural coherence or integrity) and outside of the story—how well the narrative speaks to stories of family, emotion, secrecy, and identity.

Moreover, these questions structure the gaze of the researcher and need to be examined as the relationship between the researcher and the frames themselves. Richardson asks, "Have the concepts of sociology (and by extension here, communication) been so reified that even interpretivists cannot believe they know about a person's life without refracting it through a sociologically prescribed lens?" (p. 127).

Although Richardson's queries are important, they perhaps function better as boundaries or cautionary markers for researchers utilizing an interpretive or social constructionist perspective. Much of what makes interpretive research—or any research—good is the ability to work creatively within the confines of the form. Although some interpretive scholarship has the goal of extending our notions of proper form for writing research, other work speaks to us through telling a story that speaks to readers, while at the same time reflexively examining its own position in the storytelling.

For those who might read this chapter as an example of (in)appropriate self-disclosure, I should address the personal and political aspects of its performance, especially in my own position as a woman, a feminist communication professor, and a daughter, among other things. Baker and Benton (1994) caution:

> Although we advocate a feminist approach to self-disclosure, we are concerned with how individual women can unwittingly lose themselves in the struggle to gain a voice. In freeing up that voice, might we violate ourselves? Might we become enmeshed with another? Is telling secrets detrimental? Are there times when the detriment is worth it because of something we gain? . . . We agree that there are tensions between naming and silence; yet, we are concerned about how self-disclosure is both empowering and violating. (p. 226)

These are the terms that often frame the debates over the creation, institutionalization, and legislation of public and private lives. Feminist critical scholars often theorize all private relations as oppressive to women based on the relationship between the law and property protections in patriarchal society. This characterization of privacy assumes that self-disclosure can only ever be political, and thus is inherently tied to power relations. Other feminist theorists and cultural scholars, while not disagreeing with this characterization, point to the need to expand our thinking about power to look at the ways that the notions of equality and impartiality imparted to "public" communication have marginalized and excluded many groups, perspectives, and voices. Boling (1996) observed that the feelings, desires, and commitments relegated to the private realm do not disappear; they are merely driven underground, rendered invisible in everyday discourse. Young (1990) noted that the slogan "the personal is political expresses the principle that no practices or activities should be excluded as improper subjects for public discussion, expression or collective choice" (pp. 120–121). Young argued that, although meaningful distinctions between public and private information should be made, and are possible, no persons or issues should be forced into the invisibility of the private realm. He also argued that "no social institutions or practices should be excluded a priori from being a proper subject for public discussion and expression" (pp. 120–121).

Such arguments, although giving voice to the oppressive conditions and power relations which might position self-disclosure, pit public and private as god and devil terms, and fail to look at the relationships or episodes in which public or private relationships might be empowering or oppressive or both simultaneously. In CMM terms, the consequences of self-disclosure, as empowering or violating, happen through the affordances and constraints produced in the actor's primary context of meaning. Thus, if primary importance is placed on the relational level of meaning, then the creation (or disclosure) of a self apart from important relationships *feels* like a constraint. If the grammar of action is changed, thus transcending the loop, new affordances that enhance the self can be created that change the stories lived and told about the self. However, as stories told by and about women are both personal and political, self-disclosure is violating when the story told is constrained by the social/cultural interpretations of its place and importance in the larger society. Women (and men too) will only be empowered when the stories we tell create affordances for ourselves in relation to our interactions with others.

Whether researching self-disclosure or self-creation, then communication scholars must acknowledge the complexities and nuances of multiple selves that are enacted on multiple levels of meaning. Here the metaphor of balance discussed throughout this volume can be extended to a call for equilibrium between the empowerment that the protection of private lives affords, with the empowerment that comes with giving voice to areas of our lives that have previously been silenced, and with acknowledgment of the constraints imposed by oppressive relations. Self-disclosure is not simply about the presentation of a self as a precondition of intimacy or competency in relationships, nor is it simply a political issue that privatizes oppressive power relations. Through elaborating the meanings enacted and created in stories lived and told, this chapter has demonstrated the multiple levels upon which the disclosure of "private" information, in this case family secrets, are given meaning. It is in these moments, these episodes of enacting identity within or without the physical context of family interaction, that openings or options for new stories are created or old patterns are substantiated, thus limiting possibilities for change.

VI

BALANCING PRIVATE
DISCLOSURES IN THE MEDIA
AND ACROSS CULTURES

15

▼▼▼▼▼▼▼▼

A Comparison of Self-Reported
Self-Disclosure Among Chinese
and North Americans

Donald L. Rubin
The University of Georgia

Hanbi Yang
Baker & McKenzie, Chicago

Michael Porte
University of Cincinnati

The concept of "balance" is central to mainstream East Asian world views (Wright, 1975). For example, optimal flow of life energy (*chi*) is typically regarded as requiring a balance between a number of counterpoised tensions, including the tension between *ying* (largely masculine) and *yang* (feminine). The notion of balance between competing principles inspires the general Confucian approbation for moderation in all things (*chung yung*; Young, 1994). This tenet of the Confucian value system, in turn, exerts a profound impact on communication norms throughout East Asia (Yum, 1991). Thus, Confucian doctrine enjoins people to maintain interpersonal equilibrium (*jen-lum*), including balance between expressing true emotion and desire by the individual and regulating that expression by propriety (*li*; Chang & Holt, 1991).

Within Western Anglo-American communication paradigms, self-disclosure is generally regarded as central to communication competence (Wiemann, 1977). To forge meaningful relationships, we must make ourselves known to others (Derlega et al., 1993). From its earliest formulations, however, Western social scientific research and theory about self-disclosure has also acknowledged that the impulse to disclose is counterbalanced by other communication variables relating to context. In particular, situational and topical constraints govern appropriate disclosure. Thus Jourard's influential Self-Disclosure Questionnaire (JSDQ; Jourard, 1971a; Jourard & Lasakow,

1958) inquires about willingness to disclose across several target inter-locutors (e.g., intimate friends, parents, strangers) and across several domains of subject matter (e.g., the topics of tastes and preferences, work, and body image). In a similar vein, Chelune (1979) identifies flexibility in self-disclosing across situational factors as the core of the self-disclosure construct.

In addition to varying across situations and topics of conversation, norms for what counts as appropriate self-disclosure appear to vary across cultures (Wheeless, Erickson, & Behrens, 1986). From the general perspective of the ethnography of communication, cultures can be arrayed along a continuum of expressiveness ranging from voluble to taciturn (Hymes, 1974). Indeed, a number of cross-cultural studies have attempted to verify contrasting norms and practices for self-disclosure. In one typical study, for instance, Cunning-ham (1981) asked participants to rate the degree of intimacy associated with a series of supplied topics, and determined that Australians were more open to communicating about these topics than were North Americans. In another study contrasting Germans and Americans (Plog, 1965), an interaction be-tween culture and target of interaction emerged; whereas North Americans were overall more open than Germans, that cross-cultural disparity dimin-ished when people communicated with intimate others.

Particular interest resides in contrasting the norms and meanings of self-disclosure for Anglo-American/Western cultures relative to East Asian (e.g., Chen & Starosta, 1998). That is because—as a prototypical individualist culture—Anglo-American values privilege strongly differentiated ego and individual autonomy. The interpersonal patterns associated with these West-ern values embody open expressiveness and interpersonal assertiveness (Tri-andis, 1995). East Asian patterns, in contrast, derive from prototypical collectivist cultures and tend to subjugate the self in order to focus on group harmony and group outcomes. Because self-disclosive behaviors direct at-tention to the individual and compete with the face demands of other mem-bers of a group, they are eschewed (Yum, 1991). Thus, for Westerners, East Asians may appear nondisclosive, that is, stereotypically inexpressive, in-scrutable, even impassive.

Empirical findings comparing Anglo-American and East Asian self-dis-closure are mixed, however. Ting-Toomey (1991) developed scales to examine disclosure in relationship maintenance, and found lower disclosiveness among Japanese than among either North Americans or the French. Simi-larly, Chen (1995) found lower self-reported disclosure among Taiwanese as compared with North Americans. The effect of nationality in this study was consistent across all conversational topics and interlocutors examined. Won-Doornink (1985), on the other hand, examined actual interaction data under controlled conditions and found few differences between North Americans and Koreans.

Several other studies found cultural differences in self-disclosure to be mediated by additional factors. For example, Wheeless and colleagues (1986) examined the interactive effect of culture with the personality variable locus of control. Their results suggest that people with internal loci of control are relatively impervious to diverse cultural expectations regarding disclosive communication. In contrast, people with high external loci of control are especially subject to social pressures for conformity. Therefore cross-cultural differences in self-disclosure are more prominent among people with predominantly external loci of control.

Investigating the mediating effects of social context in conjunction with culture, Argyle Henderson, Bond, Iizuka, and Contarello and colleagues (1986) asked respondents from Japan, Hong Kong, Italy, and England the degree to which they subscribed to a series of relational rules. Their findings indicated that, overall, the Japanese were most restrained about disclosing affect, relative to the other three nationalities. However, the Japanese in this study were significantly more willing to express affect when their interlocutors were intimates, compared with strangers.

In addition to culture, gender seems an obvious status variable affecting self-disclosure. Yet the myriad of empirical studies investigating gender differences in self-disclosure offer a frustrating lack of consensus (Hill & Stull, 1987). Male and female norms for self-disclosure diverge most in same-sex interactions, but seem quite similar in cross-sex conversations (see review in Derlega et al., 1993). In a number of studies males actually obtain higher self-disclosure ratings on the average than women (see review in Cline, 1986), and this appears to be especially true in initial male–female encounters in which men may be using self-disclosure to engender romantic interest on the part of their female conversational partner (Derlega et al., 1993).

Conflicting empirical findings aside, gender differences in self-disclosure are well grounded in gender theory, with women generally conceptualized as more oriented toward disclosing affect and other intimate information, whereas men are generally oriented toward disclosing a more limited range of personal information, mostly about activity (Tannen, 1990). The prototypical male communication style in Anglo-American/Western culture is controlled, unemotional, and laconic (Balwick & Peek, 1971), whereas women tend to adopt a relational style (Gilligan, 1982). Derlega et al. (1993) posit three possible mechanisms that may explain these gender-related differences in self-disclosure. One model adopts the view that women and men themselves constitute distinct subcultures, and that they are differentially acculturated regarding communicative norms (Malz & Borker, 1982; but see Uchida, 1997, for an opposing view). According to this model, boys and girls, men and women, are subject to different modeling and sanctions by others members of their respective "subcultures." An alternative model proposes that men and women within any given culture adopt differing norms for expressiveness. Presumably, the more strongly individuals adhere to traditional gender role schemas, the greater the distance separating male and female self-disclosure. The third alternative explanation suggests that social norms govern the topics that people address to males and females, such that males are provided with fewer opportunities to engage in highly disclosive conversations, whereas women often encounter interlocutors who introduce personal topics of conversation.

Particularly in light of models postulating cultural/normative explanations for gender differences in self-disclosure, some interaction between culture and gender is likely in this domain (Collier, 1986). Specifically, in Anglo-American/Western cultures, women generally have greater autonomy and latitude of sex-role enactment, compared with women in traditional East Asian cultures (Iwao, 1993). Consequently, North American women may be more free to disclose across a wider range of interlocutors and subjects of conversation. That is, one might predict an interaction between gender and culture such that women and men in the West diverge significantly with regard to expressiveness, whereas women and men in East Asia are less divergent in this regard. This is precisely the pattern reported by Ting-Toomey (1991), who found North American women higher in self-disclosure than North American men, but no gender differences in the Japanese sample. Chen (1995), in contrast, found no interaction between gender and nationality (U.S. vs. Taiwanese), and indeed, a main effect for gender on only one out of nine dependent variables: Taiwanese and U.S. women alike reported higher levels of disclosiveness directed to intimates than was the case for men (regardless of nationality) communicating with intimates.

One explanation for conflicting findings regarding gender and cultural differences in self-disclosure may relate to inadequacies in measurement instruments. The JSDQ has been criticized for failing to correlate strongly with directly observed discourse practices (Cozby, 1973), and for failing to adequately distinguish between target-specific disclosure and generalized disclosiveness (Wheeless et al., 1986). Still, it remains the dominant measurement technique in this research domain (Tardy, 1988). Hill and Stull (1987), for example, answer the critique that JSDQ fails to predict behavioral observations of self-disclosure. They rejoin that JSDQ reflects long-term past behavior with known individuals, whereas most observational studies are based on very superficial interactions with strangers in laboratory settings. The JSDQ has been used successfully in intercultural research—both interethnic (Jourard & Lasakow, 1958) and international (Melikian, 1962). Tardy (1988) concluded that "an asset of the Jourard scales is their applicability to a variety of subject populations" (p. 326).

Indeed, Jourard's (1971) self-disclosure instrument was closely adapted by Barnlund (1989) in his pivotal studies of Japanese communication patterns. Overall, Barnlund concluded that North American college students were more willing to disclose than were their Japanese counterparts. However, essential similarities between the two groups emerged in terms of rank orderings of most readily disclosed (tastes and opinions) and least readily disclosed (body and personality attributes) topics of conversation. North Americans and Japanese were also similar in their ranking of targets along a continuum of trust and intimacy. Barnlund, unlike Ting-Toomey (1991), found no gender differences in this study, nor any interactions between gender and culture that would be predicted based on the wider expressive latitude for Anglo-American women compared to East Asian women. Chen (1995) also used a close adaptation for the JSDQ in a contrastive study of North Americans and Taiwanese. Because of the design of that study, however, it is not possible to draw conclusions about differences among conversational topics, nor about differences among interlocutors, nor about the interaction of these factors with nationality or gender.

Given the lack of consistency in studies comparing self-disclosure in East-Asian cultures with Anglo-American/Western cultures, there is strong warrant for additional research on this topic. For example, much research purporting to investigate East Asian/collectivist patterns of disclosiveness have relied on Japanese participants. China, the most populous cultural entity in the world, has sustained relatively little empirical research in communication. (Chen, 1995, is one exception.) This is surprising because students of Chinese national origin (Taiwan and mainland China) represent the greatest source of East Asian influx to the United States, at least in the world of higher education ("Foreign Students' Countries of Origin, 1995–96," 1997). Moreover, there is reason to suspect that certain Chinese patterns of communication are unique, as Confucian influences may have evolved in nation-specific ways across the Pacific Rim, and have been widely overlooked (Chang & Holt, 1991).

Accordingly, the present study undertakes a comparison between self-reported self-disclosure among Chinese and North American men and women. Closely adapting the JSDQ, it examines cultural and gender differences across six topics of conversation and five target interlocutor roles. Research questions of particular interest include the following:

RQ1: A. Do Chinese differ from U.S. respondents in reported level of self-disclosure?

   B. If so, on which conversational topics and for which interlocutors do these differences emerge?

RQ2: A. Does culture interact with gender in affecting level of reported disclosiveness?

   B. If so, for which conversational topics and for which interlocutors do these interaction effects manifest?

METHODS

Participants

Research participants were students attending a large, urban university in the midwestern United States. North Americans were Caucasian citizens of the United States. The North American sample included 22 females and 22 males. Chinese participants were citizens of either the People's Republic of China or the Republic of China (Taiwan). All had resided in the United States fewer than 3 years. The Chinese sample included 20 males and 20 females.

Instrumentation and Procedure

In individual sessions, participants were briefed, and then each filled out a modified form of the JSDQ (see Appendix). The original JSDQ (Jourard & Lasakow, 1958) contains 10 items for each of 6 subjects of conversation: (1) attitudes and opinions, (2) tastes and interests, (3) work or studies, (4) money, (5) personality attributes, and (6) body attributes. In the present version, items judged by native Chinese investigators in this study to be either ill-defined in Chinese culture (e.g., bonds and interest as sources of income) or else rigidly standardized in that culture (e.g., feelings about parent–child relations) were eliminated. The resulting instrument contained 47 items (5 attitudes and opinions; 8 tastes and interests; 10 work or studies; 6 money; 11 personality; 7 body).

Participants reported their actual communication behaviors for each of these 47 items when interacting with 5 different target interlocutors. The targets, drawn from the original JSDQ, were a (1) spouse/fiancé/lover, (2) parent, (3) intimate friend, (4) acquaintance, and (5) stranger. In each case, they reported their disclosure on a four-point scale indicating (a) misrepresentation, (b) nondisclosure, (c) vague disclosure, or (d) full and open disclosure.

Analysis

Prior to averaging the items within each of the six subjects of conversation, subscale reliabilities (Cronbach's alpha) were calculated separately for Chinese and for North American participants. Table 15.1 displays the reliabilities of the six topic subscales for Chinese and for North American participants. It indicates that reliabilities are high and approximately equivalent across nationalities.

After ascertaining adequate reliability, the data were submitted to a 2 (nationality) × 2 (gender) × 5 (target interlocutors) × 6 (topics) mixed factorial analysis of variance (ANOVA), with participants nested in nationality and

TABLE 15.1
Subject Matter Subscale Reliabilities by Nationality

Subject	Chinese	American
Attitude	0.857	0.869
Taste	0.933	0.927
Work	0.955	0.960
Money	0.944	0.929
Personality	0.948	0.965
Body	0.923	0.934

gender and crossed with the repeated measures, target interlocutor and subject of conversation. Because of some unbalanced cells, a hierarchical approach to ANOVA was taken. Statistically significant effects were explored via post hoc Bonferroni ts (Dunn's multiple comparisons) to protect family-wise errors. A significance level of .01 was set for all tests.

RESULTS

Nationality by gender by target interlocutor by topic of conversation cell means are shown in Table 15.2. The ANOVA of reported disclosure appears in Table 15.3. The ANOVA reveals a statistically significant main effect for target interlocutor [$F(4, 1560) = 151$, $p < .001$; $M_{intimate} = 1.60$; $M_{parent} = 1.28$; $M_{friend} = 1.38$; $M_{acquaint} = 0.56$; $M_{stranger} = 0.22$]. Post hoc multiple comparisons indicated that all pair-wise contrasts were statistically significant. Topic of conversation likewise exerted a significant main effect [$F(4, 1560) = 12.87$, $p < .001$; $M_{taste} = 1.22$; $M_{att} = 1.10$; $M_{work} = 1.06$; $M_{body} = 0.97$; $M_{pers} = 0.88$; $M_{money} = 0.80$]. Multiple comparisons among these cell means indicated that each was significantly different from all others.

These two main effects were modified by several interactions. However, these two-way interactions between the two repeated measures, target and topic [$F(4, 1560) = 213.35$, $p < .001$], was itself further modified by two three-way interactions. The two-way effects are thus not generalizable, and therefore will not be addressed here.

Interaction Between Nationality, Target Interlocutor, and Topic of Conversation

Cell means for the interaction between nationality, target, and topic [$F(4, 1560) = 2.49$, $p < .001$] appear in Fig. 15.1. Dunn's Multiple Comparisons were run for each pair-wise contrast within simple effects. Note that respondent gender did not participate in this interaction and therefore is not a factor in any of these contrasts.

TABLE 15.2
Gender by Nationality by Target by Topic Cell Means

Target	Gender	Attitude		Taste		Work		Money		Personality		Body	
		Chinese	American	Chinese	American	Chinese	American	Chinese	American	Chinese	American	Chinese	American
Spouse/Lover	Male	1.60	1.60	1.69	1.61	1.67	1.57	1.69	1.33	1.55	1.44	1.59	1.45
	Female	1.71	1.42	1.89	1.70	1.80	1.60	1.62	1.48	1.67	1.66	1.61	1.49
Parents	Male	0.94	1.30	1.19	1.38	1.21	1.32	1.14	1.27	0.90	0.93	1.11	1.39
	Female	1.43	1.43	1.49	1.68	1.47	1.49	1.49	1.24	1.14	1.26	1.45	1.43
Friend	Male	1.47	1.60	1.48	1.54	1.49	1.37	0.82	1.07	1.22	1.24	1.17	1.28
	Female	1.67	1.50	1.77	1.70	1.51	1.59	0.98	1.02	1.42	1.50	1.41	1.40
Acquaintance	Male	0.64	0.94	0.67	0.96	0.48	0.73	0.04	0.33	0.36	0.36	0.39	0.58
	Female	0.74	0.62	0.99	1.01	0.47	0.69	0.22	0.29	0.36	0.44	0.51	0.46
Stranger	Male	0.28	0.47	0.29	0.56	0.13	0.36	-.12	0.16	0.06	0.07	0.90	0.32
	Female	0.37	0.25	0.43	0.42	0.13	0.28	-.04	0.06	0.50	0.12	0.16	0.13

TABLE 15.3
Nationality by Gender by Target by Topic ANOVA of Disclosiveness

Source of Variation	DF	SS	F
Nationality	1	1.15	0.55
Gender	1	4.65	2.23
Nationality by Gender	1	2.52	1.21
Error_between	78	162.72	
Target	4	90.60	146.13
Nationality by Target	4	0.41	0.66
Gender by Target	4	1.51	2.44
Nationality by Gender by Target	4	1.56	2.52
Topic	5	9.65	12.45
Nationality by Gender by Topic	5	0.77	0.99
Gender by Topic	5	0.12	0.15
Nationality by Target by Topic	20	7.72	2.49
Gender by Target by Topic	20	6.81	2.20
Nationality by Gender by Target by Topic	20	2.89	0.94
Error_within	1560	241.26	

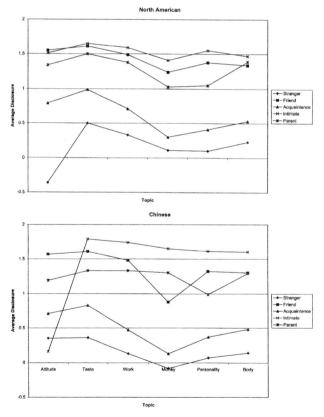

FIG. 15.1. Interaction between nationality, target, and topic on degree of disclosiveness.

Contrasting Chinese and U.S. Respondents Within Each Combination of Target Interlocutor and Conversational Topic. No pair-wise contrast between Chinese and U.S. respondents within any of the 30 target by conversational topic combinations was statistically significant.

Contrasting Target Interlocutors Within Each Combination of Nationality and Conversational Topic. The next set of simple effects explore differences among the five targets within each of the twelve nationalities by conversational topic combinations. For Chinese nationals within the topic of attitudes, the intimate target engendered significantly more disclosure than did parents, acquaintances, or strangers; but intimate targets (spouse/fiancé/lover) did not differ from close friends for the Chinese. The same pattern held for Americans within that same conversational topic (i.e., attitudes), except that parents did not differ from intimates or friends. That is, for Americans, the same amount of disclosiveness about attitudes was directed toward intimates, parents, and friends. For both Chinese as well as for Americans, all other pair-wise contrasts between targets within the topic of attitudes were significant. As can be seen from Fig. 15.1, for both nationalities, acquaintances engendered less disclosure about attitudes than did the more familiar targets, and strangers engendered even less.

For the topic of tastes and opinions, neither Chinese participants nor U.S. participants distinguished between intimate others and close friends. U.S. participants (but not Chinese) also included parents within that cluster of targets. Otherwise all other contrasts between targets within nationality and the topic of tastes and opinions were statistically significant. Again, acquaintances rated less disclosure about tastes and opinions, and strangers rated even less than acquaintances.

Similarly, within the conversational topic of work, Chinese participants did not distinguish in terms of disclosiveness between intimates and good friends, but parents engendered less disclosiveness than intimates. (Parents and friends did not differ significantly for this conversational subject among Chinese participants.) U.S. respondents, in contrast, did not distinguish among parents, friends, or intimates in terms of disclosure about work. For Chinese participants, acquaintances and strangers received equal levels of disclosure on this topic. U.S. participants, on the other hand, registered more disclosiveness to acquaintances than to strangers. For both nationalities, acquaintances and strangers garnered less disclosure about work than either of the other three more familiar target interlocutors.

For the subject of money, however, the pattern was rather different. The Chinese reported equally high disclosure about money to parents and to intimates. Close friends, for the Chinese, were significantly lower than parents or intimates when the subject was money, and all of these targets rated higher disclosure than acquaintances and strangers. Acquaintances and strangers were not significantly different from each other. For U.S. participants talking about work, the pattern was identical to the Chinese except that the Westerners were equally likely to disclose about work to parents and to close friends.

When disclosing about personality attributes like sources of worry or depression, Chinese reported higher levels of disclosure to intimates than to parents, acquaintances, or strangers. They disclosed about personality attributes more openly to parents and to friends than to either strangers or acquaintances. No other contrasts were significant among Chinese participants for the topic of personality attributes. Americans revealed the same pattern of means as did Chinese in this case. That is, U.S. participants also reported that they revealed information about personality attributes most readily to intimates, next most readily to parents and friends, and least readily to acquaintances and strangers.

For the topic of body image, Chinese and American participants manifested an identical pattern. For this combination, no significant differences held among the intimate, parent, and friend targets. Nor were the acquaintance and stranger targets significantly different. However reported disclosure to intimates, parents, and friends all exceeded reported disclosure to acquaintances and strangers.

Contrasting Conversational Topics Within Each Combination of Target Interlocutor and Nationality. The next set of simple effects for this three-way interaction contrasts across the six topics of conversation within each of the 10 nationality by target combinations. When the target was an intimate, neither Chinese nor U.S. participants differed in level of disclosiveness as a function of topical variation. That is, they reported equal likelihood of disclosure to an intimate regardless of topic of conversation.

When parents were the target of disclosiveness, the only significant difference to emerge was that Americans had reduced levels when the subject was personality traits, relative to the subject of tastes and opinions.

When communicating with good friends, however, Chinese reported lower levels of disclosure regarding the subject of money, relative to all the other topics of conversation. When U.S. respondents communicated with close friends, they reported disclosing less openly about money than about tastes and opinions. No other pair-wise contrasts between topic cell means were statistically significant when the target interlocutor was a good friend.

When the target interlocutor was a mere acquaintance, Chinese participants reported less disclosure regarding the topic of money than the topics of either attitudes or tastes. By the same token, the Chinese were less likely to disclose to acquaintances about personality traits than about tastes and opinions. U.S. respondents communicating with acquaintances reported lower levels of disclosure regarding the topic of money, relative to the topics of work, tastes, and attitudes. The North Americans were also less likely to disclose to acquaintances about personality traits than about tastes or attitudes, and they were less likely to disclose to acquaintances about body image than about tastes.

When the target was designated as a stranger, the Chinese were less likely to disclose about money than about either attitudes or tastes. For the stranger target, U.S. participants registered lower levels of disclosure regarding both money and personality traits relative to the subject of tastes.

Interaction Between Gender, Target Interlocutor, and Topic of Conversation

The three-way interaction between gender, target, and topic [$F(4, 1560) = 2.20$, $p < .005$] on reported levels of disclosiveness was also statistically significant. Cell means are presented in Fig. 15.2. Dunn's Multiple Comparisons were run for each pair-wise contrast within simple effects. Note that respondent nationality did not participate in this interaction and therefore is not a factor in any of these contrasts.

Contrasting Males and Females Within Each Combination of Target Interlocutor and Conversational Topic. The first set of simple effects examined bears on the contrast between males and females within the 30 target by

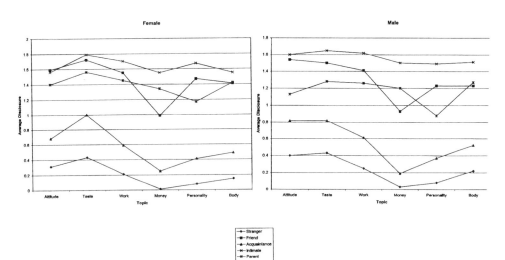

FIG. 15.2. Interaction between gender, target, and topic on degree of disclosiveness.

conversational topic combinations. Pair-wise Dunn's Multiple Comparisons indicated no such significant gender contrast.

Contrasting Target Interlocutors Within Each Combination of Gender and Conversational Topic. The second set of simple effects were those comparing levels of disclosure reported among the 5 target interlocutors within each of the twelve gender by subject matter combinations. When the topic of conversation was attitudes, males reported more disclosure to intimates and to close friends relative to their reported interactions with parents, acquaintances, and strangers. Males were significantly less disclosive to strangers than to any of the other four targets. Women discussing the topic of attitudes differed from males in their reported disclosure to parents. Disclosure to intimates, close friends, and parents were all at a similar level, and all greater than disclosure to acquaintances and strangers. As was the case for men, women were also less disclosive about attitudes to strangers than to any of the other four targets.

For the topic of tastes and opinions, both women and men were more disclosive to intimates, parents, and close friends than to acquaintances and strangers. For both women and men, the stranger was the target of less self-disclosure than any of the other four target interlocutors.

With regard to the topic of work, men disclosed more to intimates than to parents, and more to intimates and close friends than to acquaintances and strangers. Men disclosed more about work to parents than to acquaintances and strangers, and more to acquaintances than to strangers. Again, women differed from men chiefly in terms of their treatment of parents. Women disclosed more to intimates, parents, and close friends than to acquaintances and strangers. Like men, they were less disclosive on the topic of work to strangers than to any of the other four targets.

For the topic of money, men disclosed more to intimates than to any of the other targets. They disclosed more to parents and to close friends than to acquaintances or strangers. For women communicating about the subject of money, more disclosure was addressed to intimates than to close friends, acquaintances, and strangers. Women were more disclosive to parents and close friends than to acquaintances and strangers. Women did not distinguish between parents and intimates on this variable.

Regarding the subject of personality traits, men reported more disclosure to intimates and to close friends than to parents, acquaintances, or strangers. They disclosed more to parents than to acquaintances or strangers. Women, regarding personality traits, disclosed more to intimates than to parents, acquaintances, or strangers, and more to parents and to close friends than to acquaintances or strangers. Women reported disclosing significantly less about personality traits to strangers than to any of the other four interlocutors.

With regard to the subject of body image, both women and men disclosed more to intimates, parents, and close friends than to acquaintances and strangers.

Contrasting Topics of Conversation Within Each Combination of Target Interlocutor and Gender. The final set of simple effects examined differences among the 6 topics of conversation within each of the 10 gender by target combinations. When communicating with the intimate target, neither women nor men significantly differentiated among topics of conversation.

When communicating with close friends, men reported disclosing less about money than about attitudes, tastes, and work, but for men the topic of money did not differ from the topic of opinions. When women communicated with close friends, they disclosed less about money than about any of the other five topics.

When the target person was a parent, men reported less disclosure about the subject of personality traits than about tastes, work, or body image. When women communicated with parents, they were less disclosive about personality traits than about tastes. No other pair-wise contrasts among conversational topics were statistically significant within this combination of factors.

For a target who was a mere acquaintance, men reported disclosing more about attitudes and tastes than about money or personality traits. They also were more disclosive about work and body image than about money. When women communicated with acquaintances, they were more disclosive about tastes than about work, money, personality, and body image. Women were also more disclosive about attitudes than about money for acquaintance target person.

Finally, for the stranger target, men reported disclosing less about money than about attitudes or tastes. Women disclosed to strangers less about money than about tastes.

DISCUSSION

The purpose of this study was to examine differences between Chinese and North American communicators in their reported patterns of self-disclosure. A considerable body of intercultural theory and research (e.g., Barnlund, 1987; Chen, 1995; Chen & Starosta, 1998) warrants the expectation that East Asians would report substantially less self-disclosure than Anglo-Americans. The findings of this study contradict that expectation, however. These data revealed no main effect for nationality in self-disclosure.

Because self-disclosure is conceptualized as contingent upon target interlocutor and topic of conversation, it was further expected that culture would interact with these situational variables in affecting levels of disclosure. Accordingly, research question 1.B directly inquired about differences between Chinese and North Americans across combinations of target and topic. A three-way interaction between these factors yielded considerable information regarding this question. First, it is important to acknowledge that no statistically significant outcome emerged for any pair-wise contrast directly comparing Chinese and U.S. responses in the 30 combinations of interlocutor and conversational topic.

On the other hand, patterns of adapting to targets and topics vis-à-vis disclosiveness did seem to differ for the two nationalities. For four of the topics of conversation (attitudes, tastes and opinions, work, and body image), North Americans displayed especially tightly clustered levels of reported disclosure to intimates, close friends, and parents (see Fig. 15.1). The Chinese means for these interlocutors on the topics of attitudes, tastes and opinions, and personality were rather less tightly clustered. In particular, Chinese participants reported somewhat lower levels of disclosure directed toward parents compared to their communication to other intimates. Moreover, U.S. participants varied their level of disclosure to parents according to conversational topic, whereas Chinese disclosed to their parents with similar levels of openness across the several subjects of conversation (note in Fig. 15.1 the relatively flat line for the Chinese parent target).

In light of the strong family ties and deference to parents that is well known among East Asians (e.g., Yum, 1991), this finding of relatively lower levels of disclosure to parents is, at first glance, quite surprising. Consider, however, that these Chinese respondents were all sojourning several thousands of miles away from their places of origin. It is likely they were communicating with their parents with much less frequency than was the case for U.S. students. Moreover, the greater geographic distance over which the Chinese needed to communicate with their parents no doubt dampened the intimacy with which they might otherwise have interacted with their parents who were still living in their homelands. It remains for future research, then, to determine whether Chinese living in close proximity to their parents would display a pattern similar to that found for the U.S. participants in this study, or whether U.S. participants sojourning abroad would display a pattern in this regard similar to the Chinese in the present study.

The topic of money and one's financial affairs engendered considerable variability in reports of self-disclosure across target interlocutors. As is evident in Fig. 15.1, for both North Americans and Chinese, levels of self-disclosure to close friends dropped below levels of disclosure directed toward parents—just for the topic of money. The reluctance to reveal information about one's financial status to one's friends was especially marked among Chinese participants, however. Again, this was an anomalous finding, considering that it is not considered especially gauche among Chinese and other East Asians to ask another the amount of his or her salary (Centers for Disease Control, 1987).

Besides these few differing patterns of disclosure, Chinese and North Americans displayed identical configurations in a number of other comparisons. When communicating with spouses or other intimates, neither group, for example, altered its level of disclosiveness in reaction to different conversational topics. Both nationalities evinced nearly a ceiling effect on self-disclosure to intimates. Both nationalities also reduced their level of disclosure to parents on the topic of personality. The likely reason for this is that the personality scale included items regarding sexual practices and attractions. Sexual matters are not easily broached with parents in either culture (but even less easily discussed with acquaintances and strangers, according to these data).

Research question 2 inquired about differential gender effects across cultures (RQ2.A) and about the topics and interlocutors for which those differences might be most pronounced (RQ2.B). The results, however, supported no finding of interaction between culture and gender. Reported disclosiveness of men and women in across the two nationalities were not significantly distinguishable. In this regard this study stands in opposition to the findings of Ting-Toomey (1991), but is mainly in support of Chen (1995).

Gender role enactment is, of course, part and parcel of what culture is. It is important to note that no main effect for gender on reported self-disclosure emerged in this study. That negative finding, in conjunction with the fact that gender did not interact with culture in this study, can be taken as evidence supporting the position that levels of disclosiveness are not highly gender-determined (Hill & Stull, 1987).

Rather than linked simply to demographic status, it is likely that any gender differences in self-disclosure are context-determined, as indeed appears to be the case for communication behavior in general (Aries, 1996; Crawford, 1995). Although the research questions motivating this study do not inquire about gender apart from its interaction with culture, it is worth briefly noting that the interaction between gender, topic of conversation, and conversational interlocutor yielded information bearing on exactly this point (see Fig. 15.2). Analyses of the simple effects within this interaction indicated first that no direct comparison between males and females within any of the 30 combinations of target interlocutor and conversational topic was statistically significant. On the other hand, males and females did differ in at least one pattern of situation-specific self-disclosure. For most of the conversational topics, women reported levels of self-disclosure to parents at about the same rates they disclosed to intimates and to close friends. Men, in contrast, reported disclosing relatively less to parents than to intimates or close friends.

On the whole, results of this study showed that both gender and nationality were eclipsed by the potency of situational variables (target person and conversational topic) in determining levels of self-disclosure. With respect to target interlocutor, the hierarchy of self-disclosiveness progressed from stranger (least disclosure), to acquaintance, to parent, to close friend, to intimate other (highest disclosure). With respect to conversational subject, the topic of money engendered the least disclosure, followed by personality traits, body image, work, attitudes, and tastes (highest disclosure). With the few exceptions just discussed, men as well as women, Chinese as well as North Americans tended to adhere to these situational hierarchies of self-disclosure.

Certainly these findings must be considered in light of certain methodological caveats. In particular, it is worth restating that the instrument used in this study was adapted from the JSDQ, and thus is a self-report measure which may have limited correlations with observable behaviors (Cline, 1986). On the other hand, one need not expect strong correlations between a measure inquiring about *general* self-disclosure practices and observations of *particular* behaviors in laboratory conditions (Hill & Stull, 1987). In addition, it is possible that this instrument lacked sufficient sensitivity to detect any cultural differences that may, in fact, exist. In defense of the instrument used in this study, however, it should be noted that the reliability of the self-disclosure questionnaire appeared strong for both cultural groups (see Table 15.1). Moreover, previous studies that used different adaptations of the JSDQ did in fact detect cultural differences (e.g., Barnlund, 1987).

ACKNOWLEDGMENT

The authors express appreciation to Wang (Ida) Te-Jeung of Taichung, Taiwan. Ms. Wang assisted in data analysis.

APPENDIX

Adaptation of the JSDQ

How far do you disclose your personal opinions about the following topics to these targets?

1) Spouse, fiancé, or lover   2) Parents   3) Intimate friend
4) Acquaintances   5) Strangers

Please rate your levels of self-disclosure according to the following scale:

2: Have talked in full and complete detail about this item to the target. He/she knows me fully in this respect, and could describe me accurately.

1: Have talked in general terms about this item. The target has only a general idea about this aspect of me.

0: Have told the target nothing about this aspect of me.

−1: Have said something other than my true personal opinions about the topic so that the target has a false picture of me.

Questionnaire

*1. What I think and feel about religion: my personal religious views.

*2. My personal opinions and feelings about other religious groups than my own, for example, Protestants, Catholics, Jews, atheists.

*3. My views on the present government—the president, government policies, and so on.

4. My personal standards of beauty and attractiveness in women—what I consider to be attractive in a woman.

5. The things that I regard as desirable for a man to be—what I look for in a man.

6. My favorite foods, the ways I like food prepared, and my food dislikes.

7. My likes and dislikes in music.

8. My favorite reading matter.

9. The kinds of movies that I like to see best; the TV shows that are my favorites.

10. My taste in clothing.

11. The kind of party or social gathering that I like best, and the kind that would bore me or that I wouldn't enjoy.

12. My favorite ways of spending spare time.

13. What I would appreciate most for a present.

14. What I find to be the worst pressures and strains in my work (or studies).

15. What I find to be the most boring and unenjoyable aspects of my work.

16. What I enjoy most and get the most satisfaction from in my present work.

17. What I feel are my shortcomings that prevent me from working as I'd like to or that prevent me from getting further ahead in my work.

18. What I feel are my special strong points and qualifications for my work.

19. How I feel that my work is appreciated by others (e.g., boss, fellow-workers, teacher, husband, etc.).

20. My ambitions and goals in my work.
21. My feelings about the salary or rewards that I get for my work.
22. How I feel about my career—whether or not I'm satisfied with it.
23. How I really feel about the people that I work for, or work with.
24. How much money I make at my work, or get as an allowance.
25. Whether or not I have savings, and the amounts.
26. Whether or not I owe money; if so, how much.
27. Whom I owe money to at present; or whom I have borrowed from in the past.
28. Whether or not others owe me money; the amount and who owes it to me.
29. How I budget my money—the proportion that goes to necessities, luxuries, etc.
30. The aspects of my personality that I dislike, worry about, that I regard as a shortcoming in me.
31. What feelings, if any, that I have trouble expressing or controlling.
32. My personal views on sexual morality—how I feel that I and others ought to behave in sexual matters.
33. The facts of my present sex life—any problems that I might have.
34. Whether or not I feel that I am attractive to the opposite sex; my problems, if any, about getting favorable attention from the opposite sex.
35. Things in the past or present that I feel ashamed and guilty about.
36. The kinds of things that just make me furious.
37. What it takes to get me feeling real depressed.
38. What it takes to get me real worried, anxious and afraid.
39. What it takes to hurt my feelings deeply.
40. The kinds of things that make me especially proud of myself, full of self-esteem or self-respect.
41. How I wish I looked; my ideals for my appearance.
42. Any problems and worries that I had with my appearance in the past.
43. Whether or not I now have any health problems.
44. Whether or not I have any long-range worries or concerns about my health, e.g., cancer.
45. My past record of illness and treatment.
46. Whether or not I now make special efforts to keep fit, healthy and attractive, e.g., exercise, diet.
47. My present physical measurements, e.g., height, weight, etc.

Items with "*" have the following versions for the Chinese subjects:

*1. What I think about horoscope.

*2. My personal opinions and feelings about Buddhism, Taoism, Confucianism and other religions.

*3. My views on the government policies of my own country.

16

▼▼▼▼▼▼▼▼

"Egocasting" in the Avoidance of Disclosure: An Intercultural Perspective

Sally O. Hastings
Western Kentucky University

A central theoretical strand recurrent in many chapters in this volume is a concern with the "dialectic of expressiveness and protectiveness" (Rawlins, 1983b), the "express/repress dilemma" (Duck, 1982), or communication boundary management (CBM) theory (Petronio, 1993). Although dialectical tensions between competing desires to express and repress occur at an individual level, decisions about how these tensions are negotiated are culturally informed. Successful balancing of self-disclosure hinges on creating harmony between the performance of the individual and the beliefs, values, rules, and expectations associated with the cultural context of the performance. This chapter explores how one form of disclosure avoidance, *egocasting*, can be a cultural form of communication which enables individuals to display an "appropriate" cultural identity and to produce competent performance within a cultural context.

Egocasting is a term used here to describe the intrapersonal communication process that guides disclosure avoidance. Egocasting is an inversion of *altercasting*, a concept frequently used in compliance-gaining research. Weinstein and Deutschberger (1963) suggest that altercasting is a process where a social actor (the "Ego") attempts to influence the behavior of an interlocutor (the "Alter"). Influence is exerted by "casting Alter into a particular identity or role type" (p. 456). If Ego successfully persuades Alter to think and respond as one in the targeted identity or role would, then that which is "a task response for Ego will become a line of action for Alter" (p. 455). In egocasting, instead of Ego attempting to influence Alter, Ego attempts to exert self-control. Ego does this by assessing which identity or role Alter might define for Ego. Ego then uses this perception to determine what actions are and are not performable, and what words are and are not sayable. Of interest in this chapter, specifically, are occasions in which potential disclosures are averted due to conclusions drawn during egocasting.

The concept of "Ego," as developed by Weinstein and Deutschberger (1963), incorporates a sense of rational, structured, informed agency, as Ego is goal directed. The successful achievement of goals is contingent on careful analysis (i.e., of roles, role relationships, and normative conduct within specific roles) and on the use of information derived from the analysis to make choices during a given interaction. When Mead (1934) discussed the "self," he differentiated between the "I" and the "me." Mead suggested that "I" expresses individual uniqueness that, in popular American discourse, is coterminous with "self." Mead also recognized, however, that selves exist in a social context. "Me" is responsive to the social structures in which the self exists. The "me" recognizes the cultural identity inherent in the individual. Applying Mead's notion of self to the analysis herein, Ego manifests both elements of self, but appears to privilege the "me" dimension of self. Ego draws upon the structure which culture supplies to each interactional scene, then uses the structure to creatively (the "I"), yet intelligibly (the "me") select a line of action.

As senses of the self vary across cultures, so too does the comparative importance of the "I" and "me" dimensions of self. In individualistic cultures, individual freedom of action ("I") may be promoted, whereas in collectivistic cultures, individual adherence to norms and expectations of the group ("me") may be more valued. Such a claim is somewhat paradoxical, to the extent that the promotion of individual freedom of action ("I") is a culturally informed imperative, and is thus reflective of "me." The distinction is useful in that it points to the extent to which the "I" is seen as a culturally desirable component of self. In collectivistic cultures, the need for egocasting may assume considerable importance in effective self-presentation.

To demonstrate how egocasting functions as cultural communication, data from ethnographic interviews with Asian Indians living in the United States will be used to examine how and why this form of disclosure avoidance occurs among Indians. Continual points of contrast will be drawn between the disclosure avoidance of Asian Indians and that of Americans. The contrast between Asian Indians and Americans is a particularly interesting one due to the markedly divergent cultural values about the expression of the "I" and "me" components of self and the importance of talk.

The analysis of egocasting as a form of cultural communication provides an explanation for the reasons why members of a given culture are likely to make the decisions they make regarding whether to self-disclose. This can enhance the appreciation and tolerance for cultural differences in disclosure. The understanding can also lead to improved intercultural communication competence, as differences are understood as sensible within their cultural context.

CONCEPTUAL FRAMEWORK

Carbaugh (1990) provided the conceptual framework around which the study of egocasting is developed. Carbaugh links three interrelated elements of a cultural communication system: cultural frames, structuring norms, and cultural identity. Cultural frames are "a culturally coded term, such as *defense*, which identifies a kind of speaking familiar to, identified, performed, and evaluated by 'native' speakers" (Carbaugh 1990, p. 160). Such frames are guided by structuring norms and are both reflective of and constitutive of cultural identities. The particular cultural frame studied in this chapter is *egocasting*. Although performed intrapersonally, this frame is a form of "speaking" since it involves a languaged word choice and a verbal, meaningful reasoning process. The thought process is culturally coded and informs the performance which is evaluated by other members of the speech community.

The second aspect of cultural communication suggested by Carbaugh (1990) is *structuring norms*. Structuring norms involve those commonplace behaviors that unite a group of people. Of interest here are norms about speaking. Once egocasting has provided information about what types of roles are held by Ego and Alter, Ego then needs to evaluate what kinds of talk are normally appropriate within that role relationship. The information about norms that is acquired during the evaluation process will instruct Ego on how to best balance the conflicting possibilities to disclose or suppress.

The third element of cultural communication is *cultural identity*. Cultural identity provides a model for what a member of the group is like. Each culture, for example, holds different ideas about the nature of a member's positive face. Goffman (1967) acknowledged that facework includes the response of the audience to an individual performance. Efforts, then, to present a positive face are situationally constrained. Likewise, the enactment of roles is guided by cultural definitions of roles. The presentation of a positive face is contingent on cultural models of personhood. Carbaugh (1990) suggested that "a cultural model of personhood [consists of] targeted goals, loci of motives, and bases of social relations" (p. 157). The study of the relationship of cultural identity to egocasting will explore how disclosure avoidance accomplishes certain goals, is prompted by certain cultural motives, and reflects cultural definitions of social relationships.

METHOD

The data collected and used in this chapter were part of a larger study exploring Asian Indian adaptation to living in the United States. Ethnographic interviews were the primary method of data collection. However, some participant observation and triangulation of findings with key informants were used to assess the validity of conclusions drawn. Fifteen Asian Indians were interviewed, all of whom were attending the same university in the northeastern United States. Fourteen were graduate students, and one was an undergraduate student. Of the 14 interviewed, 9 were male and 5 were female. Ages of the participants ranged from about 21 years to 35 years. Although the university featured a large population of Asian Indian undergraduates, participants were chosen based on the ethnographic principle of studying a "speech community" (Hymes, 1972). In other words, the participants in this project identified themselves as comprising a speech community separate and distinct from the undergraduates. The participants had come from different regions of India during the past 3 weeks to 3 years. Most interviews were conducted individually, but three interviews were conducted with pairs of informants.

The interviews invited the Asian Indian sojourners to describe their experiences in America and to contrast Americans and Indians through the use of highly open questions. Examples of questions inviting descriptions of experiences include: "What has been your most frustrating moment since coming to the U.S.?" and "Who are your best friends here?" Examples of questions inviting contrast are: "Do you think the structure of the family is different here?" and "Is there anything about some Americans that put you off?" Although the latter question does not inherently request a contrast, contrasts were normally produced in response. Although interviewees were not questioned specifically about disclosure, the amount and types of talk produced by Americans as opposed to Indians was a point of discussion in almost every interview.

Two participants were interviewed on more than one occasion due to availability and interest in participation. The subsequent interviews helped in achieving a nonlinear research effort. A cyclical research process is preferred as a method for evaluating the quality of the theories used and for adapting the research methods more specifically to the findings of the particular case (Carbaugh & Hastings, 1992). The prolonged contact with participants was also helpful in developing credibility and contacts, which facilitate research within this close-knit speech community.

Data were transcribed using Jefferson's (1984) transcriptional notation system. A modified use of the transcriptions is included in this chapter. The modification of the transcriptional system occurred in reference to recording pause lengths. Jefferson's system measures pauses by the tenth of a second. This precise measurement seemed unnecessary for the type of analysis herein so, in the interest of concision and fluency, pauses were rounded up and down to half-second measurements with some rare exceptions. Brief pauses were coded if inclusion of the pause was seen as helpful for the reader to understand the content of the speaker's message. Unless the dash was needed to enable the reading of the transcription, pauses measuring less than 0.25 seconds were not noted. Although Jefferson's notational system does not indicate the rate of speech, Asian Indians tend to use a faster rate of speech. The faster rate of speech was noted by several informants who commented upon the slow rate of American speech. Participants' claims about the faster rate of speech by Indians are consistent with my own observations. The interview data presented in this chapter were uttered rapidly and with little hesitation.

Once data were transcribed, they were reviewed for patterns. One pattern sought was symbols used to characterize the Indian and the American identity. Data were reexamined with specific attention to discussions of norms that created the symbolic characterization of each. Both interview data and readings about Indian culture were used to amplify the cultural factors accounting for the norms. As explanations for Indian disclosure avoidance were isolated and reviewed, the concept of egocasting was identified as a potential label for typifying this type of cultural communication.

Although ethnographic data were only gathered from Asian Indians, the analysis will contrast Indian and American uses of this frame of communication. Characterizations of American communication practices will be based on published scholarship about American communication and from Asian Indian characterizations of the use of talk by Americans. The central claim of this chapter posits egocasting as a type of cultural communication that guides decisions about disclosure avoidance. The contrast between two cultures is conducive to elaborating how this communication strategy is distinctively performed by Indians. The contrast between Americans and Indians is particularly dramatic given the different perspectives toward the communication process. A. Rahim (1987) explains:

In all three of the main schools of Hindu thought, the primary focus of human communication was, unlike the Western concept of source-oriented communication, the *receiver*. The importance of the receiver-listener in the process of communication has always been the hallmark of Hindu philosophy. (p. 175)

The contrast between Indian and American communication practices highlights the outcomes associated with cultural identities privileging opposing ends of several dialectical tensions. Because dialectical tensions involve the existence of two potentially appealing, opposing forces, all speech communities are faced with using cultural information to discern how best to balance self-disclosures. Each group, however, differently defines that which constitutes a "good" balance.

ANALYSIS

Interviews with Indian sojourners to the United States yield interesting contrastive data about distinctions in communication patterns between Indians and Americans. Informants provided perceptions of American communication patterns and, in doing so, provided information about their own communication patterns. In the interest of conciseness, a representative data segment that exemplifies the intrapersonal process associated with egocasting will be presented. The cultural frame of egocasting will then be linked to the structuring norms and cultural identity (i.e., loci of motives, bases of sociation, targeted goals, and face) of Indians. Analysis of egocasting will be accomplished through a combination of interview data, literature about Indians, and contrasting information about Indian and American norms and identity.

Cultural Frame

Since egocasting is an intrapersonal process, reports from Indians about decision making and self-disclosure are needed. While interviewing Deepa and Padma, I revealed that some Indians with whom I had spoken mentioned that Padma was a good example of a "typical Indian." Deepa responded that she thought people might have said that of Padma because she is very polite. An important part of Deepa's ideas about "politeness" involve a process of disclosure avoidance. Deepa claims that Padma is "not very aggressive," and does not "dismiss the other person's argument." She elaborates:

```
 1  D  I also have this problem or I don't know what the sense that you always—
 2     before doing something you always think—hey it's not whether you think
        it's
 3     right or wrong it's also what other people think of that act you know
        it's uh I
 4     think most
 5  P  Yeah
 6  D  typical Indians will suffer from that kind
 7  P  =yeah=
 8  D          =of thing cause you always get (.5) what are people gonna say—uh
 9     it doesn't matter what—that you think it's right and you have to do
10     it it's more of what are other people going to say and what if it
11     means like suppose it's not the done thing but you're going to do it
12     because you like it and it's:—you feel it's correct and you always
13     feel oh but it's going to—if it's going to be too agog then maybe it
14     will involve the family name basically you know and—it's not a nice
15     thing
```

Deepa's description exemplifies the egocasting process. Egocasting is initiated when a potentially discordant act or utterance is conceived. The discordant thought triggers an intrapersonal process of considering what others will think (lines 3–4) and say (lines 8–10), and whether it will involve the family name (line 14). As Deepa considers the implications of her words and actions, she does so by imaginatively placing herself in the position of others who might immediately or subsequently learn of it. She imaginatively assumes the role of "daughter" as she considers the implications of her actions for the entire family. Deepa thinks in terms of role relationships which are not immediately relevant to the present interaction. Consideration of one's roles as a means of accomplishing self-restraint in disclosure is central to egocasting.

Fareena gives another example, noting the role of the family in the process of suppression.

```
16  F   there the concept of respecting your elders is so strong that you (1)
17      you would live in fear of what would my mother my aunt my uncle
18      my parents—what would they feel like if they knew that my
19      daughter is doing something una—unacceptable because you
20      depend so much you live in that family
```

Fareena's comments indicate that the extended family, and the danger of the family hearing something negative, is a weighty consideration for her. Informants were in agreement about the importance of the family in Indian life. Hierarchy, in India, extends well beyond caste boundaries. Indian hierarchy can also be seen through the respect for age and social roles.

Even in symmetrical relationships, Indians describe greater tolerance. Shivaji pointed out his difficulty in telling a friend when something he or she did was upsetting to him. Although friends talk about controversial issues, several informants noted that they were irritated by Americans who assert opinions too strongly. Indians also described the kind of public self-disclosure evident on American television talk shows as something that would "never happen" in India. In both personal and public scenes, Indians characterized themselves as not disclosing as readily.

Structuring Norms

A salient influence in egocasting is assessment of cultural norms for specific relationships. One Indian norm impacting disclosure avoidance is the amount of talk typically used. In discussing differences between Americans and Indians, several informants cited the American tendency to speak to strangers as initially disconcerting. For example, Anita explains:

```
21  A   we are not uh so effusive with words (.5) like uh you people use it
22      I don't know whether you mean it or not but have a nice day and
23      take care to anyone and all—we don't do that
```

Although all references by Indians to interaction among themselves pointed to enjoyment of extensive discussions, talk tended to revolve around pros and cons of issues, rather than the personal assertion of individual positions. In other words, less of the "self" was presented in the discussions. In the Indian context, talk more often occurs between people who are close and "interdependent" rather than to "anyone and all."

Even in interdependent relationships, taboo topics and disclosures restrict the conversational range of possibilities. Fareena elaborates how this caution extends to some topics of speech between friends.

```
24  F   I can't talk—ask—a friend of mine—uh an Indian friend of mine
25      has your boyfriend kissed you yet—I mean I could ask my closest
26      friends but (2) see they don't—they don't communicate on that
27      level because I think it's so deeply (.5) set in your mind that this
28      is not right it's not right (.5) this is not allowed and it's not right
29      it's not right
```

An understanding of this segment can be fostered through considering that dating, while more common in India than in the past, remains nonnormative. From all accounts provided by informants, discussions surrounding the topic of physical intimacy are nonnormative. Fareena's description is instructive not only of the contexts in which suppression of speech is demanded, but her statement that it's "not right" was repeated four times (lines 28–29), with the final statement made quite strongly. The vehemence in her statement, in addition to the convergence between interviewees regarding suppression of speech, reveals the force of the norms for avoiding certain types of discourse.

Further insight into the force of a norm can be gleaned by considering the social consequences for violating a norm. Due to the structure of society, role-discrepant disclosures can invoke serious consequences. Shivaji discusses the gossip network in India as he describes the difficulty he experiences in saying "no" to others in India.

```
30  S   I couldn't have—I couldn't have possible because it's so? tightly
31      webbed uh you—you say no you're the misinterpretation flows
32      down so far it's very tough for you to correct it (1) ya' gotta be
33      cautious—I'm not saying it's like a communist regime or
34      something like that but it happens that that's how social interaction
35      is. (1) I mean it's something like a small colony of people staying
36      together and they all know each other so well that—that you say
37      something it spreads off over the place?—so fast
```

Shivaji's comment gives a sense of both the scope and rationale for suppression among Indians. Due to the breadth and efficiency of the gossip network among Indians, many interactions are not merely construed "interpersonal" interactions. Even face-to-face interaction between peers may have wide-scale implications if the behavior and discourse of one participant become a topic for gossip. This characterization of the cultural context illuminates the cultural reasoning grounding normative restrictions on some speech.

Said also provides insight into how the cultural setting in India creates a context in which careless discourse is more problematic. Said is explaining the arranged marriage system, and the ways that information is obtained about a potential marriage partner when he states:

```
38   S    you make inquiries it's a very closed society (1) a lot of gossip
39        and a lot of (.5) everyone knows everything about everyone else
```

Said's reference to the gossip network as an influential part of arranged marriage was echoed by many informants, both in interviews and participant observation. If an unmarried person makes role-discrepant disclosures, gossip may be initiated which could later limit marriage options. Reputation was specified as an important "qualification" in arranged marriage.

As noted earlier, violations of norms for speaking can be a source of conflict and misunderstanding interculturally. Some Indians expressed surprise at the way certain Americans expressed their thoughts and opinions to others. Although several informants described distaste for situations in which students had spoken too harshly to a professor, and some described classroom discussions in which they observed that American students were prone to "take sides," the harshest account was offered by Tariq. Tariq characterized American communication by referencing a Hindi phrase which means "hit and make two pieces." The following dialogue occurred while asking him to expound upon that statement:

```
40   I    does that mean very direct or uh
41   T    yeah very direct=
42   I    =very direct and
43   T    unpolite (1) unpolished (1) mannerless (1) uh these are the mean
44        and crude words which I use to describe the people with whom I
45        met or read about
46        so they don't take enough consideration for the other person=
47        =not at all means not at all
```

These data suggest that some Indians see American directness as an unfavorable characteristic. Although most informants did not react to the directness as strongly as Tariq, the distaste for abrupt speech, especially toward people of higher status, such as teachers and parents, was consistently described negatively. While directness and openness is a value cited by Americans in discussing their friendships (Rawlins, 1983b) and in American public discourse in general (Carbaugh, 1988), this value does not appear to be as salient to these Indian relationships.

Cultural Identity

The ways in which key dialectical tensions are negotiated are a significant aspect of one's cultural communication system. The balance struck between such "dialectically elastic" tensions is reflective of important cultural values that distinguish the cultural identity of a group (Carbaugh, 1990, p. 6). Dialectical tensions influencing the types of communication favored by a speech community include the opposing forces: (a) express versus repress, (b) individualism versus collectivism, (c) self versus society, and (d) rights versus responsibilities. The prominent dialectical pulls for Americans and Indians will be concisely contrasted, then applied to egocasting as a cultural frame of communication.

Americans display a high level of verbal expressiveness. This cultural value is encoded in locations such as the Bill of Rights, conversational values of openness between friends (Katriel & Philipsen, 1990), and in some universities requiring public speaking as a general education requirement. American communication practices are characterized as privileging the individual self, and conferring the individual with rights (Carbaugh, 1988).

In contrast, Indians favor the opposing ends of each of the dialectical forces. Already noted in the "normative rules" section is the less effusive use of talk by Indians. The restraint is consistent with the duty-based code Shweder and Miller (1991) attribute to Indian Hindus:

Duty-based codes are concerned with the moral quality of individual action, the conformity of individual action to a code of proper conduct. The code itself takes precedence over individuals, their appetites, wants, or habits. (p. 168)

In such a code, proper conduct is determined by the role occupied within the society. The well-being of the collective, rather than the individual, is punctuated. In this social order, responsibilities are acknowledged more readily than rights.

Almost all interviewees were Hindu, but even non-Hindu informants readily recognized that Hindu philosophy affects all Indians. To understand the loci of motives of the Indian who forfeits "rights" of disclosure in favor of suppressing self-disclosure as a part of one's role enactment, it is necessary to look to Hindu philosophy. Throughout the interviews, the most commonly cited imperative of Hindu philosophy was to ignore the "fruit of one's labor": This means Indians should not look to benefit from efforts. Instead, the "right" motive for an Indian is to perform the labor because it is right to do so. A central belief enabling the perpetuation of a hierarchical caste system is that people occupy their current position in life due to actions in previous lives. In this respect, one's roles are seen as just; thus, the individual is expected to accept and adopt that role. Balagangadhara (1988) explains that "total suspension of all choices is the first requirement to be a 'moral' (used in the sense of an enlightened or liberated) person" (p. 121). Hindus believe the path to enlightenment is through "right action." The actions that are "right" are dictated by roles.

Since roles are viewed as just and appropriate, bases for sociation among Indians reflect the hierarchical organization of society. Descriptions of respect for elders, or for the person of higher status in asymmetrical role relationships (e.g., professor–student), provide a cultural logic in which the force of prescriptions not to self-disclose in a role-discrepant manner is affirmed. Put simply: hierarchy intensifies the need for caution in asymmetrical Indian relationships. Although Americans may also be more prone to avoid certain self-disclosures in asymmetrical relationships, a greater degree of flexibility would be expected due to the privileging of discourses of equality. Among Hindus, a code of equality does not resonate with expectations about social interaction.

Even in symmetrical relationships, such as friendships, the defined social roles strongly influence peer behavior. Shivaji's aforementioned inability to say "no" or to express negative feelings toward a friend is exemplary. Likewise, Deepa's typification of Padma's "politeness" demonstrates the recognition of peers as one link in the hierarchy that could learn of a role-discrepant disclosure.

The moral order of Hinduism points to the motives guiding egocasting. Hinduism may be seen as influencing the long-term goals of a person who is avoiding role-discrepant disclosures through egocasting. Hindus believe that the cycle of death and rebirth can be accomplished through "devotion to God, fulfillment of obligatory and ordained duties [and] ethical behavior" (Dandekar, 1988, p. 300). One goal of egocasting, then, could be seen as liberation from the cycle of rebirth.

A more immediate goal can be discerned by considering face wants. P. Brown and Levinson (1987) suggested that positive face, or the want to be socially desirable to some people on some occasions, is universal. Through certain forms of disclosure avoidance, Indians are able to present a face that is accepted and affirmed by the collective. The symbol "interdependence" was used consistently by informants in discussing relationships with friends and family. To preserve interdependence and maintain harmony, restraint is needed. In order to be a "good" or "moral" person in a predominantly Hindu culture, Ego needs to carefully consider which roles may be salient in a given scene, then avoid any disclosures which might violate proper role enactment.

The threats to an Indian's positive face identified in Shivaji's description of the gossip network (lines 31–37) display the difficulty entailed in repairing a damaged face in the Indian context. Once a positive face threat has occurred, it may become so widespread that apologies or clarification are infeasible. The gossip network impels Ego to consider her or his own positive face in addition to that of the family. In a culture where social harmony is prized more than individual assertiveness, the ability to threaten one's own negative face by suppressing disruptive disclosures becomes an important trait of an effective communicator. Through egocasting, an Indian cultural identity is instantiated and affirmed.

DISCUSSION

The data demonstrate that a significant factor in the thought processes about whether to disclose was the perceived role of Ego. Further, the importance of the information provided in the assessment of roles was guided by the structuring norms about talk in Indian culture and the cultural identity of Ego. The importance of certain proscriptions about self-disclosure was correlated with social structures, such as the gossip network and the extended family, which perform a cultural function in maintaining the force of certain norms. The logic behind the normative structure is informed by looking at dialectical forces, loci of motives, bases of sociation, goals, and positive face wants.

Disclosure avoidance is a communicative outcome created in a culturally informed manner. Application of "egocasting" contributes to an understanding of the *intrapersonal process* of disclosure avoidance as a culturally situated form of communication. Egocasting is not posited as a factor in all instances in which talk is restricted. When Anita indicates that Indians do not use phrases such as "have a nice day" and "take care," this is merely suggestive of differences in the cultural norms surrounding the quantity of casual speech behaviors by Americans and Indians. There is no evidence that if an Indian were to utter such a phrase, significant social ramifications would be incurred by Ego. Although this type of utterance would violate cultural norms about speaking to strangers, the use of such a phrase would not appear to be a very significant violation of norms about being less effusive.

Egocasting is involved when Ego is considering making a statement that is very open and very direct. Qualitatively, this type of speech act is out of the ordinary and constitutes a disclosure that could stimulate gossip. As Fareena indicates, there are some topics that are taboo because "they don't communicate on that level" (lines 26–27) because "it's *not right*" (line 29). The force of normative rules prohibiting some types of talk is quite strong. Dangerous forms of self-expressions can include disclosures about individual preferences, such as saying "no" (line 31), doing or saying something that diverges from salient norms (lines 2–13), and disclosing, or inviting disclosure, of information about nonnormative topics, such as dating (lines 25–26). When Ego considers making a disclosure that is "open" or "direct," the egocasting process is initiated. Ego imaginatively casts herself or himself in the position of a variety of Alters in order to assess the potential consequences associated with certain disclosures. Possible Alters for the Indian Ego to select include the immediate hearer, participants in the gossip network, and family members. As with altercasting, egocasting can also be seen as an efficacious communicative strategy. By using this strategic intrapersonal communication device, Alter's evaluation of Ego's ultimate self-presentation is more likely to be construed favorably, thus enabling Ego to maintain a positive face in the interaction.

For the Asian Indian, "face" is an important factor guiding egocasting. Shivaji's description of the gossip network conveys the difficulty entailed in repairing a damaged face in the Indian context. Cultural preferencing of dialectical pulls toward concern for the collective and producing responsible, role-appropriate speech and action provide the definition for Indian notions of personhood. This, in turn, instructs the Indian about how to present a positive face.

While egocasting may occur in all cultural groups, the roles assumed by the Ego, the topics initiating the egocasting, and the cultural reasons guiding the decision of whether to disclose would vary cross-culturally. For example, many Americans would never consider members of their extended family (i.e., aunts and uncles) in deciding whether to make a disclosure. In an American setting, Ego's perception of the existence of a close-knit, highly efficient gossip network would also change the importance placed upon this "Alter." Even if a strong gossip network did exist in an American context, given its location within an individualistic society, the importance of "what others think" would be evaluated differently given the disparate nature of American cultural codes. Although all cultures may use a form of egocasting in deciding whether to express or protect, different cultures would certainly have different topics, bases for reasoning, and imagined Alters that would be factored into the balancing of disclosures.

Egocasting as a socially situated, intrapersonal process is an example of one type of cultural communication. By applying Carbaugh's (1990) model linking cultural frames with structuring norms and cultural identity, egocasting can be seen as a frame of communication for examining interactionally significant intrapersonal processes. This communicative frame is subject to certain structuring norms about what roles Ego considers in deciding to disclose, about topics that prompt egocasting, and about how Ego can present a positive speaker face. This type of communication and the structuring norms have also been shown to form a strong link to the cultural identity of those invoking this frame. In the Asian Indian example, central values are displayed and maintained through enactment of this communicative frame. The collective identity of the Indian, especially the collective identity of family members is honored through egocasting. A value on the maintenance of social harmony through the self-constraint of the individual is affirmed. Egocasting is a cultural frame guided by Indian norms for communication and is reflective and constitutive of a uniquely Indian cultural identity.

17

▼▼▼▼▼▼▼▼

Disclosure and Privacy Issues
on Television Talk Shows

Victoria O. Orrego
Sandi W. Smith
Monique M. Mitchell
Amy Janan Johnson
Michigan State University

Kimo Ah Yun
California State University, Sacramento

Bradley Greenberg
Michigan State University

Television is an important socializing agent that shapes and creates viewers' attitudes and behavior (Bandura, 1994). With an estimated 10 million viewers a day, 750,000 of whom are under 13 years old (Mifflin, 1995), talk shows function as socializing agents that expose viewers to very distinctive and nonnormative patterns of public disclosures. Much of talk shows' increasing popularity is due to their increase in the controversial and sensational nature of guests' disclosures (Heaton & Wilson, 1995). Talk shows are "public confessionals" that encourage private revelations of intimate personal information (Priest, 1995). Private disclosures are then transformed into televised disclosures. Priest (1994) conceptualizes a televised disclosure as "the televised outpouring of personal information usually revealed only to one's close friends, family, rabbi, minister or therapist" (p. 75).

The primary vehicle through which talk show content is communicated to the audience is in the form of televised disclosures (Smith, Ah Yun, et al., in press). For example, Heaton and Wilson (1995) noted in their book *Tuning in Trouble,* that guests are invited to appear on the shows because of some unusual or bizarre experience, and the details of this experience form the focal point of the show. Additionally, Priest tracked down former guests on *Donahue* and reported on the guests' motivations to "tell all" on television (Priest, 1995; Priest & Dominick, 1994). The assumption that

249

underlies both the Heaton and Wilson and Priest research is that televised disclosures are synonymous with self-disclosure. That is, it is the guests themselves who reveal their own private experiences and feelings on talk shows.

Televised disclosures, however, have not been limited to self-disclosures. In their study on the content of talk shows, B. S. Greenberg et al. (1995) found that less than half (42%) of the disclosures were self-disclosures, but 28% were disclosures by the host, and 30% were disclosures by personal relations of the person to whom the disclosures refer. There are important implications when the sources of televised disclosures are not the guests who have experienced these events and feelings, but are instead the hosts or personal relations of the featured guests. For instance, the more severe problems associated with televised disclosures may occur when someone other than the featured guest discloses intimate details about another's life, thus ambushing him or her (Smith, Ah Yun et al., in press). These disclosures may engender negative outcomes, thus stretching the balance between revealing and concealing information. This imbalance may then lead to loss of control over private information and loss of face. In the talk show context, the ambush disclosures reflect breaches in privacy because what was once considered privately shared information has now been misused by someone whom the guest had considered a trusted friend. Thus, a comprehensive analysis of televised disclosures in talk shows must address both self-disclosures and other "ambush" disclosures.

This chapter provides an overview of television talk shows and relevant literature on self-disclosure, privacy, and face issues. Within this framework the process of *self*-disclosures on T.V. talk shows including the revelation, as well as the valence and type of the two immediate responses to the self-disclosure, will be discussed. Next, disclosures by others, also known as ambush disclosures, are presented followed by the valence and type of the two immediate responses to them. These data are analyzed in terms of whether or not and in what ways televised disclosures of either type differ from disclosures in close personal relationships. Implications of balancing disclosure and privacy issues where negative emotional outcomes, such as betrayal, loss of face, and trust, occur as a function of breaches in privacy are discussed.

TELEVISION TALK SHOWS

In 1994, daytime talk shows earned between 400 and 500 million dollars—about the same amount earned by all of NBC (Gregorian & Kuntzman, 1995). These shows typically follow a formula in that they focus on featured guests who have problems or issues concerned with sexual activity (Chad,

1995), physical health (Welles, 1992), career or celebrity status (Rosen, 1991), or criminal activity (Keller, 1993) that become the focus of the show. The shows also include a host, audience members, and, in some cases, "experts" (Heaton & Wilson, 1995). The hosts of these shows claim that they offer a public service because talk shows depict people who are coping with personal and relational problems, and these hosts further claim that their shows are positive in that they focus on the value of openness (Heaton & Wilson, 1995).

Critics, however, have characterized talk shows as sordid (Mifflin, 1995), raunchy, immoral, sleazy (Gregorian & Kuntzman, 1995), bizarre, trashy (Allen & Schwartzman, 1995), degrading (Oldenburg, 1995), revolting (Alter, 1995), and rot (Cass, 1995). Abt and Seesholtz (1994) assert that talk shows are causing "a crisis in the social construction of reality" (p. 195) in that they show persons who are breaking cultural rules, and that these portrayals serve to redefine deviance and appropriate reactions to it. Two areas in which talk show formats have broken socially appropriate norms are in their portrayal of personal relationships and in the disclosure of private information.

Current research has revealed that talk shows are characterized by intimate and private topics that are normally reserved for relational partners. In their analysis of talk show topics, Smith, Mitchell, et al. (in press) found that 847 of 955 topics featured private information about the guests' interpersonal relationships and/or personal attributes. Additionally, the majority of topics focused on negative familial and personal aspects. For example, family relationships tended to be portrayed in a negative manner (61%) rather than a neutral (32%) or positive (7%) one. Personal relationships, such as friendships or acquaintance, coworker, and romantic relationships, tended to be portrayed as neutral (45%) or negative (51%), but not as positive (4%). Individual attributes often portrayed were sexual activity, personality traits, criminal behavior, celebrity status, anger, and appearance. An analysis of the valence of the personality traits revealed that they, too, tended to be portrayed as negative (74%) rather than positive (10%) or neutral (16%). These portrayals have serious implications in that these televised depictions of personal relationships may function to distort the viewers' judgments about reality.

TELEVISED DISCLOSURES

Evidence also has been found for the general category of televised disclosures, including self-disclosures by the guest and disclosures by others (host or personal relation of the guest). These televised disclosures consist of very intimate and detailed information about the guests' personal lives (Smith, Ah Yun, et al., in press). A content analysis of 80 talk show transcripts identified 1,212 instances of six categories of televised disclosures (Smith,

Ah Yun, et al., in press). The six categories were sexual activity (23%), sexual orientation (6%), abuse (17%), embarrassing situations (12%), criminal activity (13%), and personal attributes, such as addictions, personality traits, or negative self-feelings (30%). Furthermore, after rounding the estimates to whole numbers, the typical one-hour talk show in this sample had four sexual activity disclosures, one sexual orientation disclosure, three abuse disclosures, two embarrassing situation disclosures, two criminal activity disclosures, and four personal attribute disclosures. Thus, the Smith, Ah Yun, et al. (in press) data lend support to the claim that televised disclosures encompass highly personal information usually reserved for private interactions, and that they occur with high frequency on television talk shows.

RESPONSES TO TELEVISED DISCLOSURES

Given the interactive nature of talk show formats, reactions (i.e., verbal responses) to televised disclosures have also been examined. The explicit nature of the disclosures elicited a variety of responses that were coded. Greenberg et al. (1995) categorized the first two responses to each televised disclosure, generating 20 response categories. Certain responses were categorized as punishing and negatively reinforcing, while others were found to be more neutral or positive.

First, the negative responses reflected disapproval and negative affect towards the disclosure and the person who performed the behavior that was disclosed. The punishing responses included: aggression, self-disconfirmation, other disconfirmation, moralizing/leading questions, and responses emphasizing the severity of the disclosure. Aggressive responses consisted of name-calling, attacks on character or competence, ridicule, threats, profanity, and physical attacks. Self-disconfirmation responses were statements that devalued and put down the self: "I hate myself right now; I just want to die." In this situation the discloser and respondent were the same person. Other disconfirmation responses were statements that devalued the other. The responder in this situation was anybody on the talk show except for the discloser, including audience members, the host or hostess, and other guests. An example is, "You are a sexist pig; no wonder you don't have a girlfriend!" Moralizing/leading questions were questions that emphasized the inappropriateness or immorality of the action, for example, "You knew that was wrong, didn't you?" The responses that increased distance included avoidance, aggression, denial, interruption, self-disconfirmation, and other disconfirmation.

Second, the neutral responses included: requesting more information about the disclosure, asserting the truth, and back-channeling. These responses were primarily objective, and they solicited informational content. They did not reflect overt negative or positive affect. More information about the disclosure and asserting the truth were responses given by the discloser herself or himself. They merely provided elaboration and clarification of disclosures or they validated and confirmed the truthfulness of the content, although when offered after an ambush disclosure, they served as face-saving techniques. Back-channeling were statements that prompted the discloser to continue: "uh-huh," "yes," or "go on," or at times part of the disclosure was repeated: "He swung at you with the baseball bat." Questions that requested more information were used to ask for clarification or more detail and for elaboration of the disclosure.

Third, positive responses were defined as responses that validated and confirmed the discloser. These responses to self-disclosure demonstrate support for the discloser by the host or hostess, the audience members, or other guests: "You are a beautiful person who has a lot going for her; you don't need him!" The responses that decreased distance were apology, remediation, humor, empathy, advice, self-confirmation, and other confirmation. Positive responses occurred less frequently than either negative or neutral responses, and they rewarded the discloser for opening up and discussing their personal problems and issues.

Greenberg et al. (1995) found specific response patterns for televised self-disclosures as opposed to televised other-disclosures. They coded the first two responses for each televised disclosure. The responses to televised disclosures were analyzed according to whether they followed (a) a self-disclosure where the featured guest revealed information about himself or herself, or (b) an other-disclosure by the host or a personal relation of the featured guest. For each type of disclosure, self or other, the two most proximal responses were coded as to whether they were offered by the featured guest, host, or other (personal relation, expert, or audience member), and the type of response that was offered.

Responses to Self-Disclosure

A total of 331 first responses were coded. Response one was most often offered by the host or hostess (240), and was most often a request for more information or a back-channel response that encouraged more interaction by the guest who offered the self-disclosure (58%). However, 10% of these responses were moralizing questions and 10% increased distance and emphasized the severity of the disclosure. The first response by another party was most often a disconfirmation of the guest who offered the self-disclosure (22%), and emphasizing severity, moralizing questions, and increasing distance accounted for 12% of the first responses by others.

A total of 286 second responses were coded. The second response by the featured guest who offered the self-disclosure was often an offer of more information or to assert the truth of the disclosure (78%). The second response by the host was most often a request for more information (20%), but negative responses accounted for 39%. The second response by another party was most often to offer more information (27%) or to give a response that was negative or increased distance (25%). The responses to self-disclosure focused on hosts and others instead of the featured guest who offered the self-disclosure. Hosts were likely to try to elicit more information about the disclosures, and both hosts and relational others responded negatively to the self-discloser about 30% of the time.

Responses to Other-Disclosures

A total of 506 first responses to other-disclosures were coded. The first response by a host to an other-disclosure was most often a request for more information (37%), while he or she was also likely to offer negative responses 24% of the time. The first response by another party was most often an offer of more information about the disclosure (25%), an assertion of the truth of the disclosure (19%), or a negative response (21%). Featured guests who had been ambushed engaged in face-saving strategies, such as giving more information, asserting the truth, making excuses, and denial, 85% of the time.

A total of 467 second responses to other-disclosures were coded. Similarly, the second response to an other-disclosure by the featured guest was most often a face-saving strategy (89%). The second response by the host was most often a request for more information, while 28% were negative responses such as moralizing questions or emphases of the severity of the disclosure. The second response by another party was most often an offer of more information (37%) or an assertion of the truth (19%), with 15% negative responses.

The pattern that emerges from ambush disclosures is clear. The featured guests about whom a disclosure has been offered were highly likely to use face-saving strategies such as giving information, asserting the truth, making excuses, or offering denial about 85% of the time. The data reveal that ambush disclosures stretch the balance between revealing information and concealing information. The use of face-saving strategies suggests that the ambushed guests felt that some degree of their privacy was violated by someone whom they had considered a trusted confidant. The hosts were likely to ask for more information about the disclosure (38%) and to offer general negative responses (26%). The other parties are likely to offer more information (31%), but they also assert the truth of disclosures (19%) and provide negative feedback through disconfirming the featured guests and offering responses that increase distance (17%).

It appears that self-disclosures versus other-disclosures in a mediated context engender more negative responses by the host of the talk show and the relational partner of the discloser. Due to the sensationalistic nature of talk show forums, it makes sense that the host's responses are moralizing questions that emphasize the severity and inappropriateness of the behavior in the disclosure and disconfirm the actions of the featured guest 30% of the time. Additionally, the host would be the only person who would not suffer any breach of privacy as a result of the disclosure. Self-disclosures, when told in the presence of a relational other, might engender loss of face and relational embarrassment for the other, thereby eliciting immediate negative verbal responses, as they did here 30% of the time by the relational other.

The abundance of televised disclosures and their subsequent response patterns have been demonstrated. The next step is to elaborate on the distinctions between self-disclosures and other-disclosures as well as the implications for face and privacy issues. These implications can best be discussed within the context of balancing self-disclosure, privacy, and face issues.

SELF-DISCLOSURE VERSUS TELEVISED SELF-DISCLOSURE

Self-disclosure has generally been considered a positively valued activity (Chelune, 1975). Self-disclosure is an essential component for relational development and maintenance (Cozby, 1973; Derlega et al., 1993). The core attributes of self-disclosure, as well as the social rules and norms governing this type of behavior, are discussed below. The definition of self-disclosure encompasses certain parameters that determine how self-disclosure is measured. Fisher (1984) defines self-disclosure as "verbal behavior through which individuals truthfully, sincerely and intentionally communicate novel, ordinarily private information about themselves to one or more others" (p. 288). Traditionally, self-disclosure has been viewed as a trait or global personality pattern, and the importance of socio-situational factors in determining the level of behavioral disclosure was not acknowledged (Chelune, 1976). Chelune (1975) suggested that a basic parameter of self-disclosure is the degree to which an individual can adequately differentiate interpersonal variables (e.g., social situation and target person) and adapt his or her disclosures accordingly. This has certain implications for what and how much disclosure is considered appropriate.

According to Priest (1994), two consistent findings, related to appropriateness, have emerged in the self-disclosure literature. First, self-disclosure tends to be reciprocal (Cozby, 1973; Derlega et al., 1993). The norm of reciprocity refers to the tendency for recipients to match the level of intimacy in the disclosure they receive (Derlega et al., 1993). Disclosure by one member of a dyad establishes the context for appropriateness of the level of disclosure by the other member and creates an obligation to reciprocate that is enforced by social disapproval for failure to respond in kind (Brewer & Mittelman, 1980).

A second finding from the self-disclosure literature is that disclosers tend to be liked by the target (Cozby, 1973; Derlega et al., 1993). This is generally true for individuals who know each other and are comfortable around each other. However, there are exceptions to this norm, whereby highly personal, negative disclosure given too soon inhibits liking (Bochner, 1982). Chaikin and Derlega (1974) found that, in general, high disclosure to a stranger was perceived by observers as less appropriate and more maladjusted than low disclosure. Additionally, disclosure will not lead to liking if responded to in a negative manner (Derlega et al., 1993). When self-disclosure is ignored, diminished, or dismissed, the discloser feels disconfirmed or even rejected.

In comparison to self-disclosures in interpersonal relationships, televised disclosures differ in two ways. First, talk show disclosures violate the norm of reciprocity. Televised disclosures occur in the public sphere to strangers, who for the most part do not reciprocate. In talk shows, the recipients of the disclosure are usually the host or hostess, audience members, and viewers (Priest, 1995; Smith, Ah Yun, ct al., in press). The norm of reciprocity in talk shows is overridden by the norm for public revelation. Second, televised disclosures are often perceived as inappropriate and responded to in a negative manner. Perhaps due to the early timing of the disclosure paired with what is often a topic with negative valence (Smith, Mitchell, et al., in press), the results indicated neutral or negative responses, not positive responses which would indicate liking.

On the other hand, additional research conducted by Priest (1995) has found that self-disclosing on talk shows has some benefits. In line with L. C. Miller and Read's (1987) model of self-disclosure, which includes the goals, resources, beliefs, and strategies of disclosers, Priest (1995) documented that the talk show participants on *Donahue* in her study reported one of four purposes as the motivation behind appearing as guests on talk shows. Specifically, these guests were outliers who were members of marginalized groups at the fringes of society. The most frequent motivation was a desire to remedy stereotypes and to educate a national audience about discrimination and alternative lifestyles. Disclosers also reported wanting their "15 minutes of fame," the forum to plead cases against those who had victimized them, or the opportunity to market a book or business venture as motivations for televised disclosure. In general, these former guests reported positive outcomes from engaging in televised self-disclosure that included satisfaction with the opportunity to "talk back" to society, self-esteem, and positive feedback from the public. It may be difficult to generalize these reactions to guests who engaged in televised self-disclosure on all talk shows, however, because Phil Donahue, along with current talk show hosts Oprah Winfrey and Rosie O'Donnell, was noted for his more socially responsible approach.

Although televised self-disclosures break norms for self-disclosure in close personal relationships, there appear to be some benefits to the practice (Priest,

1995). Disclosers have the ability to attempt to meet their goals, they can choose what to disclose about their personal lives, and they have control over the timing of the televised disclosures. While negative consequences may ensue, such as negative responses, televised self-disclosers have some degree of control and empowerment. On the other hand, the more severe problems associated with televised disclosures occur when someone other than the featured guest discloses intimate details about the featured guest, thus ambushing him or her. These problems center on balancing disclosure, privacy, and face issues.

BALANCING DISCLOSURE, PRIVACY, AND FACE IMPLICATIONS

In their book *Facework,* Cupach and Metts (1994) discuss three primary types of relational embarrassment: revealing relational secrets, inappropriate actions, and awkward situations. Clearly the talk show context is an ideal setting for creating relational embarrassment, whether through self- or other-disclosure. Additionally, the degree of balance between sharing information and maintaining a level of privacy differs depending on whether an individual self-discloses or is ambushed.

The self-discloser may reveal something very intimate about his or her own past, and this would still create an embarrassing situation for the partner because it may challenge the partner's perception of the discloser and possibly the relationship. The revelation of private information will create an awkward, disruptive situation. The partner experiences loss of face and embarrassment, which result in the elicitation of negative or relationally distancing responses. Even though the partner may already have known about the disclosure, it would still produce feelings of awkwardness or discomfort. As Derlega et al. (1993) note, there is a great risk in self-disclosure. Undesirable outcomes such as rejection, indifference, ridicule, the revelation of personal information to others, betrayal, and exploitation may occur. This is only compounded in a public context, such as on a talk show.

Balancing the level of revealed information with what should remain concealed is accomplished by the self-discloser. The self-discloser maintains control of what information is publicly shared and what is withheld. The self-discloser willingly chooses what to reveal to the television audience, and in doing so she or he is not put in a position of unanticipated misuse of information by another. Thus, the balance between disclosure and privacy is maintained.

Televised ambush disclosures negate the benefits of control and empowerment that one would have if he or she were the self-discloser rather than the ambushee. When hosts or personal relations of the featured guests, in particular, offer disclosures about the featured guests, important norms of privacy, trust, and saving face are violated, creating an awkward, disruptive, and distressing situation. All of these negative outcomes can occur when a host or personal relation of the featured guest offers private information to the viewing public that was told to him or her in private by the featured guest. The featured guest may feel guilt, shame, betrayal, and/or embarrassment as a result of this violation of privacy and loss of face, and "relationships can be terribly—and perhaps irrevocably—strained when public revelations include intimate details about others" (Priest, 1995, p. 185).

Additionally, loss of face occurs when the identity that the featured guest wishes to portray is challenged (Cupach & Metts, 1994). Loss of face tends to occur in problematic communication situations where the person who creates the problematic situation may not be the person who loses face. One type of predicament that Cupach and Metts detail is the "breach of privacy" in which personal and secret information is revealed to others. As documented in our research on the responses, talk show guests who were the targets of ambush disclosures were motivated to rectify the embarrassing situation by engaging in specific face-saving strategies such as giving information, asserting the truth, making excuses, or denial.

The balance between disclosure and privacy is severely stretched in the ambush disclosure situations. Even though talk show guests revealed certain information, they still reserved other information for a few trusted confidants. Ambush disclosure puts the featured guest in an uncomfortable situation, where loss of face and breaches of privacy occur (as discussed previously). Ultimately, ambush disclosures may result in relationship degeneration between the partners involved. Maintaining our interpersonal relationships requires careful judgments about what information to reveal and what to conceal. This balance is even harder to attain in a mediated context such as the talk show forum.

CONCLUSION

This chapter outlines the current research on television talk show disclosures and their subsequent implications for privacy and face issues. First, current research on televised disclosures and their subsequent responses were reviewed. Essentially, research has documented that talk shows focus on confidential and personal topics that have been usually reserved for intimates (Priest, 1995; Smith, Ah Yun, et al., in press). Every day, talk show guests willingly and publicly self-disclose very private information to millions of viewers. Talk show protocol, then, breaks traditional norms for socially appropriate levels of self-disclosure in interpersonal interactions. As a result, Priest (1995) has distinguished televised disclosures, which occur on talk shows, from disclosures in interpersonal interaction, which include self-disclosures and other-disclosures. Televised self-disclosures typically engendered negative outcomes from both the host and the relational partner an average of 30% of the time. This was not the case, however, with ambush disclosures (other-disclosures), and the subsequent problems that arise are centered on privacy and face issues. Responses to ambush disclosures were characterized as face-saving strategies designed to rectify the embarrassing breach in privacy that occurred to the featured guest. Guests who were ambushed, on average, employed face-saving strategies 85% of the time.

Second, televised disclosures were compared to self-disclosures that occur in an interpersonal context. Televised disclosures differed because (a) they occur in the public sphere to strangers who do not generally reciprocate, and (b) they are perceived and responded to in a negative manner, which decreases liking of the source. Despite the fact that televised disclosures break the norms for self-disclosure, there are some benefits to this practice. The choice to self-disclose on television was done to fulfill specific goals (i.e., gain fame, remedy stereotypes, or educate national audiences), and the timing and content are controlled by the discloser herself or himself.

Finally, we discussed the implications that televised disclosures have for balancing disclosure, privacy, and face. Televised self-disclosures did not breach privacy or offset the balance between revealing and concealing information because the featured guests were able to control the content, timing, and severity of the disclosure themselves. They did, however, lead to embarrassment and awkwardness that was evidenced by negative responses elicited from the host or the relational other. In contrast, ambush disclosures resulted in loss of face and an imbalance between revealing and concealing information because the identity of the featured guest was challenged, which led to face-saving response strategies. Essentially, the featured guest is not prepared for the disclosure and may not even want certain hidden secrets revealed, and when this does occur, that person's privacy is breached. Thus, televised disclosures, whether self-disclosures or other-disclosures, have the ability to yield embarrassment and potentially breach privacy, which can ultimately endanger the relationship between the parties involved. Lastly, viewers who are exposed to talk shows may, then, develop unrealistic or distorted views of disclosures in close personal relationships. More research on the effects of television talk shows would clarify this.

VII

BALANCING THE SECRET
BOUNDARIES OF PRIVATE
AND PUBLIC DISCLOSURES

18
▼▼▼▼▼▼▼

Sex Offender Community Notification Policies: Balancing Privacy and Disclosure

Pamela D. Schultz
Alfred University

On August 22, 1997, when a federal appeals court ruled that New York's "Megan's Law" was constitutional, thus paving the way for the state to release the names of 5,000 sex offenders after they leave prison, state Attorney General Dennis Vacco exclaimed, "The essence of today's ruling is that community notification does not amount to punishment. This is indeed a great day for victims' rights" ("Court Upholds," 1997, p. 1A).

Although popular sentiment holds that sex offender community notification policies are effective means of combating child sexual abuse, this assumption is fraught with controversy, not the least of which involves the constitutionality of such measures. The real issue revolves around whether usurping a sex offender's privacy is a deterrent to the crime, or if this lack of privacy may actually inspire more offenses. The factors which motivate an individual to molest a child are complex, with the desire to feed an erotic impulse merely one of myriad triggers. Opponents of notification policies caution that the belief that such laws can solve the problem may actually draw attention from more effective measures to control and combat sexual crimes.

This essay explores the implications of community notification policies by focusing on the balance of privacy and disclosure surrounding sexual offenses. While some states debate the constitutionality of the issue, other states such as New Jersey and New York have upheld these laws despite a number of appeals. Now is the time to ask the tough questions: Is public disclosure ammunition to combat child sexual abuse, a crime traditionally shrouded in silence? Will community notification act as a deterrent to child sexual abuse, or will it merely put more children at risk?

THE PROBLEM OF CHILD SEXUAL ABUSE

In recent years, the fear of sexual offenses has preoccupied the public. This fear is well founded since, at least statistically, sexual crimes appear to be increasing. In 1979, 12,000 people in the United States were serving state prison time for sexual offenses (Henderson, 1995). This figure rose to 20,500 in 1980 and to 63,600 just a decade later (J. M. Brown, Gilliard, Snell, Stephan, & Wilson, 1996). At least 20% of the adult prison populations in 10 states were sex offenders in 1991 (J. M. Brown et al., 1996). By 1994, state prisons held 88,100 sex offenders (English, Pullen, & Jones, 1997). The vast majority of incarcerated sex offenders are male. Although a large number of male victims report having been molested as children by females, few of these individuals are ever reported, let alone convicted. Consequently, the average first-time convicted sex offender is a White male between the ages of 33 and 35 (Henderson, 1995).

Why do prisons seem to be so filled with sex offenders? One reason is simply an apparent increase in the number of crimes being perpetrated. For example, between 1988 and 1994, reported rapes nationwide rose by 14% (Henderson, 1995). This statistic is even more startling when one considers that sexual crimes against children are commonly assumed to be underreported. However, self-reports of convicted rape and sexual assault offenders serving time in state prisons indicate that two-thirds of such offenders had victims under the age of 18, and 58% of those—or nearly four in ten imprisoned violent sex offenders—said their victims were age 12 or younger (Greenfeld, 1997). In addition, a telephone survey of a national probability sample of 2,000 children between the ages of 10 and 16 revealed that 3.2% of girls and 0.6% of boys had suffered sexual abuse involving physical contact. If one infers that those statistics can be generalized to the rest of the United States, children have experienced but not reported levels of victimization that far exceed those reported for adults (Finkelhor & Dziuba-Leatherman, 1994).

No one really knows how many children have been sexually victimized, although a commonly accepted estimate is that one in five girls and one in ten boys suffer sexual abuse before age 18 (Finkelhor & Dziuba-Leatherman, 1994). The statistics change depending on the type of variables, such as the population surveyed and the definition of sexual abuse employed by the researcher(s). Child sexual abuse is used to describe acts ranging from voyeurism and exhibitionism to sodomy and intercourse. Although the common public perception may be that sexual abusers are violent rapists who randomly kidnap and even kill their victims, in reality the crime is generally one of manipulation and seduction. Children know that adults hold power over them, and child molesters exploit this position of trust.

Why do sexual crimes appear to be increasing? Some researchers theorize that changes in society such as the breakdown of cohesive local communities, the increasing isolation of individuals and families, the sexualization of culture, and a greater tolerance for violent behavior may have contributed to this increase (Gelles & Straus, 1988). Others maintain that sexual abuse is an inevitable offshoot of patriarchal society, and that this social emphasis on power and hierarchy has caused sexual abuse not only to exist but to flourish throughout history (e.g., Crewdson, 1988; Rush, 1980). Still other researchers claim that current rates of sexual abuse are actually not much higher than in other times during this century. The major difference is that today crimes once shrouded in secrecy are being reported with more frequency.

In the 19th century, sexual abuse was primarily a home-based concern. One early accomplishment of the women's movement in the United States was to shed light on the rampant abuse of children in the home. In the early 20th century, incest underwent an interpretive transformation and the culprit of sexual abuse changed from that of relative to perverted stranger. Although the current focus on child sexual abuse exploded into the nation's consciousness during the 1970s, there were actually two other peak hysterias over sex crimes in this century. One peak was between the years 1937 and 1940, during which J. Edgar Hoover declared a war on the sex criminals who threatened American childhood and womanhood, which reflected the concurrent obsessions with nationalism, racism, and anti-communism. The other peak occurred between 1949 and 1955, following the publication of Alfred Kinsey's *Sexual Behavior in the Human Female*. Kinsey reported that nearly one quarter of 4,000 women surveyed said that they either had sex with adult males when they were children, or were approached by men seeking sex (Crewdson, 1988, pp. 24–25).

The crisis faded from national consciousness until the late 1970s. Between 1977 and 1978, almost every national magazine published a story on child sexual abuse. A national campaign against the making and sale of child pornography gained national attention in a matter of weeks; in record-breaking time, protective legislation was passed nationally and in 35 states (Finkelhor, 1979). Following the arrests of alleged members of a "sex ring" in Jordan, Minnesota, and the emergence of the McMartin Preschool case in 1984, media interest in the issue increased dramatically (Beckett, 1996). This interest has not waned in ensuing years, despite evidence that the hysteria has resulted in false arrests and the backlash of "recovered memory syndrome." Although at times hysteria has threatened to overwhelm fact, it is impossible to ignore the compelling truth that children are molested, and at great frequency. Sexual offenses, which once flourished in secrecy, are now much more likely to be prosecuted to the fullest extent of the law.

The dialectical tensions between silence and disclosure are endemic to the problem of sexual abuse. Historically, sexual abuse has been shrouded in taboo, characterizing a crime that communicates hierarchy and power to victims and perpetrators alike, unexpressed because it has been relegated to the realm of the unthinkable:

> The unthinkable has two faces. It is either what literally cannot be said—that is, verbal symbols are not available to permit saying; or it is taboo—that is, it could very well be said but should not be and if said, it is said at the risk of punishment. (Scott, 1993, p. 15)

From this perspective, the experience of child sexual abuse constitutes a form of knowledge, a paradigm through which survivors and offenders perceive personal and social reality. The delicate balance between secrecy and disclosure is thus an integral part of child sexual abuse. Today, there is a push to expose victims and perpetrators to public scrutiny. The assumption is that breaking the historical silence surrounding sexual offenses will create a safer atmosphere for children, yet indiscriminate public disclosure of sexual abusers may actually reinforce the secrecy that surrounds the crime.

COMMUNITY NOTIFICATION LAWS

As of 1985, only five states had enacted legislation requiring sex offenders to register with a central registry agency or with the law enforcement agency in the community in which they would be living (Walsh, 1997). The 1994 Violent Crime Control and Law Enforcement Act encouraged states to enact their own registration policies through a provision that threatened to withhold federal funding from states that did not implement sex offender registration programs. Consequently, by August 1995, 43 states had enacted sex offender registration laws (Henderson, 1995). By 1997, all states had devised registration laws.

Registration legislation is intended to deter offenders from committing new offenses and to create a registry to assist law enforcement investigations. A 15-year follow-up study of California's registration statute found that police investigators reported that the state's registration system was effective in helping them to apprehend suspected offenders (Finn, 1997). Sex offender registration laws generally include six features (Thomas & Lieb, 1995).

1. The registry is usually maintained by a state agency.
2. Local law enforcement is generally responsible for collecting information and forwarding it to the administrating state agency.

3. Typical information obtained includes an offender's name, address, fingerprints, photo, date of birth, social security number, criminal history, place of employment, and vehicle registration. Some states also collect blood samples for DNA identification.

4. The time frame for initial registration varies from "prior to release" or "immediately" to one year; the most common time frame is 30 days or less.

5. In most states the duration of the registration requirement is over 10 years, with some states requiring lifetime registration.

6. Most registries are updated only when the offender notifies law enforcement that he has changed residences.

By 1996, at least 32 states had taken the additional step of enacting notification statutes that either make information about sex offenders available on request or authorize probation and parole departments, law enforcement agencies, or prosecutor offices to disseminate information about released offenders to the community at large (Finn, 1997). These notification statutes are popularly known as Megan's Law after Megan Kanka, a 7-year-old girl who was raped and murdered in New Jersey in 1994. On May 17, 1996, President Clinton signed a federal version of Megan's Law. By December 1997, all states had enacted their own versions of Megan's Law (Walsh, 1997).

Community notification reflects the perception that registration alone is inadequate to protect the public against released sex offenders and that notification can help society protect itself from sexual abusers. Notification statutes have diverse provisions. Some statutes permit notification only in response to community requests, and may even charge a fee for the information (for example, Alaska charges a $10 fee to individuals who request information on a sex offender). Statutes usually assign responsibility for conducting notification to state or local criminal justice system agencies, although at least one state (Louisiana) requires that the offenders themselves do the notification.

New York's Sex Offender Registration Act

The underlying premise is that legislation should allow for local jurisdictions to develop and apply their own criteria for deciding which offenders should be subject to notification and the nature of the notification. For example, New York's Sex Offender Registration Act (SORA) of 1995 uses a number of factors to assign sex offenders one of three levels of notification. A five-member Board of Examiners of Sex Offenders, appointed by the governor, was created to assess the risk of a repeat offense of a sex offender and the threat posed to public safety. The instrument formulated to assess sex offenders is completed by corrections officials and filed with the Board in Albany, New York, who then assign the designations. A Level One designation is made when the risk of a repeat offense is low. In this case, the law enforcement agency having jurisdiction and the law enforcement agency that had jurisdiction at the time of conviction are notified (although a limited amount of information about the offender may be obtained for a fee via telephone). A Level Two designation is made when the risk of repeat offense is moderate. The law enforcement agencies then have the discretion to release information such as the offender's approximate address based on a zip code, a photograph, and the offender's criminal record. If the risk of repeat offense is high, and the offender is considered a "sexually violent predator," the offender is deemed a Level Three. In this case, law enforcement agencies are permitted to release to the community specific details regarding the offender's address and any special conditions imposed on the offender. All Level Three offenders are included in a subdirectory of sexually violent predators that is distributed to local police departments.

Regarding New York's SORA, it is important to note that the community notification procedures apply only to sex offenders imprisoned on or subsequent to January 21, 1996. On March 7, 1996, a U.S. District Court judge issued a temporary restraining order preventing people from gaining access to a $5-per-call hot line with information about newly released sex offenders stipulated in New York's Megan's Law, as well as preventing law enforcement officials from revealing information to communities. This restraining order was issued due to a class action lawsuit filed by the Legal Aid Society on behalf of approximately 6,000 sex offenders who claimed the law violated their constitutional rights. On August 22, 1997, a three-judge panel of the 2nd Circuit Court of Appeals unanimously rejected the lawsuit. A subsequent appeal in New York on behalf of the Legal Aid Society once again delayed community notification. On February 23, 1998, the U.S. Supreme Court rejected this second appeal, which claimed that Megan's Law constituted ex post facto.

New York's debate over Megan's Law reflects other states' legal wrangling over the constitutionality of community notification. For example, in 1997 the 3rd Circuit Court of Appeals in Philadelphia upheld New Jersey's version of Megan's Law, where notification policies were first proposed. Although future appeals are inevitable, it seems apparent that some measure of community notification will prevail. The issue thus becomes balancing the public's demand for information against the offender's right to privacy. Although some people might claim that sex offenders relinquished their right to privacy when they committed their crimes, the question is also whether this form of punishment will prevent recidivism or actually inspire it.

The Controversy Over Public Disclosure

Community notification policies reflect the popular sentiment that sex offenders are irredeemable. Although research exists that claims treatment can be effective to reduce recidivism amongst offenders, public fear is not assuaged by the possibility of rehabilitation. Consequently, proponents of notification statutes believe that informing the public about the presence of a convicted sex offender in a community will allow neighbors to take action to protect their children from the offender's inevitable attack. According to Lieutenant Lisa McGinn, commander of the sex crimes unit of the St. Paul, Minnesota, Police Department, "[Community notification] lessens the hysteria that surrounds this [crime]. . . . Now [citizens] have the opportunity to take this information and do some positive crime-prevention in their community" ("Put on Notice," 1997, p. 10).

Proponents of notification believe that the statutes will improve public safety because the public will be able to recognize and report risky behaviors by sex offenders, such as purchasing pornography or talking to children. For example, as the result of a flier distributed at a community meeting in Seattle, a woman reported that a man had appeared at her house and said he was a high school math tutor. The man turned out to be a registered Level II sex offender (Finn, 1997). Proponents of notification point to studies showing that anonymity is a factor in many crimes and claim that criminals are more apt to commit crimes in neighborhoods where they do not know the neighbors and the neighbors do not know each other. The assumption is that a criminal will be less likely to commit crimes where the neighbors recognize him or her, particularly if they know he or she has a criminal record.

In addition, some proponents claim that community notification may allow informed neighbors to help sex offenders rehabilitate themselves. The hope is that public disclosure of an offender's presence will inspire an outpouring of support for the offender. One proponent of community notification writes of a man who was paroled in 1990 after serving two years for selling cocaine. The man was released to the same neighborhood where he grew up, and credited his neighbors for helping him to keep his record clean after his parole (Carlson, 1997).

Overall, proponents of notification believe that such policies are necessary due to a perception that sex offenders are much more likely than are other criminals to re-offend. In actuality, research shows that about 50% of sex offenders engage in recidivistic activity (Bench, Kramer, & Erickson, 1997). This figure is about equal to the recidivism rate of other criminals; as researchers have pointed out, within 3 years of sentencing, while still on probation, nearly half of all probationers commit a new crime or abscond (Carlson, 1997). Some researchers have even found that sex offender recidivism rates are actually lower than those of other criminals. For example, a 1989 Justice Department study found that 32% of burglars were rearrested for burglary within 3 years after their release, compared to 8% of sex offenders rearrested for rape (Bernstein, 1995).

Opponents of notification claim that such policies are ill advised on a number of points. First, opponents claim that notification statutes are unconstitutional. As reported earlier, a number of states have had their notification statutes legally challenged, including New York, New Jersey, and Connecticut. Many critics believe community notification unjustly continues the punishment of an offender after he has served prison time. However, sex offender registration statutes that have been challenged on the basis that they violate due process rights, punish after the fact, or constitute "cruel and unusual punishment" have resulted in merely minor modifications (Henderson, 1995). Sex offender registration has never been judged unconstitutional, and now it appears that notification policies will be upheld as well, even though it singles out a particular group of criminals for special treatment.

Second, opponents threaten that notification policies may result in decreased reporting of sexual offenses. Reports from New Jersey and Colorado indicate that there is a decrease in the reporting of juvenile sex offenses and incest offenses by family members and victims who do not want to cope with the impact of public notification on their family (Freeman-Longo, 1996). In cases of incest, public disclosure of a sex offender's whereabouts also acts as public exposure of his victims.

Third, opponents note that these policies ignore the largest number of sexual abusers by focusing on "stranger danger." According to STOP IT NOW!, a Vermont-based organization devoted to educating the public about sexual abuse and sexual abusers, at least 90% of victims nationally are molested by someone they trust. STOP IT NOW! maintains that using notification policies as a panacea for public fears perpetuates the stereotype of the child molester as a dirty old man lurking in the bushes, attacking any child who happens to cross his path. In reality, most child molesters prey on children they know.

Fourth, notification policies may undermine treatment for offenders. Drama therapy, cognitive behavior therapy, psychoeducation groups, and pharmacological treatment are potential means of reducing recidivism in sex offenders (Prentky, Knight, & Lee, 1997). Yet, opponents claim that public disclosure of sex offenders undermines treatment on two fronts. First, public notification may put therapists in the ethically untenable position of violating the confidentiality of their clients. Second, public notification may reinforce the problems that contribute to the offender's behavior in the first place, including poor anger management and communication skills, fear, lack of trust, low self-esteem, lack of empathy, and isolation (Prentky et al., 1997). Ultimately, the offender may choose to avoid treatment (whether court-ordered or not) due to fear of disclosure, which could further exacerbate the symptomatology.

Fifth, opponents believe that notification policies may promote violence against convicted sex offenders or those purported to be sex offenders. Despite proponents' belief that community notification may inspire neighbors to help ex-cons become upstanding citizens, the disclosure of personal information about sex offenders in particular has already led to assaults, harassment, and job loss. For example, when a community was notified of a sex offender's return to their neighborhood in Washington State, his future "neighbors" burned down his home. In New Jersey, a father and son broke into a home and beat a man they mistakenly believed was a sex offender (Walsh, 1997).

Sixth, opponents claim that Megan's Law provides a false sense of security. Opponents maintain that it is the parents' responsibility to educate their children regarding danger, not the state's responsibility. Believing the government is taking care of that education may lull parents into complacency regarding their children's moral upbringing. In addition, the belief that Megan's Law is an effective deterrent to the crime may cause people to persist in their ignorance concerning the dangers and causes of child sexual abuse. If the public believes Megan's Law solves the crime, there is little incentive for understanding the roots of the problem.

Seventh, opponents believe that notification policies raise controversial issues regarding confidentiality and privacy. As Freeman-Longo (1996) related, the American Psychiatric Association's *Diagnostic and Statistical Manual of Mental Disorders* (4th ed.; 1994) classifies the sexual abuse of children under a diagnostic category known as pedophilia. Notification laws require that this mental health/medical diagnosis be publicly disclosed, while many other medical diagnoses of dangerous diseases, such as tuberculosis and HIV, are protected from public scrutiny. Admittedly, it is potentially offensive to place pedophiles in the same category as persons suffering from contagious diseases, since this medical diagnosis in no way justifies the crime. Yet communities are not notified about the presence of other individuals diagnosed with potentially dangerous mental illnesses or criminals convicted of heinous offenses such as drug dealing or homicide. How can we justify extending privacy to one group of potentially dangerous individuals, yet not another? How do we balance an individual's right to privacy versus the public's right to know?

Privacy Versus the Right to Know

The essential problem with trying to balance public disclosure and individual privacy is that, legally, the concept of privacy is vague and even undefined. Some legal scholars argue that the right to privacy in the United States is an intrinsic good, therefore fundamental and irreducible. Others contend that privacy is an instrumental good emanating from other rights such as freedom and personal security. Legal conceptions of privacy stem from an 1890 article in *The Harvard Law Review,* in which Louis D. Brandeis and Samuel D. Warren made the case that the Lockean notion of the natural right to life included the right to be left alone. Although philosophically supportive of an individual's right to privacy, Brandeis and Warren's argument excluded information that was in the public interest.

The idea of information that is in the public interest pertains to the issue of sex offender community notification policies. Are the records of sex offenders no one's business because offenders have paid their debts to society and should be left alone? Or is it in the community's best interest to know about a convicted sex offender's presence? Proponents of notification laws maintain that people have the right to know whether convicted sex offenders reside in their community, and that perpetrators gave up their rights to privacy when they committed their offenses.

Opponents of notification policies, such as New York's Legal Aid Society, argue that various Supreme Court rulings have held that the Constitution bestows on individuals some right of privacy in accordance with the First, Fourth, Ninth, and Fourteenth Amendments. They believe that the Fourteenth Amendment protects the sort of "informational" privacy that notification laws address. Grounded in the Fourteenth Amendment's concept of personal liberty, the right of privacy safeguards two different types of interests: the interest in avoiding disclosure of personal matters and the interest in independence in making certain kinds of decisions. Opponents also note that several laws enacted by Congress have been designed to protect the right to privacy. However, these laws are not comprehensive (for example, the 1974 Privacy Act, which deals with the protection of privacy in the use or distribution of government records but applies only to federal agencies).

In general, courts confronted with a right-to-privacy claim in a challenge to registration or notification requirements for sex offenders have held that there is no protected privacy right to information that is a matter of public record, within the public domain, or exposed to the public, because there is no *reasonable* expectation of privacy. Courts have held that in sex offender cases, the interests of the government in assisting law enforcement efforts and public safety outweigh the private interest (Walsh, 1997). In other words, sex offenders have waived their right to privacy by committing their crimes, as have persons convicted of other crimes while under the strictures of a criminal sentence.

Therefore, focusing the debate on whether or not notification statutes are constitutional is ultimately fruitless. Given the assumption that society's general interests supersede individual rights of privacy, the pressing issue becomes whether public notification is an effective means of combating the crime of sexual abuse by empowering victims and reducing offender recidivism. When considering the balance of privacy and disclosure regarding notification laws, three important issues need to be addressed. First is the idea that, while the offenders may have relinquished their rights to privacy by committing their crimes, their victims have not—yet notification laws put victims' privacy at risk. In some cases, publicly identifying offenders could result in violating the privacy of the offenders' victims. If an offender has been convicted of incest, in particular, his or her victim's identity may be impossible to hide. In this sense, public demand for disclosure may actually revictimize the victims of sexual abuse by forcing them to endure public scrutiny.

Second is the danger that public notification may actually feed the crime by forcing offenders into isolation and secrecy. During the past two decades, increasing numbers of sexual abuse survivors have publicly disclosed their experiences. Perpetrators of these crimes, however, have been forced to remain secretive, particularly since the pedophile has become the public's most recent bogeyman. Notification policies are attempts to break through this silence by forcing offenders into public self-disclosure. The idea is that tagging perpetrators with a scarlet letter will flush them out into the open, and public exposure will make it impossible for them to repeat their crimes.

Researchers note that self-disclosure is a means of empowering the self and controlling the environment. The key to successful self-disclosure is the individual's ability to regulate the information, since social norms inhibiting or forcing self-disclosure can have an isolating effect (Derlega & Grzelak, 1979). Public notification interferes with an offender's ability to readjust to life outside of prison. The community may shun him or her, and subsequently may shun his or her family. As a result, the offender may be unable to find housing or employment, may drop out of therapy programs, or may turn to drugs or alcohol to sublimate the rejection. In effect, the public's demand for disclosure may actually encourage the offender to be secretive for fear of rejection, thus reinvigorating the environmental stresses that triggered his crimes. The end result could be to increase his or her risk of recidivism.

Third, public notification may victimize the neighborhood into which a convicted offender moves. For example, property values may plummet, and inhabitants may be gripped by fear. Even carefully planned notification procedures can inspire hysteria amongst citizens, especially children. This latter issue is especially potent when one considers that the underlying goal of notification policies is to identify offenders so that community citizens can legally keep them from engaging in high-risk behaviors such as loitering near playgrounds or schools. Yet, this becomes problematic when piggy-backing the cry of public notification is a movement away from paroling convicted sex offenders.

To understand the impact that not paroling sex offenders can have on recidivism, it is necessary to understand the nature of a crime conviction. At sentencing, offenders are given a conditional release (CR) as well as a maximum release (MR) date. If offenders are not granted parole, they serve in prison until their CR date. If they are released upon that date, they are subject to strict supervision by parole until their MR date. Any minor violation of parole restrictions sends them back into prison. Increasingly, public outcry due to notification policies has caused offenders to stay in prison until their MR date, which means they are subject to vastly less supervision on their release. The irony is that public notification may thus create a more dangerous environment for sexual offenses.

In summary, the courts have upheld the notion that the public has the right to know of a convicted sex offender's presence. The real question is whether public notification may tip the balance in favor of increased risk to children, rather than improved safety for society.

CONCLUSION

Overall, the argument in favor of publicly identifying convicted sex offenders rests on a premise of Millsian utilitarianism. The prevailing assumption is that the privacy of sex offenders is less important than the safety of the communities in which they reside. The likelihood is that sex offender notification statutes will withstand legal challenge. The punishment of sex offenders continues to spiral and notification statutes are only one aspect of the public's demand for retribution. Perhaps sex offenders have more to worry about than their right to privacy. California recently passed a statute to chemically castrate repeat child molesters, and offenders have the option of surgical castration. Other states are following suit, although the American Civil Liberties Union has vowed to challenge these statutes. Overall, state and federal governments are swiftly passing legislation in this area.

At this point, most registration and notification statutes have not been in action long enough for researchers to be able to gauge their effectiveness as a deterrent to crime. What is clear about these scarlet letter conditions is that they are controversial, and they seem to raise more questions than they address. For example, are notification statutes designed to protect the public? Or are they a means to exact revenge? Are they intended as further punishment for offenders, or to assist in their rehabilitation? Will these notification laws result in a safer society—or will they merely fuel the problem of sexual abuse by reinforcing the secrecy that invigorates the crime?

Sex offender community notification laws are aimed at soothing the public's fear of sexual offenses. Yet a closer examination of the crime reveals it to be spawned by myriad factors, internal and external to the offender. Given the delicate balance of secrecy and disclosure regarding sexual offenses, community notification may exacerbate the stressors that trigger the crime. In effect, the public may reap the opposite of what it seeks.

19
▼▼▼▼▼▼▼▼

Private Secrets and Public
Disclosures: The Case
of Battered Women

Lara E. Dieckmann
California State University, Los Angeles

The focus of this chapter is an analysis of ethnographic data collected through research at an agency for battered women and their children located in Chicago, Illinois. The data were collected in a 10-month period from the summer of 1992 through the spring of 1993. Data were generated through three key methods. The major source of data comes from in-depth interviews with regular agency clients conducted over the course of 6 months. The initial interviews involved a core group of eight informants. All of the interviewees, whose names have been changed to protect anonymity, knew of my research project. I verified the transcriptions of the first set of interviews with each of them. Of the core group, three of the women were European American, two were African American, and three were Hispanic American. Their ages ranged from 20 to 38, though only one informant was willing to specify her exact age (a European American woman, aged 23).

Interviews with other agency and shelter volunteers and activists in the battered women's movement constitute another source of data in this study. These interviews were less formal. In some cases, volunteers or activists were only interviewed once. The data from these interviews are used to describe the relationship between the agency clients and the counselors who attempt to aid them, as well as to illuminate the process by which abused women are encouraged to disclose narratives of abuse in counseling.

The third method of data collection in this study was the documentation of observations in the field. The "field" in this context refers to the afore-mentioned agency and to the Skokie, Illinois, courthouse at which agency

volunteers, including the author, served as legal advocates. Much of the
observed interaction between agency volunteers and battered women or the
interactions among allegedly abused women, alleged abusers, lawyers, judges,
and legal advocates were informal, singular, and fleeting and, therefore,
difficult to verify from outside sources. Observations are used in this chapter
as a way to describe the context of domestic violence and to support the
data collected in the interviews. The conclusions reached herein, although
potentially applicable to a wider population, reflect the experiences and
opinions of this particular group of women in this particular context.

   In addition to the interviews and field observations, this study benefitted
from extensive participation in the local community, composed of various
activist groups and organizations devoted to ending violence against women.
The choice to employ the method of participant observation reflects the
feminist politics that the agency, volunteers, and activists espouse (Abu-Lughod, 1990). Reinharz (1992) synthesized the goals of feminist ethnography
in the following schema: "1) to document the lives and activities of women,
2) to understand the experience of women from their own point of view, and
3) to conceptualize women's behavior as an expression of social contexts"
(p. 51). Reinharz's first point is self-evident; this study documents some
experiences of a particular set of abused women seeking help from an agency
for battered women. The second and third points require some explication.

   In order to comprehend abused women's experiences from their vantage
point, the narratives of disclosure generated from interviews are considered
the primary source of information about abuse within the scope of this study.
This represents an attempt to situate the interviewees as interlocutors within
the scholarly discussion about communication and domestic violence (Ray,
1996). Moreover, this choice emphasizes the imperative that Alcoff (1991)
stated: "We should strive to create wherever possible the conditions for
dialogue and the practice of speaking with and to rather than speaking for
others" (p. 23). Speaking for others (in this context, battered women) is
perhaps unavoidable in this chapter. But, according to Alcoff (1991), "there
is no neutral place to stand free and clear in which one's words do not
prescriptively affect or mediate the experience of others, nor is there a way
to decisively demarcate a boundary between one's location and all others"
(p. 20). Interpreting abused women's experience in relation to their social
and political context and with reference to their own words is an attempt to
construct an ethical representation of this particular research project.

   Reinharz's (1992) final point about feminist ethnography is particularly
salient in relation to the balance of privacy, secrecy, and disclosure in battered
women's experiences. The abused women interviewed in this project chose
to disclose their narratives in relation to the social context of the agency of
which they became temporary members. Similarly, abused women's behaviors, decisions, fears, and hopes are comprehensible only in relation to the

context of domestic violence that conditions every aspect of their lives. Given the importance of Reinharz's methodological principles for a feminist analysis of abused women's experience, the next section describes at some length an observation of an abusive interaction in order to evoke the complex context of disclosure within which abused women must negotiate.

OBSERVATION FROM THE FIELD:
THE COMPLEX CONTEXT OF DISCLOSURE

The following observation was documented during a session in the domestic criminal court of the Old Orchard Courthouse in Skokie, Illinois, on November 3, 1992. The transcription excerpt is intended to describe the social, political, and institutional context in which abuse occurs and to reflect the intense conflation of privacy, publicity, secrecy, and disclosure within abused women's daily lives. By demonstrating the degree to which publicity and privacy are conflated within the experience of abuse, the aptness of the balance metaphor to describe the operations of disclosure and secrecy in battered women's lives is revealed.

The first case of the docket was reviewed by the judge. Apparently, the attorney asked for, and received, a continuance. The woman, allegedly abused by her husband, returned to her seat in the court, two rows in front of me. Her appointed lawyer tells her to wait in the courtroom, as her request for an order of protection is a separate matter from the criminal charges she is bringing against her partner. She appears confused about why a legal distinction is made between the two complaints. The husband, one of the few alleged abusers to appear in court in response to official summons, walks down the center aisle. Blank-faced, he takes a seat behind his wife, just one row in front of me. He begins to whisper in her ear, but loud enough for me to hear. "I hate you for doing this to me, you fucking bitch. I'm getting tired of your bullshit. You're lucky I don't kill you right here. You're gonna regret fucking with me, bitch." She shifts away from him, but he shifts toward her. He is far enough away from her so as not to draw attention to himself, but close enough to communicate to her. I wonder if I should call over the bailiff? I've been warned that my presence in the courtroom is a courtesy. I am not to draw attention to myself in any way while the judge is speaking. I try to get his attention, but the bailiff's back is turned. I catch a sudden movement out of the corner of my eye, a flash of skin.

The man has hooked his hand under her arm over the bench separating their seats. He is attempting to force her to get up. The man's attorney approaches them. The husband immediately releases his grip and appears composed. The lawyer signals the man to follow him out of the courtroom for consultation. I shift in my seat to look at the woman. She appears impassive, her face devoid of expression. I enter the row ahead of mine, walk toward her and sit down. I retrieve from my bag a business card with a series of emergency numbers and a list of local resources for battered women and their children and pass it to the woman in front of me. She takes the card, but seems disturbed and not altogether happy about my intrusion. She glances down at the card and hurriedly stashes it in her purse. She turns to face the front of the court and nods twice. I get up and return to my seat. She never looks at me and we never speak.

The courtroom observation documented above exemplifies the extreme complexity of privacy, secrecy, and disclosure in the lives of battered women (Fineman & Mykitiuk, 1994). Balance is an extremely appropriate metaphor to describe the experience of domestic violence, as this extended excerpt demonstrates. In this context, the abused woman attempted to negotiate the legal institution by lodging a formal complaint against her husband. However, her request for an order of protection was separated by the judge from her complaint of abuse, though the *experience* of the violence, of course, was the same. Therefore, she was required to balance her understanding of her experience with her desire to remedy her situation through legal means.

The abuser, too, was attempting to balance the appearance of his innocence, a public persona, with his abusive, but private, attempt to squelch the legal action his wife was taking against him. Furthermore, the interaction between the abused woman and her potential advocate was conditioned by competing interests: the imperative to maintain personal privacy, even in a highly public place, with the imperative to receive help from outside sources. In this context, then, domestic violence was rendered highly visible and mediated by the court system, but was also invisible, occurring under the watchful eye of the judge and bailiff. In other words, it was simultaneously public and private, disclosed and secret.

The conflation of privacy and publicity that this experience represents seems to point to a condition of domestic violence best understood as the precarious balance between safety and danger, disclosure and secrecy (Ray, 1996). For the battered women interviewed in this study:

> The dissolution of the boundary between inside and outside gives rise to an almost obscene conflation of private and public. It brings with it all the solitude of absolute privacy with none of its safety, all the self-exposure of the utterly public with none of its possibility for camaraderie or shared experience. (Scarry, 1985, p. 53)

Although the desire for privacy, the habit of secrecy, and the act of disclosure may be common features of human interaction, the interplay of these communicative elements is particularly heightened for women in abusive relationships.

THE DECISION TO DISCLOSE

Disclosure is always ambivalent. For abused women in particular, disclosure represents imminent danger (D. Martin, 1976; L. E. Walker, 1979). Derlega et al. (1993) referred to the "duality of self-disclosure: it can indeed be a frightening venture, opening the teller to rejection or indifference, but at the same time it can be confirmation of one's worth" (p. 14). The risk of consequence is considered a normal function of self-disclosure. "Decisions that persons make about self-disclosure have consequences for the individual partners in a relationship but also for the relationship itself" (Derlega et al., 1993, p. 8). However, for abused women, this condition is greatly exacerbated. What is simply frightening about the venture of self-disclosure for others has life-threatening implications for them. Though she may fear rejection by or indifference from her listener, increased violence from her abuser becomes a more immediate threat. Although disclosure is a method by which abused women seek help, it is also a source of extreme danger. The power that disclosure signifies in abusive relationships, however, also represents its liberatory potential, as keeping abuse secret is itself a form of psychological or emotional abuse. Clearly, disclosing abuse may function as the first step in disengaging from a violent relationship (Derlega & Berg, 1987).

The decision to disclose is complicated by the fact that many abused women consider the abuse they suffer so horrible and shameful that they do not wish to share it and potentially expose themselves to ridicule or misunderstanding. As Susan, a regular agency client interviewed for this study, stated:

> Telling you about this . . . making that first call was the hardest thing I have ever done in my entire life. I was so afraid to even pick up the phone! I mean I had the number for weeks. A friend gave it to me. She knew about what was going on. Who was I trying to kid? So I finally called. I guess I realized that if I didn't do something soon, one of us would end up killing somebody. I didn't want to be dead, but I almost wished it. At some point, it just seemed like it would be better to be dead than to be where I was. Thank God I don't feel like that anymore.

Common responses to revelations of abuse, such as "why don't you just leave him?," "how could you let him do that to you?," or "I would never put up with that kind of treatment," though reflective of a simplistic understanding of domestic violence, nonetheless may serve to decrease a battered woman's already low self-esteem (Crocker & Schwartz, 1985). Loss of self-esteem is compounded even further by external factors such as economic dependence, concern about children, religious conviction, and familial or cultural pressure to remain within a relationship, among many others (Stein-

metz, 1977). Juanita, a key informant, reiterates Susan's experience in deciding to disclose the domestic violence she suffered: "Nothing seemed like
it would be harder [than to disclose the abuse]. I mean, I been through a
lot, but thinking I could do this: Now *that* was hard." Fear, shame, and low
self-esteem may be the most significant obstacles in the decision to disclose.
    According to the battered women interviewed for this study, several
factors mitigated the difficulty that surrounded their decision to disclose.
These factors can be summarized in the following way: (a) anonymity afforded by crisis hotlines and other forms of mediated communication; (b)
inclusion in a group context in which shared knowledge of abuse is fore-
grounded (Kreckel, 1981); (c) a sudden increase in intensity or frequency of
abuse, in which threats against disclosure in the future become less frightening
than the violence in the present; (d) discovery of accessible, safe services for
victims of domestic violence; (e) revelation of the experience of similar abuse
by a friend, coworker, relative, or counselor; (f) institutional intervention,
such as a hospital worker who recognizes signs of abuse in treating a victim
or a lawyer or legal advocate who represents or advises a victim during a
legal proceeding; and (g) a "trigger effect" in communication with others,
such as a phrase or reference that "triggers" a particularly volatile or sensitive
memory of abuse.
    Interviewees who shared narratives of abuse cited the aforementioned
factors in various combinations as reasons that prompted their decision to
disclose. For Gloria, a regular agency client:

> It had to be without anybody knowing. No way was I going to spill my guts
> to somebody I didn't know. But then I had no options. No choice. I couldn't
> stay home even though I wanted to hide, and I couldn't leave the house. He'd
> find me for sure. Plus I look like shit. Everyone would know. What could I
> do? I called you guys. At least I could talk to someone when I wanted. Hell,
> *when I could.*

Gloria's narrative reveals the difficult balance of privacy and publicity, secrecy and disclosure within abused women's experience. Gloria would only
reveal her abuse to someone she knew, though she felt that she could not
risk that type of interpersonal disclosure. For Gloria, the mere act of leaving
her home would constitute unwanted exposure; the evidence of abuse was
visible on her body. Though "spilling her guts to a stranger" was not ideal,
it provided her with the privacy of her home, in which she could monitor
how and when she disclosed her abuse, and the limited publicity of an anonymous call. In this way, Gloria was able to disclose without unwanted exposure. In other words, she could balance her need for communication with
her need for safety under the condition of anonymity. Anonymity in this
context, then, functions as a tactic in de Certeau's (1984) sense:

Without leaving the place where he has no choice but to live and which lays down its law for him, he establishes within it a degree of plurality and creativity. By an art of being in between, he draws unexpected results from his situation. (p. 30)

Tactics deployed by women in abusive situations, such as anonymous disclosure, are creative and often subversive (at least in the short term); they are "the result of calculated assessments; that is, women rationally, and automatically, take account of the situation and do a mental calculation of the dangers present before deciding how to behave" (Gordon & Riger, 1989, p. 4). Asserting a sense of agency within an imagined community of other women represents in many cases a gesture, albeit limited, toward resistance.

THE BALANCE OF PUBLIC AND PRIVATE SPACES
IN FEMINIST ANALYSES

Although the perceived split between the public sphere and the private sphere has been helpful in elucidating gendered power relations in feminist theory, this dichotomy clearly fails to represent battered women's experiences. According to Haraway (1991):

> If it was ever possible ideologically to characterize women's lives by the distinction of public and private domains suggested by images of the division of working class life into factory and home, of bourgeois life into market and home, and of gender existence into personal and political realms, it is now a totally misleading ideology, even to show how both terms of these dichotomies construct each other in practice and in theory. I prefer a network ideological image, suggesting the profusion of spaces and identities and the permeability of boundaries in the personal body and in the body politic. (p. 170)

Perhaps the only consistent element that cuts across lines of age, race, ethnicity, class, religion, education, and sexuality in narratives of abuse involves the permeability of personal and political spatial boundaries (Ray, 1996). The courtroom incident and the various excerpts from women's narratives in this chapter exemplify the fluid boundaries between public and private.

Feminist analyses contingent on the public–private binary collude with what Phelan (1993) terms "the trap of visibility politics" (p. 198). The assertion that women's "addition" into "the public sphere," and the concomitant public "visibility" of their experiences, will result in liberation is naive, at best, as Gloria's narrative demonstrates. However, this fallacy is common to many feminist studies of space and social context. For example, Spain (1992) notes that:

Spatial segregation is one of the mechanisms by which a group with greater power can maintain its advantage over a group with less power. By controlling access to knowledge and resources through the control of space, the dominant group's ability to retain and reinforce its position is enhanced. Thus, spatial boundaries contribute to the unequal status of women. For women to become *more knowledgeable, they must also change places* [italics added]. (p. 16)

Spain's argument, and other theories like it that depend on the private–public dichotomy, have limited use-value for feminist activists concerned with systemic social transformation. Significantly, personal and political transformation is the explicit and primary goal of activism against domestic violence (Burstow, 1992; Curry & Allison, 1996; Kinstlinger-Bruhn, 1997; Ney & Peters, 1995).

Spain's (1992) analysis links power and freedom with public space and links restriction and domination with the private sphere. However, as Fraser (1992) argues, "it is not correct to view publicity as always and unambiguously an instrument of empowerment and emancipation. For members of subordinate groups, it will always be a matter of *balancing* the potential political *uses of publicity against the dangers of loss of privacy*" [italics added] (p. 610). Two informants corroborated this claim in their interviews. Juanita:

> I want the right to stay in one place. I don't really care where it is. That's the only way I can get my life back together again. Stable, you know. Some place of my own, where I can be. You know, by myself when I want and with people when I want. Control I guess is what I'm saying.

Susan:

> I never felt at home in my own house, you know that? I feel more at home walking on the street or in a mall or wherever than I do at home. I miss that feeling, of being at home.

As these narratives testify, there is no simple way to conceptualize the spectrum of privacy and publicity experienced by battered women.

Fraser (1990) argued that there has never been one monolithic public sphere, but rather "a host of competing counterpublics" (p. 61). These alternative competing arenas coexist with what is considered the traditionally male-dominated public sphere. The major example Fraser (1990) cited is the set of public spaces established by second-wave American feminist communities and composed of "a variegated array of journals, bookstores, publishing companies, film and video distribution networks, lecture series, research centers, academic programs, conferences, conventions, festivals and local meeting places" (p. 67). Significantly, Fraser (1990) did not include battered women's shelters in her examples of recent U.S. feminist counterpublics, although these sites were an important contribution of the second-wave women's movement.

Battered women's shelters certainly meet the definitional criteria of a counterpublic. According to Loeske (1992), "the collective representation of shelters constructed the battered woman as a victim needing to increase faith in herself, something to be accomplished through self help and peer support" (later the term *survivor* is substituted for victim, p. 60). This alternative, shared construction was formulated by a feminist community that Loeske characterizes as a "*smaller public*" that made claims about the needs and interests of battered women notably absent from "*the public stage*" [italics added] (p. 30). Agencies and shelters constitute a counterpublic in Fraser's framework.

Perhaps one explanation for the exclusion of agencies and shelters in Fraser's analysis is the construction of these spaces as "private" enterprises, operating in public without attendant publicity. Many agencies and shelters create their simultaneously private and public status through explicitly coded naming practices: "A Safe Place," "My Sister's House," "A Friend's Place." Such designations are intended to communicate directly to a woman in crisis; the names address a perceived need for a safe place outside the home, but promise anonymity and privacy by eschewing reference to abuse, battery, or violence. In the interviews a crisis volunteer articulated the rationale for this naming practice. "It's important that we're obvious in the yellow pages. It takes enormous courage to make that first call. We want her to know that we're someplace safe she can call, she can go." One feminist organizer interviewed conceptualized the relationship between the public and the private in the following way: "Since we can't sit over a cup of coffee in her kitchen, her coming out to the shelter is the next best thing." Conceding that the home is at least temporarily unsafe, this interviewee reconfigures the public space of the shelter for the private work of conversation and intimate intervention. In accomplishing the goal of privacy, albeit in a public place, the shelter represents the safest available alternative. The limits of public and private epitomized by the battered women's shelter illuminate the complex spatial practices of abused women.

THE BALANCE OF PUBLIC AND PRIVATE SPACES
WITHIN NARRATIVES OF DISCLOSURE

Contrary to theoretical models that insist on stable, discrete, and separate spheres, individuals conceptualize their own "public" and "private" spaces differently over time. Fluctuations in the ways individuals differentiate between public space and private space certainly depend in part on their ability

to define these "personal/private" and "political/public" boundaries for themselves. Moreover, how women feel about and experience the range of public
and private spaces they inhabit shifts constantly. Though the courthouse,
for example, may represent liberation in one sense, it may represent another
kind of danger, to which the earlier description points. Susan's narrative
demonstrates the fluidity of, and limitations within, these conceptualized
spaces. In responding to the question of what she wanted most in her life,
she replied:

> I'm a really private person. I like to have my own space and not be bothered
> all the time and watched. I suppose if I could get anything I wanted it would
> be my own body back. Yeah, my body.

In this case, Susan defined the boundaries of the personal and private at the
limits of her own physical body.

In addition to the ways that designations between public and private space
shift, cultural values greatly impact a woman's relationship to the issues of
publicity and privacy. A Latina interviewee said that she thought her circumstances would be different if she were White.

> If I was a White woman, I could walk outta here easier. There is a lot of
> stigma where I come from about keeping a man. And a lot of women get hit
> once in a while. It's not like it's a good thing, but it's just something that
> happens. What makes me so special? My family is very traditional you know.

Other pressures based on race and ethnicity were commonly featured in
women's narratives of abuse (Gresson, 1995). An African-American client
related the following in an interview:

> I can't say anything about the shit that goes on behind the door. That's our
> business. I feel so bad as it is: Black men have it real hard. I don't want to
> make it harder on him. Course I don't want the abuse neither. It makes me
> so angry that he takes it out on me.

Clearly, any conceptualization of publicity and privacy must consider the
multiple ways that cultural differences impinge on lived experiences of domestic violence.

Just as heterosexual women's experiences of domestic violence differ based
on cultural values, traditions, and imperatives, lesbians in abusive relationships face particular difficulties compounded by homophobia and the isolation it often engenders. "Outing" a partner to family or coworkers is a
common form of domination in abusive lesbian relationships. Although a
verbal threat may be considered less abusive than physical violence by others,
it is often experienced by women as *more* life threatening. Toni said in this

interview, "I'm terrified of her. She could ruin my life in just a few words if I leave her. I'm tied to her in a way I can't even believe." The intersection of verbal and physical violence creates in many women's lives a sense that public disclosure, whether chosen or compelled, invites retribution and increased abuse more than any other single act.

METAPHORIC CONSTRUCTIONS OF ABUSE
WITHIN NARRATIVES OF DISCLOSURE

Geertz's (1973) axiom that ethnography is "not an experimental science in search of law but an interpretive one in search of meaning" (p. 5) provides the rationale for the following section. The analysis of metaphors employed by abused women to describe their experience of domestic violence participates in the effort to construct meaning through interpretation (Ray, 1996). Many of the abused women interviewed for this study used a set of somatic metaphors to describe their experiences dealing with isolation and secrecy (Carter & Presnell, 1994). The most common metaphoric constructions involved illness and pregnancy, two conditions closely associated with deeply embodied experience. Juanita's narrative features an extended metaphor relating her experience of abuse to the flu:

> The abuse is that kind of flu that sticks with you all winter long. It sort of comes and goes without a real warning or really even because of how well you take care of yourself. It's always lurking there, waiting for the time to send you to bed with a crash. You know, low grade fever. That's what the fear is like. And your loneliness. I feel it in my bones.

Audre's metaphor relates disclosure to pregnancy and birthing. "I can't talk about this anymore. It's too hard. Too much to bear. Like giving birth again and again. Too painful. Ripping you up inside." The experience of illness and pregnancy foreground the deeply embodied nature of pain, discomfort, and liminality. Within our society, one is set apart from the "normal" functions of human interaction by illness and pregnancy, even though many people share these physical experiences.

Significantly, the centrality of pain and liminality within these narratives suggests the desire to name abuse as something recognizable, something potentially shared, while maintaining the sense that each experience of abuse is unique, just as each person's experience of an illness or pregnancy is her own. Again, this communicative tactic simultaneously registers the shared public nature of the experience as well as its privacy, for, as Scarry (1985) noted, "whatever pain achieves, it achieves in part through its unsharability, and it ensures this unsharability through its resistance to language" (p. 4). Though "physical pain has no voice" (Scarry, p. 3), the descriptions of abuse in this context invoke the concept of personal voice through the deeply embodied nature of their metaphoric constructions.

Although the women used evocative expressions of embodiment in their narratives, many of them constructed their sentences in the second person: "and *your* loneliness," "ripping *you* up inside." Though these descriptions are clearly personal, the women do not assume the first person. The simultaneous invocation of embodied knowledge was, therefore, countered by the distancing technique of attributing this somatic, experiential reality to a general "you," an external construction, separate from the self. The simultaneous act of personalizing the experience through somatic metaphors of illness and pregnancy and distancing the experience through the construction of the second person voice suggests yet another balancing act within abused women's lives: the balance between claiming an experience as one's own and sharing the experience with others, between physical embodiment and discursive distance.

CONCLUSION

The conflation of privacy and publicity in battered women's experiences complicates the decision to disclose and conditions the ways in which abuse is conceptualized. However, the attempt to balance privacy, secrecy, and disclosure through counseling may be seen also as a source of resistance and agency. As demonstrated earlier in this chapter, anonymity within the agency and over the telephone provided one way that the women could maintain a sense of privacy while reaching out for assistance in the (counter)public sphere. Disclosing abuse to other abused women and counselors who listen and empathize creates the sense of an imagined, discursive community, a common refrain in narratives of abuse. Gloria states that: "When I called earlier and I got a busy signal, I guess I felt happy. Not happy that someone needed to call, God knows, but glad. Y'all must talk to a lot of us." In this case, the conflation of privacy and publicity worked on behalf of abused women's needs. Within the context of counseling, abused women may be able to assert agency through their choice of self-disclosure as a communicative practice.

VIII

BALANCING FUTURE
CONSIDERATIONS

20
▼▼▼▼▼▼▼▼

Some Possible Directions
for Future Research

Leslie A. Baxter
Erin M. Sahlstein
University of Iowa

Self-disclosure is one of the most researched topics of the past three decades in the fields of interpersonal communication, social psychology, and social and personal relationships. However, as the chapters in this volume demonstrate, important and interesting research questions continue to emerge. Existing research traditions have been moved forward in interesting directions, and new lines of inquiry have been advanced. Using these chapters as a springboard, our goal in this concluding chapter is to identify some possible directions for future research on balancing disclosure, privacy, and secrecy. Our comments are grouped into five major points: taking the concept of balance seriously, decentering the sovereign self, moving beyond target intimates, developing theory, and enlarging the methodological tool kit.

TAKING THE CONCEPT OF BALANCE SERIOUSLY

Balance is one of the guiding themes of this volume. However, it is not clear what balance means and how we can use the concept to further our thinking about disclosure, privacy, and secrecy. The first issue that we need to address is the site of balance: Where is the balancing taking place? If the site of balance is taken to be the body of scholarship on the topics of disclosure, privacy, and secrecy, then balancing is a simple matter of counting up the number of studies on disclosure and the number of studies on informational closedness in its many forms (privacy and secrecy, among others) and aspiring to an equal number in each column. A very different way to proceed is to locate balancing in social actors and their relationships. With this alternative conception of the site of balance, research attention of necessity must shift away from the study of disclosure and informational closedness in isolation of one another to their simultaneous consideration in a given study. About a third of the chapters in this volume subscribe to the latter conception of balancing, and it is this conception we would like to encourage in future research. Consistent with a dialectical perspective (e.g., Altman, Vinsel, & Brown, 1981; Baxter & Montgomery, 1996; Montgomery & Baxter, 1998; Rawlins, 1983a, 1983b), our position is that informational openness and closedness exist as *unified opposites* that cannot be understood in isolation of one another. They are inseparable at the same time that they are opposed to one another. Disclosure comes to mean only in relation to privacy and secrecy, and vice versa. The fact that openness and closedness are functional opposites means that their unity, of necessity, will be a dynamic, tension-filled process of interplay. Existing research suggests that people in developing relationships experience this unified opposition between openness and closedness on an ongoing basis (Baxter, 1990; Baxter & Erbert, 1997; Baxter & Montgomery, 1996; Rawlins, 1983b).

If, then, the site of balance is social actors and their relationships, the next issue of relevance is how to conceptualize the process of balancing. One way to proceed is to locate balancing as an intrapersonal mental calculation inside an actor's head; the actor weighs the benefits and risks of disclosure more or less like an accountant sizing up a ledger book's debits and assets. Within this conceptualization, the benefit/risk analysis is an antecedent cognitive decision that results in an act of direct disclosure, an indirect or ambiguous act of disclosure, or a refrain from disclosure. The majority of chapters in this volume that address balancing are of this sort, with chapter 4, by Derlega, Winstead, and Folk-Barron, serving as an example of this tradition.

An alternative way to conceive of balancing is to examine, over time, how a given social actor or relational pair attempts to achieve both openness and closedness as outcomes of interaction. Scholars have argued for at least the past 15 years that both privacy and disclosure are requisite to intimacy (e.g., Altman et al., 1981; Bochner, 1982; Parks, 1982). Research on the praxis of balance suggests that several communicative options are available to relational parties (for a review, see Baxter & Montgomery, 1996). For example, an actor or a relational pair could segregate topic domains, such that some topic areas are taboos or sites of privacy and other topics are "fair game" for expectations of openness. Alternatively, an actor or pair could cycle back and forth between openness and closedness (e.g., Altman et al., 1981). An actor or pair could also opt for compromise, engaging in communication that is only partially disclosive; for example, use of indirect disclosure or equivocation. Existing research suggests that both segregation and cycling are frequently enacted ways in which relationship parties accomplish balance, achieving both openness and closedness (for a review of research, see Baxter & Montgomery, 1996). This alternative conception of balancing looks outward, not inside the individual, to interaction outcomes through time, and it is this conception we would like to encourage in future research on disclosure, privacy, and secrecy.

Consistent with a dialectical perspective, however, we are suspect of any approach to balance that is dualistic (Baxter & Montgomery, 1996). In a dualistic approach to balance, openness and closedness remain as stable entities; what counts as openness is stable and what it means to have privacy or secrecy remains intact. In dualistic thinking, the metaphor of a balancing scale is apt; the phenomena to be balanced are placed in opposite sides of the balancing scale and adjustments are made until the two sides of the scale are counterpoised. The phenomena to be balanced are self-contained and separate from one another. However, to a dialectical way of thinking, the metaphor of a balancing scale is nonsensical. Because they are unified opposites, always in dynamic interplay with one another, the phenomena to be balanced are not separable; they are unstable and subject to transformation as a result of their dynamic interplay. A dialectical approach to balancing, then, would examine not only how openness and closedness are in ongoing tension but how that dynamic opposition transforms what it means to be open and closed and the interplay between them.

The third issue we wish to consider is what it is that is being balanced. The title and chapters of this volume would suggest that disclosure is balanced against privacy and secrecy. From a dialectical standpoint, we know that a phenomenon is always defined by, through, and with its paired opposites. In pairing these three concepts with and against each other, a certain system of meaning for all three concepts is created. It is important to recognize that the opposition of disclosure and privacy/secrecy is not without tendency. For example, this triad is framed within a Euro-American, highly individualistic orientation, as Hastings' chapter (chap. 16) usefully reminds us. From a different cultural perspective, this particular opposition may make no sense. Further, other oppositions may exist that could alter our understandings of what exactly it is that is being balanced. For example, in the opposition of disclosure and deception, disclosure is understood more in terms of a moral/ethical framework of meaning in contrast to the logic of individual rights that organizes the opposition of disclosure and privacy. Even within a framework of rights, disclosure takes on a different meaning when the opposition is right-to-privacy against right-to-know (e.g., Cline & McKenzie, chap. 5 of this volume). Our point is that if we take balance seriously, we ought not to take for granted the opposition of disclosure against privacy and secrecy but instead ask what is (are) the relevant oppositions in play with and against disclosure in the particular situation under study. "Disclosure," "privacy," and "secrecy" may mean different things depending on the sea of oppositions in which they swim.

If the site of balance is intrapersonal, as it is for the majority of chapters in this volume that address the matter of balance, then it is not surprising to note that the agent who accomplishes balance is the individual. The individual is cast as the exclusive gatekeeper of a knowledge domain and decides whether or not information within that domain is revealed or concealed. An alternative conception positions social actors as jointly responsible in the process of balancing. It is this latter position that we develop further in our next section.

DECENTERING THE SOVEREIGN SELF

At the center of modern social scientific inquiry is the presumption of a sovereign self. As Sampson (1993) argued:

> The dominant . . . tradition of inquiry into human nature has increasingly sought the human essence in the characteristics of self, mind and personality said to be found within what I have termed the self-contained individual. . . . Conventional wisdom tells us that each one of us is like a small container designed to prevent our "inner essence" from leaking out. We believe that in order to be a proper container, each individual must become a coherent, integrated, singular entity whose clear-cut boundaries define its limits and separate it from other similarly bounded entities. (p. 17)

The contained, or sovereign, self is a unitary, intact, rational agent who acts autonomously on the world based on the internal workings of the individual mind.

Self-disclosure scholars typically have approached the act of disclosing as an individual process that is rational and driven by choice. Derlega et al. (1993) conceptualize this process as "what individuals verbally reveal about themselves to others (including thoughts, feelings, and experiences)" (p. 1). This conceptualization focuses on the "sender" and his or her decision to disclose to a "receiver." One major assumption of this definition is that individuals consciously decide to reveal their private information for personal reasons. Individuals weigh the pros and cons of disclosing; if the costs are too high they do not "open up" to the other person. The content of the self-disclosure is treated as if it were representative of a preformed, intact individual. The individual's prior life experiences, personality traits, feelings, and ideas are presumed to exist "inside" the individual who decides (or not) to give others informational access.

Over the past decade, however, the sovereign self has been decentered in favor of an alternative conception of the self, one we call a social or dialogic self (Baxter & Montgomery, 1996; Gergen, 1994; Sampson, 1993). Actually, the intellectual roots of this alternative conception are long ones, including such early 20th-century social thinkers as Vygotsky, Voloshinov, Bakhtin, Mead, and Cooley, among others. From this alternative conception, self is constructed with and through others, not separate from others. Self is not preformed but instead is fluid and emergent, characterized by fragmentation and multiplicity. Self cannot be separated from other; rather, other helps to construct self in an ongoing dialogue. In contrast to the perspective of the sovereign self, which directs our gaze within the individual, the perspective of the social self directs our gaze *between* individuals. Or, as Voloshinov and Bakhtin (1973) expressed it, "The organizing center . . . is not within but outside—in the social milieu surrounding the individual being" (p. 93). In short, "self" is a social product, a discursive production that emerges through interaction with others. From the perspective of a social self, then, self-disclosure cannot be understood as the representation of some stable, intact, inner essence. Instead, self-disclosure is a process between parties in which selves are constructed and performed.

The research implications of a social or dialogic self are substantial, but we would emphasize five issues in particular. First, more attention should be given to the "between," that is, the interaction that transpires between the individual and other(s). One consequence of focusing on the between would be a tempering of the view that disclosure (or lack thereof) is the consequence of a prior rational decision by the individual (e.g., Derlega et al., chap. 4; Afifi & Guerrero, chap. 12). As Hopper and Drummond (1990) nicely illustrated, a focus on interaction underscores the emergent nature of goals. Interaction is not a process in which actors each implement the decisions they formulated prior to the beginning of the exchange. Rather, goals and actions emerge through interaction with each other. Stamp and Knapp (1990) have made a similar point in critiquing the concept of intent, shifting attention to the emergent and joint construction of intentions as actors interact with one another. Put simply, self-disclosure, both as intended goal and as behavioral action, is not something exclusively under the control of the sovereign self, but rather is a negotiated, emergent process between parties.

The second research implication involves recognition of how we are disclosed by others. Through gossip (i.e., talk about others in their absence) and the related communicative phenomenon of reported speech (i.e., talk in which others' communication is reproduced, mimicked, or paraphrased), social actors disclose others to third parties. Both of these communication practices are frequently enacted in everyday life (Bakhtin, 1981; Goldsmith & Baxter, 1996). Although gossip and reported speech have received research attention (e.g., Bergmann, 1993; Holt, 1996), conceptualizing them as socially regulated disclosure and privacy is a novel idea grounded in the perspective of the social self. Both practices illustrate powerful ways in which others are in control of disclosures about a person's self or identity. Furthermore, others' control is not limited to potentially unwanted disclosures about oneself. Others also can gatekeep in order to prevent information from being transmitted to others; when one wants news to be spread widely, this control for concealment purposes is as undesirable as unwanted disclosures. Gossip and reported speech vividly demonstrate that disclosure and privacy are social processes, not actions exclusively controlled by sovereign selves.

The third research implication involves the realization that an utterance of self-disclosure is but one link in a longer conversational chain whose outcome is to construct selves; how utterances we have labeled as "self-disclosure" function to fashion selves-in-becoming should receive greater attention. For example, when a person reveals some detail of background information, that information is subject to affirmation, criticism, reinterpretation, or neglect in subsequent conversation with another. Through subsequent conversation, the background information is subject to new meaning, which occupies a new place in the person's conception of self.

The fourth implication for research is recognition of the multiplicity of our social selves. The social self is not only fluid and emergent, but also multiple depending on the others with whom one is relationally interdependent. As a consequence, issues of disclosure, privacy, and secrecy extend beyond autonomous individuals to larger social units, including dyadic relationships, work teams, families, neighborhoods, and so forth. In a family, for example, the individual simultaneously is implicated in negotiating issues of disclosure and privacy for himself or herself, for each of the family subsystems in which membership is held, and for the family as a whole system. The issue here is not to whom the individual reveals or conceals; rather, the issue is the social relation about which revelation or concealment occurs. As Petronio (chap. 3) suggested, each of these social units establishes boundaries of openness and closedness, and the individual simultaneously is implicated directly in negotiating revelation and concealment for each social unit. Such multiplicity positions the individual to experience fragmented and incompatible sites of disclosure and privacy at any given point in time.

The fifth, and final, implication for research is recognition that "disclosure" is a socially meaningful act; how something gets understood as an act of "disclosure" between interactants, and what that means, should not be taken for granted but studied in its own right. Katriel and Philipsen (1981) provided an example of this in their classic ethnographic study of the "really communicating" communication ritual. Needless to say, the same point could be made about "privacy" and "secrecy." For example, it is not only important to study that someone "keeps a secret" from a researcher's point of view, but additionally, it is important to study the meanings that participants themselves make of "keeping a secret," "sharing secrets," and those who "keep secrets" (e.g., Katriel, 1990/1991).

The majority of the chapters in this volume reflect the perspective of the sovereign self, and certainly that tradition is a well established one that deserves to be continued. However, a significant number of the chapters speak in the alternative voice of the social self. Cooks' auto-ethnography (chap. 14) vividly captures the process by which utterances of disclosure take on social significance in constructing selves-in-becoming. Brouwer's analysis (chap. 7) of gay men's choreographies of HIV discovery and disclosure emphasizes how something counts as a "disclosure" and how disclosure is as much in the control of the other as oneself. The chapter by Schultz (chap. 18) on sex offender community notification policies documents the social negotiation surrounding disclosure and the social significance of acts of disclosure for implicated individuals. Similarly, the chapter by Cline and McKenzie (chap. 5) on HIV disclosures speaks cogently to the social stakes of an act of disclosure and the social negotiation surrounding that act. Orrego et al. (chap. 17) summarize a program of research whose upshot is the televised public spectacle of selves-in-the-making through guests' disclosures and reactions by hosts and audience members.

We encourage further work on disclosure from the perspective of the social self. We place significance on the fact that the title of this volume uses the term "disclosure" rather than "self-disclosure." By omitting the term "self," the title of the volume functions to create a space for the scholarly recognition that we are disclosed, and thus constructed, by and with others.

MOVING BEYOND TARGET INTIMATES

Existing disclosure research is biased towards intimacy, intimate relationships, and information exchange in the so-called private spheres of everyday life. Early theorizing about disclosure (e.g., interdependence theory, social penetration theory, uncertainty reduction theory) constructed and perpetuated an ideology of intimacy (Parks, 1995). As a consequence of the attention given to disclosure in private life, little attention has been given to the public side of disclosure. However, as several chapters in this volume demonstrate, disclosure holds currency in interactional contexts other than our most intimate relations. Including such diverse contexts as health care settings (Cline & McKenzie, chap. 5; Parrott, Duncan, & Duggan, chap. 10), TV talk shows (Orrego et al., chap. 17), sex offender community notifications (Schultz, chap. 18), and crisis hotlines and homes for battered women (Dieckmann, chap. 19), scholars in this volume are moving beyond the context of romantic and familial relationships to study the disclosure process in the so-called public sphere.

However, consistent with a dialectical view, we think it is important not to let "public" and "private" spheres exist in separate programs of research that are isolated from one another. Thus, in addition to research that specializes in disclosure (and privacy) in private life and research that specializes in disclosure (and privacy) in public life, we would encourage research that examines how public and private spheres interface in the conduct of disclosure (and privacy). For example, following de Certeau's (1984) view that the social actor is more than a passive and powerless player in society, we would ask how persons creatively make use of their social world in enacting their everyday lives. For example, in the context of the military, how do gay and lesbian military personnel use the "don't ask, don't tell" policy as a social resource in their conduct of everyday life? How do people invoke the "right to privacy" as a social resource in communicatively giving legitimacy to their everyday conduct? How is the notion of "the general good" invoked as a resource by social actors in the micropractices of everyday life? By posing questions such as these, we are asking for research that brings so-called public and private spheres into play with one another.

The private and the public domains of social reality are inextricably intertwined. Personal relationships, whatever their intimacy level, are simultaneously private and public phenomena, and we cannot ignore this in our disclosure theory and research. Our private havens of relating are shaped by, and in turn shape, societal and cultural expectations. "Culture" is not some entity "out there" in the distant and remote public sphere but is voiced, and given voice, in our everyday relating. In our everyday revelations and concealments, we construct and reproduce our cultural premises of personhood, social relations, and communication, or what Fitch (1998) referred to as a culture's interpersonal ideology. In this sense, then, the mundane disclosures of everyday life bring private and public spheres together as much as the "big" issues of widely recognized social significance such as HIV/AIDS, sexual aggression, and domestic violence.

Of course, as Dieckmann (chap. 19) usefully demonstrated, the public–private binary easily blurs. Her chapter more than any other in the volume challenges the very distinction between "public" and "private." It moves us beyond an agenda of bringing public and private spheres into play with one another, because the notion of an interface still gives conceptual legitimacy to the distinction between the spheres. Dieckmann, through her study of the experiences of battered women, questions the usefulness of the public–private distinction to begin with.

We have oversimplified our treatment of "public" and "private" spheres by giving the impression that each domain is unitary. Given our discussion above of the social self, it would be more accurate to refer to the multiple, fluid spheres of social relations that we equate with the conduct of everyday life. Similarly, it is a fiction to refer to the public sphere as if it were singular. "Society," "culture," and "the public order" are far from stable, unitary social entities. Such unitizing terms gloss a multiplicity of social collectives and their respective institutions and normative practices. Such collectives are likely to be fuzzy around the edges, with fluctuating memberships and dynamics. Further, each collective is likely to have distinctive interests that partially repeat, reformulate, rebut, and contradict one another (Streeck, 1994).

DEVELOPING THEORY

An amazing range of theories was invoked by the contributors to this volume, including communication boundary management, coordinated management of meaning, dialectical theory, feminist theory, force-field analysis, narrative theory, politeness theory, privacy regulation, social exchange theory, social penetration theory, and uncertainty reduction theory. On the one hand, we celebrate this diverse array of theories, for disclosure research historically has been dominated by a narrow band of theories that reflected in one way or another a social-exchange perspective. This perspective has focused our gaze narrowly on individual rewards and costs of disclosing. Alternative theoretical perspectives provide the obvious benefit of opening up new research questions and issues.

However, despite the wide range of theories invoked in this volume, we think that a top priority for future research must be theory development. By "theory," we do not wish to limit ourselves to a traditional conception of deductively derived, axiomatic statements testable through hypothesis-testing. Like Turner (1986), we legitimate a variety of kinds of theories and theorizing. To us, a theory is a rhetorical and symbolic tool that renders sensical some facet of the social world. The crucial issue facing researchers who study disclosure, privacy, and secrecy is to determine the facet(s) of interest: What are we theorizing about?

Considered collectively, the chapters in this volume point to three crucial nodal points about which theorists need to make careful decisions: *phenomenon, unit of analysis,* and *context.* With respect to phenomenon, we have pointed to four possibilities about which to theorize: informational openness (disclosure); informational closedness (privacy, secrecy); the dualistic balance between openness and closedness; or the dialectical interplay of openness with closedness. With respect to unit of analysis, we have pointed to a basic choice between the sovereign self and the relational or social self (or "the between"). With respect to context, we have pointed to four possibilities:

- *private sphere,* in which issues of disclosure, privacy, and secrecy are examined in personal relationships such as close friendships, romantic relationships, and familial relationships;
- *public sphere,* in which issues of disclosure, privacy, and secrecy are examined in social settings outside of personal relationships, including role-based relationships, communities, and public policy and law;

- *public–private interface,* in which researchers probe the ways in which everyday "private life" and the practices that guide society's public life are mutually shaped and sustained; and
- *public–private implosion,* in which the fundamental distinction between "private" and "public" is made suspect.

This treatment produces a 4 X 2 X 4 matrix by which to organize and position various theoretical perspectives. About a third of the chapters in this volume align with the phenomenon of openness, about a third with the phenomenon of closedness, and about a third with the phenomenon of dualistic balance. A majority of the chapters focus on the sovereign individual self as the unit of analysis. A preponderance of the chapters center on disclosure, privacy, and secrecy in the private sphere.

An obvious direction for future theorizing is to flush out the underrepresented cells of this matrix. We have particularly emphasized the value of taking balance seriously (whether dualistically or dialectically), with a relational, or "between" analytic focus, and with attention to both private and public spheres (whether to interface them or to implode the distinction).

Existing theories that take balancing seriously include communication Boundary Management Theory (e.g., Petronio, chap. 3) and dialectical theory (Baxter & Montgomery, 1996; Montgomery & Baxter, 1998). Integral to both of these theoretical approaches is the interplay of openness with and against closedness. From the standpoint of both of these theories, balance is more than the ratio of benefits to risks calculated in an individual's mind. Although empirical work guided by these theoretical orientations is relatively recent, it is nonetheless promising.

Social constructionist approaches (e.g., Gergen, 1994; Pearce, 1995) can prove useful to scholars interested in disclosure, privacy, and secrecy from the perspective of the social self. By using these approaches, our gaze is directed away from the individual revealing himself or herself and instead is focused on how disclosure socially constructs and is constitutive of selves, relating, and society. Communication and relating, the "between," becomes the center of attention from a social constructionist position.

Critical theories are virtually absent from disclosure and privacy scholarship and could provide productive ways of looking at how power relations are implicated in disclosure, privacy, and secrecy (e.g., Lannaman, 1991, 1994). Several of the chapters in this volume highlight the contestedness of disclosure and privacy, but more work from a critical perspective awaits. By adopting a critical-theory lens, we can productively interrogate the political nature of our disclosure negotiations. Who, for example, has a choice to disclose, as opposed to being silenced or denied voice? Who can disclose and who can't in our society? What can they say that others cannot? Who is protected from unwanted disclosure and who is not? To what extent is the widespread cultural bias toward "openness and honesty" an ideology of tyranny to which we are all communicative prisoners? By posing questions such as these, critical theorists push us to consider issues of power and our own place as scholars in the complex matrix of power relations.

ENLARGING THE METHODOLOGICAL TOOL KIT

Traditionally, research on self-disclosure and privacy has been dominated by experimental designs and self-report questionnaires. As several of the chapters in this volume demonstrate, these methods continue to reap useful information. We also applaud the move taken in many of the chapters in this volume to enlarge the methodological tool kit to include ethnography, interpretive text analysis, autobiographical narrative, and meta-analysis. We would, however, urge future researchers to enlarge the tool kit even more, particularly if attention is to be given to the concept of balance and the perspective of the social self.

Existing research typically focuses on informants' self-reports of thoughts, feelings, and strategies used in disclosure. Consistent with this research tradition, a researcher interested in the insider perspective on dilemmas of openness and closedness can simply ask informants to reflect on the dilemmatic nature of their communication practices. When guided by the perspective of the sovereign self, this task can be accomplished either through interviewing, in which data can take a more qualitative form (e.g., Baxter, 1990) or through self-report questionnaires, in which data can take a more quantitative form (e.g., Baxter & Erbert, 1997). However, if one's theoretical perspective is that of a social self, then a method that we think holds substantial promise is the couple interview (Acitelli, 1997). Couple interviewing emphasizes the "between," interviewing couples (or larger social units) with an emphasis on the unstructured talk that takes place between the parties themselves in the context of the interview. When applied to dilemmas of openness and closedness, couple interviewing would enable a researcher to address insider reflections about the praxis of balance in a way that appreciates the social self, because the method embraces the emergent co-construction of meaning among informants.

Furthermore, from the perspective of the social self, more research attention needs to be given to the actual dialogues that take place between parties as they negotiate, perform, and enact disclosure, privacy, and secrecy. Discourse analysis is an underutilized method that holds much potential. The method encompasses a family of analytic approaches, all of which are committed to an interpretive understanding of how meaning-making gets done in naturally occurring texts (whether oral or written) (Schiffrin, 1994). The analysis of openness/closedness dilemmas, and the praxis of balance, could fruitfully be

pursued through the discourse analytic method used by Billig and his colleagues (1988) to identify ideological dilemmas in talk. Basically, Billig et al.
paid close analytic attention to a variety of discourse markers (Schiffrin, 1987)
whose meaning points to a disjuncture of some kind. For example, utterances
that contain the markers "but," "nonetheless," "however," "on the other
hand," and so forth potentially display moments of fissure.

Couple interviewing and discourse analysis are not the methodological
equivalents of Swiss Army knives; they, like other methods, are designed to
perform a very narrow range of functions. Existing research methods are
well suited to the study of openness and closedness as discrete phenomena
from the perspective of a sovereign self. Couple interviewing and discourse
analysis hold particular potential for scholars committed to the perspective
of the social self and scholars interested in studying the process of balance.

CONCLUSION

The Russian social theorist Mikhail Bakhtin once observed that "The utterance . . . is a considerably more complex and dynamic organism than it
appears when construed simply as a thing that articulates the intention of
the person uttering it" (quoted in Clark & Holquist, 1984, p. 220). In this
chapter, we have attempted to flush out some of this complexity by emphasizing a social approach to the interplay of openness and closedness. Do not
misunderstand our agenda. We do not wish to argue for the abandonment
of the rich tradition of research on self-disclosure and on privacy that has
fruitfully brought us to the present. We see that tradition alive and well, as
demonstrated in several chapters in this volume. However, we think the
intellectual conversation on disclosure, privacy, and secrecy can only be
enhanced with the addition of more perspectives at the scholarly table. Several chapters in this volume represent new and different perspectives that we
eagerly embrace, for we all stand to benefit from the scholarly feast that is
sure to ensue from a future grounded in a multiplicity of conceptual, theoretical, and methodological commitments.

Epilogue
Taking Stock

Susanne M. Jones
Sandra Petronio
Arizona State University

The concern over the ever-changing boundaries that divide private from public information has increased in the past 20 years. More than ever, controlling private information is perplexing. Yet, as this volume illustrates, the calculus for balance moderates the ways people are public while remaining private. Doctors believe that knowing intimate information helps their patients become well. Patients want the right to decide who knows test results. Spouses want to both keep secrets and have their partners tell secrets to them, employers want to make salaries public, and employees see their salaries as private information. In every instance, balancing the demands for public revelations with private expectations is a dominant theme. The paradoxical world we live in hampers our ability to manage these often-competing needs.

These chapters bring us a diversity of methodology to decipher the public–private paradox bringing to bear philosophical treatises, experimental observations conducted under tight scientific rigor, and interpretive perspectives relevant to these issues.

These chapters also highlight the changing nature of privacy, disclosure, and secrecy in today's society. We may be more concerned with the risks of relinquishing our private information and our secrets than ever before. The proliferation of ways to invade privacy and secrecy appears to be on the increase (Alderman & Kennedy, 1995). The loss of privacy is especially obvious with the invention of the Internet (Meeks, 1997). The underlying assumption is our right to own information. The frustration is that this presumed right is violated every day. Perhaps this explains one reason the themes of disclosure avoidance and privacy/secrecy protection circulate throughout a number of chapters.

For example, we learn that people make choices to avoid revealing HIV test results to their partners and within interpersonal relationships (Derlega, Winstead, & Folk-Barron, chap. 4; Yep, chap. 6). People try to protect their HIV/AIDS status within the health care system (Cline & McKenzie, chap. 5). Stigma contributes to an unwillingness to disclose chronic illness (Greene, chap. 9). Individuals often avoid full disclosure of health problems to health care givers (Parrott, Duncan, & Duggan, chap. 10). People manage topic and conflict avoidance through rendering certain information taboo (Roloff & Ifert, chap. 11; Afifi & Guerrero, chap. 12). Often people aggressively seek privacy (Buslig & Burgoon, chap. 13). People protect their family secrets (Cooks, chap. 14). Individuals avoid disclosure in an intercultural context (Hastings, chap. 16). There are face-saving problems that people experience with disclosures on television talk shows (Orrego, Smith, Mitchell, Johnson, Ah Yun, & Greenberg, chap. 17). In addition, often privacy protection is problematic for battered women (Dieckmann, chap. 19) and paradoxical for sex offenders (Schultz, chap. 18).

In many social areas such as health care, intimate relationships, the media, across cultures, and in policymaking, the balancing act is tricky. The weight of avoidance and privacy protection leads to a heightened awareness of the need for balance. However, the significance of balance is more evident because we also learn in these chapters that revealing is beneficial. For instance, we find that there is a relationship between disclosure and liking (Dindia, chap. 2), gay men reveal HIV status through nonverbal messages (Brouwer, chap. 7), there are health benefits of self-disclosure (Tardy, chap. 8), and, in some cases, there are similar patterns of self-disclosure intercultur-ally (Rubin, Yang, & Porte, chap. 15). In all, people wish to preserve a sense of control over privacy and secrecy. Therefore the way they are dis-closive matters greatly.

In closing these chapters provide multiple perspectives and address an array of issues that are crucial to the continued study of privacy, secrecy, and disclosure. As the chapters in this book demonstrate, the functional approach to disclosure continues to inform many of the fundamental as-sumptions researchers hold about the secrets of private disclosures. However, these chapters also expand this traditional perspective. Although individual characteristics have an impact, social and cultural issues are equally impor-tant to the balance calculus. They advance our knowledge about the outcome of considering the public and private for a host of life situations. *Balancing the Secrets of Private Disclosures* offers new paths to follow that will help unravel the puzzle of how to balance the paradox of remaining private or secret while continuing to build bridges through disclosure.

References

Abt, V., & Seesholtz, M. (1994). The shameless world of Phil, Sally and Oprah: Television talk shows and the deconstructing of society. *Journal of Popular Culture, 35,* 195–215.

Abu-Lughod, L. (1990). Can there be a feminist ethnography? *Women and Performance, 5,* 7–27.

Ace, T. (1995). Dire diaries. *Diseased Pariah News, 10,* 31–32.

Acitelli, L. K. (1997). Sampling couples to understand them: Mixing the theoretical with the practical. *Journal of Social and Personal Relationships, 14,* 243–261.

Adam, B. D., & Sears, A. (1996). *Experiencing HIV: Personal, family, and work relationships.* New York: Columbia University Press.

Adamopoulos, J. (1991). The emergence of interpersonal behavior: Diachronic and cross-cultural processes in the evolution of intimacy. In S. Ting-Toomey & F. Korzenny (Eds.), *Cross-cultural interpersonal communication* (pp. 155–170). Newbury Park, CA: Sage.

Adamopoulos, J., & Bontempo, R. N. (1986). Diachronic universals in interpersonal structures. *Journal of Cross-Cultural Psychology, 17,* 169–189.

Adler, R. B., Rosenfeld, L. B., Towne, N., & Proctor, R. F., II. (1998). *Interplay: The process of interpersonal communication* (7th ed.). Fort Worth, TX: Harcourt Brace.

Afifi, W. A. (1999). Harming the ones we love: Relational attachment and perceived consequences as predictors of safe-sex behavior. *Journal of Sex Research, 36,* 198–206.

Afifi, W. A., & Burgoon, J. K. (1998). "We never talk about that:" A comparison of cross-sex friendships and dating relationships on uncertainty and topic avoidance. *Personal Relationships, 5,* 255–272.

Afifi, W. A., & Guerrero, L. K. (1998). Some things are better left unsaid II: Topic avoidance in friendships. *Communication Quarterly, 36,* 231–249.

Albas, D., & Albas, C. (1988). Aces and bombers: The post-exam impression management strategies of students. *Symbolic Interaction, 11*(2), 289–302.

Alberts, J. K. (1988). An analysis of couples' conversational complaints. *Communication Monographs, 55,* 184–196.

Albrecht, T. L., & Adelman, M. B. (1987). *Communicating social support.* Newbury Park, CA: Sage.

Alcoff, L. (1991). The problem of speaking for others. *Cultural Critique, 20,* 5–32.

Alderman, E., & Kennedy, C. (1995). *The right to privacy.* New York: Knopf.

Allen, M. O., & Schwartzman, P. (1995, October 28). Talk TV trash bash. *New York Daily News, 7.*

Alter, J. (1995, November 6). Next: The revolt of the revolted. *Newsweek,* 46–47.

Altman, I. (1973). Reciprocity of interpersonal exchange. *Journal for the Theory of Social Behavior, 3,* 249–261.

Altman, I. (1975). *The environment and social behavior: Privacy, personal space, territory, and crowding.* Monterey, CA: Brooks/Cole.

Altman, I., & Taylor, D. A. (1973). *Social penetration: The development of interpersonal relationships.* New York: Holt, Rinehart & Winston.

Altman, I., Vinsel, A., & Brown, B. (1981). Dialectic conceptions in social psychology: An application to social penetration and privacy regulation. In L. Berkowitz (Ed.), *Advances in experimental social psychology* (Vol. 14, pp. 107–160). New York: Academic Press.

Amaro, H. (1988). Considerations for prevention of HIV infection among Hispanic women. *Psychology of Women Quarterly, 12,* 429–443.

American Heart Association (1998). Biostatistical fact sheets [On-line]. Available in HTML: www.amhrt.org/Heart_and_Stroke_a_z_guide/biolc.html and www.amhrt.org/Heart_and-Stroke_a_z_guide/bioho.html.

American Psychiatric Association. (1994). *Diagnostic and statistical manual of mental disorders* (4th ed.). Washington, DC: Author.

Anderson, C. M., & Martin, M. M. (1995, November). *Motives, self-disclosure, and satisfaction in families: A communication study of mothers and adult children.* Paper presented at the annual Speech Communication Association convention, San Antonio, TX.

Anderson, E. A. (1989). Implications for public policy: Towards a pro-family AIDS social policy. In E. Macklin (Ed.), *AIDS and families* (pp. 187–228). New York: Harrington Park.

Apsler, R. (1975). Effects of embarrassment on behavior toward others. *Journal of Personality and Social Psychology, 32,* 145–153.

Archer, R. L. (1979). Anatomical and psychological sex differences. In G. J. Chelune (Ed.), *Self-disclosure: Origins, patterns, and implications of openness in interpersonal relationships* (pp. 80–109). San Francisco: Jossey-Bass.

Archer, R. L. (1987). Commentary: Self-disclosure, a very useful behavior. In V. J. Derlega & J. H. Berg (Eds.), *Self-disclosure: Theory, research and therapy* (pp. 329–342). New York: Plenum.

Argyle, M. (1975). *Bodily communication.* New York: International Universities Press.

Argyle, M., Henderson, M., Bond, M., Iizuka, Y., & Contarello, A. (1986). Cross-cultural variation in relationship rules. *International Journal of Psychology, 21,* 287–315.

Aries, E. (1996). *Men and women in interaction: Reconsidering the differences.* New York: Oxford University Press.

Arkin, R. M. (1981). Self-presentation styles. In J. T. Tedeschi (Ed.), *Impression management theory and social psychological research* (pp. 311–333). New York: Academic Press.

Aronson, E. (1984). *The social animal* (4th ed.). New York: Freeman.

Austin, J. T., & Vancouver, J. B. (1996). Goal constructs in psychology: Structure, process and content. *Psychological Bulletin, 3,* 338–375.

Backlar, P. (1996). Ethics in community mental health care: Confidentiality and common sense. *Community Mental Health, 32,* 513–518.

Baker, B. L., & Benton, C. L. (1994). The ethics of feminist self-disclosure. In K. Carter & M. Presnell (Eds.), *Interpretive approaches to interpersonal communication* (pp. 219–246). Albany: State University of New York Press.

Baker, H. A., Jr. (1984). *Blues, ideology, and Afro-American literature: A vernacular theory.* Chicago: The University of Chicago Press.

Baker, R. (1996, December). More good news on combination therapy using protease inhibitor drugs. *Beta: Bulletin of Experimental Treatments for AIDS,* 43–44.

Bakhtin, M. M. (1981). *The dialogic imagination: Four essays by M. M. Bakhtin* (M. Holquist, Ed.; C. Emerson & M. Holquist, Trans.). Austin: University of Texas Press.

Balagangadhara, S. N. (1988). Comparative anthropology and moral domains. *Cultural Dynamics, 1,* 98–128.

Balwick, J., & Peek, C. W. (1971). The inexpressive male: Tragedy of American society. *Family Coordinator, 20,* 363–368.

Bandura, A. (1994). Social cognitive theory of mass communication. In J. Bryant & D. Zillman (Eds.), *Media effects: Advances in theory and research* (pp. 61–90). Hillsdale, NJ: Lawrence Erlbaum Associates.

Baran, A., & Pannor, R. (1993). *Lethal secrets: The psychology of donor insemination problems and solutions.* New York: Amistad.

Barnes, D. B., Gerbert, B., McMaster, J. R., & Greenblatt, R. M. (1996). Self-disclosure experience of people with HIV infection in dedicated and mainstreamed dental facilities. *Journal of Public Health Dentistry, 56,* 223–225.

Barnlund, D. (1989). *Communicative styles of Japanese and Americans.* Belmont, CA: Wadsworth.

Bartholomew, K. (1990). Avoidance of intimacy: An attachment perspective. *Journal of Social and Personal Relationships, 7,* 147–178.

Bartholomew, K. (1993). From childhood to adult relationships: Attachment theory and research. In S. Duck (Ed.), *Understanding relationship processes: Vol. 2. Learning about relationships* (pp. 30–62). Newbury Park, CA: Sage.

Bartholomew, K., & Horowitz, L. M. (1991). Attachment styles among young adults: A test of a four-category model. *Journal of Personality and Social Psychology, 61,* 226–244.

Baumeister, R. F. (1982). A self-presentational view of social phenomena. *Psychological Bulletin, 91,* 3–26.

Baumeister, R. F. (1991). *Meanings of life.* New York: Guilford.

Baumeister, R. F. & Leary, M. R. (1995). The need to belong: Desire for interpersonal attachments as a fundamental human motivation. *Psychological Bulletin, 117,* 497–529.

Baumeister, R. F., Stillwell, A., & Wotman, S. R. (1990). Victim and perpetrator accounts of interpersonal conflict: Autobiographical narratives about anger. *Journal of Personality and Social Psychology, 59,* 994–1005.

Bavelas, J. B., Black, A., Chovil, N., & Mullett, J. (1990). *Equivocal communication.* Newbury Park, CA: Sage.

Baxter, L. A. (1982). Strategies for ending relationships: Two studies. *Western Journal of Speech Communication, 46,* 223–241.

Baxter, L. A. (1984a). An investigation of compliance-gaining as politeness. *Human Communication Research, 10,* 427–456.

Baxter, L. A. (1984b). Gender differences in the heterosexual relationship rules embedded in break-up accounts. *Journal of Social and Personal Relationships, 3,* 289–306.

Baxter, L. A. (1988). A dialectical perspective on communication strategies in relationship development. In S. Duck (Ed.), *Handbook of personal relationships* (pp. 257–273). New York: Wiley.

Baxter, L. A. (1990). Dialectical contradictions in relationship development. *Journal of Social and Personal Relationships, 7,* 69–88.

Baxter, L. A. (1991, November). *Bakhtin's ghost: Dialectical communication in relationships.* Paper presented at the annual meeting of the Speech Communication Association, Atlanta, GA.

Baxter, L. A., & Erbert, L. (1997, November). *Perceptions of dialectical contradictions in the turning points of development in heterosexual romantic relationships.* Paper presented at the National Communication Association Convention, Chicago.

Baxter, L. A., & Montgomery, B. M. (1996). *Relating: Dialogues and dialectics.* New York: Guilford.

Baxter, L. A., & Wilmot, W. W. (1984). Secret tests: Social strategies for acquiring information about the state of the relationship. *Human Communication Research, 11,* 171–201.

Baxter, L. A., & Wilmot, W. W. (1985). Taboo topics in close relationships. *Journal of Social and Personal Relationships, 2,* 253–269.

Bayer, R. (1994, February 15). AIDS: Human rights and responsibilities. *Hospital Practice, 29*(2), 155–157, 161–164.

Beasley, D. (1993, January 9). Trying to stop a dirty habit: Macon doctor behind drive against unhealthy, age-old craving for kaolin. *Atlanta Journal & Constitution,* B2.

Beauchamp, T., & Childress, J. (1989). *Principles of biomedical ethics* (3rd ed.). New York: Oxford University Press.

Beckett, K. (1996). Culture and the politics of signification: The case of child sexual abuse. *Social Problems, 43,* 57–76.

Beckman, H. B., & Frankel, R. M. (1984). The effect of physician behavior on the collection of data. *Annals of Internal Medicine, 101,* 692–696.

Behringer v. The Medical Center of Princeton, 592 A 2d. (NJ Super. 1991).

Beisecker, A. E., & Beisecker, T. D. (1990). Patient information-seeking behaviors when communicating with doctors. *Medical Care, 28,* 19–28.

Bench, L. L., Kramer, S. P., & Erickson, S. (1997). A discriminant analysis of predictive factors in sex offender recidivism. In B. K. Schwartz & H. R. Cellini (Eds.), *The sex offender: New insights, treatment innovations, and legal developments* (pp. 15-1–15-15). Kingston, NJ: Civic Research Institute.

Benn, S. I., & Gaus, G. F. (1983). The public and the private: Concepts and action. In S. I. Benn & G. F. Gaus (Eds.), *Public and private in social life.* New York: St. Martin Press.

Benoit, W. J., & Benoit, P. J. (1987). Everyday argument practices of naive social actors. In J. W. Wentzel (Ed.), *Argument and critical practices* (pp. 465–473). Annandale, VA: Speech Communication Association.

Berg, J. H., & Archer, R. L. (1980). Disclosure or concern: A second look at liking for the norm breaker. *Journal of Personality, 48*(2), 245–257.

Berg, J. H., & Archer, R. L. (1982). Responses to *self*-disclosure and interaction goals. *Journal of Experimental Social Psychology, 18,* 501–512.

Berg, J. H., & Derlega, V. J. (1987). Themes in the study of self-disclosure. In V. J. Derlega & J. H. Berg (Eds.), *Self-disclosure: Theory, research, and therapy* (pp. 1–18). New York: Plenum.

Berg, J. H. & Peplau, L. A. (1982). Loneliness: The relationship of self-disclosure and androgyny. *Personality and Social Psychology Bulletin, 8,* 624–630.

Berger, C. R. (1987). Communicating under uncertainty. In M. E. Roloff & G. R. Miller (Eds.), *Interpersonal processes: New directions in communication research* (pp. 39–62). Thousand Oaks, CA: Sage.

Berger, C. R. (1988). Uncertainty and information exchange in developing relationships. In S. Duck (Ed.), *Handbook of personal relationships: Theory, research, and interventions* (pp. 239–256). Chichester, England: Wiley.

Berger, C. R. (1993). Uncertainty and social interaction. In S. Deetz (Ed.), *Communication yearbook 16* (pp. 491–502). Newbury Park, CA: Sage.

Berger, C. R., & Bradac, J. J. (1982). *Language and social knowledge: Uncertainty in interpersonal relations.* London: Edward Arnold.

Berger, C. R., & Calabrese, R. J. (1975). Some explorations in initial interaction and beyond: Toward a developmental theory of interpersonal communication. *Human Communication Research, 1,* 99–112.

Berger, C. R., & Kellermann, K. (1994). Acquiring social information. In J. A. Daly & J. M. Wiemann (Eds.), *Strategic interpersonal communication* (pp. 1–31). Hillsdale, NJ: Lawrence Erlbaum Associates.

Berger, J. T., Rosner, F., & Farnsworth, P. (1996). The ethics of mandatory HIV testing in newborns. *The Journal of Clinical Ethics, 7,* 77–84.

Berglas, S. & Jones, E. E. (1978). Drug choice as a self-handicapping strategy in response to a non-contingent success. *Journal of Personality and Social Psychology, 36,* 405–417.

Bergmann, J. R. (1993). *Discreet indiscretions: The social organization of gossip.* New York: Aldine de Gruyter.

Berke, R. L. (1998, April 19). In new climate, more politicians surmount imperfect private lives. *New York Times,* p. 1.

Berkman, L. F. (1995). The role of social relations in health promotion. *Psychosomatic Medicine, 57,* 245–254.

Bernstein, A. (1995). Should you be told that your neighbor is a sex offender? In R. E. Long (Ed.), *Rights to privacy* (pp. 21–24). New York: H. W. Wilson.

Billig, M., Condor, S., Edwards, D., Gane, M., Middleton, D., & Radley, A. (1988). *Ideological dilemmas: A social psychology of everyday thinking.* Newbury Park, CA: Sage.

Birchler, G. R. (1979). Communication skills in married couples. In A. S. Bellack & M. Hersen (Eds.), *Research and practice in social skills training* (pp. 273–315). New York: Plenum.

Birchler, G. R., Wiess, R. L., & Vincent, J. P. (1975). Multimethod analysis of social reinforcement exchange between maritally distressed and nondistressed spouse and stranger dyads. *Journal of Personality and Social Psychology, 31,* 349–360.

Black, L. W. (1993). AIDS and secrets. In E. Imber-Black (Ed.), *Secrets in families and family therapy* (pp. 355–369). New York: Norton.

Blair, A., & Zahm, S. H. (1991). Cancer among farmers. *Occupational Medicine: State of the Art Reviews, 6,* 335–354.

Blos, P. (1962). *On adolescence: A psychoanalytic interpretation.* New York: The Free Press.

Blotcky, A. D., Carscaddon, D. M., & Grandmaison, S. L. (1983). Self-disclosure and physical health: In support of curvilinearity. *Psychological Reports, 53,* 903–906.

Bochner, A. P. (1982). On the efficacy of openness in closed relationships. In M. Burgoon (Ed.), *Communication yearbook 5* (pp. 109–124). New Brunswick, NJ: Transaction Books.

Bochner, A. P., Kaminski, E. P., & Fitzpatrick, M. A. (1977). The conceptual domain of interpersonal communication behavior: A factor-analytic study. *Human Communication Research, 3,* 291–302.

Bok, S. (1982). *Secrets: On the ethics of concealment and revelation.* New York: Pantheon.

Boling, P. (1996). *Privacy and the politics of intimate life.* Ithaca, NY: Cornell University Press.

Bolund, C. (1990). Crisis and coping: Learning to live with cancer. In J. C. D. Holland & R. Zittoun (Eds.), *Psychosocial aspects of oncology* (pp. 13–26). Berlin: Springer-Verlag.

Bowen, S. P., & Michal-Johnson, P. (1989). The crisis of communicating in relationships: Confronting the threat of AIDS. *AIDS & Public Policy Journal, 4,* 10–19.

Bowlby, J. (1969). *Attachment and loss: Vol. 1.* New York: Basic Books.

Bowman, M. L. (1990). Coping efforts and marital satisfaction: Measuring marital coping and its correlates. *Journal of Marriage and the Family, 52,* 463–474.

Bradac, J. J., Hosman, L. A., & Tardy, C. H. (1978). Reciprocal disclosures and language intensity: Attributional consequences. *Communication Monographs, 5,* 1–17.

Branscomb, A. W. (1994). *Who owns information? From privacy to public access.* New York: Basic Books.

Brewer, M. B., & Mittelman, J. (1980). Effects of normative control of self-disclosure on reciprocity. *Journal of Personality, 48,* 89–102.

Brouwer, D. (1995). *The charisma of "responsibility": A comparison of U.S. mainstream representations of gay men with AIDS and representations of gay men with AIDS in U.S. AIDS zines.* Unpublished master's thesis, Northwestern University, Chicago.

Brown, J. M., Gilliard, D. F., Snell, T. L., Stephan, J. J., & Wilson, D. J. (1996). *Correctional populations in the United States, 1994.* Washington, DC: U.S. Department of Justice, Bureau of Justice Statistics.

Brown, P., & Levinson, S. C. (1978). Universals in language use: Politeness phenomena. In E. Goody (Ed.), *Questions and politeness: Strategies in social interaction* (pp. 56–289). Cambridge, MA: Cambridge University Press.

Brown, P., & Levinson, S. C. (1987). *Politeness: Some universals in language usage.* Cambridge, England: Cambridge University Press.

Bruni, F. (1998, April 19). Psychiatrist's silence at issue in a lawsuit. *New York Times,* p. 24.

Buhrmester, D. (1992). The developmental courses of sibling and peer relationships. In F. Boer & J. Dunn (Eds.), *Children's sibling relationships: Developmental and clinical issues* (pp. 19–40). Hillsdale, NJ: Lawrence Erlbaum Associates.

Buller, D. B., & Burgoon, J. K. (1996). Interpersonal deception theory. *Communication Theory, 6,* 203–242.

Burgoon, J. K. (1982). Privacy and communication. In M. Burgoon (Ed.), *Communication yearbook 6* (pp. 206–288). Beverly Hills, CA: Sage.

Burgoon, J. K., Buller, D. B., & Woodall, W. G. (1996). *Nonverbal communication: The unspoken dialogue* (2nd. ed.). New York: McGraw-Hill.

Burgoon, J. K., & Hale, J. L. (1984). The fundamental topoi of relational communication. *Communication Monographs, 51,* 193–214.

Burgoon, J. K., & Koper, R. J. (1984). Nonverbal and relational communication associated with reticence. *Human Communication Research, 10,* 601–626.

Burgoon, J. K., Parrott, R., Le Poire, B. A., Kelley, D. L., Walther, J. B., & Perry, D. (1989). Maintaining and restoring privacy through communication in different types of relationships. *Journal of Social and Personal Relationships, 6,* 131–158.

Burke, R. J., Weir, T., & Harrison, D. (1976). Disclosure of problems and tensions experienced by marital partners. *Psychological Reports, 38,* 531–542.

Burstow, B. (1992). *Radical feminist therapy: Working in the context of violence.* Newbury Park, CA: Sage.

Buslig, A. L. S. (1994). *Controlling privacy: Environmental, nonverbal, and verbal mechanisms.* Unpublished manuscript, University of Arizona, Tucson.

Buss, D. M., Gomes, M., Higgins, D. S., & Lauterbach, K. (1987). Tactics of manipulation. *Journal of Personality and Social Psychology, 52,* 1219–1229.

Cahn, D. D. (1992). *Conflict in intimate relationships.* New York: Guilford Press.

Cameron, M. E. (1993). *Living with AIDS: Experiencing ethical dilemmas.* Newbury Park, CA: Sage.

Campbell, E. (1990). Mandatory AIDS testing and privacy: A psychological perspective. *North Dakota Law Review, 66,* 448–494.

Canary, D. J., Emmers-Sommer, T. M., & Faulkner, S. (1997). *Sex and gender differences in personal relationships.* New York: Guilford Press.

Canary, D. J., & Spitzberg, B. H. (1989). A model of the perceived competence of conflict strategies. *Human Communication Research, 15,* 630–649.

Canary, D. J., & Stafford, L. (1994). Maintaining relationships through strategic and routine interaction. In D. J. Canary & L. Stafford (Eds.), *Communication and relational maintenance* (pp. 3–22). San Diego, CA: Academic Press.

Canterbury v. Spence, 464 F. 2d (DC Cir. 1972), *cert. denied,* 409 U.S. 1064 (1973).

Cappella, J. N., & Street, R. L. (1985). A functional approach to the structure of communicative behavior. In R. L. Street & J. N. Cappella (Eds.), *Sequence and pattern in communicative behavior.* London: Edward Arnold.

Carbaugh, D. (1988). *Talking American.* Norwood, NJ: Ablex.

Carbaugh, D. (1990). *Cultural communication and intercultural contact.* Hillsdale, NJ: Lawrence Erlbaum Associates.

Carbaugh, D., & Hastings, S. O. (1992). A role for communication theory in ethnography and cultural analysis. *Communication Theory, 2,* 156–164.

Carlson, T. (1997). Community notification laws will reduce sexual violence. In D. L. Bender, B. Leone, S. Barbour, B. Stalcup, M. E. Williams, & T. L. Roleff (Eds.), *Sexual violence: Opposing viewpoints* (pp. 155–161). San Diego: Greenhaven.

Carrese, J. A., & Rhodes, L. A. (1995). Western bioethics on the Navajo reservation. *Journal of the American Medical Association, 274,* 826–829.

Carroll, J. M. (1975). *Confidential information sources: Public and private.* Los Angeles: Security World.

Carter, K., & Presnell, M. (Eds.). (1994). *Interpretive approaches to interpersonal communication.* New York: State University of New York Press.

Cass, C. (1995, October 27). Gangster rap foes attack trash on TV. *Lansing State Journal,* p. 3A.

Cassidy, J. (1994). A confidence betrayed. *Nursing Times, 90,* 16–17.

Catania, J. A., Turner, H. A., Choi, K., & Coates, T. J. (1992). Coping with death anxiety: Help-seeking and social support among gay men with various HIV diagnoses. *AIDS, 6,* 999–1005.

Centers for Disease Control. (1987, June 12). Update: Human immunodeficiency virus infection in health care workers exposed to blood of infected patients. *Morbidity & Mortality Weekly Reports, 361*(16). Atlanta, GA: U.S. Department of Health and Human Services.

Centers for Disease Control. (1987, August). *Crossing cultures? Some suggestions to smooth the way. IV Regional Annex: Southeast Asian mainland.* Atlanta: U.S. Department of Health and Human Resources, Public Health Service, Centers for Disease Control.

Centers for Disease Control and Prevention. (1997, June). *HIV/AIDS surveillance report, 9*(1). Atlanta, GA: U.S. Department of Health and Human Services.

Chackes, E., & Christ, G. (1996). Cross cultural issues in patient education. *Patient Education and Counseling, 27,* 13–21.

Chad, N. (1995, May). Talk stupid to me. *Gentlemen's Quarterly,* 156–159, 194.

Chaikin, A. L., & Derlega, V. J. (1974). Variables affecting the appropriateness of self-disclosure. *Journal of Consulting and Clinical Psychology, 42,* 13–19.

Chang, H. C., & Holt, G. R. (1991). The concept of yuan and Chinese interpersonal relationships. In S. Ting-Toomey & F. Korzenny (Eds.), *Cross-cultural interpersonal communication* (pp. 28–57). Newbury Park, CA: Sage.

Chatters, L. M., Taylor, R. J., & Jackson, J. S. (1985). Size and composition of informal helper networks of elderly blacks. *Journal of Gerontology, 40,* 605–614.

Chawla, P., & Krauss, R. M. (1994). Gesture and speech in spontaneous and rehearsed narratives. *Journal of Experimental Social Psychology, 30,* 580–601.

Chelune, G. J. (1975). Self-disclosure: An elaboration of its basic dimensions. *Psychological Reports, 36,* 79–85.

Chelune, G. J. (1976). The self-disclosure situations survey: A new approach to measuring self-disclosure. *JSAS Catalog of Selected Documents in Psychology, 6*(1367), 111–112.

Chelune, G. J. (1979). Measuring openness in interpersonal communication. In G. J. Chelune (Ed.), *Self-disclosure: Origins, patterns, and implications of openness in interpersonal relationships* (pp. 1–27). San Francisco: Jossey-Bass.

Chelune, G. J. (Ed.). (1979). *Self-disclosure: Origins, patterns, and implications of openness in interpersonal relationships.* San Francisco: Jossey-Bass.

Chelune, G. J. (1979). Summary, implications, and future perspectives. In G. J. Chelune (Ed.), *Self-disclosure: Origins, patterns, and implications of openness in interpersonal relationships* (pp. 243–260). San Francisco: Jossey-Bass.

Chen, G.-M. (1995). Differences in self-disclosure patterns among Americans versus Chinese: A comparative study. *Journal of Cross-Cultural Psychology, 26,* 84–91.

310

REFERENCES

Chen, G.-M., & Starosta, W. J. (1998). *Foundations of intercultural communication.* Needham Heights, MA: Allyn & Bacon.

Cherry, K., & Smith, D. H. (1993). Sometimes I cry: The experience of loneliness for men with AIDS. *Health Communication, 5,* 181–208.

Chidwick, A., & Borrill, J. (1996). Dealing with a life-threatening diagnosis: The experience of people with the human immunodeficiency virus. *AIDS Care, 8,* 271–284.

Choi, K., Yep, G. A., & Kumekawa, E. (1998). HIV prevention among Asian and Pacific Islander men who have sex with men: A critical review of theoretical models and directions for future research. *AIDS Education and Prevention, 10*(Supplement A), 19–30.

Christensen, A. (1987). Detection of conflict patterns in couples. In K. Hahlweg & M. J. Goldstein (Eds.), *Understanding major mental disorder: The contribution of family interaction research* (pp. 250–265). New York: Family Process Press.

Christensen, A. (1988). Dysfunctional interaction patterns in couples. In P. Noller & M. A. Fizpatrick (Eds.), *Perspectives on marital interaction* (pp. 31–52). Clevedon, Avon, England: Multilingual Matters.

Christensen, A., & Heavey, C. L. (1990). Gender and social structure in the demand/withdraw pattern of marital conflict. *Journal of Personality and Social Psychology, 59,* 73–81.

Christensen, A. J., & Smith, T. W. (1993). Cynical hostility and cardiovascular reactivity during self-disclosure. *Psychosomatic Medicine, 55,* 193–202.

Christie, J. (1996, April). Club medicine: Legal cultivation and distribution of marijuana. *Reason, 27,* 54.

Clark, K., & Holquist, M. (1984). *Mikhail Bakhtin.* Cambridge, MA: The Belknap Press of Harvard University Press.

Clemo, L. (1992). The stigmatization of AIDS in infants and children in the United States. *AIDS Education and Prevention, 4,* 308–318.

Cline, R. J. (1986). The effects of biological sex and psychological gender on reported and behavioral intimacy and control of self-disclosure. *Communication Quarterly, 34,* 41–54.

Cline, R. J., & McKenzie, N. J. (in press). Interpersonal roulette and HIV/AIDS as disability: Stigma and social support in tension. In D. Braithwaite & T. Thompson (Eds.), *Handbook of communication and people with disabilities.* Mahwah, NJ: Lawrence Erlbaum Associates.

Cline, R. J. W. (1989). Communication and death and dying: Implications for coping with AIDS. *AIDS and Public Policy, 4,* 40–50.

Cline, R. J. W., & Boyd, M. F. (1993). Communication as threat and therapy: Stigma, social support, and coping with HIV infection. In E. B. Ray (Ed.), *Case studies in health communication* (pp. 131–147). Hillsdale, NJ: Lawrence Erlbaum Associates.

Cline, R. J. W., & Johnson, S. J. (1992). Mosquitoes, doorknobs, and sneezing: Relationships between homophobia and AIDS mythology among college students. *Health Communication, 4,* 273–289.

Cline, R. J. W., & McKenzie, N. J. (1996). Women and AIDS: The lost population. In R. Parrott & C. Condit (Eds.), *Evaluating women's health messages: A resource book* (pp. 382–401). Thousand Oaks, CA: Sage.

Closen, M. L. (1991). Mandatory disclosure of HIV blood test results to the individuals tested: A matter of personal choice neglected. *Loyola University Chicago Law Journal, 22,* 445–478.

Cloven, D. H., & Roloff, M. E. (1991). Sense-making activities and interpersonal conflict: Communicative cures for the mulling blues. *Western Journal of Speech Communication, 55,* 134–158.

Cloven, D. H., & Roloff, M. E. (1993a). Sense-making activities and interpersonal conflict, II: The effects of communicative intentions on internal dialogue. *Western Journal of Communication, 57,* 309–329.

Cloven, D. H., & Roloff, M. E. (1993b). The chilling effect of aggressive potential on the expression of complaints in intimate relationships. *Communication Monographs, 60,* 199–219.

Cloven, D. H., & Roloff, M. E. (1994). A developmental model of decisions to withhold relational irritations in romantic relationships. *Personal Relationships, 1,* 143–164.

Cloven, D. H., & Roloff, M. E. (1995). Making sense of interpersonal conflict: Interpersonal communication effects on intrapersonal sense-making processes. In J. E. Aitken & L. J. Shedlestsky (Eds.), *Intrapersonal communication processes* (pp. 250–255). Plymouth, MI: Midnight Oil Multimedia.

Cochran, S. D., & Mays, V. M. (1990). Sex, lies, and HIV [Letter to the editor]. *New England Journal of Medicine, 322,* 774–775.

Cohen, J. (1969). *Statistical power analysis for the behavioral sciences.* New York: Academic Press.

Cole, S. W., Kemeny, M. E., Taylor, S. E., Visscher, B. R., & Fahey, J. L. (1996). Accelerated course of human immunodeficiency virus infection in gay men who conceal their homosexual identity. *Psychosomatic Medicine, 58,* 219–231.

Coleman, P. G., & Shellow, R. A. (1995). Privacy and autonomy in the physician-patient relationship. *The Journal of Legal Medicine, 16,* 509–543.

Collier, M. J. (1986). Culture and gender: Effects on assertive behavior and communication competence. In M. L. McLaughlin (Ed.), *Communication yearbook 9* (pp. 576–592). Newbury Park, CA: Sage.

Collins, N. L., & Miller, L. C. (1994) The disclosure-liking link: From meta-analysis toward a dynamic reconceptualization, *Psychological Bulletin,* 116, 457–475.

Court upholds Megan's Law. (1997, August 23). *Rochester Democrat & Chronicle,* p. 1A.

Cozby, P. C. (1973). Self-disclosure: A literature review. *Psychological Bulletin, 79*(2), 73–91.

Craig, R. J., Tracy, K., & Spisak, F. (1986). The disclosure of requests: Assessment of politeness approval. *Human Communication Research, 12,* 437–468.

Crandall, C. S., & Coleman, R. (1992). AIDS-related stigmatization and the disruption of social relationships. *Journal of Social and Personal Relationships, 9,* 163–177.

Crawford, A. M. (1996). Stigma associated with AIDS: A meta-analysis. *Journal of Applied Social Psychology, 26,* 398–416.

Crawford, M. (1995). *Talking difference: On gender and language.* London: Sage Publications.

Crewdson, J. (1988). *By silence betrayed: Sexual abuse of children in America.* Boston: Little, Brown.

Crocker, J., & Schwartz, I. (1985). Prejudice and ingroup favoritism in a minimal intergroup interaction: Effects of self-esteem. *Personality and Social Psychology Bulletin, 11,* 379–386.

Cronen, V. E. (1995). Practical theory and the tasks ahead for the social approaches to communication. In W. Leeds-Hurwitz (Ed.), *Social approaches to communication.* New York: Guilford.

Cumes, D. P. (1983). Hypertension, disclosure of personal concerns, and blood pressure response. *Journal of Clinical Psychology, 39,* 376–381.

Cunningham, J. D. (1981). Self-disclosure intimacy: Sex, sex-of-target, cross-national, and "generational" differences. *Personality and Social Psychology Bulletin, 7,* 314–319.

Cupach, W. R., & Canary, D. J. (1997). *Competence in interpersonal conflict.* New York: McGraw-Hill.

Cupach, W. R., & Metts, S. (1994). *Facework.* Thousand Oaks, CA: Sage.

Curran, J. W. (1988). AIDS in the United States. In R. F. Schinazi & A. J. Nahmias (Eds.), *AIDS in children, adolescents, and heterosexual adults: An interdisciplinary approach to prevention* (pp. 10–12). New York: Elsevier.

Curry, R. R., & Allison, T. (1996). *States of rage: Emotional eruption, violence, & social change.* New York: State University of New York Press.

Cutrona, C. E. (1996). *Social support in couples.* Thousand Oaks, CA: Sage.

Dandekar, R. N. (1988). The Bhagavad Gita: Action and devotion. In A. T. Embree (Ed.), *Sources of Indian tradition* (pp. 276–296). New York: Columbia University Press.

Daniolos, P. T., & Holmes, V. F. (1995). HIV public policy and psychiatry: An examination of ethical issues and professional guidelines. *Psychosomatics, 36,* 12–21.

Davidson, B., Balswich, J., & Halverson, C. (1983). Affective self-disclosure and marital adjustment: A test of equity theory. *Journal of Marriage and the Family, 45,* 93–102.

Davis, D., & Holtgraves, T. (1984). Perceptions of unresponsive others: Attributions, attraction, understandability, and memory of their utterances. *Journal of Experimental Social Psychology, 20,* 383–408.

Davis, D., & Perkowitz, W. T. (1979). Consequences of responsiveness in dyadic interaction: Effects of probability of response and proportion of content-related response on interpersonal attraction. *Journal of Personality and Social Psychology, 37,* 534–550.

Davis, D. T., Bustamante, A., Brown, C. P., Wolde-Tsadik, G., Savage, E. W., Cheng, X., & Howland, L. (1994). The urban church and cancer control: A source of social influence in minority communities. *Public Health Reports, 109,* 500–506.

Deaux, K. (1996). Social identification. In E. T. Higgins & A. W. Kruglanski (Eds.), *Social psychology: Handbook of basic principles* (pp. 777–798). New York: Guilford.

de Carpio, A. B., Carpio-Cedraro, F. F., & Anderson, L. (1990). Hispanic families learning and teaching about AIDS: A participatory approach at the community level. *Hispanic Journal of Behavioral Sciences, 12,* 165–176.

Decker, S. D., & Knight, L. (1990). Functional health pattern assessment: A seasonal migrant farmworker community. *Journal of Community Health Nursing, 7,* 141–51.

de Certeau, M. (1984). *The practice of everyday life.* (S. F. Randall, Trans.). Berkeley: University of California Press.

DePaulo, B. M., Kashy, D. A., Kirkendol, S. E., & Wyer, M. M. (1996). Lying in everyday life. *Journal of Personality and Social Psychology, 70,* 779–795.

Derlega, V. J. (1984). Self-disclosure and intimate relationships. In V. J. Derlega (Ed.), *Communication, intimacy, and close relationships* (pp. 1–9). Orlando, FL: Academic Press.

Derlega, V. J., & Barbee, A. P. (Eds.). (1998). *HIV and social interaction.* Thousand Oaks, CA: Sage.

Derlega, V. J., & Berg, J. H. (Eds.). (1987). *Self-disclosure: Theory, research and therapy.* New York: Plenum Press.

Derlega, V. J., & Chaikin, A. L. (1977). Privacy and self-disclosure in social relationships. *Journal of Social Issues, 33,* 102–115.

Derlega, V. J., & Grzelak, J. (1979). Appropriateness of self-disclosure. In G. J. Chelune (Eds.), *Self-disclosure: Origins, patterns, and implications of openness in interpersonal relationships* (pp. 151–176). San Francisco: Jossey-Bass.

Derlega, V. J., Lovejoy, D., & Winstead, B. A. (1998). Personal accounts of disclosing and concealing HIV-positive test results: Weighing the benefits and risks. In V. J. Derlega & A. P. Barbee (Eds.), *HIV and social interaction* (pp. 147–164). Thousand Oaks, CA: Sage.

Derlega, V. J., Metts, S., Petronio, S., & Margulis, S. T. (1993). *Self-disclosure.* Newbury Park, CA: Sage.

Derse, A. R. (1995). HIV and AIDS: Legal and ethical issues in the emergency department. *Emergency Clinics of North America, 13,* 213–223.

Deutsch, M. (1973). *The resolution of conflict: Constructive and destructive processes.* New Haven, CT: Yale University Press.

Diaz, R. M. (1998). *Latino gay men and HIV: Culture, sexuality, and risk behavior.* New York: Routledge.

DiClemente, R. J. (1990). The emergence of adolescents as a risk group for human immunodeficiency virus infection. *Journal of Adolescent Research, 5,* 7–17.

Dillard, J. P., & Spitzberg, B. H. (1984). Global impressions of social skills: Behavioral predictors. In R. N. Bostrom (Ed.), *Communication yearbook 8* (pp. 446–463). Beverly Hills, CA: Sage.

DiMatteo, M., Linn, L. S., Chang, B. L., & Cope, D. W. (1985). Affect and neutrality in physician behavior: A study of patients values and satisfaction. *Journal of Behavioral Medicine, 8,* 397–409.

Dindia, K. (1982). Reciprocity of self-disclosure: A sequential analysis. In M. Burgoon (Ed.), *Communication yearbook 6* (pp. 506–530). Beverly Hills, CA: Sage.

Dindia, K. (1984, May). *Antecedents and consequents of self-disclosure.* Paper presented at the meeting of the International Communication Association, San Francisco.

Dindia, K. (1988). A comparison of several statistical tests of reciprocity of self-disclosure. *Communication Research, 15,* 726–752.

Dindia, K. (1994). The intrapersonal-interpersonal dialectical process of self-disclosure. In S. Duck (Ed.), *Dynamics of relationships* (pp. 27–57). Thousand Oaks, CA: Sage.

Dindia, K. (1998). "Going into and coming out of the closet": The dialectics of stigma disclosure. In B. M. Montgomery & L. A. Baxter (Eds.), *Dialectical approaches to studying personal relationships* (pp. 83–108). Mahwah, NJ: Lawrence Erlbaum Associates.

Dindia, K., & Allen, M. (1992). Sex-differences in self-disclosure: A meta-analysis, *Psychological Bulletin, 112,* 106–124.

Dindia, K. & Allen, M. (1995, June). *Reciprocity of self-disclosure: A meta-analysis.* Paper presented at the International Network on Personal Relationships conference, Williamsburg, VA.

Dindia, K., Fitzpatrick, M. A., & Kenny, D. A. (1997). Self-disclosure in spouse and stranger dyads: A social relations analysis. *Human Communication Research, 23,* 388–412.

Doll, L. S., Harrison, J. S., Frey, R. L., McKirnan, D., Bartholow, B. N., Douglas, J. M., Joy, D., Bolan, G., & Doetsch, I. (1994). Failure to disclose HIV risk among gay and bisexual men attending sexually transmitted disease clinics. *American Journal of Preventive Medicine, 10*(3), 125–129.

Douard, J. (1990). AIDS, stigma, and privacy. *AIDS and Public Policy Journal, 5,* 37–41.

Dowell, K. A., Lo Presto, C. T., & Sherman, M. F. (1991). When are AIDS patients to blame for their disease? Effects of patients' sexual orientation and mode of transmission. *Psychological Reports, 69,* 211–219.

Driscoll, J. M. (1992). Keeping covenants and confidence sacred: One point of view. *Journal of Counseling and Development, 70,* 704–708.

Duck, S. (1982). A topography of relationship disengagement and dissolution. In S. Duck (Ed.), *Personal relationships 4: Dissolving personal relationships* (pp. 1–30). London: Academic Press.

Duck, S., & Miell, D. E. (1986). Charting the development of personal relationships. In R. Gilmour & S. Duck (Eds.), *The emerging field of personal relationships* (pp. 133–143). Hillsdale, NJ: Lawrence Erlbaum Associates.

Duck, S., & Pittman, G. (1994). Social and personal relationships. In M. L. Knapp & G. R. Miller (Eds.), *Handbook of interpersonal communication* (2nd ed., pp. 676–695). Thousand Oaks, CA: Sage.

Dumois, A. O. (1995). The case against mandatory screening for HIV antibodies. *Journal of Community Health, 20,* 143–159.

Dunkel-Schetter, C., Feinstein, L. G., Taylor, S. E., & Falke, R. L. (1992). Patterns of coping with cancer. *Health Psychology, 11,* 79–87.

Earl, W. L., Martindale, C. J., & Cohn, D. (1991). Adjustment: Denial in the styles of coping with HIV infection. *Omega, 24,* 35–47.

Eisenberg, E. M. (1990). Jamming: Transcendence through organizing. *Communication Research, 17,* 139–164.

Eisenberg, E. M., & Witten, M. G. (1987). Reconsidering openness in organizational communication. *Academy of Management Review, 12,* 418–428.

Ekman, P., & Friesen, W. V. (1976). Measuring facial movement. *Environmental Psychology and Nonverbal Behavior, 1,* 56–75.

Ellis, C. (1991a). Sociological introspection and emotional experience. *Symbolic Interaction, 14*, 23–50.

Ellis, C. (1991b). Emotional sociology. *Studies in Symbolic Interaction, 12*, 123–145.

Ellis, C., & Bochner, A. P. (1992). Telling and performing personal stories: The constraints of choices in abortion. In C. Ellis & M. G. Flaherty (Eds.), *Investigating subjectivity: Research on lived experience* (pp. 79–101). Newbury Park, CA: Sage.

Enelow, A. J., & Swisher, S. N. (1986). *Interviewing and patient care* (3rd ed.). Oxford, England: Oxford University Press.

Eng, E., Hatch, J., & Callan, A. (1985). Institutionalizing social support through the church and into the community. *Health Education Quarterly, 12*, 81–90.

English, K., Pullen, S., & Jones, L. (1997, January). *Managing adult sex offenders in the community: A containment approach* (NCJ no. 163387). Washington, DC: U.S. Department of Justice, National Institute of Justice.

Epstein, N. (1980). Social consequences of assertion, aggression, passive aggression, and submission. *Behavior Therapy, 11*, 662–669.

Epstein, N., Pretzer, J. L., & Fleming, B. (1987). The role of cognitive appraisal in self-reports of marital communication. *Behavior Therapy, 18*, 51–69.

Evans, H. E. (1994). Public policy and AIDS. *Clinics in Perinatology, 21*, 29–38.

Falbo, T., & Peplau, L. A (1980). Power strategies in intimate relationships. *Journal of Personality and Social Psychology, 38*, 618–628.

Fallowfield, L. (1997). Truth sometimes hurts but deceit hurts more. *Annals of the New York Academy of Science, 809*, 525–536.

Felson, R. B. (1981). An interactionist approach to aggression. In J. T. Tedeschi (Ed.), *Impression management theory and social psychological research* (pp. 181–199). New York: Academic Press.

Felson, R. B. (1984). Patterns of aggressive social interaction. In A. Mummendey (Ed.), *The social psychology of aggression: From individual behavior to social interaction* (pp. 107–125). New York: Springer-Verlag.

Feyeriesen, P. (1987). Gestures and speech, interactions and separations: A reply to McNeil (1985). *Psychological Review, 94*, 493–498.

Filley, A. C. (1975). *Interpersonal conflict resolution.* Glenview, IL: Scott, Foresman.

Fincham, F. D., & Bradbury, T. N. (1989). The impact of attributions in marriage: An individual difference analysis. *Journal of Social and Personal Relationships, 6*, 69–85.

Fineman, M. A., & Mykitiuk, R. (1994). *The public nature of private violence: The discovery of domestic abuse.* New York: Routledge.

Finkelhor, D. (1979). *Sexually victimized children.* New York: The Free Press.

Finkelhor, D., & Dziuba-Leatherman, J. (1994). Children as victims of violence: A national survey. *Pediatrics, 94*, 413–420.

Finn, P. (1997, February). *Sex offender community notification* (NCJ no. 162364). Washington, DC.: U.S. Department of Justice, National Institute of Justice.

Fisher, D. V. (1984). A conceptual analysis of self-disclosure. *Journal for the Theory of Social Behavior, 14*(3), 279–296.

Fitch, K. (1998). *Speaking relationally: Culture, communication, and interpersonal connection.* New York: Guilford.

Fleischman, A. R., Post, L. F., & Dubler, N. N. (1994). Mandatory newborn screening for human immunodeficiency virus. *Bulletin of the New York Academy of Medicine, 71*, 4–17.

Folger, J. P., Poole, M. S., & Stutman, R. K. (1997). *Working through conflict: Strategies for relationships, groups, and organizations.* New York: Longman.

Foreign students' countries of origin, 1995–96. (1997, August 29). *The Chronicle of Higher Education*, p. 22.

Francis, M. E., & Pennebaker, J. W. (1992). Putting stress into words: The impact of writing on physiological, absentee, and self-reported emotional well-being measures. *American Journal of Health Promotion, 6,* 280–287.

Fraser, N. (1990). Rethinking the public sphere: A contribution to the critique of actually existing democracy. *Social Text, 25/26,* 56–80.

Fraser, N. (1992). Sex, lies and the public sphere. *Critical Inquiry, 18,* 594–612.

Frazoi, S. L. & Davis, M. H. (1985). Adolescent self-disclosure and loneliness: Private self-consciousness and parental influences. *Journal of Personality and Social Psychology, 48,* 768–780.

Freeman-Longo, R. E. (1996). Feel good legislation: Prevention or calamity? *Child Abuse & Neglect, 20,* 95–101.

Friedland, B. (1994). Physician-patient confidentiality: Time to re-examine a venerable concept in light of contemporary society and advances in medicine. *Journal of Legal Medicine, 15,* 249–277.

Frost, J. H., & Wilmot, W. W. (1977). *Interpersonal conflict.* Dubuque, IA: Brown.

Fullilove, M. T. (1989). Anxiety and stigmatizing aspects of HIV infection. *Journal of Clinical Psychiatry, 50* (Suppl), 5–8.

Funch, D. P., & Mettlin, C. (1982). The role of support in relation to recovery from breast surgery. *Social Science and Medicine, 16,* 91–98.

Gadlin, H. (1977). Private lives and public order: A critical view of the history of intimate relations in the United States. In G. Levinger & H. L. Raush (Eds.), *Close relationships: Perspectives on the meaning of intimacy* (pp. 33–72). Amherst, MA: University of Massachusetts Press.

Gard, L. H. (1990). Patient disclosure of human immunodeficiency virus (HIV) status to parents: Clinical considerations. *Professional Psychology: Research and Practice, 21,* 252–256.

Gates, H. L., Jr. (1988). *The signifying monkey: A theory of Afro-American literary criticism.* New York: Oxford University Press.

Geertz, C. (1973). *The interpretation of cultures.* New York: Basic Books.

Gelles, R. J., & Straus, M. A. (1988). *Intimate violence.* New York: Simon & Schuster.

Gerbert, B., Maguire, B. T., Bleecker, T., Coates, T. J., & McPhee, S. J. (1991). Primary care physicians and AIDS: Attitudinal and structural barriers to care. *Journal of the American Medical Association, 266,* 2837–2842.

Gergen, K. (1994). *Realities and relationships: Soundings in social construction.* Cambridge, MA: Harvard University Press.

Gilbert, S. J. (1976). Empirical and theoretical extensions of self-disclosure. In G. R. Miller (Ed.), *Explorations in interpersonal communication* (pp. 197–216). Beverly Hills, CA: Sage.

Gilligan, C. (1982). *In a different voice: Psychological theory and women's development.* Cambridge, MA: Harvard University Press.

Glaser, B., & Strauss, A. L. (1967). Awareness contexts and social interaction. *American Sociological Review, 29,* 669–679.

Gochros, H. L. (1992). The sexuality of gay men with HIV infection. *Social Work, 37,* 105–109.

Goffman, E. (1959). *The presentation of self in everyday life.* Garden City, NY: Doubleday Anchor.

Goffman, E. (1963). *Stigma: Notes on the management of spoiled identity.* Englewood Cliffs, NJ: Prentice-Hall.

Goffman, E. (1967). *Interaction ritual.* New York: Pantheon Books.

Goldsmith, D., & Baxter, L. A. (1996). Constituting relationships in talk. *Human Communication Research, 23,* 87–114.

Goodwin, R. (1990). Taboo topics among close friends: A factor-analytic investigation. *Journal of Social Psychology, 130,* 691–692.

Gordon, M., & Riger, S. (1989). *The female fear.* New York: The Free Press.

Gormly, J. (1974). A comparison of predictions from consistency and affect theories for arousal during interpersonal disagreement. *Journal of Personality and Social Psychology, 30,* 658–663.

Gostin, L. O. (1995). Informed consent, cultural sensitivity, and respect for persons. *Journal of the American Medical Association, 274,* 844–845.

Gottman, J. M. (1993). The roles of conflict engagement, escalation, and avoidance in marital interaction: A longitudinal view of five types of couples. *Journal of Consulting and Clinical Psychology, 61,* 6–15.

Gottman, J. M. (1994). *What predicts divorce: The relationship between marital processes and marital outcomes.* Hillsdale, NJ: Lawrence Erlbaum Associates.

Gottman, J. M., & Krokoff, L. J. (1989). Marital interaction and satisfaction: A longitudinal view. *Journal of Consulting and Clinical Psychology, 57,* 47–52.

Graziano, W. G., Jensen-Campbell, L. A., & Hair, E. C. (1996). Perceiving interpersonal conflict and reacting to it: The case for agreeableness. *Journal of Personality and Social Psychology, 70,* 820–835.

Green, S. A. (1995). The ethical limits of confidentiality in the therapeutic relationship. *General Hospital Psychiatry, 17,* 80–84.

Greenberg, B. S., Smith, S., Ah Yun, J., Busselle, R., Rampoldi-Hnilo, L., Mitchell, M., & Sherry, J. (1995). *The content of television talk shows: Topics, guests, and interactions* (Technical Report). East Lansing: Michigan State University, Departments of Communication and Telecommunication.

Greenberg, J., Pyszczynski, T., & Solomon, S. (1986). The causes and consequences of a need for self-esteem: A terror management theory. In R. F. Baumeister (Ed.), *Public self and private self* (pp. 189–206). London: Springer-Verlag.

Greenberg, M. A., & Stone, A. A. (1992). Emotional disclosure about traumas and its relation to health: Effects of previous disclosure and trauma severity. *Journal of Personality and Social Psychology, 63,* 75–84.

Greenberg, M. A., Wortman, C. B., & Stone, A. A. (1996). Emotional expression and physical health: Revisiting traumatic memories or fostering self-regulation? *Journal of Personality and Social Psychology, 71,* 588–602.

Greenblatt, M., Becerra, R. M., & Serafetinides, E. A. (1982). Social networks and mental health: An overview. *American Journal of Psychiatry, 139,* 977–984.

Greene, K. L., Parrott, R., & Serovich, J. M. (1993). Privacy, HIV testing, and AIDS: College students' versus parents' perspectives. *Health Communication, 5,* 59–74.

Greene, K. L., & Serovich, J. M. (1995, November). *Predictors of willingness to disclose HIV-infection to nuclear family members.* Paper presented at the annual meeting of the Speech Communication Association, San Antonio, TX.

Greene, K. L., & Serovich, J. M. (1996). Appropriateness of disclosure of HIV-testing information: The perspective of PLWAs. *Journal of Applied Communication Research, 24,* 50–65.

Greenfeld, L. A. (1997, February). *Sex offenses and offenders: An analysis of data on rape and sexual assault* (NCJ No. 163392). Washington, DC: U.S. Department of Justice, Bureau of Justice Statistics.

Greenhalgh, L. (1986, Summer). Managing conflict. *Sloan Management Review, 27,* 45–51.

Greenwald, A. G., & Breckler, S. J. (1985). To whom is the self presented? In B. R. Schlenker (Ed.), *The self and social life* (pp. 126–145). New York: McGraw-Hill.

Gregorian, D., & Kuntzman, G. (1995, October 28). Talk-TV titans meet in apple to accentuate the positive. *New York Post,* p. 1A.

Gresson, A. D. (1995). *The recovery of race in America.* Minneapolis: University of Minnesota Press.

Griffith, E. E. H., English, T., & Mayfield, V. (1980). Possession, prayer, and testimony: Therapeutic aspects of the Wednesday night meeting in a Black church. *Psychiatry, 43,* 120–129.

Gross, A. E., Green, S. K., Storck, J. T., & Vanyur, J. M. (1980). Disclosure of sexual orientation and impressions of male and female homosexuals. *Personality and Social Psychology Bulletin, 6,* 307–314.

Gudykunst, W. B. (1986). The influence of cultural variability on perceptions of communication behavior associated with relationship terms. *Human Communication Research, 13*, 147–166.

Guendelman, S. (1983). Developing responsiveness to the health needs of Hispanic children and families. *Social Work in Health Care, 8*, 1–15.

Guerrero, L. K., & Afifi, W. A. (1995a). Some things are better left unsaid: Topic avoidance in family relationships. *Communication Quarterly, 43*, 276–296.

Guerrero, L. K., & Afifi, W. A. (1995b). What parents don't know: Taboo topics and topic avoidance in parent-child relationships. In T. J. Socha and G. Stamp (Eds.), *Parents, children, and communication: Frontiers of theory and research* (pp. 219–245). Hillsdale, NJ: Lawrence Erlbaum Associates.

Guerrero, L. K., & Afifi, W. A. (1998). Communicative responses to jealousy as a function of self-esteem and relationship maintenance goals: A test of Bryson's dual motivation model. *Communication Reports, 11*, 111–122.

Hacker, H. M. (1981). Blabbermouths and clams: Sex differences in self-disclosure in same-sex and cross-sex friendship dyads. *Psychology of Women Quarterly, 5*, 385–401.

Haggard, L. M., & Werner, C. M. (1990). Situational support, privacy regulation, and stress. *Basic and Applied Psychology, 11*, 313–337.

Hahn, W. K., Brooks, J. A., & Hartsough, D. M. (1993). Self-disclosure and coping styles in men with cardiovascular reactivity. *Research in Nursing and Health, 16*, 275–282.

Halperin, E. C. (1988). The right to privacy and the duty to protect. *Southern Medical Journal, 81*, 1286–1290.

Hammer, M. (1983). "Core" and "extended" social networks in relation to health and illness. *Social Science and Medicine, 17*, 405–414.

Handkins, R. E., & Munz, D. C. (1978). Essential hypertension and self-disclosure. *Journal of Clinical Psychology, 34*, 870–875.

Haraway, D. (1991). *Simians, cyborgs, and women.* New York: Routledge.

Hard, V. K. (1993). Mandatory disclosure of AIDS status by health care workers. *Western State University Law Review, 21*, 295–319.

Hareven, T. K. (1991). The home and the family in historical perspective. *Social Research, 58*, 253–285.

Harrigan, J. A., Oxman, T. E., & Rosenthal, R. (1985). Rapport expressed through nonverbal behavior. *Journal of Nonverbal Behavior, 9*, 95–110.

Haslett, B. (1987). *Communication: Strategic action in context.* Hillsdale, NJ: Lawrence Erlbaum Associates.

Hatfield, E. (1984). The dangers of intimacy. In V. J. Derlega (Ed.), *Communication, intimacy, and close relationships* (pp. 207–220). New York: Academic Press.

Hatfield, E., Cacioppo, J. T., & Rapson, R. L. (1994). *Emotional contagion.* New York: Cambridge University Press.

Hays, R. B., Turner, H. A., & Coates, T. J. (1992). Social support, AIDS-related symptoms, and depression among gay men. *Journal of Consulting and Clinical Psychology, 60*, 463–469.

Hazan, C., & Shaver, P. R. (1994). Attachment as an organizational framework for research on close relationships. *Psychological Inquiry, 5*, 1–22.

Heaton, J. A., & Wilson, N. L. (1995). *Tuning in trouble: Talk T.V.'s destructive impact on mental health.* San Francisco: Jossey-Bass.

Heavey, C. L., Christensen, A., & Malamuth, N. M. (1995). The longitudinal impact of demand and withdrawal during marital conflict. *Journal of Consulting and Clinical Psychology, 63*, 683–687.

Heavey, C. L., Layne, C., & Christensen, A. (1993). Gender and conflict in structure in marital interaction: A replication and extension. *Journal of Consulting and Clinical Psychology, 61*, 16–27.

Heidegger, M. (1962). *Being and time.* San Francisco: Harper and Row. (Original work published 1927)

Hellinger, F. J. (1993). The lifetime cost of treating a person with HIV. *Journal of the American Medical Association, 270,* 474–478.

Henderson, A. (1995, August). The sexual criminal. *Governing,* pp. 35–38.

Henwood, K., Giles, H., Coupland, J., & Coupland, N. (1993). Stereotyping and affect in discourse: Interpreting the meaning of elderly, painful self-disclosure. In D. M. Mackie & D. L. Hamilton (Eds.), *Affect, cognition and stereotyping: Interactive processes in group perception* (pp. 269–296). San Diego, CA: Academic Press.

Herek, G. M., & Berrill, K. T. (Eds.). (1992). *Hate crimes: Confronting violence against lesbians and gay men.* Newbury Park, CA: Sage.

Herek, G. M., & Capitanio, J. P. (1993). Public reactions to AIDS in the United States: A second decade of stigma. *American Journal of Public Health, 83,* 574–577.

Herek, G. M., & Glunt, E. K. (1988). An epidemic of stigma: Public reactions to AIDS. *American Psychologist, 43,* 886–891.

Herek, G. M., & Glunt, E. K. (1991). AIDS-related attitudes in the United States: A preliminary conceptualization. *Journal of Sex Research, 28,* 99–123.

Herek, G. M., & Glunt, E. K. (1993). Public attitudes toward AIDS-related issues in the United States. In J. B. Pryor & G. D. Reeder (Eds.), *The social psychology of HIV infection* (pp. 229–261). Hillsdale, NJ: Lawrence Erlbaum Associates.

Hewitt, J., & Stokes, R. (1975). Disclaimers. *American Sociological Review, 40,* 1–11.

Hill, C. T., & Stull, D. E. (1982). Disclosure reciprocity: Conceptual and measurement issues. *Social Psychology Quarterly, 45,* 238–244.

Hill, C. T., & Stull, D. E. (1987). Gender and self-disclosure: strategies for exploring the issues. In V. J. Derlega & J. H. Berg (Eds.), *Self-disclosure: Theory, research, and therapy,* (pp. 81–100). New York: Plenum Press.

Hirsch, H. L. (1994). AIDS and the emergency room physician and staff. *Legal Medicine,* 201–228.

Hocker, J. L., & Wilmot, W. W. (1985). *Interpersonal conflict* (2nd ed.). Dubuque, IA: Brown.

Hocker, J. L., & Wilmot, W. W. (1995). *Interpersonal conflict* (3rd ed.). Dubuque, IA: Brown.

Hoge, S. K. (1995). Proposed federal legislation jeopardizes patient privacy. *Bulletin of the American Academy of Psychiatry Law, 23,* 495–500.

Hollandsworth, J. G., Jr. (1977). Differentiating assertion and aggression: Some behavioral guidelines. *Behavior Therapy, 8,* 347–352.

Hollandsworth, J. G., Jr., & Cooley, M. L. (1978). Provoking anger and gaining compliance with assertive versus aggressive responses. *Behavior Therapy, 9,* 640–646.

Holt, E. (1996). Reporting on talk: The use of direct reported speech in conversation. *Research on Language and Social Interaction, 29,* 219–245.

Holtgraves, T. M. (1988). Gambling as self-presentation. *Journal of Gambling Behavior, 4,* 78–91.

Hoppe, S. K., & Heller, P. L. (1975). Alienation, familism and the utilization of health services by Mexican Americans. *Journal of Health and Social Behavior, 16,* 304–314.

Hopper, R., & Drummond, K. (1990). Emergent goals at a relational turning point: The case of Gordon and Denise. *Journal of Language and Social Psychology, 9,* 39–66.

Huberty, C. J., & Morris, J. D. (1989). Multivariate analyses versus multiple univariate analyses. *Psychological Bulletin, 105,* 302–308.

Hull, D. B., & Schroeder, H. E. (1979). Some interpersonal effects of assertion, nonassertion, and aggression. *Behavior Therapy, 10,* 20–28.

Hyde, J. S. (1993). Gender differences in mathematics ability, anxiety, and attitudes: What do meta-analyses tell us? In L. A. Penner, G. M. Batsche, H. M. Knoff, & D. L. Nelson (Eds), *The challenge in mathematics and science education: Psychology's response* (pp. 237–249). Washington, DC: American Psychological Association.

Hymes, D. (1972). Models of the interaction of language and social life. In. J. Gumperz & D. Hymes (Eds.), *Directions in sociolinguistics: The ethnography of communication* (pp. 35–71). New York: Holt, Rinehart, and Winston.

Hymes, D. (1974). *Foundations in sociolinguistics: An ethnographic approach.* Philadelphia: University of Pennsylvania Press.

Igun, U. A. (1979). Stages in health-seeking: A descriptive model. *Social Science & Medicine, 13,* 445–456.

Infante, D. A., Chandler, T. A., & Rudd, J. E. (1989). Test of an argumentative skill deficiency model of interspousal violence. *Communication Monographs, 56,* 163–177.

In re Hershey Medical Center, 595 A. 2d. (Pa. Super. 1991).

Iwao, S. (1993). *The Japanese woman: Traditional image and changing reality.* Cambridge, MA: Harvard University Press.

Jacobson, N. S. (1989). The politics of intimacy. *Behavior Therapist, 12*(2), 29–32.

Jandt, F. E. (Ed.). (1973). *Conflict resolution through communication.* New York: Harper & Row.

Jaska, J. A., & Pritchard, M. (1994). *Communication ethics: Methods of analysis* (2nd ed.). Belmont, CA: Wadsworth.

Jefferson, G. (1984). Transcription notation. In J. M. Atkinson & J. Heritage (Eds.), *Structures of social action: Studies in conversation analysis* (pp. ix–xvi). Cambridge, England: Cambridge University Press.

Jemmott, J. B., & Jones, J. M. (1993). Social psychology and AIDS among ethnic minority individuals: Risk behaviors and strategies for changing them. In J. B. Pryor & G. D. Reeder (Eds.), *The social psychology of HIV infection* (pp. 183–224). Hillsdale, NJ: Lawrence Erlbaum Associates.

Johnson, K. L., & Roloff, M. E. (1995, November). *The nature and effects of serial arguments in dating relationships.* Paper presented at the annual convention of the Speech Communication Association, San Antonio, TX.

Jones, J. H. (1993). *Bad blood: The Tuskegee syphilis experiment* (2nd ed.). New York: The Free Press.

Jorgensen, R. S., & Houston, B. K. (1986). Family history of hypertension, personality patterns, and cardiovascular reactivity to stress. *Psychosomatic Medicine, 48,* 102–117.

Jourard, S. M. (1959). Health personality and self-disclosure. *Journal of Mental Hygiene, 43,* 499–507.

Jourard, S. M. (1971a). *Self-disclosure: An experimental analysis of the transparent self.* New York: Wiley.

Jourard, S. M. (1971b). *The transparent self* (Rev. ed.). New York: Van Nostrand.

Jourard, S., & Lasakow, P. (1958). Some factors in self-disclosure. *Journal of Abnormal and Social Psychology, 56,* 91–104.

Kalichman, S. C. (1995). *Understanding AIDS: A guide for mental health professionals.* Washington, DC: American Psychological Association.

Kalinowski, J. (1994). The myth of confidentiality. *Journal of the Association of Nurses in AIDS Care, 5*(2), 9–10.

Karpel, M. A. (1980). Family secrets: I. Conceptual and ethical issues in the relational context, II. Ethical and practical considerations in therapeutic management. *Family Processes, 19,* 295–306.

Karr, W. W. (1992, March). Examinations. *Infected Faggot Perspectives, 7,* 5.

Kashy, D. A., & DePaulo, B. M. (1996). Who lies? *Journal of Personality and Social Psychology, 70,* 1037–1051.

Katriel, T. (1990/1991). Sodot: Secret-sharing as a social form among Israeli children. *Research on Language and Social Interaction, 24,* 141–160.

Katriel, T., & Philipsen, G. (1981). "What we need is communication": "Communication" as a cultural category in some American speech. *Communication Monographs, 48,* 301–317.

Katriel, T., & Philipsen, G. (1990). "What we need is communication": "Communication" as a cultural category in some American speech. In D. Carbaugh (Ed.), *Cultural communication and intercultural contact* (pp. 77–93). Hillsdale, NJ: Lawrence Erlbaum Associates.

Keller, T. (1993). Trash TV. *Journal of Popular Culture, 26*(4), 195–206.

Kellermann, K., Reynolds, R., & Chen, J. B. (1991). Strategies for conversational retreat: When parting is not sweet sorrow. *Communication Monographs, 58,* 362–383.

Kelly, J. A., Kern, J. M., Kirkley, B. G., Patterson, J. N., & Keane, T. M. (1980). Reactions to assertive versus unassertive behavior: Differential effects for males and females and implications for assertiveness training. *Behavior Therapy, 11,* 670–682.

Kelly, J. A., St. Lawrence, J. S., Hood, H. V., Smith, S., & Cook, D. J. (1988). Nurses' attitudes towards AIDS. *Journal of Continuing Education in Nursing, 19,* 78–83.

Kelly, J. A., St. Lawrence, J. S., Smith, S., Hood, H. V., & Cook, D. J. (1987). Medical students' attitudes towards AIDS and homosexual patients. *Journal of Medical Education, 62,* 549–556.

Kelly, J. J., Chu, S. Y., & Buehler, J. W. (1993). AIDS deaths shift from hospital to home. *American Journal of Public Health, 83,* 1433–1437.

Kenny, D. A., & La Voie, L. (1984). The social relations model. In L. Berkowitz (Ed.), *Advances in experimental social psychology* (Vol. 18, pp. 141–82). Orlando, FL: Academic Press.

Kiecolt-Glaser, J. K., & Glaser, R. (1988). Psychological influences on immunity: Implications for AIDS. *American Psychologist, 43,* 892–898.

Kimberly, J. A., Serovich, J. M., & Greene, K. (1995). Disclosure of HIV-positive status: Five women's stories. *Family Relations, 44,* 316–322.

Kinstlinger-Bruhn, C. (1997). *Everything you need to know about breaking the cycle of domestic violence.* New York: Rosen Publishing Group.

Kirchler, E. (1988). Marital happiness and interaction in everyday surroundings; A time-sample diary approach for couples. *Journal of Social and Personal Relationships, 5,* 275–382.

Klinetob N. A., & Smith, D. S. (1996). Demand-withdraw communication in marital interaction: Tests of interspousal contingency and gender role hypothesis. *Journal of Marriage and the Family, 58,* 866–883.

Klopfer, P. H., & Rubenstein, D. I. (1977). The concept *privacy* and its biological basis. *Journal of Social Issues, 33,* 52–65.

Kluwer, E. S., Heesink, J. A. M., & Van de Vliert, E. (1997). The marital dynamics of conflict over the division of labor. *Journal of Marriage and the Family, 59,* 635–654.

Knapp, M. L., Stafford, L., & Daly, J. A. (1986). Regrettable messages: Things people wish they hadn't said. *Journal of Communication, 36,* 40–58.

Knapp, M. L., & Vangelisti, A. L (1992). *Interpersonal communication and human relationships* (2nd ed.). Boston, MA: Allyn & Bacon.

Kornstein, D. J. (1987). Medical privacy and the right to know. *Bulletin of the New York Academy of Medicine, 63,* 957–967.

Kottler, J. (1990). *Private moments, secret selves: Enriching our time alone.* Los Angeles: Jeremy P. Tarcher.

Krajeski, J. P. (1990). Ethical, legal, and public policy issues. *New Directions for Mental Health Services, 48,* 97–106.

Krajewski-Jaime, E. R. (1991). Folk-healing among Mexican-American families as a consideration in the delivery of child welfare and child health care services. *Child Welfare, 70,* 157–167.

Krantz, D. S., Baum, A., & Singer, J. E. (Eds.). (1983). *Cardiovascular disorders and behavior.* Hillsdale, NJ: Lawrence Erlbaum Associates.

Krauss, R., Morel-Samuels, P., & Colasante, C. (1991). Do conversational hand gestures communicate? *Journal of Personality and Social Psychology, 61,* 743–754.

Kreckel, M. (1981). *Communicative acts & shared knowledge in natural discourse.* London: Academic Press.

Kulik, J. A., & Mahler, H. I. (1989). Social support and recovery from surgery. *Health Psychology, 8,* 221–238.

Kurdek, L. A. (1994). Conflict resolution styles in gay, lesbian, heterosexual nonparent, and heterosexual parent couples. *Journal of Marriage and the Family, 56,* 705–722.

Lacoursiere, R. B. (1980). *The life cycles of groups: Group developmental stage theory.* New York: Human Sciences Press.

Laing, R. D. (1962). *Self and others.* Chicago: Quadrangle.

Lako, C. J., & Lindenthal, J. J. (1991). The management of confidentiality in general medical practice: A comparative study in the U.S.A. and the Netherlands. *Social Science Medicine, 32,* 153–157.

Lannaman, J. (1991). Interpersonal communication research as ideological practice. *Communication Theory, 1,* 179–203.

Lannaman, J. (1994). The problem with disempowering ideology. *Communication Yearbook, 17,* 136–147.

Larson, D. G., & Chastain, R. L. (1990). Self-concealment: Conceptualization, measurement, and health implications. *Journal of Social and Clinical Psychology, 8,* 439–455.

Laufer, R. S., Proshansky, H. M, & Wolfe, M. (1973). Some analytical dimensions of privacy. In R. Kuller (Ed.), *Architectural psychology: Proceedings of the Lund conference* (pp. 353–372). Stroudsburg, PA: Dowden, Hutchinson, & Ross.

Lave, J. D., & Wegner, D. M. (1995). The cognitive consequences of secrecy. *Journal of Personality and Social Psychology, 69,* 237–253.

Leary, M. R., & Kowalski, R. M. (1990). Impression-management: A literature review and two-component model. *Psychological Bulletin, 107,* 34–47.

Leary, M. R., & Schreindorfer, L. S. (1998). The stigmatization of HIV and AIDS: Rubbing salt in the wound. In V. J. Derlega & A. P. Barbee (Eds.), *HIV and social interaction* (pp. 12–29). Thousand Oaks, CA: Sage.

Leeds-Hurwitz, W. (1995). Introducing social approaches. In W. Leeds-Hurwitz (Ed.), *Social approaches to communication* (pp. 3–22). New York: Guilford.

Leong, G. B., Silva, J. A., & Weinstock, R. (1992). Reporting dilemmas in psychiatric practice. *Psychiatric Annals, 22,* 482–486.

Lewis, A. (1988). Development of AIDS awareness: A personal history. *Death Studies, 12,* 371–379.

Lewis, L. S., & Range, L. M. (1992). Do means of transmission, risk knowledge, and gender affect AIDS stigma and social interactions? *Journal of Social Behavior and Personality, 7,* 211–216.

Lewis, P. N., & Gallois, C. (1984). Disagreements, refusals, or negative feelings: Perceptions of negatively assertive messages from friends and strangers. *Behavior Therapy, 15,* 353–368.

Lim, T. S., & Bowers, J. W. (1991). Facework: Solidarity, approbation, and tact. *Human Communication Research, 17,* 415–450.

Lindenthal, J. J., & Thomas, C. S. (1982). Consumers, clinicians and confidentiality. *Social Science Medicine, 16,* 333–335.

Lloyd, S. (1987). Conflict in premarital relationships: Differential perceptions of males and females. *Family Relations, 36,* 290–294.

Lloyd, S. A. (1990). A behavioral self-report technique for assessing conflict in close relationships. *Journal of Social and Personal Relationships, 7,* 265–272.

Lo, B., Steinbrook, R. L., Cooke, M., Coates, T. J., Walters, E. J., & Hulley, S. B. (1989). Voluntary screening for human immunodeficiency virus (HIV) infection: Weighing the benefits and harms. *Annals of Internal Medicine, 110,* 727–733.

Loeske, D. (1992). *The battered woman and shelters: The social construction of wife abuse.* Albany: State University of New York Press.

Lupton, D., McCarthy, S., & Chapman, S. (1995). "Doing the right thing": The symbolic meanings and experiences of having an HIV antibody test. *Social Science & Medicine, 41,* 173–180.

Lynch, J. J. (1985). *Language of the heart.* New York: Basic Books.

Maas, P. (1998, April 19). How private is your life? *Parade,* 4–6.

Makoul, G., & Roloff, M. E. (1998). The role of efficacy and outcome expectations in the decision to withhold relational complaints. *Communication Research, 25,* 5–29.

Malz, D. N., & Borker, R. A. (1982). A cultural approach to male-female miscommunication. In J. J. Gumperz (Ed.), *Language and social identity* (pp. 195–216). Cambridge, UK: Cambridge University Press.

Mann, S. J., & Delon, M. (1995). Improved hypertension control after disclosure of decades-old trauma. *Psychosomatic Medicine, 57,* 501–505.

Mansergh, G., Marks, G., & Simoni, J. M. (1995). Self-disclosure of HIV-infection among men who vary in time since seropositive diagnosis and symptomatic status. *AIDS, 9,* 639–644.

Mariner, W. K. (1995). AIDS phobia, public health warnings, and lawsuits: Deterring harm or rewarding ignorance? *American Journal of Public Health, 85,* 1562–1568.

Marks, G., Bundek, N. I., Richardson, J. L., Ruiz, M. S., Maldonado, N., & Mason, H. R. (1992). Self-disclosure of HIV-infection: Preliminary results from a sample of Hispanic men. *Health Psychology, 11,* 300–306.

Marks, G., Mason, H. R., & Simoni, J. M. (1995). The prevalence of patient disclosure of HIV infection to doctors. *American Journal of Public Health, 85,* 1018–1019.

Marks, G., Richardson, J. L., & Maldonado, N. (1991). Self-disclosure of HIV infection to sexual partners. *American Journal of Public Health, 81,* 1321–1322.

Martin, D. (1976). *Battered wives.* New York: Simon & Schuster.

Martin, L. R. (1982). Overview of the psychosocial aspects of cancer. In J. Cohen, J. W. Cullen, & L. R. Martin (Eds.), *Psychosocial aspects of cancer* (pp. 1–8). New York: Raven.

Martin, M. M., & Anderson, C. M. (1995). The father-young adult relationship: Interpersonal motives, self-disclosure and satisfaction. *Communication Quarterly, 43,* 119–130.

Mason, R. C., Marks, G., Simoni, J. M., Ruiz, M. S., & Richardson, J. L. (1995). Culturally sanctioned secrets? Latino men's nondisclosure of HIV infection to family, friends, and lovers. *Health Psychology, 14,* 6–12.

Mays, V. M., & Cochran, S. D. (1993). Ethnic and gender differences in beliefs about sex partner questioning to reduce HIV risk. *Journal of Adolescent Research, 8,* 77–88.

McAdams, D. P., & Powers, J. (1981). Themes of intimacy in behavior and thought. *Journal of Personality and Social Psychology, 40,* 573–587.

McCampbell, E., & Ruback, B. (1985). Social consequences of apologetic, assertive, and aggressive requests. *Journal of Counseling Psychology, 32,* 68–73.

McCann, S., & Weinman, J. (1995). Empowering the patient in the consultation: A pilot study. *Patient Education and Counseling, 27,* 227–234.

McCorkle, S., & Mills, J. L. (1992). Rowboat in a hurricane: Metaphors of interpersonal conflict management. *Communication Reports, 5,* 57–66.

McCornack, S. A., & Levine, T. R. (1990). When lies are uncovered: Emotional and relational outcomes of discovered deception. *Communication Monographs, 57,* 119–138.

McGonagle, K. A., Kessler, R. C., & Gotlib, I. H. (1993). The effects of marital disagreement style, frequency, and outcome on marital disruption. *Journal of Social and Personal Relationships, 10,* 385–404.

McKerrow, R. E. (1989). Critical rhetoric: Theory and praxis. *Communication Monographs, 56,* 91–111.

McLaughlin, T. (1996). *Street smarts and critical theory: Listening to the vernacular.* Madison: University of Wisconsin Press.

Mead, G. H. (1934). *Mind, self, and society.* Chicago: University of Chicago Press.

Meeks, B. N. (1997). Privacy lost, anytime, anywhere. *Communications of the ACH, 40,* 11–13.

Mehrabian, A. (1972). *Nonverbal communication.* Chicago: Aldine-Atherton.

Mehrabian, A. (1981). *Silent messages: Implicit communication of emotions and attitudes* (2nd ed.). Belmont, CA: Wadsworth.

Melikian, L. H. (1962). Self-disclosure among university students in the Middle East. *Journal of Social Psychology, 57,* 257–263.

Meneghan, E. (1982). Measuring coping effectiveness: A panel analysis of marital problems and coping efforts. *Journal of Health and Social Behavior, 23,* 220–234.

Meneghan, E. (1983). Coping with parental problems: Panel assessments of effectiveness. *Journal of Family Issues, 4,* 483–506.

Mesters, L., Van den Borne, H., McCormick, L., Pruyn, J., de Boer, M., & Imbos, T. (1997). Openness to discuss cancer in the nuclear family: Scale, development, and validation. *Psychosomatic Medicine, 59,* 269–279.

Metts, S. (1994). Relational transgressions. In W. R. Cupach & B. H. Spitzberg (Eds.), *The dark side of interpersonal communication* (pp. 217–239). Hillsdale, NJ: Lawrence Erlbaum Associates.

Metts, S., & Cupach, W. R. (1989). Situational influence on the use of remedial strategies in embarrassing predicaments. *Communication Monographs, 56,* 151–161.

Metts, S., Cupach, W. R., & Imahori, T. T. (1992). Perceptions of sexual compliance-resisting messages in three types of cross-sex relationships. *Western Journal of Communication, 56,* 1–17.

Michal-Johnson, P., & Bowen, S. P. (1992). The place of culture in HIV education. In T. Edgar, M. A. Fitzpatrick, & V. S. Freimuth (Eds.), *AIDS: A communication perspective* (pp. 147–172). Hillsdale, NJ: Lawrence Erlbaum Associates.

Mifflin, L. (1995, October 28). Aim higher, forum urges talk shows. *New York Times,* p. L6.

Mikulincer, M., & Nachshon, O. (1991). Attachment styles and patterns of self-disclosure. *Journal of Personality and Social Psychology, 61*(2), 321–331.

Millar, F. E., & Rogers, L. E. (1987). Relational dimensions of interpersonal dynamics. In M. E. Roloff & G. R. Miller (Eds.), *Interpersonal processes: New directions in communication research* (pp. 117–139). Newbury Park, CA: Sage.

Miller, G. R., & Simons, H. W. (Eds.). (1974). *Perspectives on communication in social conflict.* Englewood Cliffs, NJ: Prentice-Hall.

Miller, L. C., Berg, J. H., & Archer, R. L. (1983). Openers: Individuals who elicit intimate self-disclosure. *Journal of Personality and Social Psychology, 44,* 1234–1244.

Miller, L. C., & Read, S. L. (1987). Why am I telling you this? Self disclosure in a goal based model of personality. In V. J. Derlega & J. H. Berg (Eds.), *Self disclosure: Theory, research, and therapy. Perspectives in social psychology* (pp. 35–58). New York: Plenum Press.

Milligan, M. A. (1987). When the lack of privacy gets to your patient. *RN, 50*(3), 17–18.

Mishel, M. H. (1984). Perceived uncertainty and stress in illness. *Research in Nursing and Health, 7,* 163–171.

Mitsuya, H. (1997). Telling the truth to cancer patients and patients with HIV-1 infection in Japan. *Annals of the New York Academy of Sciences, 809,* 279–289.

Montgomery, B. M., & Baxter, L. A. (Eds.). (1998). *Dialectical approaches to studying personal relationships.* Mahwah, NJ: Lawrence Erlbaum Associates.

Mooney, K. M., Cohn, E. S., & Swift, M. B. (1992). Physical distance and AIDS: Too close for comfort? *Journal of Applied Social Psychology, 22,* 1442–1452.

Morin, S. F., Charles, K. A., & Malyon, A. K. (1984). The psychological impact of AIDS on gay men. *American Psychologist, 39,* 1288–1293.

Motley, M. T. (1992). Mindfulness in solving communicators' dilemmas. *Communication Monographs, 59,* 306–314.

Mousel, L. M. (1992). The risk of health care workers transmitting AIDS to patients: Legal and policy implications: Is disclosure the answer? *Criminal Justice Journal, 14,* 81–104.

Nakanishi, M., & Johnson, K. M. (1993). Implications of self-disclosure on conversational logics, perceived communication competence, and social attraction. In R. L. Wiseman & J. Koester (Eds.), *Intercultural communication competence* (pp. 204–221). Newbury Park, CA: Sage.

Newell, S. E., & Stutman, R. K. (1991). The episodic nature of social confrontation. In J. A. Anderson (Ed.), *Communication yearbook 14* (pp. 359–392). Thousand Oaks, CA: Sage.

Ney, P. G., & Peters, A. (1995). *Ending the cycle of abuse: The stories of women abused as children & the group therapy techniques that helped them heal.* New York: Brunner & Mazel.

Novack, D. H., Plumer, R., Smith, R. L., Ochitill, H., Morrow, G. R., & Bennet, J. M. (1979). Changes in physicians' attitudes toward telling the cancer patient. *Journal of the American Medical Association, 241,* 897–900.

Noveck, J. (1997, October 11). Villages' DNA tested in search for killer. *The Tempe (AZ) Tribune,* p. A12.

Nuland, S. B. (1988). *Doctors: The biography of medicine.* New York: Random House.

Nyberg, D. (1993). *The varnished truth: Truthtelling and deceiving in ordinary life.* Chicago: University of Chicago Press.

Oddi, L. F. (1994). Disclosure of human immunodeficiency virus status in health care settings: Ethical concerns. *Journal of Intravenous Nursing, 17*(2), 93–102.

O'Donnell, L., O'Donnell, C. R., Pleck, J. H., Snarey, J., & Rose, R. M. (1987). Psychosocial responses of hospital workers to acquired immune deficiency syndrome (AIDS). *Journal of Applied Social Psychology, 17,* 269–285.

Officer, S. A., & Rosenfeld, L. B. (1985). Self-disclosure to male and female coaches by high school female athletes. *Journal of Sport Psychology, 7,* 360–370.

Ogilvie, D. M. (1987). The undesired self: A neglected variable in personality research. *Journal of Personality and Social Psychology, 52,* 379–385.

O'Hair, D., & Cody, M. J. (1994). Interpersonal deception: The dark side of interpersonal communication? In W. R. Cupach & B. H. Spitzberg (Eds.), *The dark side of interpersonal communication* (pp. 181–214). Hillsdale, NJ: Lawrence Erlbaum Associates.

Oken, D. (1961). What to tell cancer patients: A study of medical attitudes. *Journal of the American Medical Association, 175,* 1120–1128.

Oldenburg, A. (1995, October 31). A click trip around talk-show dial. *USA Today,* p. 3D.

Ono, K. A., & Sloop, J. M. (1995, March). The critique of vernacular discourse. *Communication Monographs, 62,* 19–46.

Opperer, J. F. (1995). Mandatory HIV testing and disclosure: A legal, ethical, and medical perspective. *Medical Trial Technique Quarterly, 41,* 624–641.

Ostrow, D. G., Joseph, J. G., Kessler, R., Soucy, J., Tal, M., Eller, M., Chmiel, J., & Phair, J. P. (1989). Disclosure of HIV antibody status: Behavioral and mental health correlates. *AIDS Education and Prevention, 1,* 1–11.

Parks, M. R. (1982). Ideology of interpersonal communication: Off the couch and into the world. In M. Burgoon (Ed.), *Communication yearbook 5* (pp. 79–108). New Brunswick, NJ: Transaction Books.

Parks, M. R. (1995). Ideology in interpersonal communication: Beyond the couches, talk shows, and bunkers. In B. R. Burleson (Ed.), *Communication yearbook 18* (pp. 480–497). Thousand Oaks, CA: Sage.

Parrott, R. (1995). Topic-centered and person-centered "Sensitive subjects": Recognizing and managing barriers to disclosure about health. In L. K. Fuller & L. M. Shilling (Eds.), *Communicating about communicable diseases* (pp. 177–189). Amherst, MA: HRD Press.

Parrott, R., Burgoon, J. K., Burgoon, M., & Le Poire, B. A. (1989). Privacy between physicians and patients: More than a matter of confidentiality. *Social Science and Medicine, 29,* 1381–1385.

Patton, C. (1996). *Fatal advice: How safe-sex education went wrong.* Durham, NC: Duke University Press.

Pearce, W. B. (1989). *Communication and the human condition.* Carbondale, IL: Southern Illinois University Press.

Pearce, W. B. (1994). *Interpersonal communication: Creating social worlds.* New York: Harper-Collins.

Pearce, W. B. (1995). A sailing guide for social constructionists. In W. Leeds-Hurwitz (Ed.), *Social approaches to communication* (pp. 88–113). New York: Guilford.

Pearce, W. B., & Cronen, V. E. (1980). *Communication, action, and meaning: The creation of social realities.* New York: Praeger.

Pearce, W. B., & Sharp, S. M. (1973). Self-disclosing communication. *Journal of Communication, 23,* 409–425.

Peck, J. (1995). TV talk shows as therapeutic discourse: The ideological labor of the televised talking cure. *Communication Theory, 5,* 58–81.

Pedersen, D. (1988). Correlates of privacy regulation. *Perceptual and Motor Skills, 66,* 595–601.

Pennebaker, J. W. (1989). Confession, inhibition, and disease. In L. Berkowitz (Ed.), *Advances in experimental social psychology* (Vol. 22, pp. 211–244). New York: Academic Press.

Pennebaker, J. W. (1990). *Opening up: The healing power of confiding in others.* New York: Morrow.

Pennebaker, J. W. (1997). *Opening up: The healing power of expressing emotions.* New York: Guilford.

Pennebaker, J. W., Barger, S. D., & Tiebout, J. (1989). Trauma and health among Holocaust survivors. *Psychosomatic Medicine, 51,* 577–589.

Pennebaker, J. W., & Beall, S. W. (1986). Confronting a traumatic event: Toward an understanding of inhibition and disease. *Journal of Abnormal Psychology, 95,* 274–281.

Pennebaker, J. W., Colder, M., & Sharp, L. K. (1990). Accelerating the coping process. *Journal of Personality and Social Psychology, 58,* 528–537.

Pennebaker, J. W., Hughes, C., & O'Heeron, R. C. (1987). The psychophysiology of confession: Linking inhibitory and psychosomatic processes. *Journal of Personality and Social Psychology, 52,* 781–793.

Pennebaker, J. W., Kiecolt-Glaser, J. K., & Glaser, R. (1988). Disclosure of traumas and immune function: Health implications for psychotherapy. *Journal of Consulting and Clinical Psychology, 56,* 239–245.

Pennebaker, J. W., Mayne, T. J., & Francis, M. E. (1997). Linguistic predictors of adaptive bereavement. *Journal of Personality and Social Psychology, 72,* 863–871.

Pennebaker, J. W., & O'Heeron, R. C. (1984). Confiding in others and illness rate among spouses of suicide and accidental death victims. *Journal of Abnormal Psychology, 93,* 473–476.

Pennebaker, J. W., & Sussman, J. R. (1988). Disclosure of trauma and psychosomatic processes. *Social Science and Medicine, 26,* 327–332.

Perry, S., Card, C., Moffatt, M., Ashman, T., Fishman, B., & Jacobsberg, L. (1994). Self-disclosure of HIV infection to sexual partners after repeated counseling. *AIDS Education and Prevention, 6,* 403–411.

Perry, S., Jacobsberg, L., Fishman, B., Weiler, P., Gold, J., & Frances, A. (1990). Psychological responses to serological testing for HIV. *AIDS, 4,* 145–152.

Perry, S., Ryan, J., Fogel, K., Fishman, B., & Jacobsberg, L. (1990). Voluntarily informing others of positive HIV test results: Patterns of notification by infected gay men. *Hospital and Community Psychiatry, 41,* 549–551.

Perry, S. W., & Markowitz, J. C. (1988). Counseling for HIV testing. *Hospital Communication Psychiatry, 39,* 731–739.

Petronio, S. (1991). Communication boundary management: A theoretical model of managing disclosure of private information between marital couples. *Communication Theory, 1,* 311–335.

Petronio, S. (1993). Communication boundary management: A theoretical model of managing disclosure of private information between marital couples. In S. Petronio, J. K. Alberts, M. L. Hecht, & J. Buley (Eds.), *Contemporary perspectives on interpersonal communication* (pp. 221–240). Madison, WI: Brown & Benchmark.

Petronio, S. (1994). Privacy binds in family interactions: The case of parental privacy invasion. In W. R. Cupach & B. H. Spitzberg (Eds.), *The darkside of interpersonal communication.* Hillsdale, NJ: Lawrence Erlbaum Associates.

Petronio, S. (1998). *Multiple boundaries: Beyond "self" disclosure.* Manuscript submitted for publication.

Petronio, S. (in press). The ramifications of a reluctant confidant. In A. C. Richards & T. Schumrum (Eds.), *Invitations to dialogue: The legacy of Sidney M. Jourard.* Dubuque, IA: Kendall/Hunt Publishers.

Petronio, S. (in press). *Boundaries of private disclosures.* New York: State University of New York Press.

Petronio, S., & Kovach, S. (1997). Managing privacy boundaries: Health providers' perceptions of resident care in Scottish nursing homes. *Journal of Applied Communication Research, 25,* 115–131.

Petronio, S., & Magni, J. (1996, November). *Being gay and HIV positive: Boundary regulation of disclosure discourse.* Paper presented to the annual meeting of the Speech Communication Association, San Diego, CA.

Petronio, S., & Martin, J. N. (1986). Ramifications of revealing private information: A gender gap. *Journal of Clinical Psychology, 42,* 499–506.

Petronio, S., Martin, J., & Littlefield, R. (1984). Prerequisite conditions for self-disclosing: A gender issue. *Communication Monographs, 51,* 268–273.

Petronio, S., Reeder, H. M., Hecht, M. L., & Mon't Ros-Mendoza, T. (1996). Disclosure of sexual abuse by children and adolescents. *Journal of Applied Communication Research, 24,* 181–199.

Pfiffner, E., Nil, R., & Battig, K. (1987). Psychophysiological reactivity and speech behavior during the Structured Type A Interview and a self-disclosure monologue. *International Journal of Psychophysiology, 5,* 1–9.

Phelan, P. (1993). *Unmarked: The politics of performance.* New York: Routledge.

Phillips, G. M., & Metzger, N. J. (1976). *Intimate communication.* Boston: Allyn and Bacon.

Pike, G. R., & Sillars, A. L. (1985). Reciprocity of marital communication. *Journal of Social and Personal Relationships, 2,* 303–324.

Planalp, S., & Honeycutt, J. M. (1985). Events that increase uncertainty in personal relationships. *Human Communication Research, 11,* 593–604.

Planalp, S., Rutherford, D. K., & Honeycutt, J. M. (1988). Events that increase uncertainty in personal relationships: II. Replication and extension. *Human Communication Research, 14,* 516–547.

Plog, S. C. (1965). The disclosure of self in the United States and Germany. *Journal of Social Psychology, 65,* 193–203.

Prentky, R. A., Knight, R. A., & Lee, A. F. S. (1997, June). *Child molestation: Research issues* (NCJ No. 163390). Washington, DC: U.S. Department of Justice, National Institute of Justice.

Price, D. M. (1991). What should we do about HIV-positive health professionals? *Archives of Internal Medicine, 151,* 658.

Priest, P. J. (1994). Pulp pulpits: Self-disclosure on "Donahue." *Journal of Communication, 44*(4), 74–97.

Priest, P. J. (1995). *Public intimacies.* Cresskill, NJ: Hampton.

Priest, P. J., & Dominick, J. R. (1994). Pulp pulpits: Self-disclosure on "Donahue." *Journal of Communication, 44,* 74–97.

Pruitt, D. G. (1981). *Negotiation behavior.* New York: Academic Press.

Pruyn, J. F. A., Van den Borne, H. W., & Stringer, P. (1986). Theories, methods and some results on coping with cancer and contact with fellow sufferers. In M. Watson & S. Greer (Eds.), *Psychosocial issues in malignant disease* (pp. 41–53). New York: Pergamon.

Pryor, J. B., & Reeder, G. D. (1993). Collective and individual representations of HIV/AIDS stigma. In J. B. Pryor & G. D. Reeder (Eds.), *The social psychology of HIV infection* (pp. 263–286). Hillsdale, NJ: Lawrence Erlbaum Associates.

REFERENCES **327**

Put on notice: Police agencies wrestle with sex-offender notification issues. (1997, June 15). *Law Enforcement News*, pp. 1, 10.

Quick, R. (1998, February 6). Don't expect your secrets to get kept on the internet. *The Wall Street Journal*, p. B5.

Quinn, T. C., Narain, J. P., & Zacarias, R. K. (1990). AIDS in the Americas: A public health priority for the region. *AIDS, 4,* 709–724.

Rabkin, R., & Rabkin, J. (1995). Management of depression in patients with HIV infection. In A. Odets & M. Shernoff (Eds.), *The second decade of AIDS: A mental health practice handbook* (pp. 11–25). New York: Hatherleigh Press.

Rahim, A. (1987). The practice of *Antyodaya* in agricultural extension communication in India. In D. L. Kincaid (Ed.), *Communication theory: Eastern and western perspectives* (pp. 173–182). New York: Academic Press.

Rahim, M. A. (1986). *Managing conflict in organizations.* New York: Praeger.

Rands, M., Levinger, G., & Mellinger, G. D. (1981). Patterns of conflict resolution and marital satisfaction. *Journal of Family Issues, 2,* 297–321.

Rawlins, W. K. (1983a). Negotiating close friendship: The dialectics of conjunctive freedoms. *Human Communication Research, 9,* 255–266.

Rawlins, W. K. (1983b). Openness as problematic in ongoing friendships: Two conversational dilemmas. *Communication Monographs, 50,* 1–13.

Rawlins, W. K. (1992). *Friendship matters: Communication, dialectics, and the life course.* New York: Aldine de Gruyter.

Ray, E. B. (1996). When the protector is the abuser: Effects of incest on adult survivors. In E. B. Ray (Ed.), *Case studies in communication and disenfranchisement* (pp. 127–140). Mahwah, NJ: Lawrence Erlbaum Associates.

Reinharz, S. (1992). *Feminist methods in social research.* New York: Oxford University Press.

Resick, P. A., Barr, P. K., Sweet, J. J., Kieffer, D. M., Ruby, N. L., & Speigel, D. K. (1981). Perceived and actual discriminators of conflict from accord in marital communication. *The American Journal of Family Therapy, 9,* 58–68.

Revenson, T. A., Wollman, C. A., & Felton, B. J. (1983). Social supports as stress buffers for adult cancer patients. *Psychosomatic Medicine, 45,* 321–331.

Richardson, L. (1992). The consequences of poetic interpretation. In C. Ellis & M. Flaherty (Eds.), *Investigating subjectivity: Research on lived experience* (pp. 125–137). Newbury Park, CA: Sage.

Robinson, I. (1991). Confidentiality for whom? *Social Science of Medicine, 32,* 279–286.

Rofes, E. (1995). *Reviving the tribe: Regenerating gay men's sexuality and culture in the ongoing epidemic.* Binghamton, NY: Haworth Press.

Rokeach, M. J. (1960). *The open and closed mind: Investigations into the nature of belief systems and personality systems.* New York: Basic Books.

Rokeach, M. J. (1968). *Beliefs, attitudes, and values: A theory of organization and change.* San Francisco: Jossey-Bass.

Roloff, M. E., & Cloven, D. H. (1990). The chilling effect in interpersonal relationships: The reluctance to speak one's mind. In D. H. Cahn (Ed.), *Intimates in conflict: A communication perspective* (pp. 49–76). Hillsdale, NJ: Lawrence Erlbaum Associates.

Roloff, M. E., & Cloven, D. H. (1994). When partners transgress: Maintaining violated relationships. In D. J. Canary & L. Stafford (Eds.), *Communication and relational maintenance* (pp. 23–44). San Diego: Academic Press.

Roloff, M. E., & Ifert, D. (1998). Antecedents and consequences of explicit agreements to declare a topic taboo in dating relationships. *Personal Relationships, 5,* 191–205.

Ronai, C. R. (1992). The reflexive self through narrative: A night in the life of an exotic dancer/researcher. In C. Ellis & M. Flaherty (Eds.), *Investigating subjectivity: Research on lived experience* (pp. 102–124). Newbury Park, CA: Sage.

Rook, K. S. (1985). The functions of social bonds: Perspectives from research on social support, loneliness and social isolation. In I. G. Sarason & B. R. Sarason (Eds.), *Social support: Theory, research and applications* (pp. 243–267). Dordrecht, the Netherlands: Martinus Nijhoff.

Rosen, J. (1991). The talk show and the terror of conversation. *et cetera, 14*(4), 366–371.

Rosenfeld, L. B. (1979). Self-disclosure avoidance: Why I am afraid to tell you who I am. *Communication Monographs, 46*, 63–74.

Rosenfeld, L. B., & Bowen, G. L. (1991). Marital disclosure and marital satisfaction: Direct-effect versus interaction-effect models. *Western Journal of Speech Communication, 55*, 69–84.

Rosenfeld, L. B., & Gilbert, J. R. (1989). The measurement of cohesion and its relationship to dimensions of self-disclosure in classroom settings. *Small Group Behavior, 20*, 291–301.

Rosenfeld, L. B., & Kendrick, W. L. (1984). Choosing to be open: Subjective reasons for self-disclosing. *Western Journal of Speech Communication, 48*, 326–343.

Rotello, G. (1997). *Sexual ecology: AIDS and the destiny of gay men.* New York: Penguin.

Rowe, W., Plum, G., & Crossman, C. (1988). Issues and problems confronting the lovers, families and communities associated with persons with AIDS. *Journal of Social Work and Human Sexuality, 6*, 71–88.

Rush, F. (1980). *The best kept secret: Sexual abuse of children.* Englewood Cliffs, NJ: Prentice-Hall.

Sampson, E. E. (1993). *Celebrating the other: A dialogic account of human nature.* Boulder, CO: Westview Press.

Samter, W. (1994). Unsupportive relationships: Deficiencies in the support-giving skills of the lonely person's friends. In B. R. Burleson, T. L. Albrecht, & I. G. Sarason (Eds.), *Communication of social support: Messages, interactions, relationships, and community* (pp. 195–214). Thousand Oaks, CA: Sage.

Scanzoni, J. (1978). *Sex roles, women's work, and marital conflict.* Lexington, MA: Lexington Books.

Scarry, E. (1985). *The body in pain.* Oxford, England: Oxford University Press.

Schain, W. S. (1990). Physician-patient communication about breast cancer: A challenge for the 1990s. *Surgical Clinics of North America, 70*, 917–936.

Scheerhorn, M. (1995). Disclosure of health care workers with HIV or AIDS. *Nursing Management, 26*, 48C, 48F–48G.

Scherer, K. R., & Tannenbaum, P. H. (1986). Emotional experience in everyday life: A survey approach. *Motivation and Emotion, 10*, 295–314.

Schiffrin, D. (1987). *Discourse markers.* New York: Cambridge University Press.

Schiffrin, D. (1994). *Approaches to discourse.* Cambridge, MA: Blackwell.

Schlenker, B. R. (1980). *Impression management: The self-concept, social identity, and interpersonal relations.* Monterey, CA: Brooks/Cole.

Schlenker, B. R. (1985). Identity and self-identification. In B. R. Schlenker (Ed.), *The self and social life* (pp. 65–99). New York: McGraw-Hill.

Schlenker, B. R., Britt, T. W., & Pennington, J. (1996). Impression regulation and management: Highlights of a theory of self-identification. In R. M. Sorrentino & E. T. Higgins (Eds.), *Handbook of motivation and cognition (Vol. 3): The interpersonal context* (pp. 118–147). New York: Guilford.

Schlenker, B. R., Britt, T. W., Pennington, J., Murphy, R., & Doherty, K. J. (1994). The triangle model of responsibility. *Psychological Review, 101*, 632–652.

Schlossberger, E., & Hecker, L. (1996). HIV and family therapists' duty to warn: A legal and ethical analysis. *Journal of Marital and Family Therapy, 22*, 27–40.

Schnell, D. J., Higgins, D. L., Wilson, R. M., Goldbaum, G., Cohn, D. L., & Wolitski, R. J. (1992). Men's disclosure of HIV test results to male primary sex partners. *American Journal of Public Health, 82*, 1675–1676.

Schoofs, M. (1994, August 16). Love stories in the age of AIDS. *The Village Voice*, p. 21.

Schwartz, G. S., Kane, T. R., Joseph, J. M., & Tedeschi, J. T. (1978). The effects of post-transgression remorse on perceived aggression, attributions of intent, and level of punishment. *British Journal of Social and Clinical Psychology, 17,* 293–297.

Scott, R. (1993). Dialectical tensions of speaking and silence. *Quarterly Journal of Speech, 79,* 1–18.

Seeman, M., & Seeman, T. E. (1983). Health behavior and personal autonomy: A longitudinal study of the sense of control in illness. *Journal of Health and Social Behavior, 24,* 144–160.

Segrin, C. (1998). Interpersonal communication problems associated with depression and loneliness. In P. A. Andersen & L. K. Guerrero (Eds.), *Handbook of communication and emotion: Research, theory, applications, and contexts* (pp. 215–242). San Diego: Academic Press.

Serovich, J. M., & Greene, K. (1993). Perceptions of family boundaries: The case of disclosure of HIV testing information. *Family Relations, 42,* 193–197.

Serovich, J. M., Greene, K., & Parrott, R. (1992). Boundaries and AIDS testing: Privacy and the family system. *Family Relations, 41,* 104–109.

Serovich, J. M., Kimberly, J. A., & Greene, K. (1998). Perceived family member reaction to women's disclosure of HIV-positive information. *Family Relations, 47,* 15–22.

Severo, R. (1977, May 4). Cancer: More than a disease, for many a silent stigma. *New York Times,* p. B1.

Sharkey, W. F., & Stafford, L. (1990). Responses to embarrassment. *Human Communication Research, 17,* 315–342.

Shilts, R. (1987). *And the band played on.* New York: St. Martin's.

Schoeman, F. D. (Ed). (1984). *Philosophical dimensions of privacy: An anthology.* London: Cambridge University Press.

Shotter, J., & Gergen, K. J. (Eds.). (1989). *Texts of identity.* London: Sage.

Shweder, R. A., & Miller, J. G. (1991). The social construction of the person: How is it possible? In R. A. Shweder (Ed.), *Thinking through cultures* (pp. 156–185). Cambridge, MA: Harvard University Press.

Siegel, K., & Krauss, B. J. (1991). Living with HIV infection: Adaptive tasks of seropositive gay men. *Journal of Health and Social Behavior, 32,* 17–32.

Siegler, M. (1982). Confidentiality in medicine? A decrepit concept. *New England Journal of Medicine, 307,* 1518–1521.

Siegman, A. W., Dembroski, T. M., & Crump, D. (1992). Speech rate, loudness, and cardiovascular reactivity. *Journal of Behavioral Medicine, 15,* 519–532.

Sillars, A. L. (1980). Attributions and communication in roommate conflicts. *Communication Monographs, 47,* 180–200.

Sillars, A. L., Coletti, S. F., Parry, D., & Rogers, M. A. (1982). Coding verbal conflict tactics: Nonverbal and perceptual correlates of the "avoidance-distributive-integrative" distinction. *Human Communication Research, 9,* 83–95.

Sillars, A. L., Pike, G. R., Jones, T. S., & Redmon, K. (1983). Communication and conflict in marriage. In R. Bostrom (Ed.), *Communication yearbook 7* (pp. 414–429). Thousand Oaks, CA: Sage.

Sillars, A. L., & Weisberg, J. (1987). Conflict as a social skill. In M. E. Roloff & G. R. Miller (Eds.), *Interpersonal processes: New directions in communication research* (pp. 140–171). Newbury Park, CA: Sage.

Simoni, J. M., Mason, H. R. C., Marks, G., Ruiz, M. S., Reed, D., & Richardson, J. L. (1995). Women's self-disclosure of HIV-infection: Rates, reasons, and reactions. *Journal of Consulting and Clinical Psychology, 63,* 474–478.

Singleton, D. C. (1993). Nonconsensual HIV testing in the health care setting: The case for extending the occupational protections of California Proposition 96 to health care workers. *Loyola of Los Angeles Law Review, 26,* 1251–1290.

Sister's silence on aunt's death was cruel. (1997, November 24). *The Arizona Republic,* p. C6.

Slaughter, D. T., & Epps, E. G. (1987). The home environment and academic achievement of black American children and youth: An overview. *Journal of Negro Education, 56*, 3–20.

Smith, M. Y., & Rapkin, B. D. (1996). Social support and barriers to family involvement in caregiving for persons with AIDS: Implications for patient education. *Patient Education and Counseling, 27*, 85–94.

Smith, S., Ah Yun, K., Orrego, V., Johnson, A., Mitchell, M., & Greenberg, B. S. (in press). The sources, types, and frequencies of personal disclosures on talk television. In L. Klein (Ed.), *Talking up a storm: The social impact of daytime programs.* Westport, CT: Greenwood.

Smith, S., Mitchell, M., Ah Yun, J., Johnson, A. J., Orrego, V. O., & Greenberg, B. (in press). The valence of close relationships, focus on individual attributes and corresponding content of personal disclosures in six months of talk show titles. *Communication Studies.*

Solomon, D. H., & Roloff, M. E. (1996). *Reasons for withholding complaints in dating relationships.* Unpublished manuscript.

Solomon, D. H., & Samp, J. A. (1998). Power and problem appraisal: Perceptual foundations of the chilling effect in dating relationships. *Journal of Social and Personal Relationships, 15*, 191–210.

Sontag, S. (1989). *AIDS and its metaphors.* New York: Doubleday.

Spain, D. (1992). *Gendered spaces.* Chapel Hill: University of North Carolina Press.

Spencer, T. (1993, November). *Testing the self-disclosure reciprocity hypothesis within the context of conversational sequences in family interaction.* Paper presented at the annual meeting of the Speech Communication Association, Miami, FL.

Spielman, B. (1992). Expanding the boundaries of informed consent: Disclosing alcoholism and HIV status to patients. *The American Journal of Medicine, 93*, 216–218.

Spigner, C. (1998). Sociology of AIDS within Black communities: Theoretical considerations. In D. Buchanan & G. Cernada (Eds.), *Progress in preventing AIDS? Dogma, dissent and innovation: Global perspectives* (pp. 203–213). Amityville, NY: Baywood.

Spitzberg, B. H. (1994). The dark side of (in)competence. In W. R. Cupach & B. H. Spitzberg (Eds.), *The dark side of interpersonal communication* (pp. 25–49). Hillsdale, NJ: Lawrence Erlbaum Associates.

Stafford, M. C., & Gibbs, J. P. (1993). A theory about disputes and the efficacy of control. In R. B. Felson & J. T. Tedeschi (Eds.), *Aggression and violence: Social interaction perspectives* (69–98). Washington, DC: American Psychological Association.

Stamp, G., & Knapp, M. (1990). The construct of intent in interpersonal communication. *Quarterly Journal of Speech, 76*, 282–299.

Steinberg, L., & Silverberg, S. B. (1986). The vicissitudes of autonomy in early adolescence. *Child Development, 57*, 841–851.

Steinmetz, S. K. (1977). *The cycle of violence: Assertive, aggressive & abuse family interaction.* New York: Praeger.

Stempel, R., Moulton, J., Bachetti, P., & Moss, A. R. (1989, June). *Disclosure of HIV-antibody tests results and reactions of sexual partners, friends, family, and health professionals.* Paper presented at the 5th International Conference on AIDS, Montreal, Quebec.

Stephan, T. D., & Harrison, T. M. (1985). Gender, sex-role identity and communicator style: A Q-sort of behavior differences. *Communication Research Reports, 2*, 53–61.

Stern, L. A. (1990). *The effect of assertive and unassertive messages and communication style on perceptions of relational messages, attractiveness, and satisfaction.* Unpublished masters thesis, University of Arizona, Tucson.

Stern, L. A. (1994). *Confrontation between friends.* Unpublished doctoral dissertation, University of Arizona, Tucson.

Sternberg, R. J., & Dobson, D. M. (1987). Resolving interpersonal conflicts: An analysis of stylistic consistency. *Journal of Personality and Social Psychology, 52*, 794–812.

Stewart, A. L., Hays, R. D., & Ware, J. E. (1988). The MOS short-form general health survey: Reliability and validity in a patient population. *Medical Care, 26*, 724–735.

Stewart, L., Cooper, P. J., Stewart, A. D., & Friedley, S. A. (1996). *Communication and gender* (3rd ed.). Scottsdale, AZ: Gorsuch Scarisbrick.

Stiles, W. B. (1987). "I have to talk to somebody": A fever model of disclosure. In V. J. Derlega & J. H. Berg (Eds.), *Self-disclosure: Theory, research, and therapy* (pp. 257–282). New York: Plenum.

St. Lawrence, J. S., Husfeldt, B. A., Kelly, J. A., Hood, H. V., & Smith, S. (1990). The stigma of AIDS: Fear of disease and prejudice toward gay men. *Journal of Homosexuality, 19,* 85–99.

Stokes, J., Fuehrer, A., & Childs, L. (1980). Gender differences in self-disclosure to various target persons. *Journal of Counseling Psychology, 27,* 192–198.

Stolberg, S. G. (1998, January 18). Quandary on donor eggs: What to tell the children. *The New York Times,* p. 1.

Strassberg, D. S., Adelstein, T. B., & Chemers, M. M. (1988). Adjustment and disclosure reciprocity. *Journal of Social and Clinical Psychology, 7,* 234–245.

Strassberg, D. S., Gabel, H., & Anchor, K. N. (1976). Patterns of self-disclosure in parent discussion groups. *Small Group Behavior, 7,* 369–378.

Streeck, J. (1994). Culture, meaning, and interpersonal communication. In M. L. Knapp & G. R. Miller (Eds.), *Handbook of interpersonal communication* (2nd ed., pp. 286–322). Thousand Oaks, CA: Sage.

Street, R. L. (1991). Physicians' communication and parents' evaluations of pediatric consultations. *Medical Care, 29,* 1146–1152.

Stulberg, I., & Buckingham, S. L. (1988). Parallel issues for AIDS patients, families, and others. *Social Casework, 69,* 355–359.

Sue, D. W., Bernier, J. E., Durran, A., Feinberg, L., Pedersen, P., Smith, E. J., & Vasques-Nuttall, E. (1982). Position paper: Cross-cultural counseling competencies. *The Counseling Psychologist, 10,* 45–52.

Sugarman, J., & Powers, M. (1991). How the doctor got gagged: The disintegrating right of privacy in the physician-patient relationship. *Law and Medicine, 266,* 3323–3327.

Susman, J. R. (1988). Disclosure of traumas and psychosomatic processes. *Social Science and Medicine, 26,* 327–332.

Swann, B. W., Jr. (1990). To be adored or to be known? The interplay of self-enhancement and self-verification. In E. T. Higgins & R. M. Sorrentino (Eds.), *Handbook of motivation and cognition: Foundations of social behavior* (pp. 408–450). New York: Guilford.

Tajfel, H., & Billig, M. (1974). Familiarity and categorization in intergroup behavior. *Journal of Experimental Social Psychology, 10,* 159–170.

Tannen, D. (1986). *That's not what I meant! How conversational style makes or breaks your relations with others.* New York: Morrow.

Tannen, D. (1990). *You just don't understand: Women and men in conversation.* New York: William Morrow.

Tannen, D. (1995). *Talking from 9 to 5. Women and men in the workplace: Language, sex and power.* New York: Avon Books.

Tarasoff v. Regents of University of California, 17 Cal. 3d 425, 551 P. 2d 334, 131 Cal Rptr. 14 (1976).

Tardy, C. H. (Ed.). (1988). Self-disclosure: Objectives and methods of measurement. In C. H. Tardy (Ed.), *A handbook for the study of human communication: Methods and instruments for observing, measuring, and assessing communication processes* (pp. 323–346). Norwood, NJ: Ablex.

Tardy, C. H. (1993). Biological perspectives on language and social interaction. *American Behavioral Scientist, 36,* 339–358.

Tardy, C. H., & Allen, M. T. (1998). Moderators of cardiovascular reactivity to speech: Discourse production and group variations in blood pressure and pulse rate. *International Journal of Psychophysiology, 27,* 247–254.

Tardy, C. H., Hosman, L. A., & Bradac, J. J. (1981). Disclosing self to friends and family: A reexamination of initial questions. *Communication Quarterly, 29,* 263–268.

Tardy, C. H., Thompson, W. R., & Allen, M. T. (1989). Cardiovascular responses during speech. *Journal of Language and Social Psychology, 8,* 371–285.

Taylor, D. A., & Altman, I. (1987). Communication in interpersonal relationships: Social penetration processes. In M. E. Roloff & G. R. Miller (Eds.), *Interpersonal processes: New directions in communication research* (pp. 257–277). Beverly Hills, CA: Sage.

Taylor, S. E., Kemeny, M. E., Schneider, S. G., & Aspinwall, L. G. (1993). Coping with the threat of AIDS. In J. B. Pryor & G. D. Reeder (Eds.), *The social psychology of HIV infection* (pp. 305–332). Hillsdale, NJ: Lawrence Erlbaum Associates.

Thomas, S., & Lieb, R. (1995). *Sex offender registration: A review of state laws.* Olympia, WA: Washington State Institute for Public Policy.

Thompson, C. (1997, November 15). Country doctor faced tough issue of HIV privacy. *The Arizona Republic,* p. A23.

Ting-Toomey, S. (1986). Interpersonal ties in intergroup communication. In W. Gudykunst (Ed.), *Intergroup communication* (pp. 114–126). London: Edward Arnold.

Ting-Toomey, S. (1987, March). *Intercultural conflict: A face negotiation model.* Paper presented at the Temple University Discourse Conference, Philadelphia.

Ting-Toomey, S. (1991). Intimacy expressions in three cultures: France, Japan, and the United States. *International Journal of Intercultural Communication, 15,* 29–46.

Tracy, K. (1990). The many faces of facework. In H. Giles & W. P. Robinson (Eds.), *Handbook of language and social psychology* (pp. 209–226). New York: Wiley.

Trenholm, S., & Jensen, A. (1990, June). *The guarded self: Toward a social history of interpersonal styles.* Paper presented at the meeting of the Speech Communication Association of Puerto Rico, San Juan.

Triandis, H. (1995). *Individualism and collectivism: New directions in social psychology.* Boulder, CO: Westview Press.

Triplet, R. G., & Sugarman, D. B. (1987). Reactions to AIDS victims: Ambiguity breeds contempt. *Personality and Social Psychology Bulletin, 13,* 265–274.

Trotter, R. T. (1990). The cultural parameters of lead poisoning: A medical anthropologist's view of intervention in environmental lead exposure. *Environmental Health Perspectives, 89,* 79–84.

Turnbull, C. M. (1972). *The mountain people.* New York: Simon and Shuster.

Turner, J. H. (1986). *The structure of sociological theory* (4th ed.). Chicago: Dorsey.

Turner, R. E., Edgely, C., & Olmstead, G. (1975). Information control in conversation: Honesty is not always the best policy. *Kansas Journal of Sociology, 11,* 69–89.

Uchida, A. (1997). Bringing the "culture" back in: A culture building approach to gender and communication. *Women and Language, 20*(2), 15–24.

Ullom-Minnich, P. D., & Kallail, K. J. (1993). Physicians' strategies for safeguarding confidentiality: The influence of community and practice characteristics. *The Journal of Family Practice, 37,* 445–448.

van der Pligt, J., Otten, W., Richard, R., & van der Velde, F. (1993). Perceived risk of AIDS: Unrealistic optimism and self-protective action. In J. B. Pryor & G. D. Reeder (Eds.), *The social psychology of HIV infection* (pp. 39–58). Hillsdale, NJ: Lawrence Erlbaum Associates.

Vangelisti, A. L. (1994). Family secrets: Forms, functions and correlates. *Journal of Social and Personal Relationships, 11,* 113–135.

Vangelisti, A. L. & Caughlin, J. P. (1997). Revealing family secrets: The influence of topic, function, and relationships. *Journal of Social and Personal Relationships, 14,* 679–708.

Van Lear, C. A. (1987). The formation of social relationships: A longitudinal study of social penetration, *Human Communication Research, 13,* 299–322.

Voloshinov, V. N., & Bakhtin, M. M. (1973). *Marxism and the philosophy of language* (L. Matejks & I. R. Titunik, Trans.). Cambridge, MA: Harvard University Press.

Vorauer, J. D., & Ross, M. (1996). The pursuit of knowledge in close relationships: An informational goals analysis. In G. J. O. Fletcher & J. Fitness (Eds.), *Knowledge structures in close relationships: A social psychological approach* (pp. 369–396). Mahwah, NJ: Lawrence Erlbaum Associates.

Vuchinich, S. (1987). Starting and stopping spontaneous family conflicts. *Journal of Marriage and the Family, 49,* 591–601.

Waitzkin, H., Cabrera, A., DeCabrera, E. A., Radlow, M., & Rodriguez, F. (1996). Patient-doctor communication in cross-national perspective: A study in Mexico. *Medical Care, 34,* 641–671.

Walker, L. E. (1979). *The battered woman.* New York: Harper & Row.

Walsh, E. R. (1997). Megan's Law—Sex offender registration and notification statutes and constitutional challenges. In B. K. Schwartz & H. R. Cellini (Eds.), *The sex offender: New insights, treatment innovations, and legal developments* (pp. 24-1–24-32). Kingston, NJ: Civic Research Institute.

Warren, S. D., & Brandeis, L. D. (1890). The right to privacy. *Harvard Law Review, 4,* 220.

Warren, C., & Laslett, B. (1980). Privacy and secrecy: A conceptual comparison. In S. K. Tefft (Ed.), *Secrecy: A cross-cultural perspective* (pp. 25–34). New York: Human Sciences.

Watson, M. S., Trasciatti, M. A., & King, C. P. (1996). Our bodies, our risk: Dilemmas in contraceptive information. In R. Parrott & C. Condit (Eds.), *Evaluating women's health messages: A resource book* (pp. 95–123). Thousand Oaks, CA: Sage.

Webster, D. M., & Kruglanski, A. W. (1994). Individual differences in need for cognitive closure. *Journal of Personality and Social Psychology, 67,* 1049–1062.

Weeks, L. (1997, September 27). 5,500 watch Jenni's every move. *The Tempe (AZ) Tribune,* p. D3.

Weinstein, E. A., & Deutschberger, P. (1963). Some dimensions of altercasting. *Sociometry, 26,* 454–466.

Weir, J., Deans, G., & Calman, K. C. (1985). Practical aspects of psychological support. In M. Watson & T. Morris (Eds.), *Psychological aspects of cancer* (pp. 85–92). New York: Pergamon.

Weitz, R. (1989). Uncertainty and the lives of persons with AIDS. *Journal of Health and Social Behavior, 30,* 270–281.

Weitz, R. (1991). *Life with AIDS.* New Brunswick, NJ: Rutgers University Press.

Welles, S. (1992). My year with talk shows and how I almost got hooked. *Television Quarterly, 26*(2), 47–59.

Werner, C. M., & Haggard, L. M. (1992). Avoiding intrusions in the office: Privacy regulation on typical and high solitude days. *Basic and Applied Social Psychology, 13,* 181–193.

Westin, A. (1970). *Privacy and freedom.* New York: Atheneum.

Wheeless, L. R. (1976). Self-disclosure and interpersonal solidarity: Measurement, validation, and relationships. *Human Communication Research, 3,* 47–61.

Wheeless, L. R., Erickson, K. V., & Behrens, J. S. (1986). Cultural differences in disclosiveness as a function of locus of control. *Communication Monographs, 53,* 36–46.

Wheeless, L. R., & Grotz, J. (1976). Conceptualization and measurement of reported self-disclosure. *Human Communication Research, 2,* 338–346.

Wiemann, J. M. (1977). Explication and test of a model of communication competence. *Human Communication Research, 3,* 195–213.

Wilkinson, D. Y., & King, G. (1987). Conceptual and methodological issues in the use of race as a variable: Policy implications. *The Milbank Quarterly, 65,* 56–71.

Williams, J. I. (1971). Privacy and health care. *Canadian Journal of Public Health, 62,* 490–495.

Wilmot, W. W. (1980). *Dyadic communication* (2nd ed.). Reading, MA: Addison-Wesley.

Wintrob, H. L. (1987). Self-disclosure as a marketable commodity. *Journal of Social Behavior and Personality, 2,* 77–88.

Wissow, L. S., Roter, D. L., & Wilson, M. E. H. (1994). Pediatrician interview style and mothers' disclosure of psychosocial issues. *Pediatrics, 93,* 289–295.

Witteman, H. (1988). Interpersonal problem solving: Problem conceptualization and communication use. *Communication Monographs, 55,* 336–359.

Witteman, H. (1992). Analyzing interpersonal conflict: Nature of awareness, type of initiating event, situational perceptions, and management styles. *Western Journal of Communication, 56,* 248–280.

Wolfson, K., & Pearce, W. B. (1983). A cross-cultural comparison of the implications of self-disclosure on conversational logics. *Communication Quarterly, 31,* 249–256.

Won-Doornink, M. J. (1985). Self-disclosure and reciprocity in conversation: A cross-national study. *Social Psychology Quarterly, 48,* 97–107.

Wood, R. E., & Mitchell, T. R. (1981). Manager behavior in a social context: The impact of impression management on attributions and disciplinary actions. *Organizational Behavior and Human Performance, 28,* 356–387.

Woolfolk, R. L., & Dever, S. (1979). Perceptions of assertion: An empirical analysis. *Behavior Therapy, 10,* 404–411.

Wright, A. (1975). *Confucian personalities.* Stanford, CA: Stanford University Press.

Wright, T. L., & Ingraham, L. J. (1985). The simultaneous study of individual differences and relationship effects in social behavior in groups. *Journal of Personality and Social Psychology, 48,* 1041–1047.

Xi, C. (1991). *Communication in China: A case study of Chinese Collectivist and Self-Interest talk in social action from the CMM perspective.* Unpublished dissertation, University of Massachusetts, Amherst.

Yep, G. A. (1992). Communicating the HIV/AIDS risk to Hispanic populations: A review and integration. *Hispanic Journal of Behavioral Sciences, 14,* 403–420.

Yep, G. A. (1993a, November). *Disclosure of HIV-infection to significant others: A communication boundary management perspective.* Paper presented at the Speech Communication Association meeting, Miami, FL.

Yep, G. A. (1993b). Health beliefs and HIV prevention: Do they predict monogamy and condom use? *Journal of Social Behavior and Personality, 8,* 507–520.

Yep, G. A. (1993c). HIV/AIDS in Asian and Pacific Islander communities in the United States: A review, analysis, and integration. *International Quarterly of Community Health Education, 13,* 293–315.

Yep, G. A. (1995). Healthy desires/unhealthy practices: Interpersonal influence strategies for the prevention of HIV/AIDS among Hispanics. In L. K. Fuller & L. McPherson Shilling (Eds.), *Communicating about communicable diseases* (pp. 139–154). Amherst, MA: Human Resource Development Press.

Yep, G. A. (1997). Changing homophobic and heterosexist attitudes: An overview of persuasive communication approaches. In J. T. Sears & W. L. Williams (Eds.), *Overcoming heterosexism and homophobia: Strategies that work* (pp. 49–64). New York: Columbia University Press.

Yep, G. A. (1998). Safer sex negotiation in cross-cultural romantic dyads: An extension of Ting-Toomey's face negotiation theory. In N. L. Roth & L. K. Fuller (Eds.), *Women and AIDS: Negotiating safer practices, care, and representation* (pp. 81–100). New York: Harrington Park Press.

Yep, G. A., Lovaas, K. E., & Pagonis, A. V. (in press). The case of "riding bareback": Sexual practices and the paradoxes of identity in the era of AIDS. *Journal of Homosexuality.*

Yep, G. A., & Pietri, M. (1999). In their own words: Communication and the politics of HIV education for transgenders and transsexuals in Los Angeles. In W. N. Elwood (Ed.), *Power in the blood: A handbook on AIDS, politics, and communication* (pp. 199–213). Mahwah, NJ: Lawrence Erlbaum Associates.

Yep, G. A., Reece, S. T., & Negron, E. L. (1997, February). *Communication, culture, and group psychotherapy: The case of Asian Americans living with HIV infection.* Paper presented to the annual meeting of the Western States Communication Association, Monterey, CA.

Young, I. M. (1990). *Justice and the politics of difference.* Princeton, NJ: Princeton University Press.

Young, L. W. L. (1994). *Cross-talk and culture in Sino-American communication.* New York: Cambridge University Press.

Yovetich, N. A., & Rusbult, C. E. (1994). Accommodative behavior in close relationships: Exploring transformation of motivation. *Journal of Experimental Social Psychology, 30,* 138–164.

Yum, J. O. (1991). The impact of Confucianism on interpersonal relationships and communication patterns in East Asia. In L. Samovar & R. Porter (Eds.), *Intercultural communication: A reader* (5th ed., pp. 66–77). Belmont, CA: Wadsworth.

Zich, J., & Temoshok, L. (1987). Perceptions of social support in men with AIDS and ARC: Relationships with distress and hardiness. *Journal of Applied Social Psychology, 17,* 193–215.

Zikoupolous, M. (1992). *Open doors 1987/1988: Report on international educational exchange.* New York: Institute of International Education.

Author Index

Subject Index

A

Abuse, decision to disclose, 279–281
  danger, 279
  mitigating factors, 280–281
  negative consequences, 279–80
Abused women, *see* Battered women
Aggression, 181–196
  and assertiveness, 182
  and composure, 183–184, 190–191, 194
  and dominance, 190–191, 193–194
  and intimacy of relationship, 184–185
  justification, 186–187
  perceived threat, 186–187
  perceptions of, 183–184, 193–194
  and pleasantness, 190–191, 194
  postinteraction effects, 194–195
  preinteraction mediators, 194–195
  relational outcomes, 182–186, 191–192, 195–196
  and satisfaction, 186, 189, 192–193
  and social appropriateness, 182
AIDS, *see* HIV/AIDS, HIV-seropositive
Asian cultures, *see* East Asian cultures, Indian culture
Attachment, 170, 172
Attachment styles, 57, 64

B

Battered women, 275–286
  balance of public and private spheres, 283–285

and feminist analyses, 281–283
in lesbian relationships, 284–285
metaphors, 285–286

C

Child sexual abuse, *see* Sexual abuse
Collectivism, 236
Communication Boundary Management
    Theory, 11–12, 37–43, 48, 84,
    86–88, 90–94, 125–126, 132,
    134, 298
  applied to cancer, 134
  applied to HIV/AIDS, 84, 86–88, 134
  boundary management system, 39–43,
      46–47
    rule coordination, 40–42, 47
    rule formation, 39–40
    rule turbulence, 42–43
    rule usage, 39–40, 46
  boundary structures, 38–39
    control, 38–39
    levels, 38–39
    ownership, 38–39
    permeability, 38–39
  discloser's message strategy selection,
      90
  expectations of discloser, 88
  informational privacy, 91
  message content, 92–93
  receiving partner, 93–94
  strategy production, 92

F

Facework, 137, 245–248, 257–259
Feminist approach to self-disclosure, 210
Feminist ethnography, 276–277
Future research, 289–300
    decentering the sovereign self, 292–295
    methodologies, 299–300
    moving beyond target intimates,
        295–297
    taking the concept of balance seriously,
        289–292
    theory development, 297–299

G

Gender differences, 217–218, 226–228,
    230
    interaction with cultural norms, 218
    and target, 226–228
    and topic, 226–228
Goals, 169–179
Gossip network, 242–243, 247

H

HIV/AIDS, *see also* HIV-seropositive,
        12–13, 71, 74–82, 85–86, 100,
        124–125
    health care worker disclosure to patient,
        80–82
    initial disclosure of testing, 74–77
    and nonverbal vernacular, 100
    patient disclosure to third parties,
        77–80
    secrecy, 71
    stigma of, 71, 85–86, 124–125
HIV-seropositive, *see also* HIV/AIDS,
        54–57, 60
    disclosure of diagnosis, 54–55
    reasons for and against disclosure, 56,
        57, 60
        to intimate partner, 57
Honesty, 9

I

Identity, *see also* Self, 197–198, 200–203,
        208–209
"Ideology of Intimacy," 34
Indian culture, 239–248
    and asymmetry of relationships, 245
    and directness, 243–244
    and effusiveness, 241–242, 246
    and face, 245–248
    and family, 247–248
    and Hinduism, 239, 244–245
    and politeness, 240
Individualism, 236
Interaction characteristics and patient's
        privacy, 145–146
Interpretive research, 209–210
Introspective accounts, 201

J

Jourard's Self Disclosure Questionnaire
        (JSDQ), 215–216, 218, 220,
        231–234

L

Locus of control, 217
Lying, 9–10

M

Medical ethics, 72–74
    in conflict, 72
Megan's Law, *see also* Sex offender
        community notification policies,
        267
Multiple caregivers and privacy, 140

O

Other-disclosure, 250, 254, 293

P

Personal characteristics and patient's
        privacy, 144–145

Politeness theory and health disclosure,
   137–139
  impression management and health,
   138–139
Praxis of boundary management, 43–48
  boundary gatekeeper, 46
  co-owned rules, 47
  exemplar, patient–physician, 44–48
Privacy, control over, 302
Privacy, loss of, 301
Privacy, protection of, 187
Public and private spheres, 283–285,
   295–298

R

Relational maintenance, 208
Restoration of privacy, 187
Right to privacy, 271–274
  constitutionality, 272

S

Secrecy, 181
Secret tests, 167
Secrets, 166
Self, *see also* Identity, 236, 292–295
  multiplicity, 294
  social, 292–295
  sovereign, 292, 295
Self-disclosure, 3–11, 14–16, 22–31, 33,
   113–120, 127–128, 216, 235,
   237, 240, 244, 246
  avoidance of, 14–15, 235, 237, 240,
   244, 246
  definition, 3–4
  direct or indirect, 62
  and HIV/AIDS, 127–128
   to parents, 128
   to partner, 127
   to siblings, 128
  and liking, 29–31
   methods issues, 29–30
   moderators, 29
   partners, 29
   theoretical implications, 31
  privacy and, 6
  reasons for, 6–7
  reciprocity of, 10–11, 24–29, 33

  actual, 26
  dyadic, 26
  moderating effects, 28
  perceived, 26
  and resistance to illness,
   113–120
   cardiovascular diseases, 115–120
  and speech reactivity, 117–120
  confession and health, 114
  risks of, 8–9
  secrecy and, 9, 16
  and sex differences, 22–24, 33
   personality trait, 22
   target, 22–23
  targets of, 5
  variation in, 216
Sex differences, *see* Gender differences,
   Self-disclosure and sex
   differences
Sex offender community notification
   policies, *see also* Megan's Law,
   263, 266–274
  controversy, 269–271
   opponents' arguments, 270–271
   proponents' arguments, 269–270
   recidivism, 269–270
  features of registration laws, 266–267
  New York's Sex Offender Registration
   Act (SORA), 267–268
   lawsuits, 268
   levels, 268
  right to privacy versus right to know,
   271–274
   isolation and secrecy, 273
   risk to victims, 273
   victimization of neighborhood, 273
Sexual abuse, 264–266
  history, 265
  increase in, 265
Social constructionist theory, *see also*
   Interpretive research, 298
Social Penetration Theory (SPT), 168
Social support, 176–178
Stigma, 123–125, 129, 132, 134, 181
  and cancer, 125, 129, 132
  and healthcare workers, 134
  and HIV/AIDS, 124–125
  of privacy, 181